The Heroic Legend of
ARSLAN

STORY BY
YOSHIKI TANAKA

MANGA BY
HIROMU ARAKAWA

9

THE HEROIC LEGEND OF
ARSLAN

TABLE OF CONTENTS

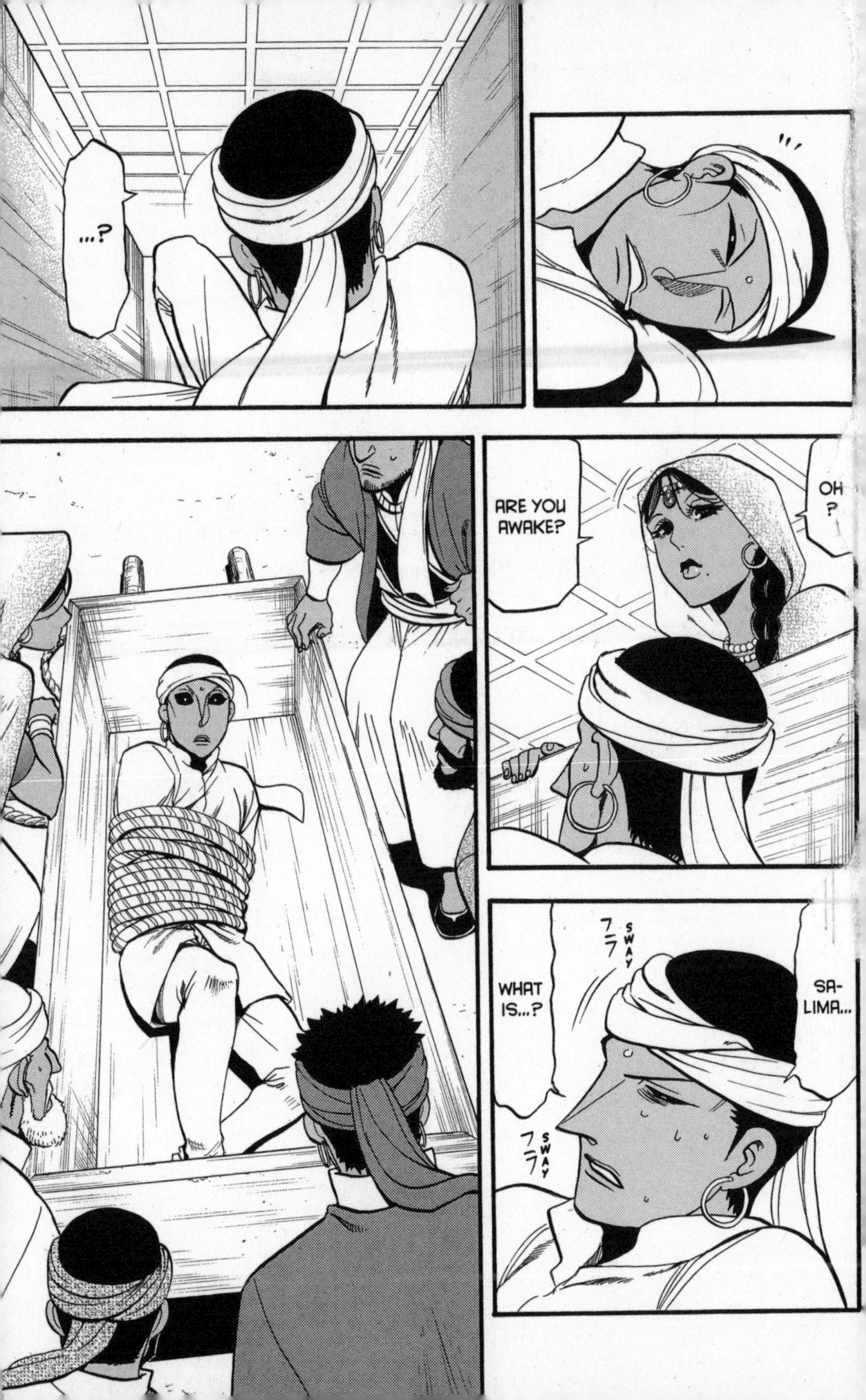
...?
OH ?
ARE YOU AWAKE?
SA-LIMA...
フラ SWAY
WHAT IS...?
フラ SWAY

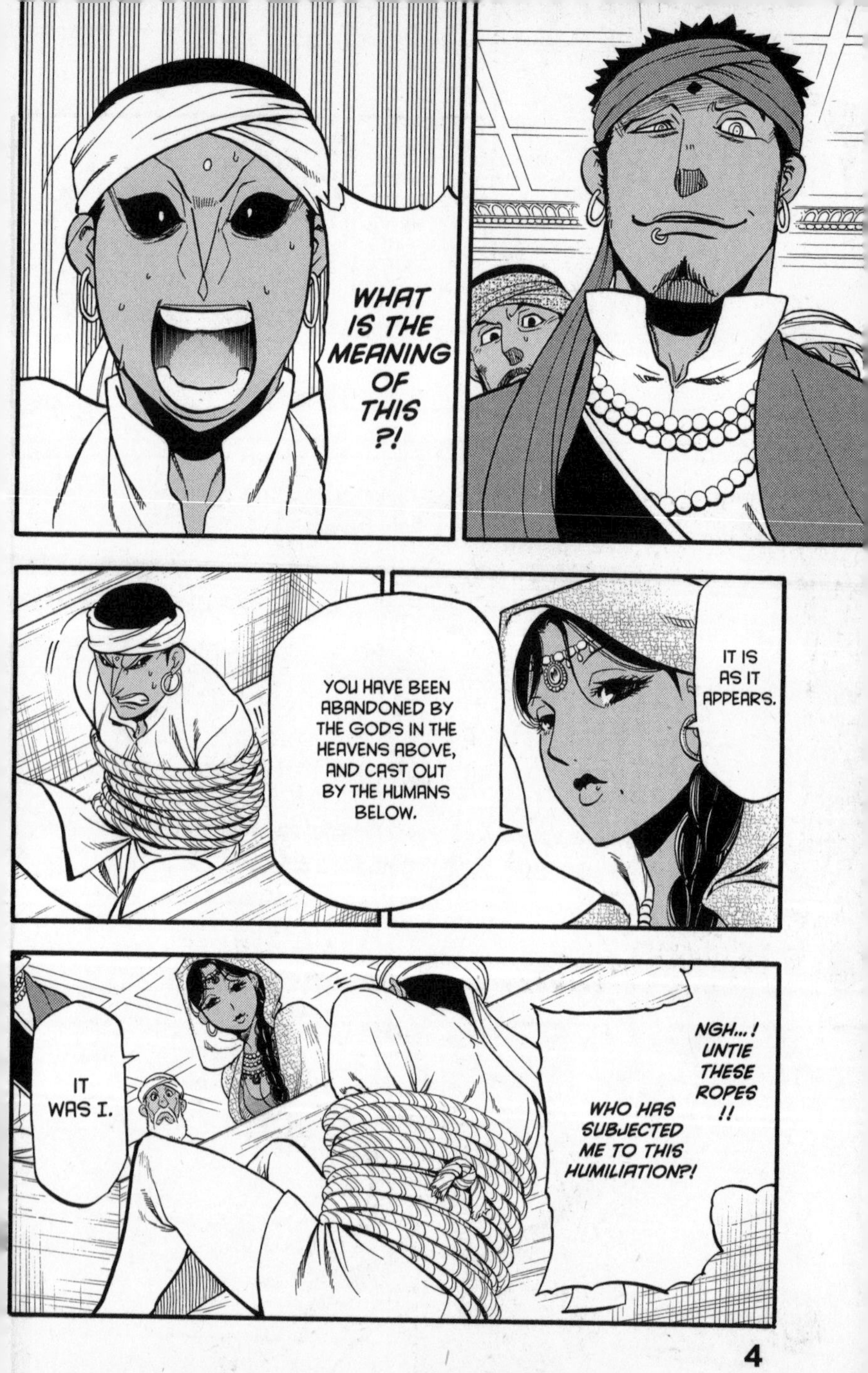
WHAT IS THE MEANING OF THIS?!
IT IS AS IT APPEARS.
YOU HAVE BEEN ABANDONED BY THE GODS IN THE HEAVENS ABOVE, AND CAST OUT BY THE HUMANS BELOW.
NGH...! UNTIE THESE ROPES!!
WHO HAS SUBJECTED ME TO THIS HUMILIATION?!
IT WAS I.

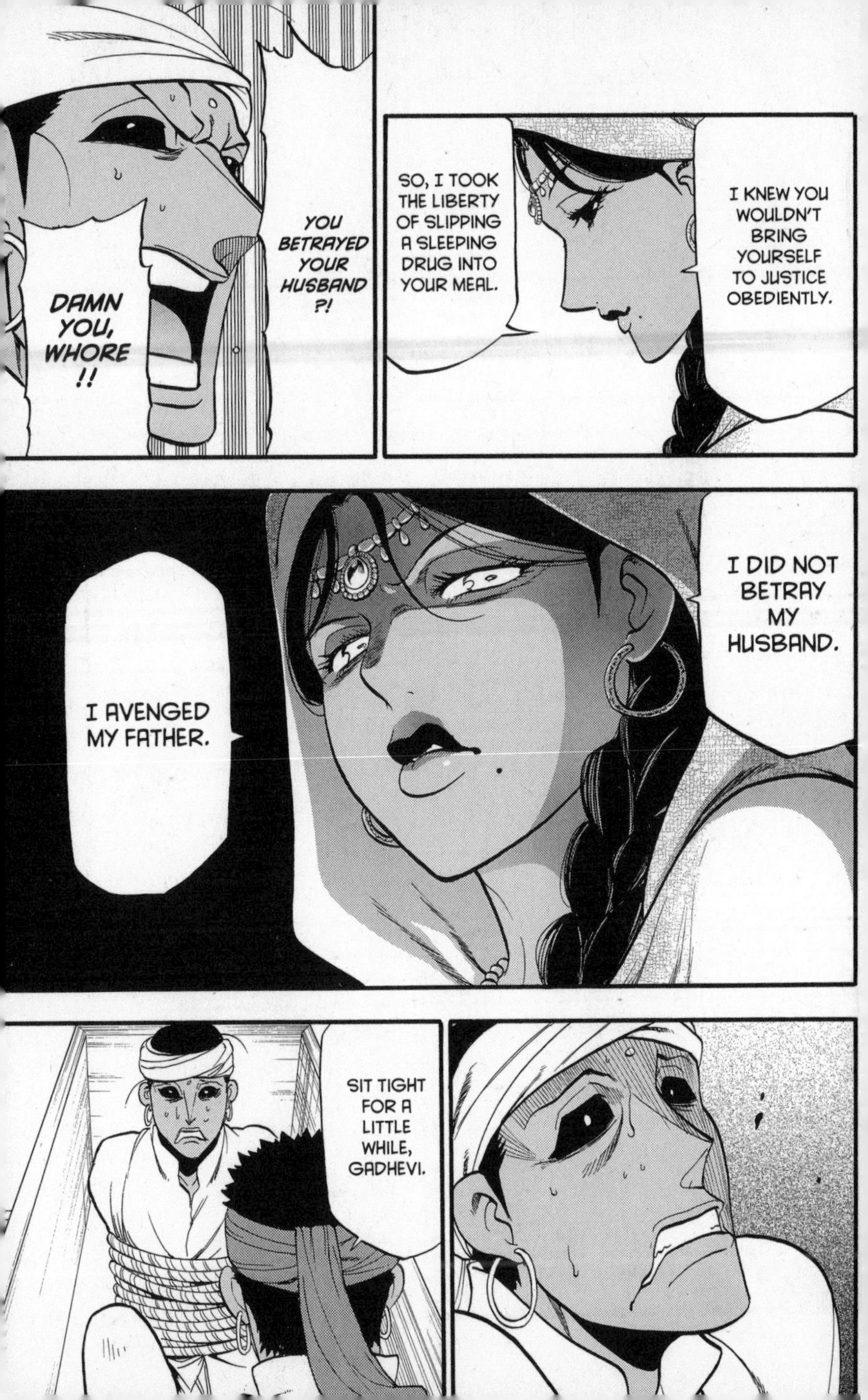
I KNEW YOU WOULDN'T BRING YOURSELF TO JUSTICE OBEDIENTLY.
SO, I TOOK THE LIBERTY OF SLIPPING A SLEEPING DRUG INTO YOUR MEAL.
YOU BETRAYED YOUR HUSBAND ?!
DAMN YOU, WHORE !!
I DID NOT BETRAY MY HUSBAND.
I AVENGED MY FATHER.
SIT TIGHT FOR A LITTLE WHILE, GADHEVI.

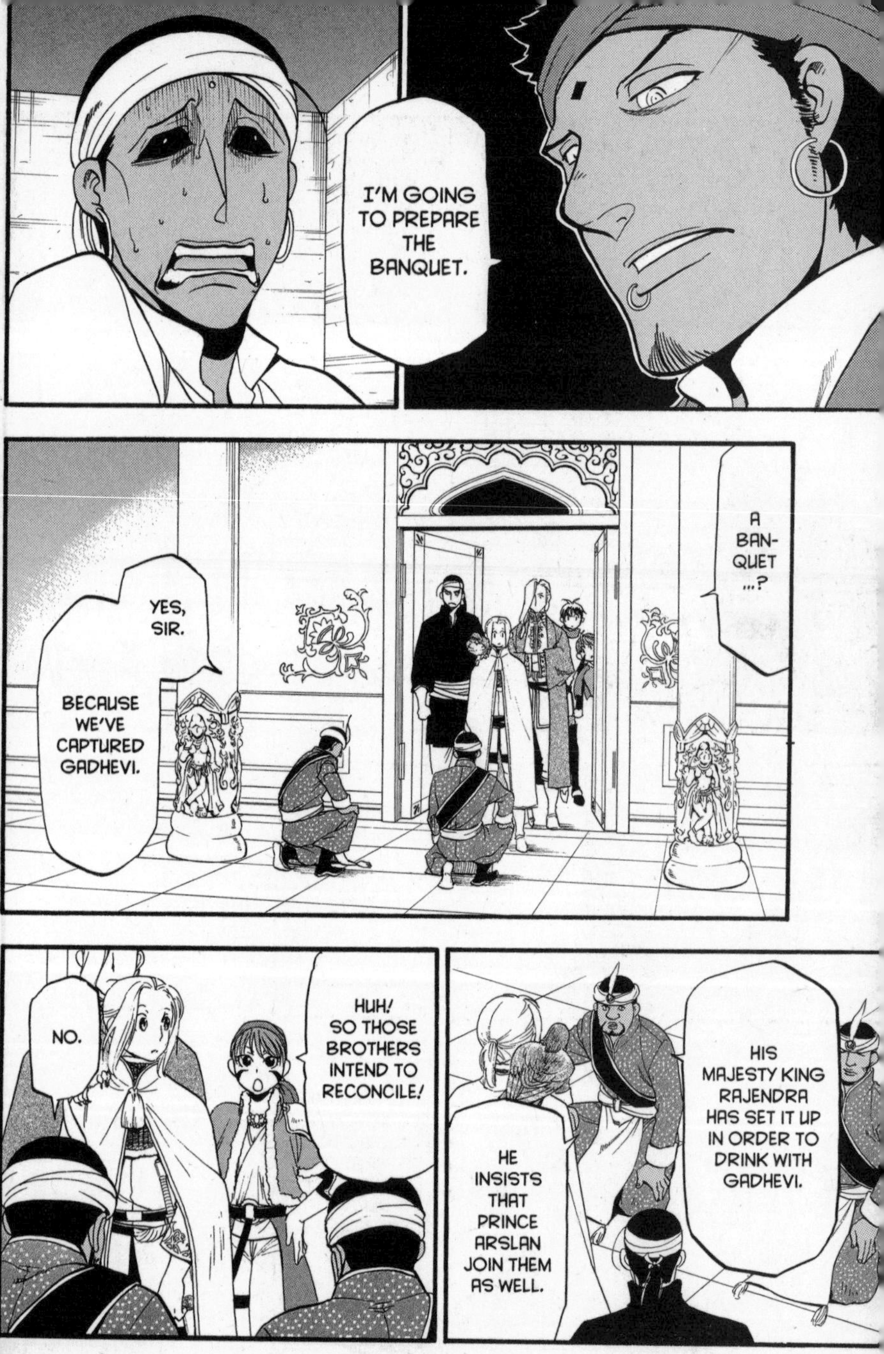
I'M GOING TO PREPARE THE BANQUET.
A BAN-QUET ...?
YES, SIR.
BECAUSE WE'VE CAPTURED GADHEVI.
HIS MAJESTY KING RAJENDRA HAS SET IT UP IN ORDER TO DRINK WITH GADHEVI.
HE INSISTS THAT PRINCE ARSLAN JOIN THEM AS WELL.
HUH! SO THOSE BROTHERS INTEND TO RECONCILE!
NO.

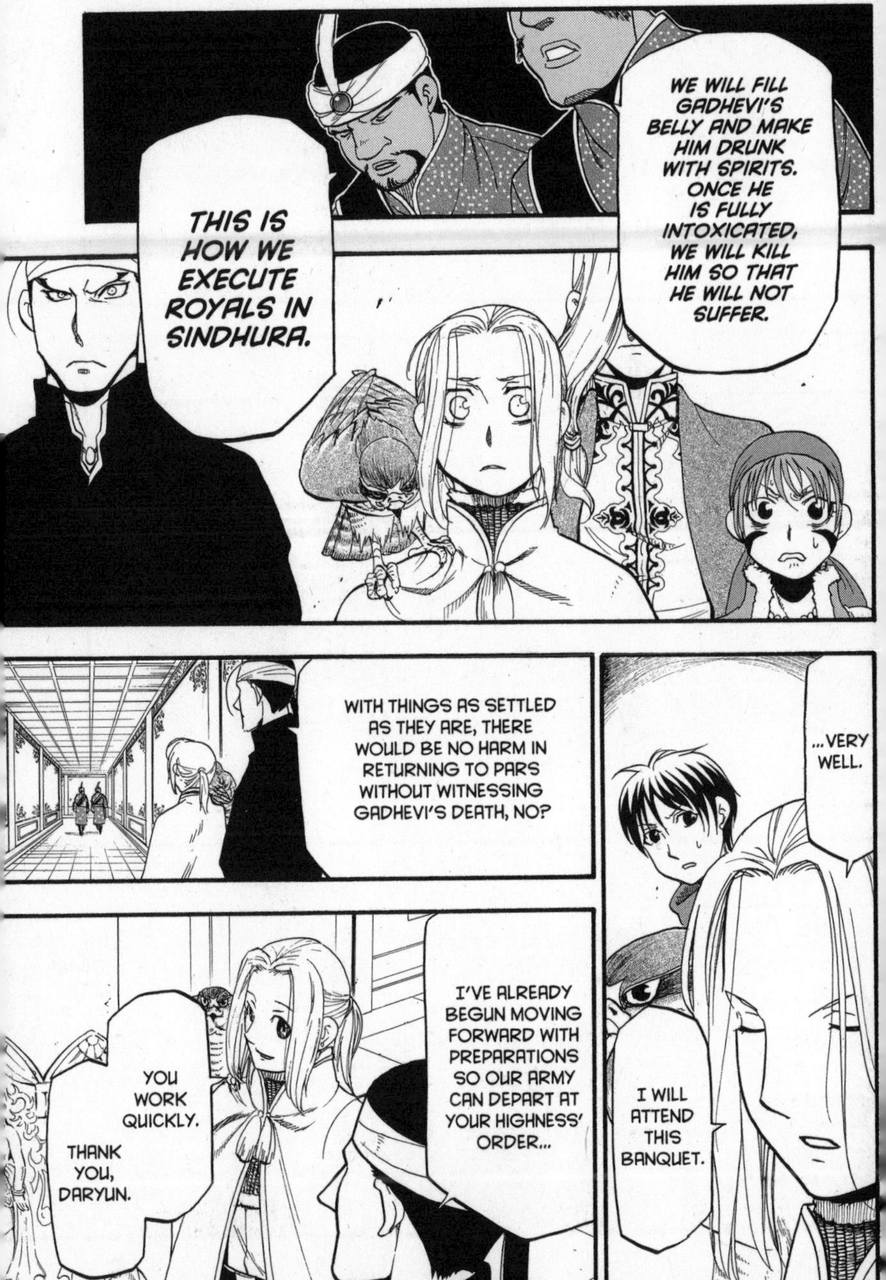
WE WILL FILL GADHEVI'S BELLY AND MAKE HIM DRUNK WITH SPIRITS. ONCE HE IS FULLY INTOXICATED, WE WILL KILL HIM SO THAT HE WILL NOT SUFFER.
THIS IS HOW WE EXECUTE ROYALS IN SINDHURA.
...VERY WELL.
I WILL ATTEND THIS BANQUET.
WITH THINGS AS SETTLED AS THEY ARE, THERE WOULD BE NO HARM IN RETURNING TO PARS WITHOUT WITNESSING GADHEVI'S DEATH, NO?
I'VE ALREADY BEGUN MOVING FORWARD WITH PREPARATIONS SO OUR ARMY CAN DEPART AT YOUR HIGHNESS' ORDER...
YOU WORK QUICKLY.
THANK YOU, DARYUN.

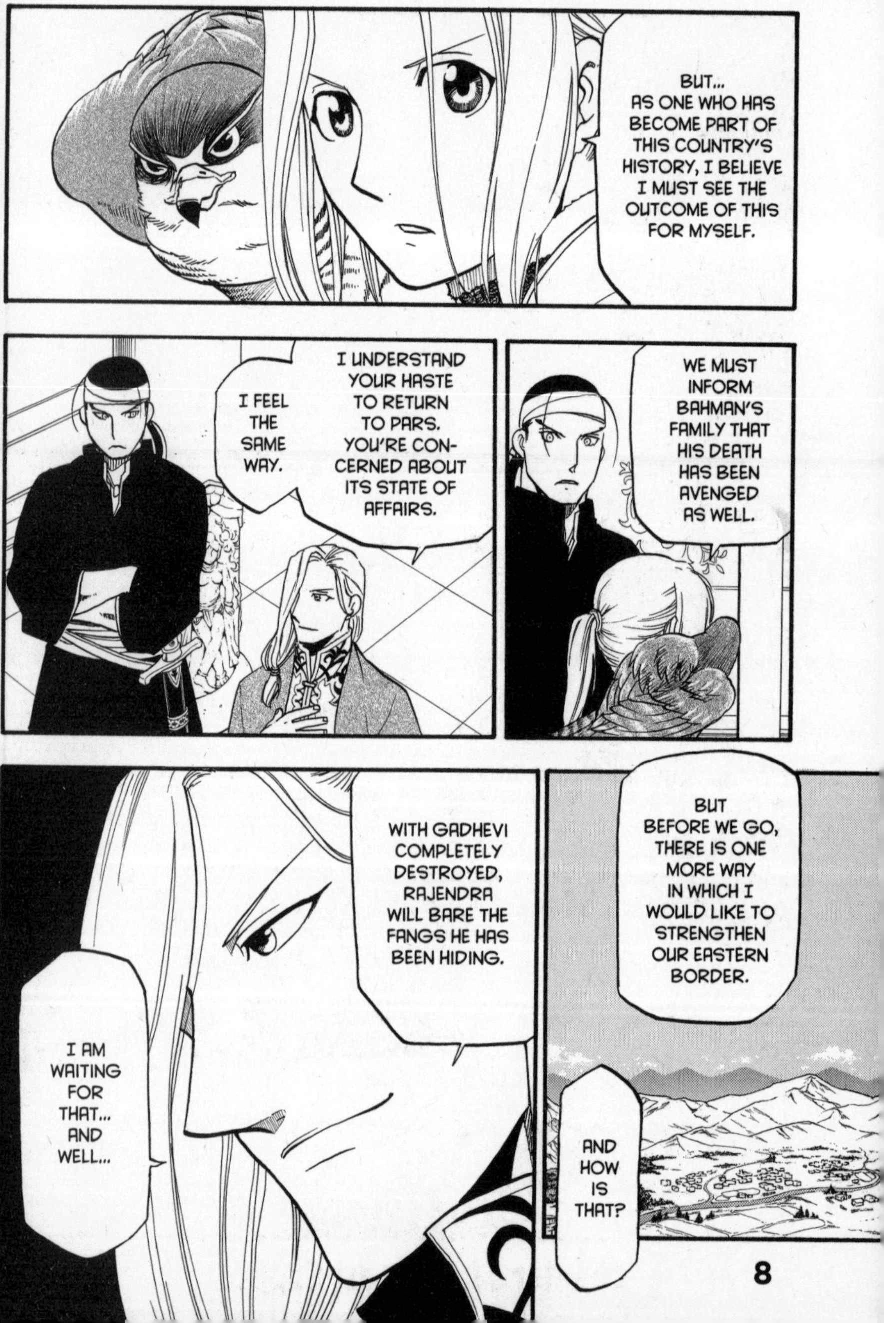
BUT... AS ONE WHO HAS BECOME PART OF THIS COUNTRY'S HISTORY, I BELIEVE I MUST SEE THE OUTCOME OF THIS FOR MYSELF.
WE MUST INFORM BAHMAN'S FAMILY THAT HIS DEATH HAS BEEN AVENGED AS WELL.
I UNDERSTAND YOUR HASTE TO RETURN TO PARS. YOU'RE CONCERNED ABOUT ITS STATE OF AFFAIRS.
I FEEL THE SAME WAY.
BUT BEFORE WE GO, THERE IS ONE MORE WAY IN WHICH I WOULD LIKE TO STRENGTHEN OUR EASTERN BORDER.
AND HOW IS THAT?
WITH GADHEVI COMPLETELY DESTROYED, RAJENDRA WILL BARE THE FANGS HE HAS BEEN HIDING.
I AM WAITING FOR THAT... AND WELL...

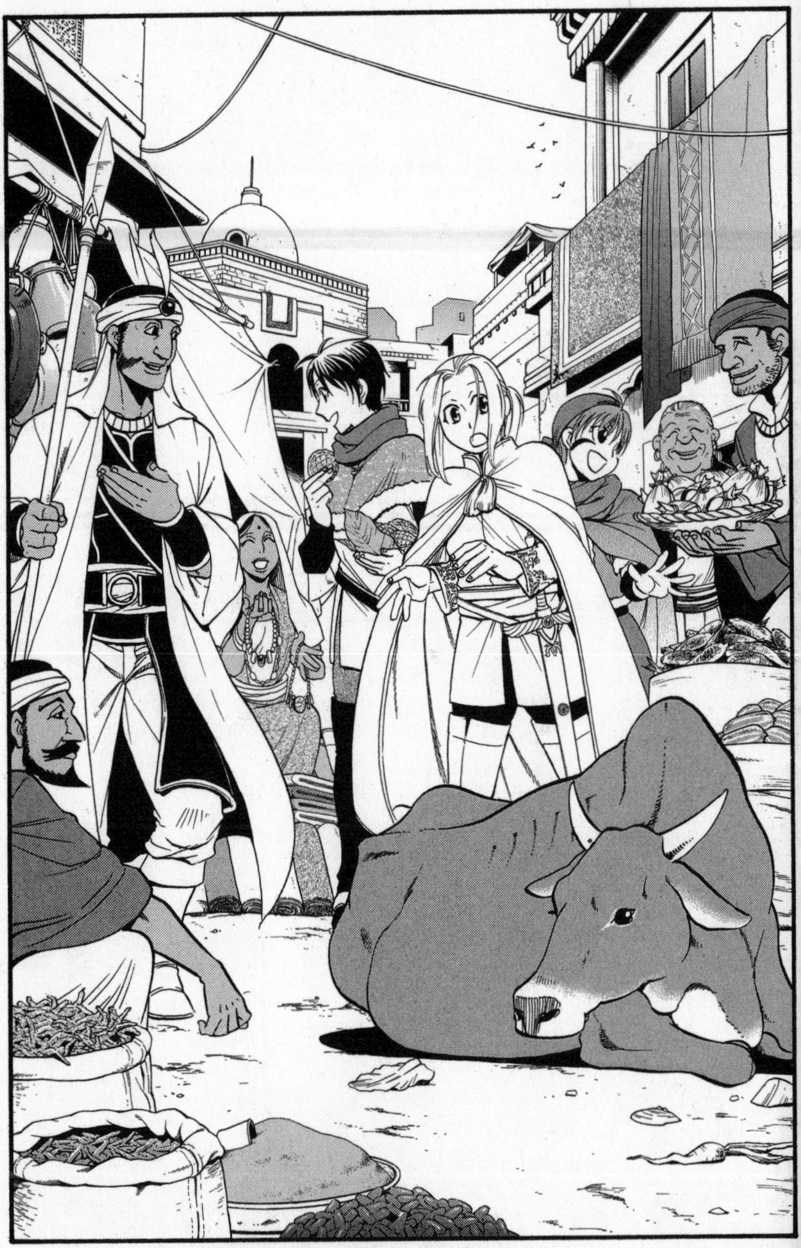

Chapter 53: The Last Supper

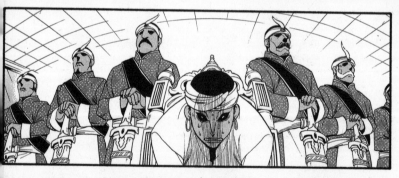

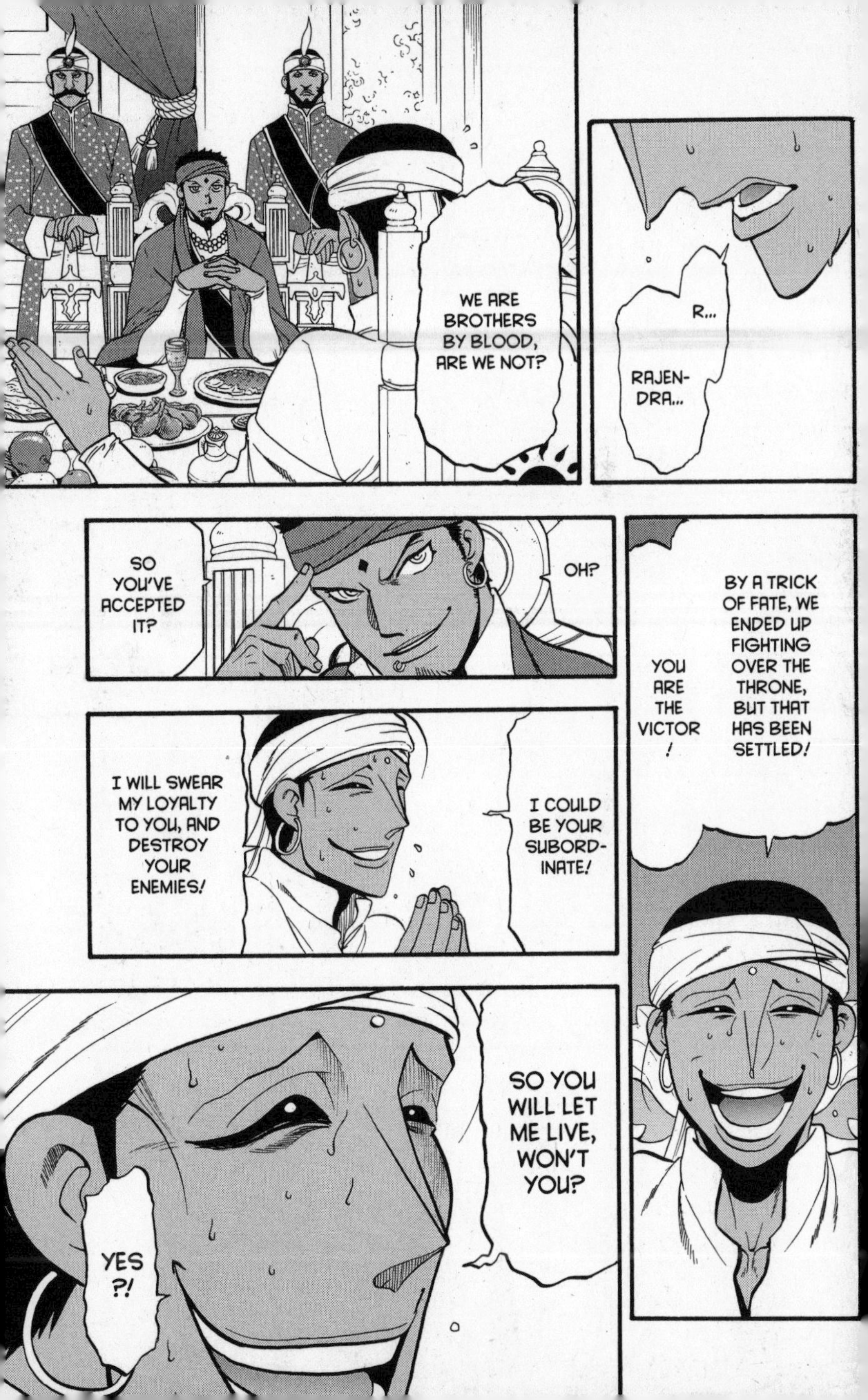
R...
RAJEN-DRA...
WE ARE BROTHERS BY BLOOD, ARE WE NOT?
BY A TRICK OF FATE, WE ENDED UP FIGHTING OVER THE THRONE, BUT THAT HAS BEEN SETTLED!
YOU ARE THE VICTOR!
OH?
SO YOU'VE ACCEPTED IT?
I COULD BE YOUR SUBORD-INATE!
I WILL SWEAR MY LOYALTY TO YOU, AND DESTROY YOUR ENEMIES!
SO YOU WILL LET ME LIVE, WON'T YOU?
YES ?!

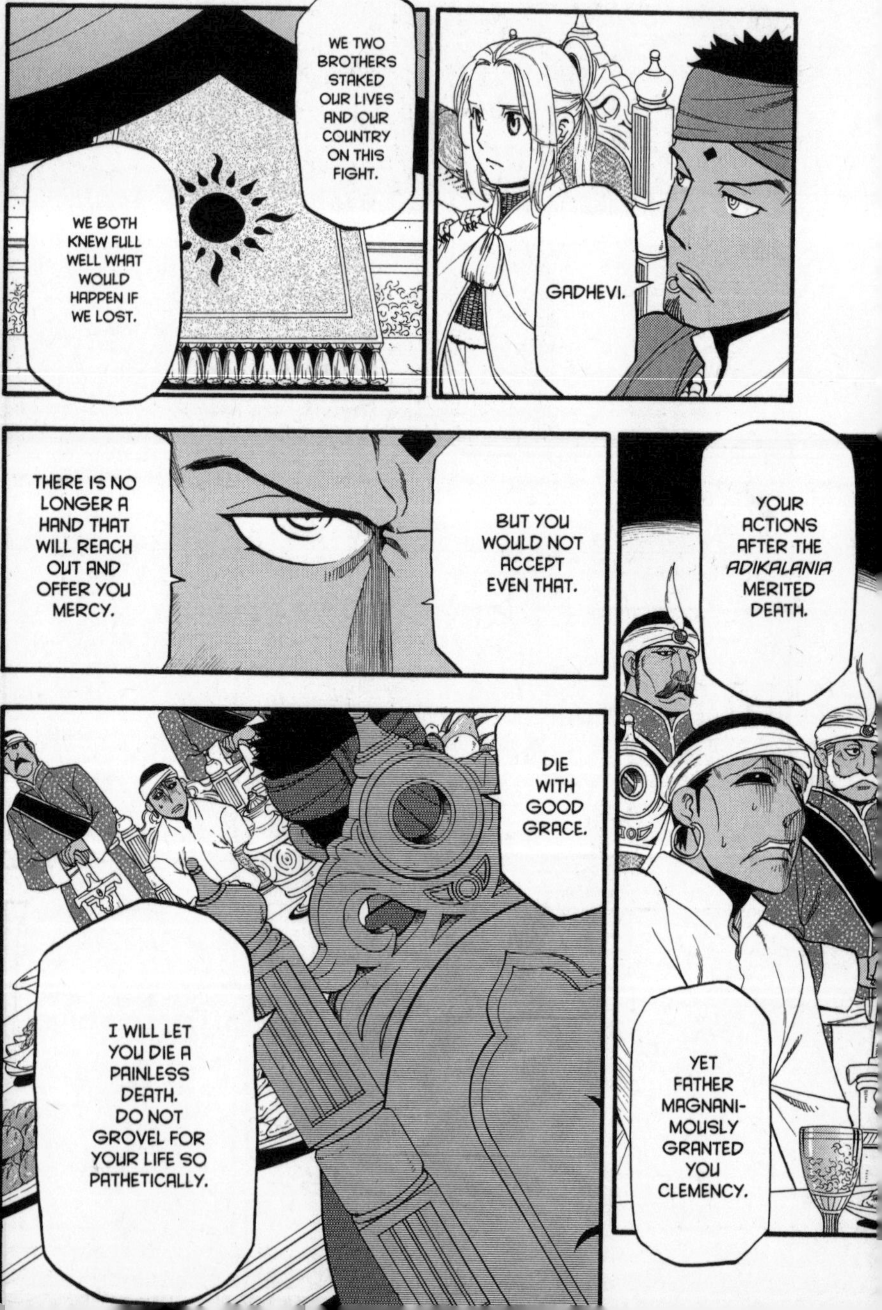
GADHEVI.
WE TWO BROTHERS STAKED OUR LIVES AND OUR COUNTRY ON THIS FIGHT.
WE BOTH KNEW FULL WELL WHAT WOULD HAPPEN IF WE LOST.
YOUR ACTIONS AFTER THE *ADIKALANIA* MERITED DEATH.
YET FATHER MAGNANI-MOUSLY GRANTED YOU CLEMENCY.
BUT YOU WOULD NOT ACCEPT EVEN THAT.
THERE IS NO LONGER A HAND THAT WILL REACH OUT AND OFFER YOU MERCY.
DIE WITH GOOD GRACE.
I WILL LET YOU DIE A PAINLESS DEATH. DO NOT GROVEL FOR YOUR LIFE SO PATHETICALLY.

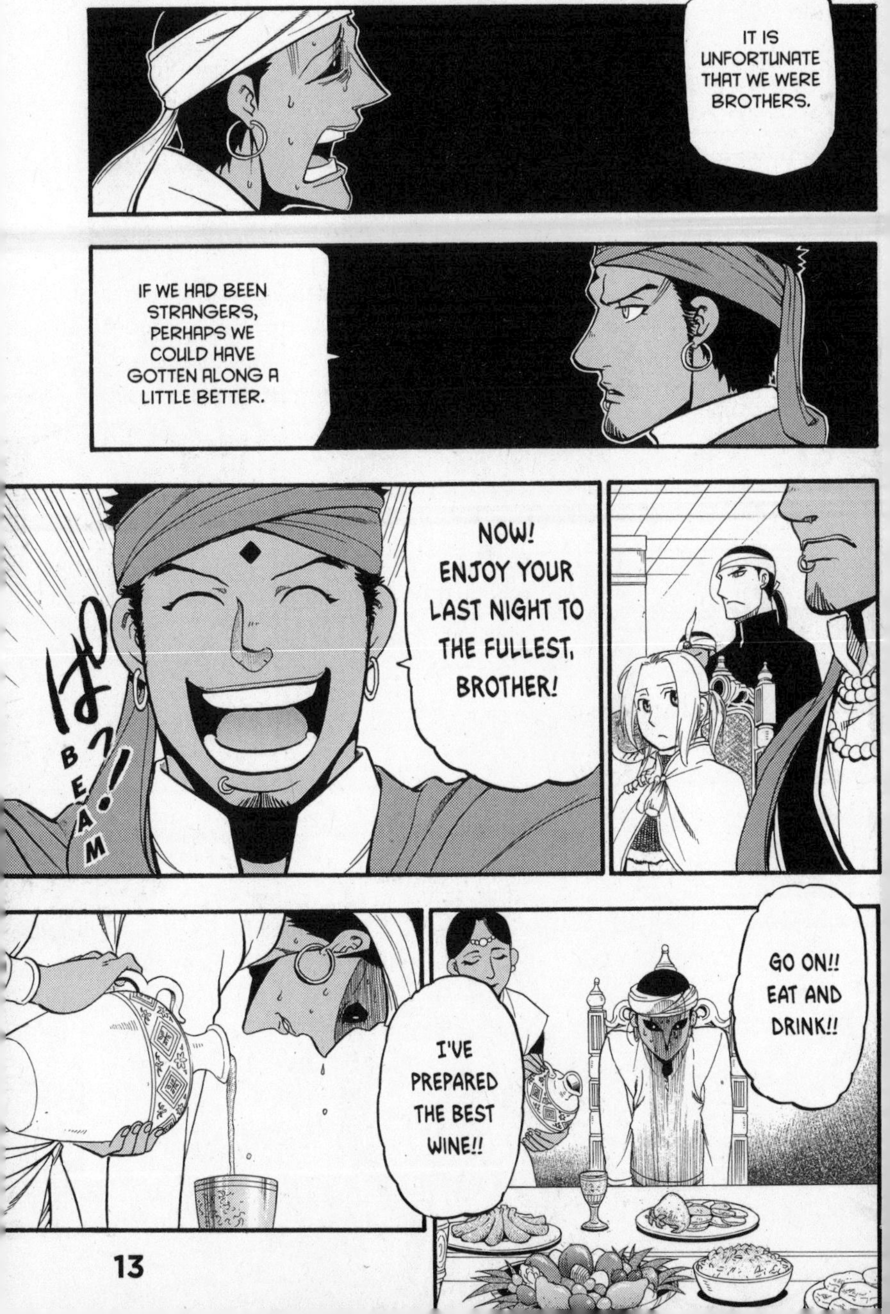
IT IS UNFORTUNATE THAT WE WERE BROTHERS.
IF WE HAD BEEN STRANGERS, PERHAPS WE COULD HAVE GOTTEN ALONG A LITTLE BETTER.
NOW! ENJOY YOUR LAST NIGHT TO THE FULLEST, BROTHER!
ぱっ!
BEAM
GO ON!! EAT AND DRINK!!
I'VE PREPARED THE BEST WINE!!

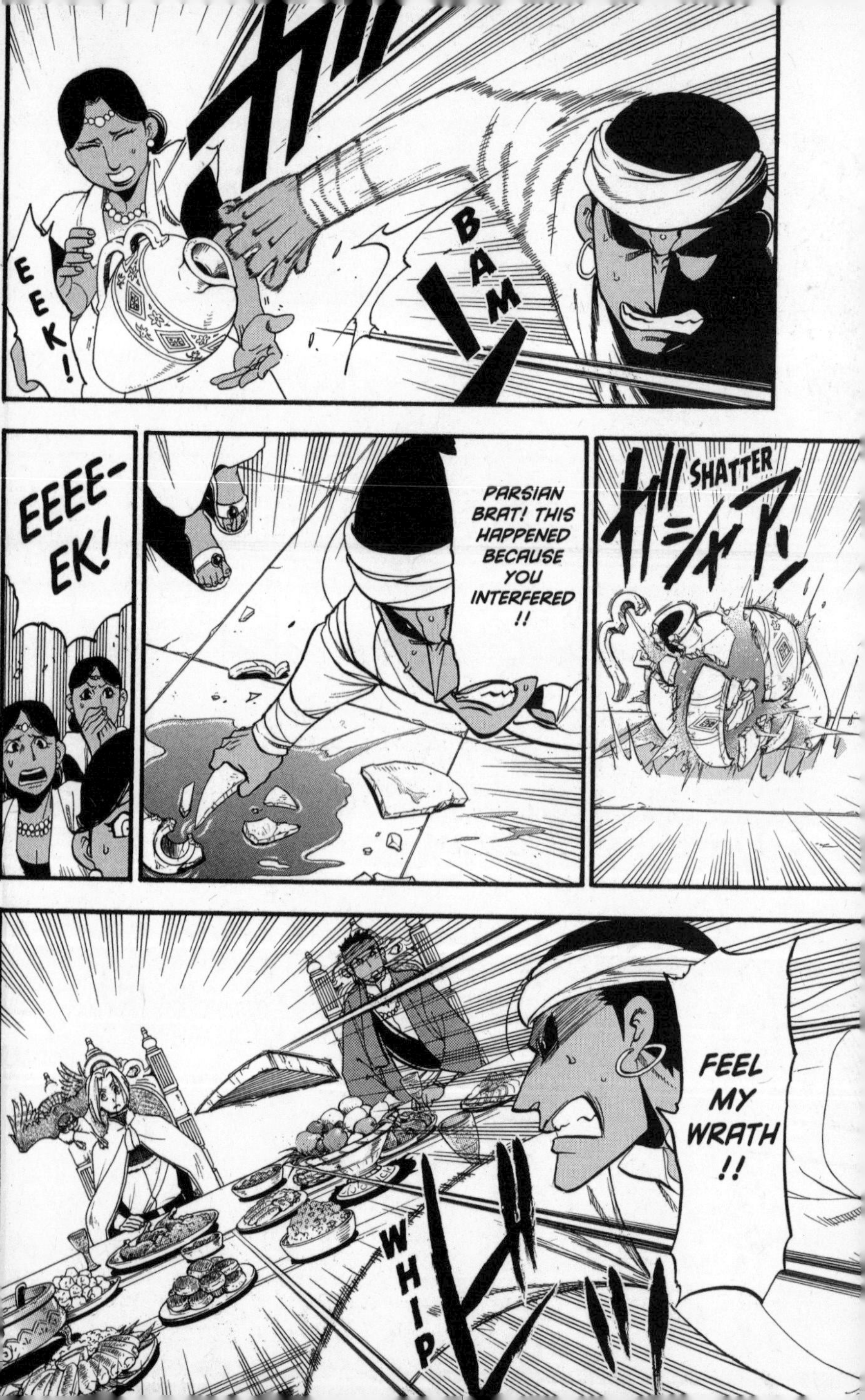

BAM
EEK!
SHATTER
PARSIAN BRAT! THIS HAPPENED BECAUSE YOU INTERFERED !!
EEEE-EK!
FEEL MY WRATH !!
WHIP

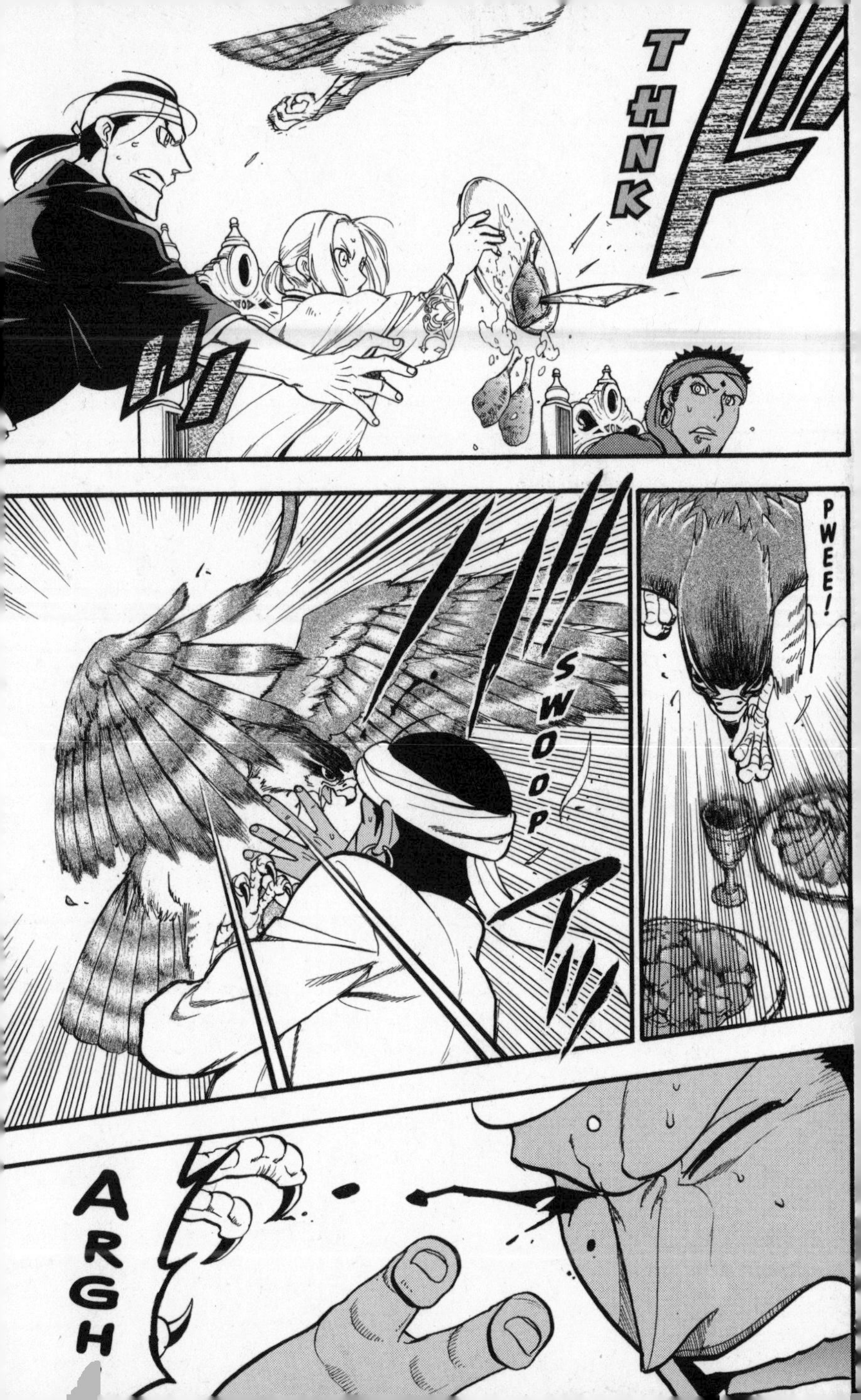
THNK
PWEE!
SWOOP
ARGH

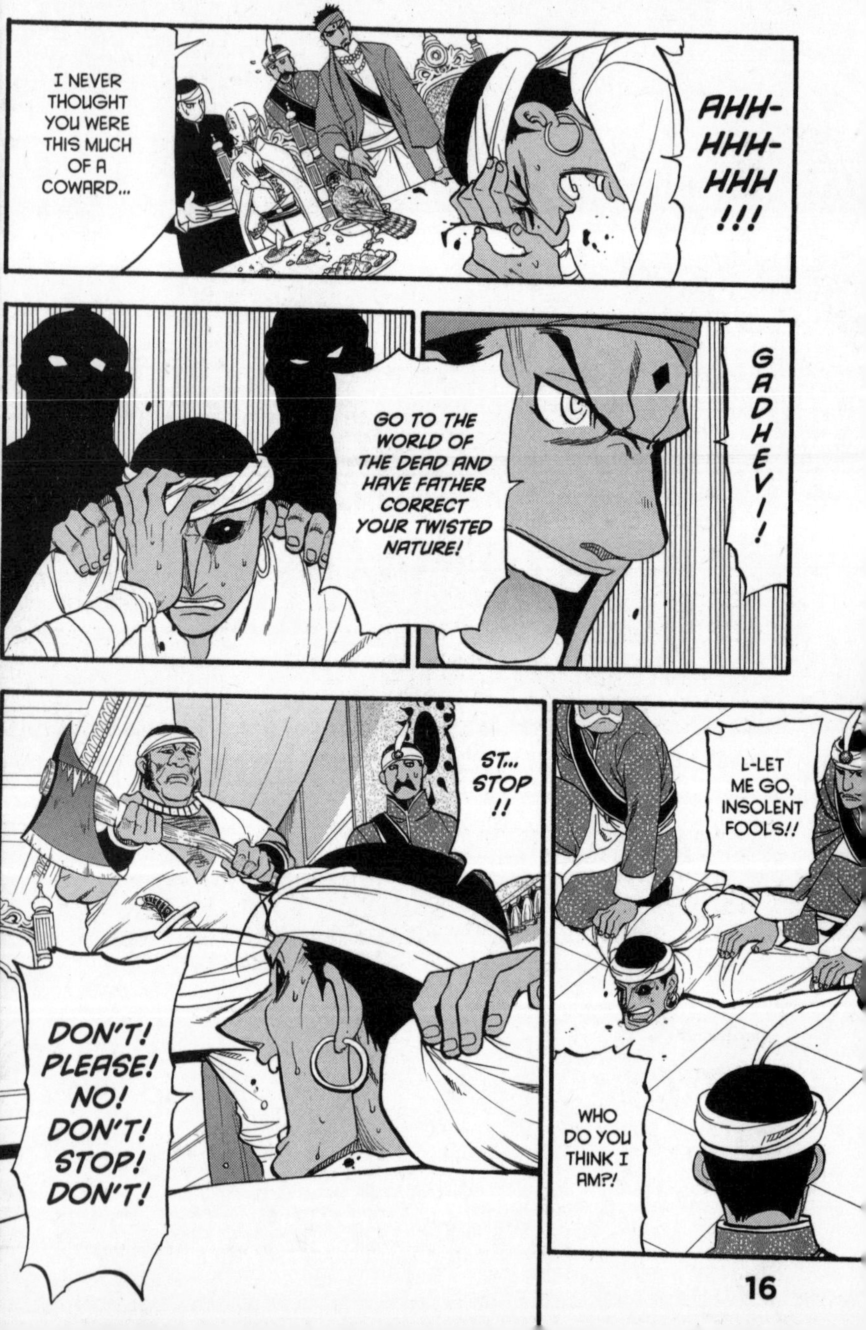
AHH-HHH-HHH!!!
I NEVER THOUGHT YOU WERE THIS MUCH OF A COWARD...
GADHEVI!
GO TO THE WORLD OF THE DEAD AND HAVE FATHER CORRECT YOUR TWISTED NATURE!
L-LET ME GO, INSOLENT FOOLS!!
WHO DO YOU THINK I AM?!
ST... STOP!!
DON'T! PLEASE! NO! DON'T! STOP! DON'T!

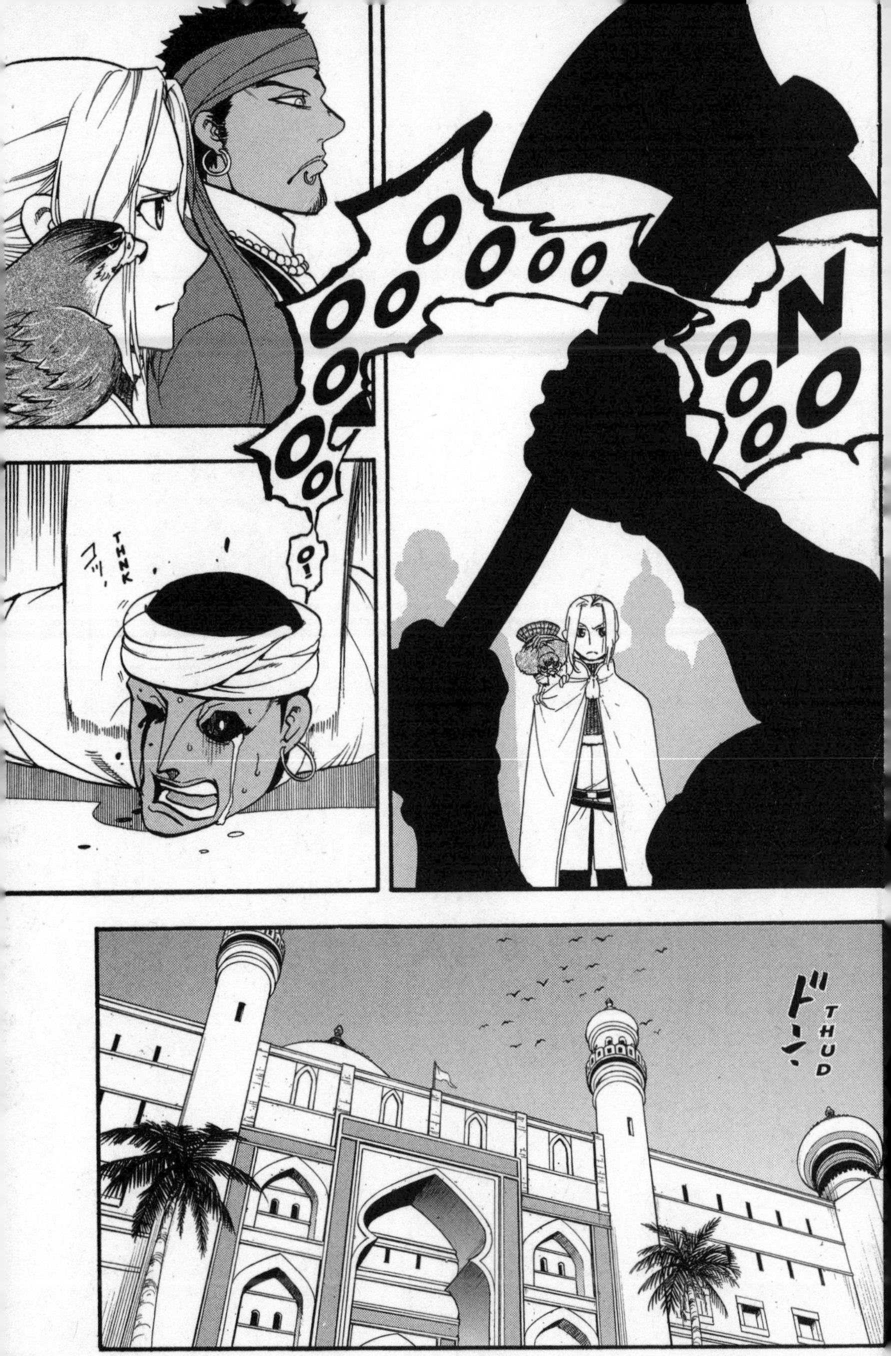
NOOOOOOOOOOOOOOOOOOO!
ゴッ THNK
ドーン THUD

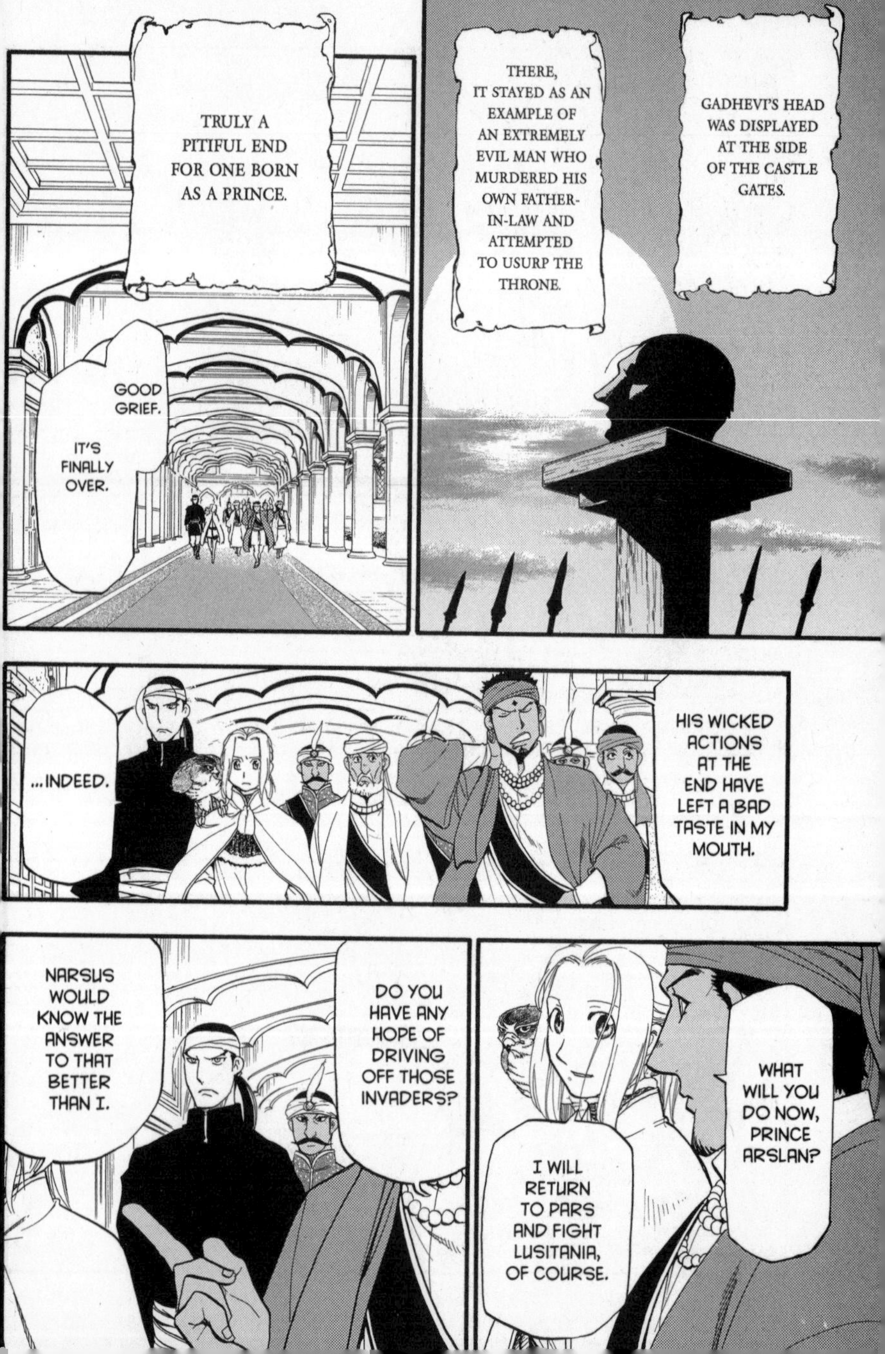
GADHEVI'S HEAD WAS DISPLAYED AT THE SIDE OF THE CASTLE GATES.
THERE, IT STAYED AS AN EXAMPLE OF AN EXTREMELY EVIL MAN WHO MURDERED HIS OWN FATHER-IN-LAW AND ATTEMPTED TO USURP THE THRONE.
TRULY A PITIFUL END FOR ONE BORN AS A PRINCE.
GOOD GRIEF.
IT'S FINALLY OVER.
HIS WICKED ACTIONS AT THE END HAVE LEFT A BAD TASTE IN MY MOUTH.
...INDEED.
WHAT WILL YOU DO NOW, PRINCE ARSLAN?
I WILL RETURN TO PARS AND FIGHT LUSITANIA, OF COURSE.
DO YOU HAVE ANY HOPE OF DRIVING OFF THOSE INVADERS?
NARSUS WOULD KNOW THE ANSWER TO THAT BETTER THAN I.

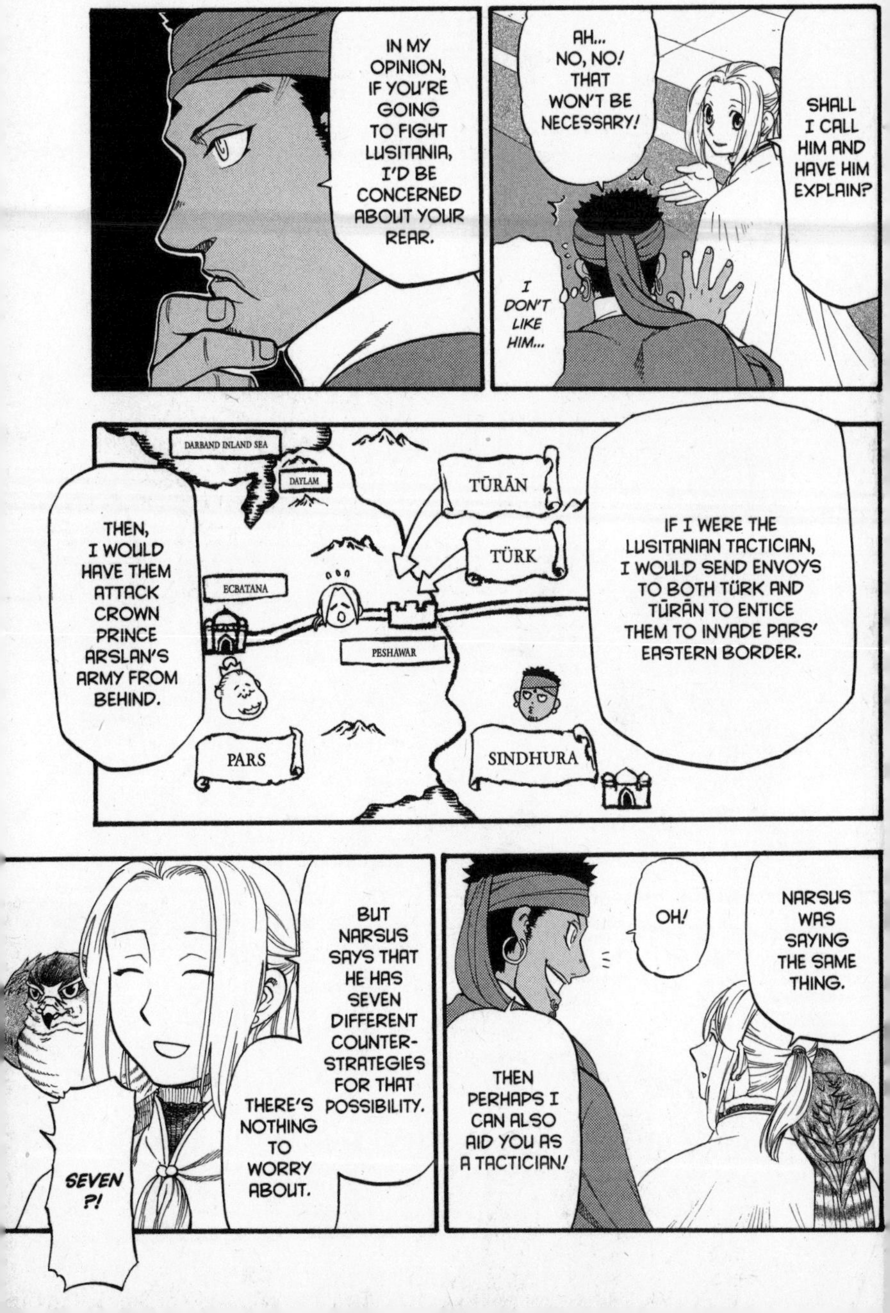
SHALL I CALL HIM AND HAVE HIM EXPLAIN?
AH... NO, NO! THAT WON'T BE NECESSARY!
I DON'T LIKE HIM...
IN MY OPINION, IF YOU'RE GOING TO FIGHT LUSITANIA, I'D BE CONCERNED ABOUT YOUR REAR.
IF I WERE THE LUSITANIAN TACTICIAN, I WOULD SEND ENVOYS TO BOTH TÜRK AND TŪRĀN TO ENTICE THEM TO INVADE PARS' EASTERN BORDER.
DARBAND INLAND SEA
DAYLAM
TŪRĀN
TÜRK
ECBATANA
PESHAWAR
PARS
SINDHURA
THEN, I WOULD HAVE THEM ATTACK CROWN PRINCE ARSLAN'S ARMY FROM BEHIND.
NARSUS WAS SAYING THE SAME THING.
OH!
THEN PERHAPS I CAN ALSO AID YOU AS A TACTICIAN!
BUT NARSUS SAYS THAT HE HAS SEVEN DIFFERENT COUNTER-STRATEGIES FOR THAT POSSIBILITY.
THERE'S NOTHING TO WORRY ABOUT.
SEVEN ?!

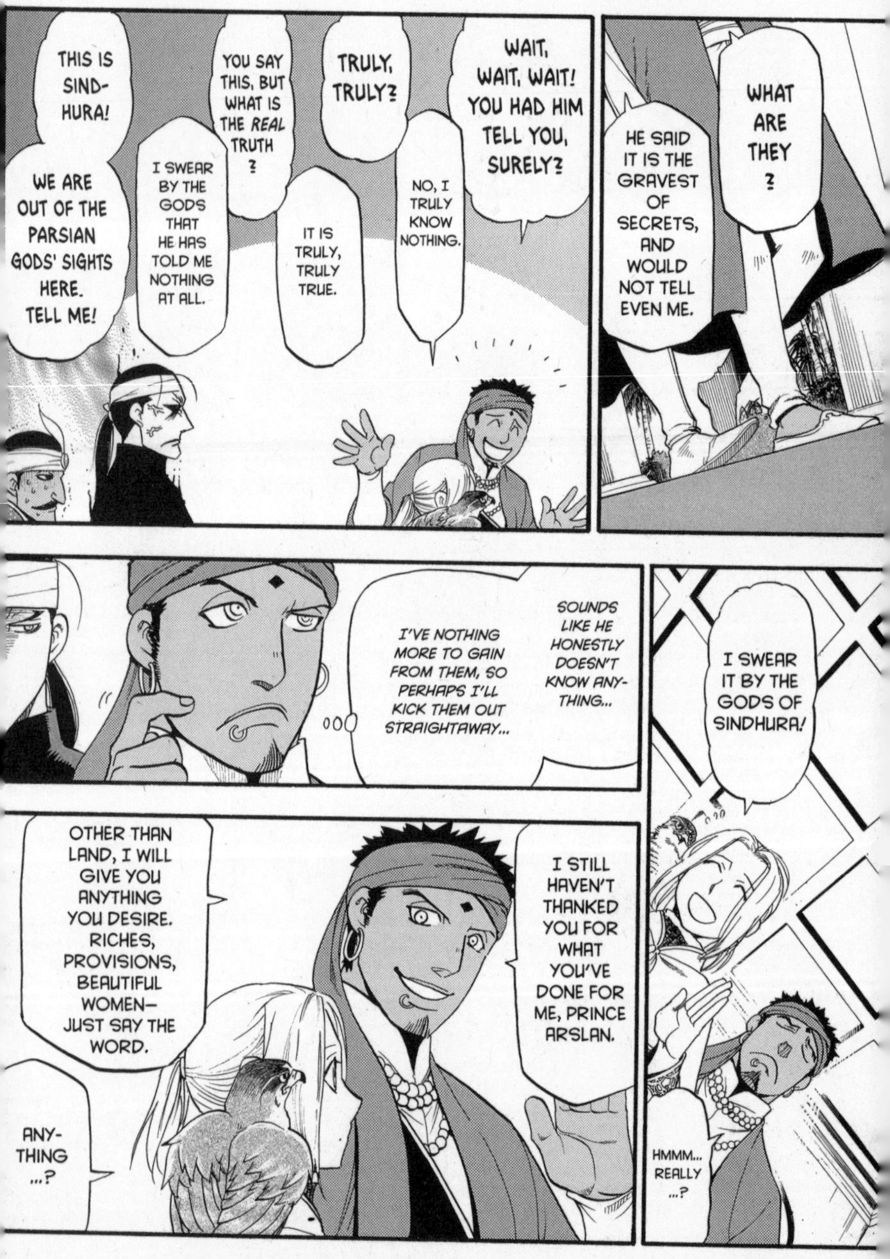
WHAT ARE THEY?
HE SAID IT IS THE GRAVEST OF SECRETS, AND WOULD NOT TELL EVEN ME.
WAIT, WAIT, WAIT! YOU HAD HIM TELL YOU, SURELY?
NO, I TRULY KNOW NOTHING.
TRULY, TRULY?
IT IS TRULY, TRULY TRUE.
YOU SAY THIS, BUT WHAT IS THE *REAL* TRUTH?
I SWEAR BY THE GODS THAT HE HAS TOLD ME NOTHING AT ALL.
THIS IS SINDHURA!
WE ARE OUT OF THE PARSIAN GODS' SIGHTS HERE. TELL ME!
I SWEAR IT BY THE GODS OF SINDHURA!
HMMM... REALLY...?
SOUNDS LIKE HE HONESTLY DOESN'T KNOW ANYTHING...
I'VE NOTHING MORE TO GAIN FROM THEM, SO PERHAPS I'LL KICK THEM OUT STRAIGHTAWAY...
I STILL HAVEN'T THANKED YOU FOR WHAT YOU'VE DONE FOR ME, PRINCE ARSLAN.
OTHER THAN LAND, I WILL GIVE YOU ANYTHING YOU DESIRE. RICHES, PROVISIONS, BEAUTIFUL WOMEN— JUST SAY THE WORD.
ANYTHING...?

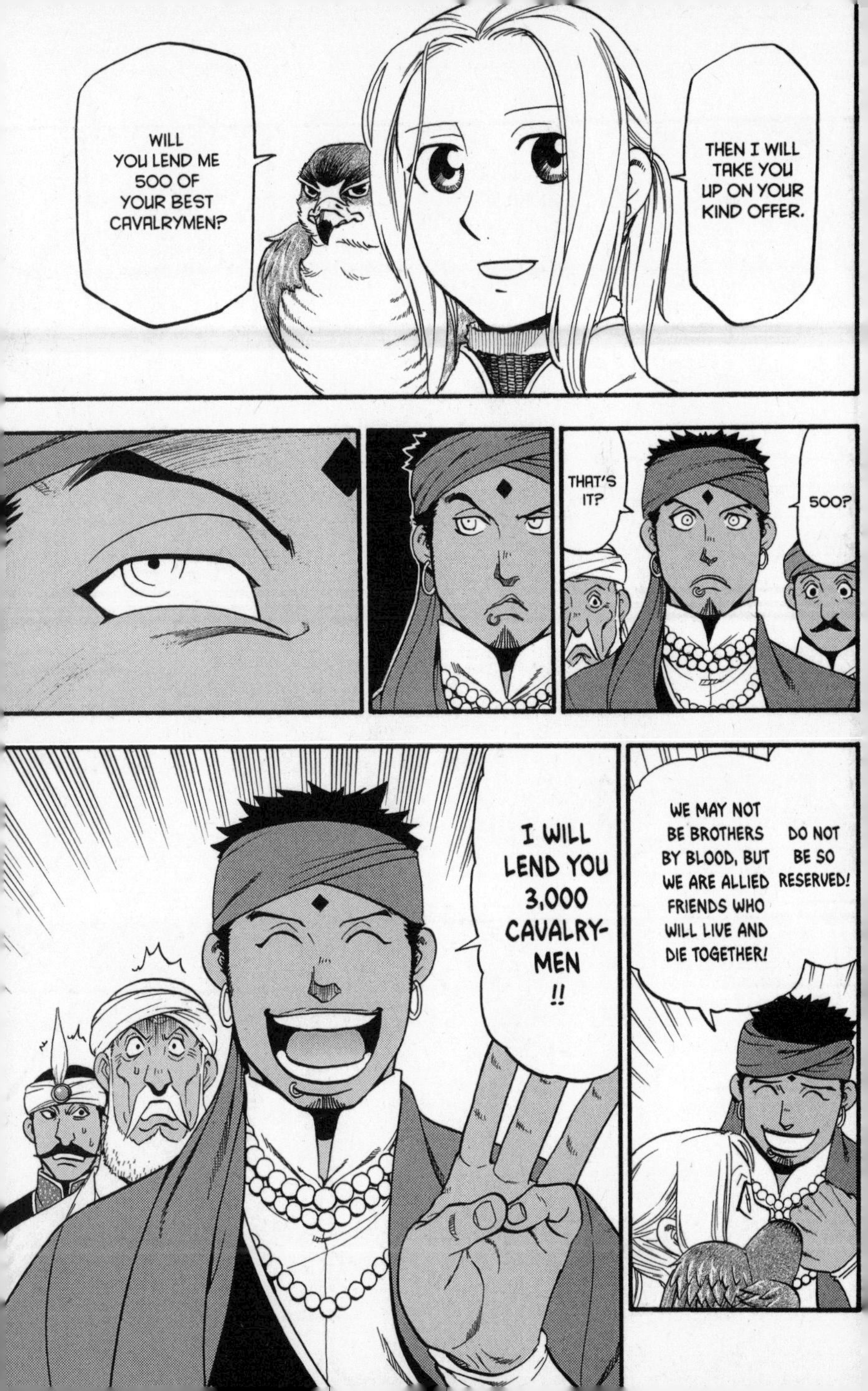
THEN I WILL TAKE YOU UP ON YOUR KIND OFFER.
WILL YOU LEND ME 500 OF YOUR BEST CAVALRYMEN?
500?
THAT'S IT?
DO NOT BE SO RESERVED!
WE MAY NOT BE BROTHERS BY BLOOD, BUT WE ARE ALLIED FRIENDS WHO WILL LIVE AND DIE TOGETHER!
I WILL LEND YOU 3,000 CAVALRY-MEN !!

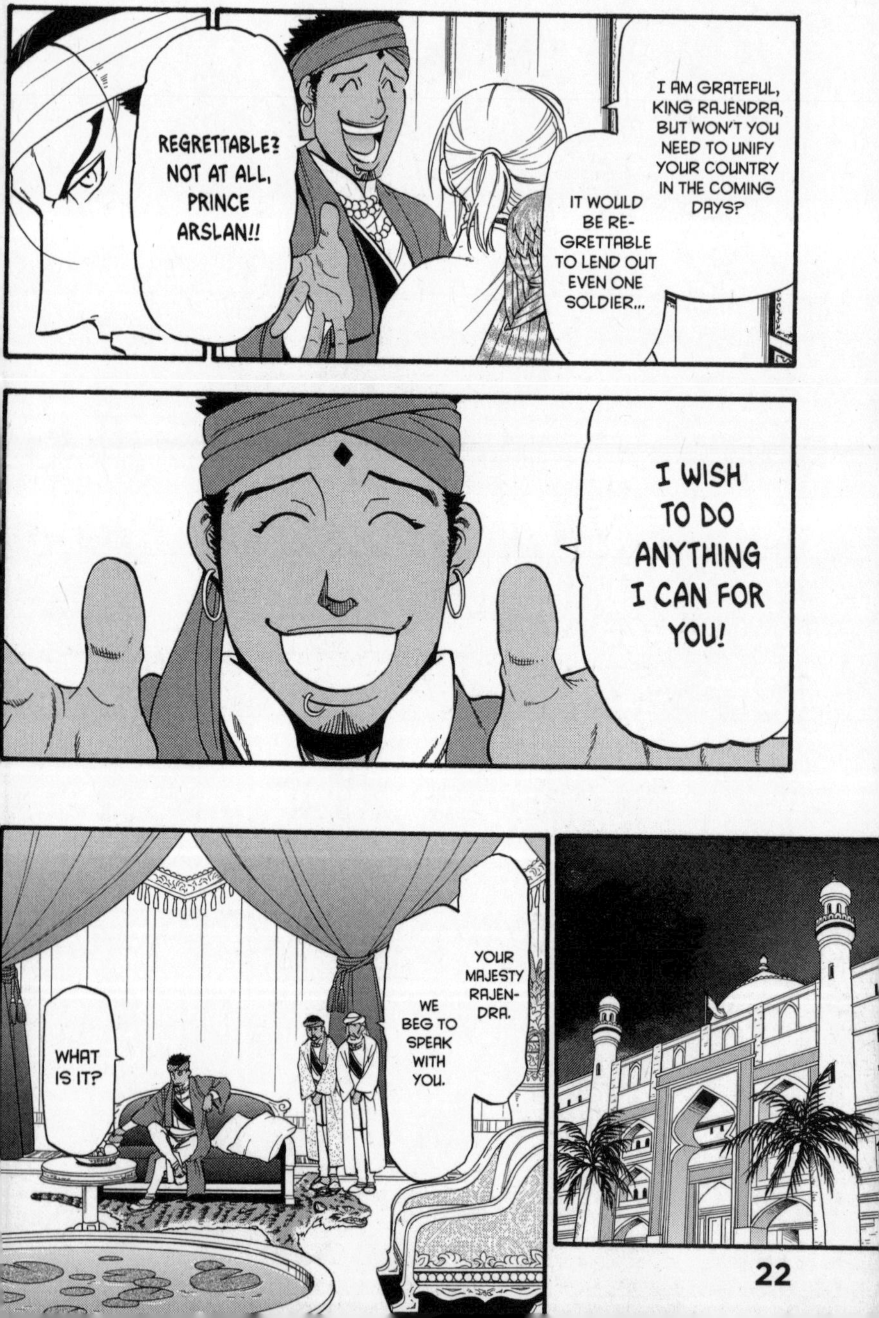
I AM GRATEFUL, KING RAJENDRA, BUT WON'T YOU NEED TO UNIFY YOUR COUNTRY IN THE COMING DAYS?
IT WOULD BE RE-GRETTABLE TO LEND OUT EVEN ONE SOLDIER...
REGRETTABLE? NOT AT ALL, PRINCE ARSLAN!!
I WISH TO DO ANYTHING I CAN FOR YOU!
YOUR MAJESTY RAJEN-DRA.
WE BEG TO SPEAK WITH YOU.
WHAT IS IT?

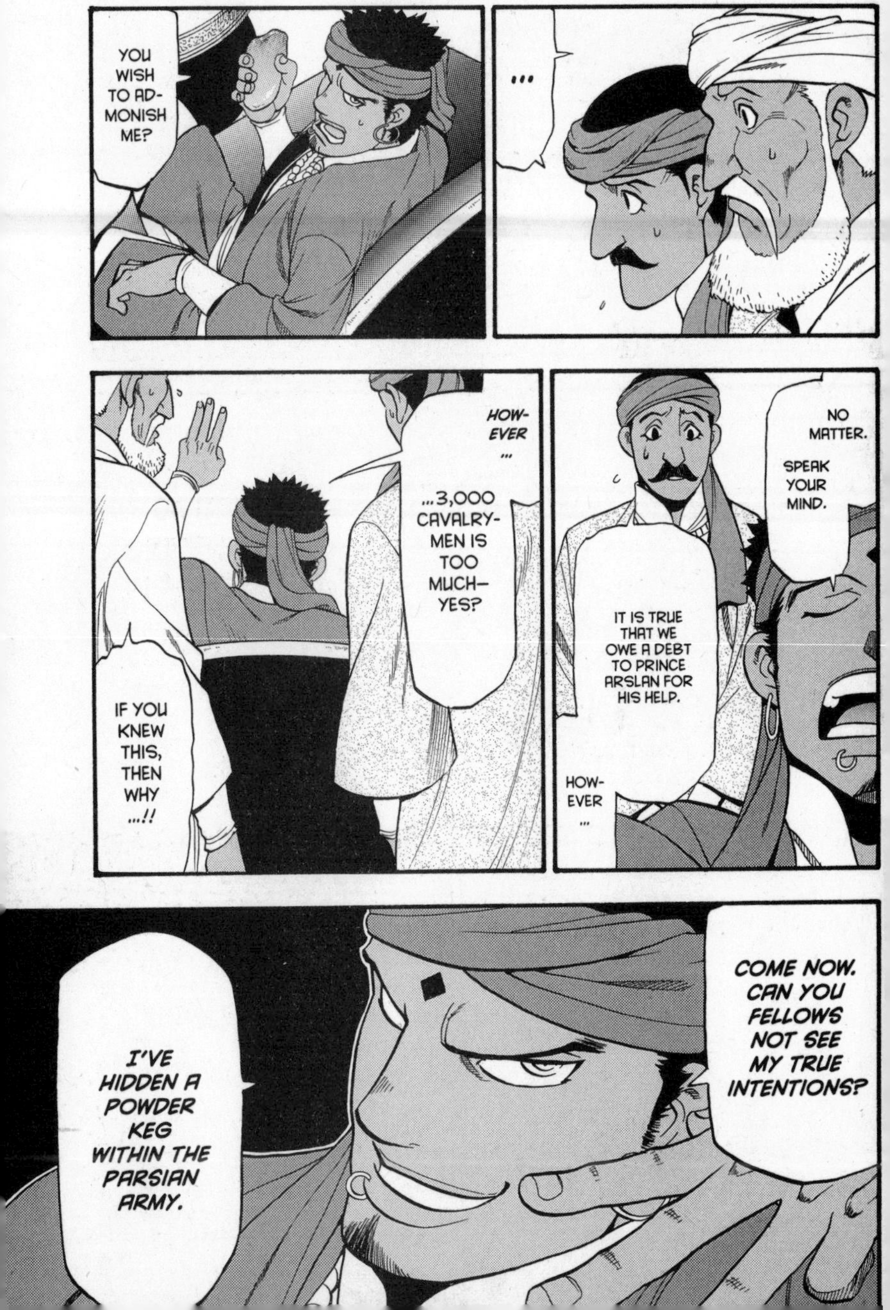
...
YOU WISH TO AD-MONISH ME?
NO MATTER.
SPEAK YOUR MIND.
IT IS TRUE THAT WE OWE A DEBT TO PRINCE ARSLAN FOR HIS HELP.
HOW-EVER ...
HOW-EVER ...
...3,000 CAVALRY-MEN IS TOO MUCH-YES?
IF YOU KNEW THIS, THEN WHY ...!!
COME NOW. CAN YOU FELLOWS NOT SEE MY TRUE INTENTIONS?
I'VE HIDDEN A POWDER KEG WITHIN THE PARSIAN ARMY.

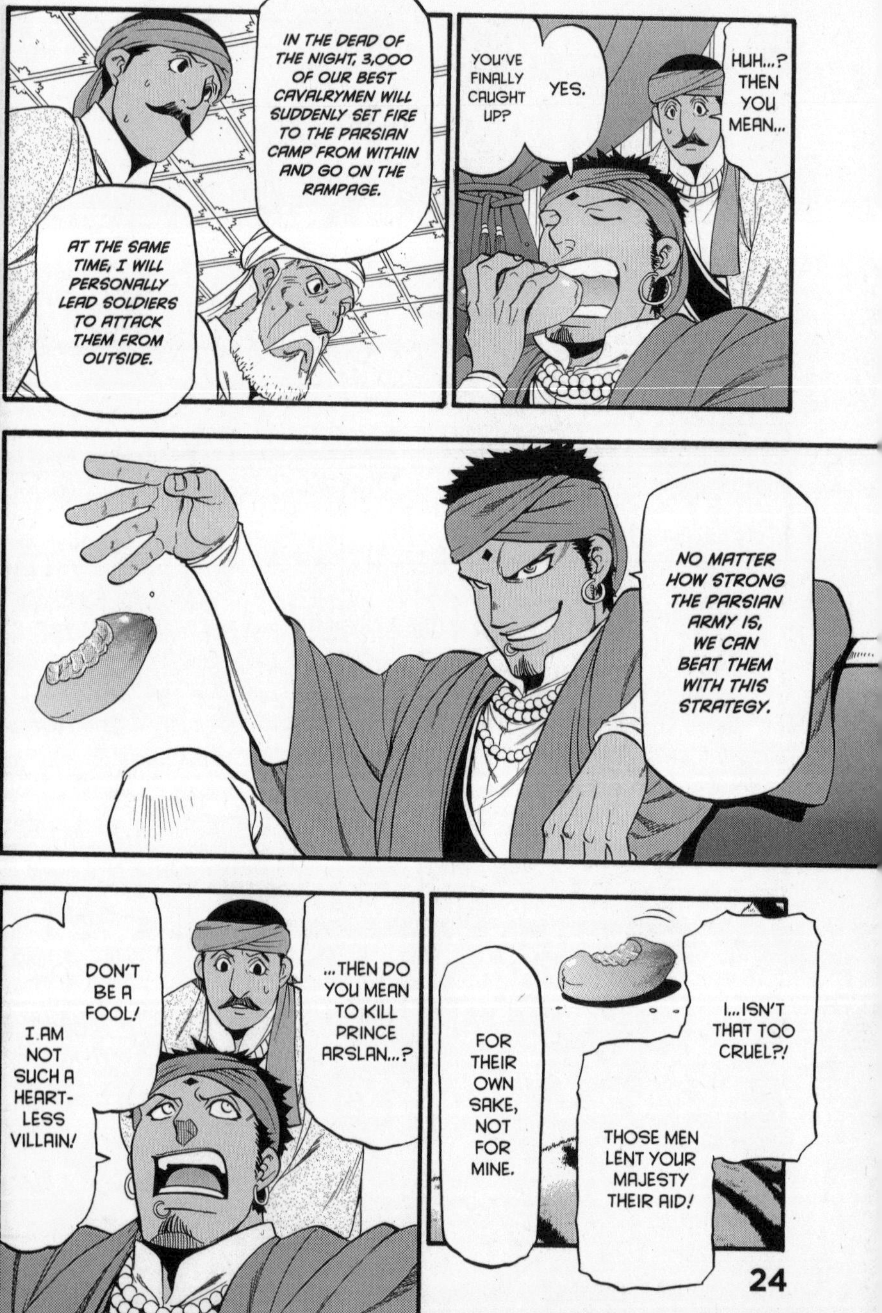
HUH...? THEN YOU MEAN...
YES.
YOU'VE FINALLY CAUGHT UP?
IN THE DEAD OF THE NIGHT, 3,000 OF OUR BEST CAVALRYMEN WILL SUDDENLY SET FIRE TO THE PARSIAN CAMP FROM WITHIN AND GO ON THE RAMPAGE.
AT THE SAME TIME, I WILL PERSONALLY LEAD SOLDIERS TO ATTACK THEM FROM OUTSIDE.
NO MATTER HOW STRONG THE PARSIAN ARMY IS, WE CAN BEAT THEM WITH THIS STRATEGY.
I...ISN'T THAT TOO CRUEL?!
THOSE MEN LENT YOUR MAJESTY THEIR AID!
FOR THEIR OWN SAKE, NOT FOR MINE.
...THEN DO YOU MEAN TO KILL PRINCE ARSLAN...?
DON'T BE A FOOL!
I AM NOT SUCH A HEART-LESS VILLAIN!

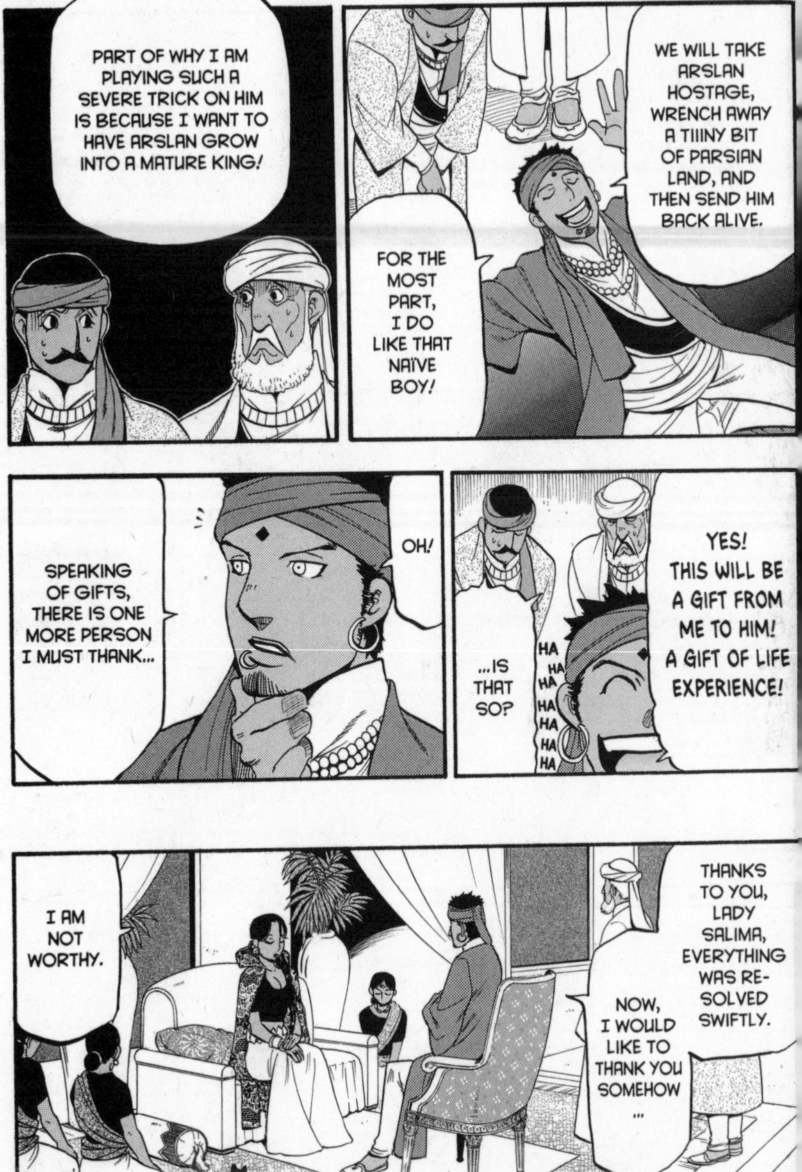
WE WILL TAKE ARSLAN HOSTAGE, WRENCH AWAY A TIIINY BIT OF PARSIAN LAND, AND THEN SEND HIM BACK ALIVE.
FOR THE MOST PART, I DO LIKE THAT NAÏVE BOY!
PART OF WHY I AM PLAYING SUCH A SEVERE TRICK ON HIM IS BECAUSE I WANT TO HAVE ARSLAN GROW INTO A MATURE KING!
YES! THIS WILL BE A GIFT FROM ME TO HIM! A GIFT OF LIFE EXPERIENCE!
HA HA HA HA HA HA HA HA
...IS THAT SO?
OH!
SPEAKING OF GIFTS, THERE IS ONE MORE PERSON I MUST THANK...
THANKS TO YOU, LADY SALIMA, EVERYTHING WAS RE-SOLVED SWIFTLY.
NOW, I WOULD LIKE TO THANK YOU SOMEHOW ...
I AM NOT WORTHY.

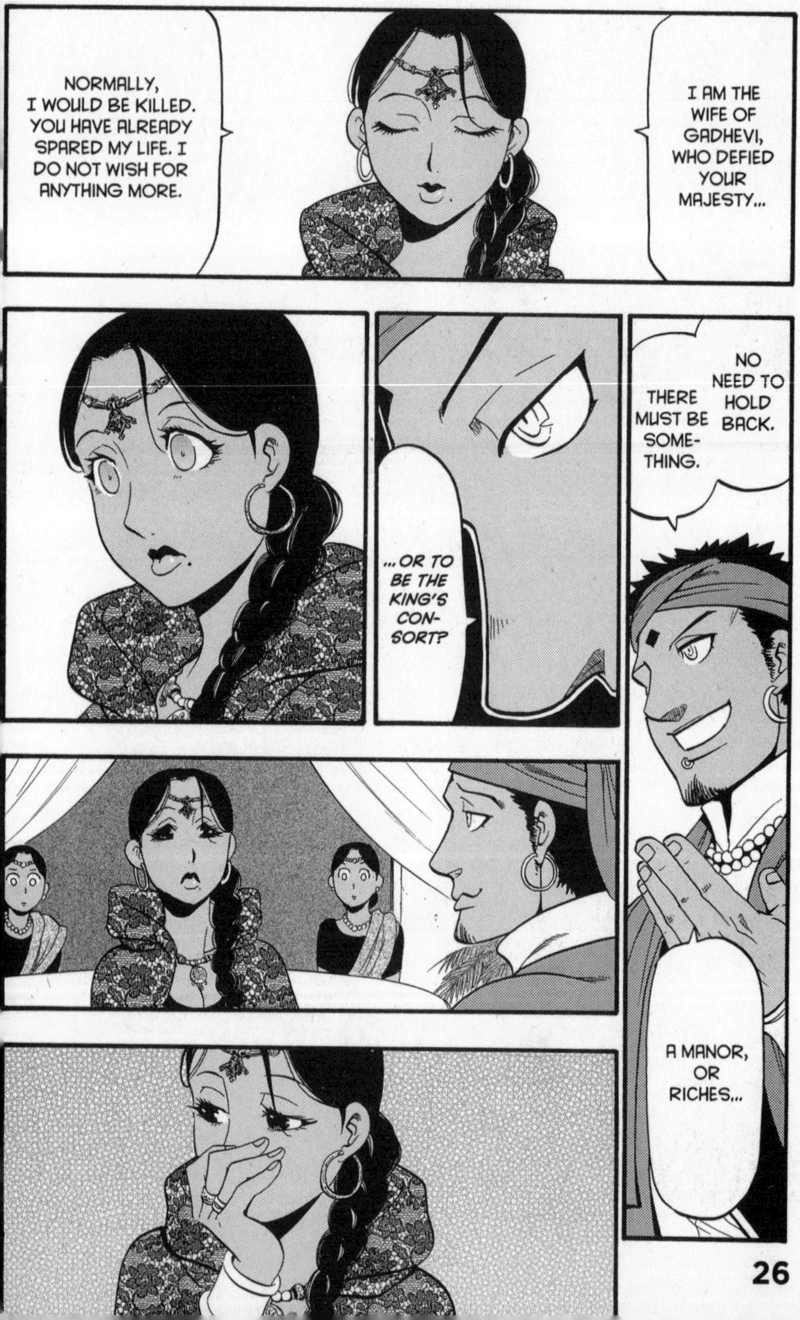
I AM THE WIFE OF GADHEVI, WHO DEFIED YOUR MAJESTY...
NORMALLY, I WOULD BE KILLED. YOU HAVE ALREADY SPARED MY LIFE. I DO NOT WISH FOR ANYTHING MORE.
NO NEED TO HOLD BACK.
THERE MUST BE SOME-THING.
A MANOR, OR RICHES...
...OR TO BE THE KING'S CON-SORT?

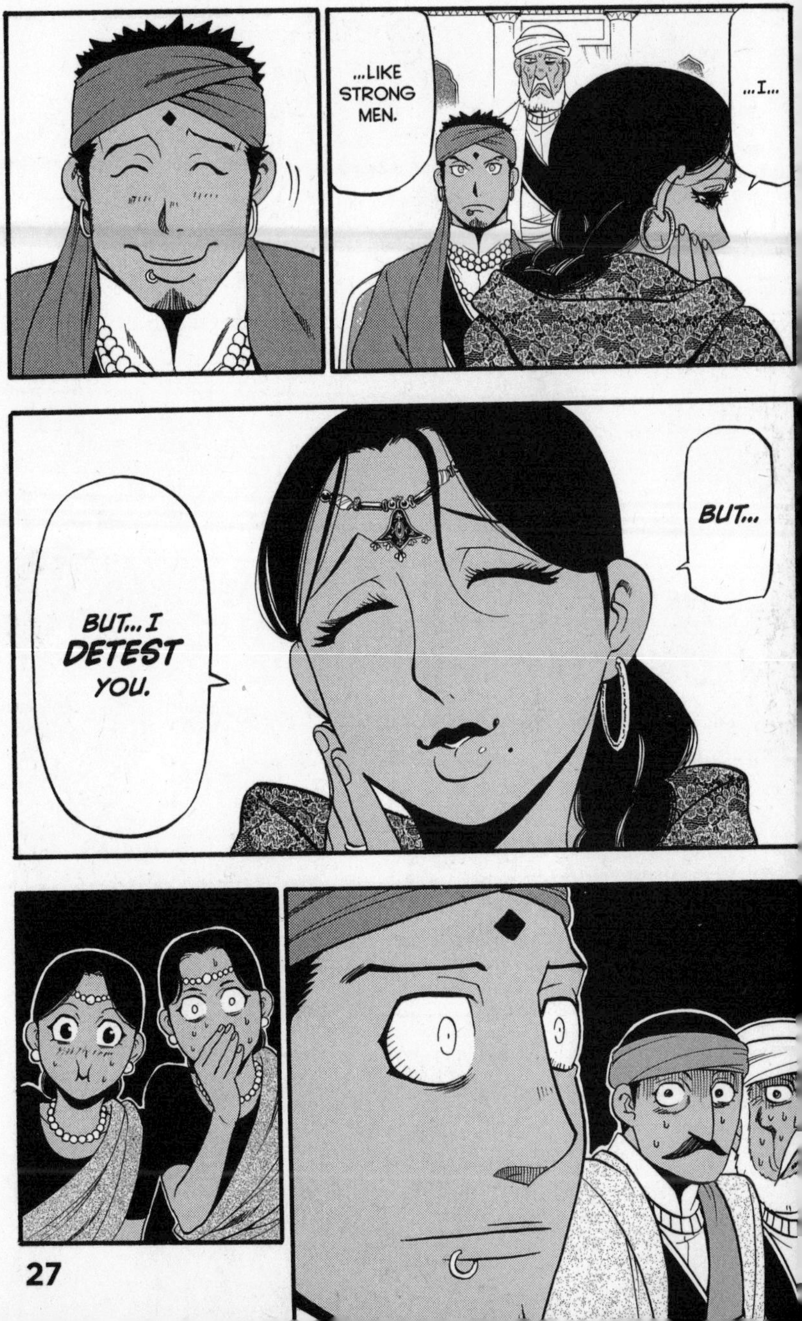

...I...
...LIKE STRONG MEN.
BUT...
BUT... I **DETEST** YOU.

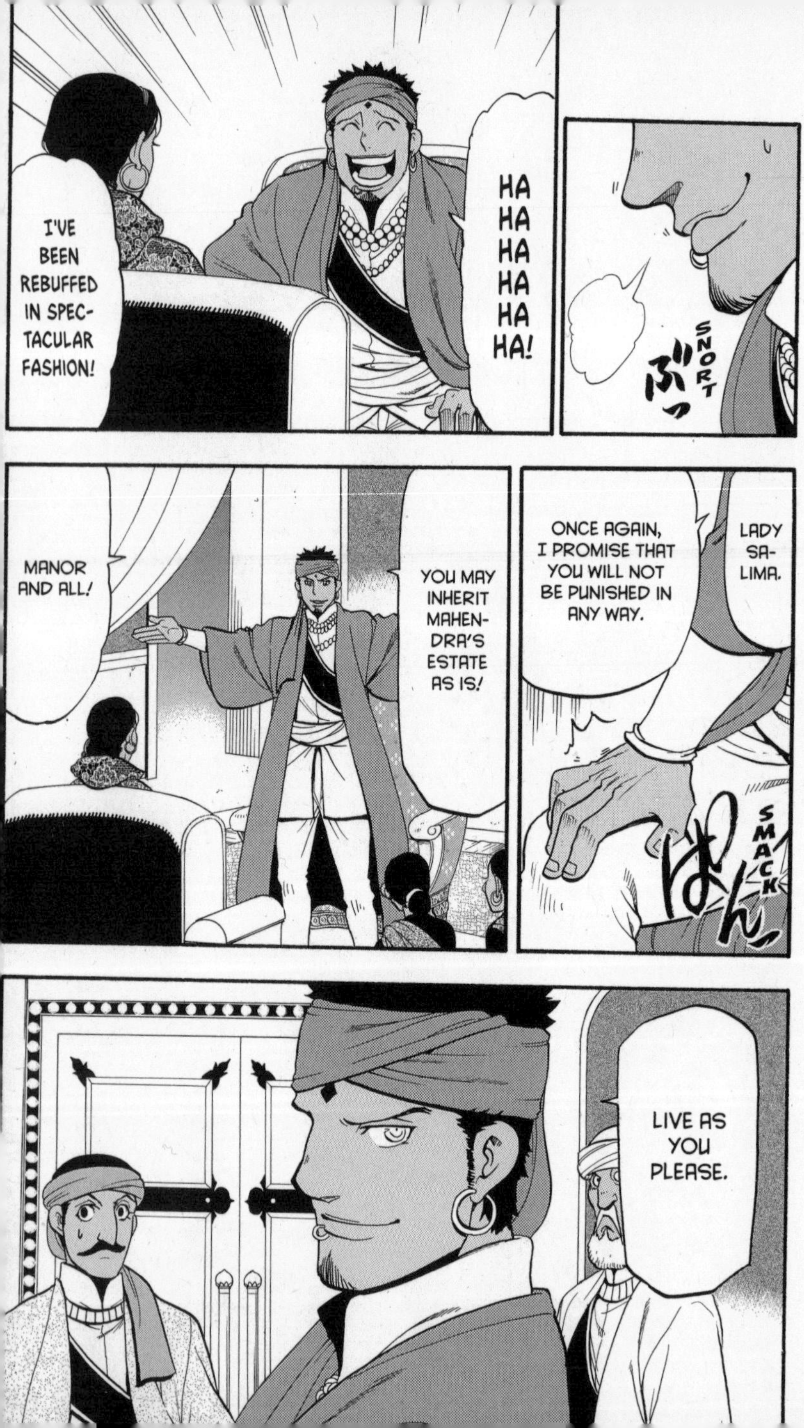
SNORT
HA HA HA HA HA HA!
I'VE BEEN REBUFFED IN SPECTACULAR FASHION!
LADY SALIMA.
ONCE AGAIN, I PROMISE THAT YOU WILL NOT BE PUNISHED IN ANY WAY.
SMACK
YOU MAY INHERIT MAHENDRA'S ESTATE AS IS!
MANOR AND ALL!
LIVE AS YOU PLEASE.

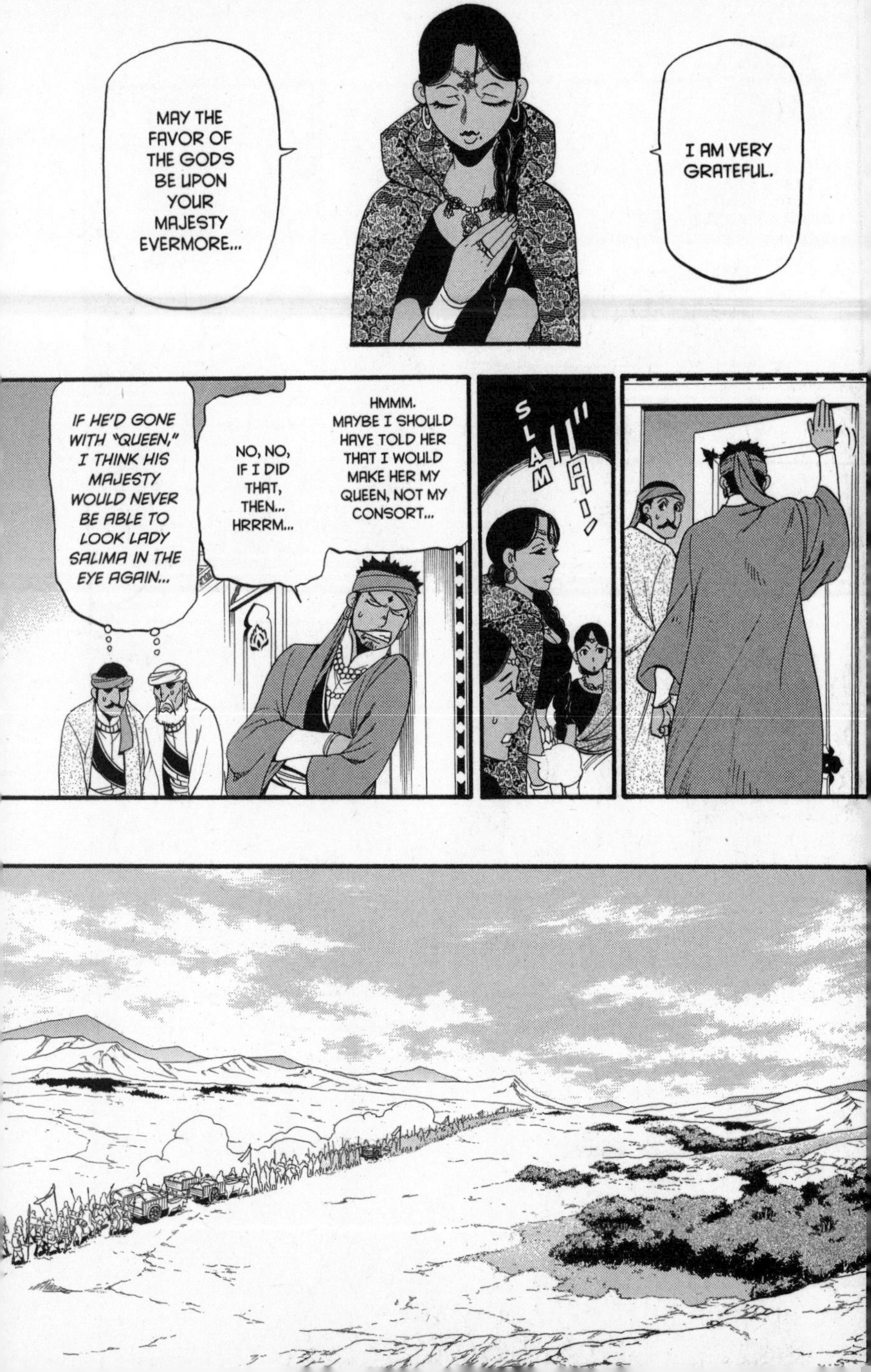
I AM VERY GRATEFUL.
MAY THE FAVOR OF THE GODS BE UPON YOUR MAJESTY EVERMORE...
SLAM
HMMM. MAYBE I SHOULD HAVE TOLD HER THAT I WOULD MAKE HER MY QUEEN, NOT MY CONSORT...
NO, NO, IF I DID THAT, THEN... HRRRM...
IF HE'D GONE WITH "QUEEN," I THINK HIS MAJESTY WOULD NEVER BE ABLE TO LOOK LADY SALIMA IN THE EYE AGAIN...

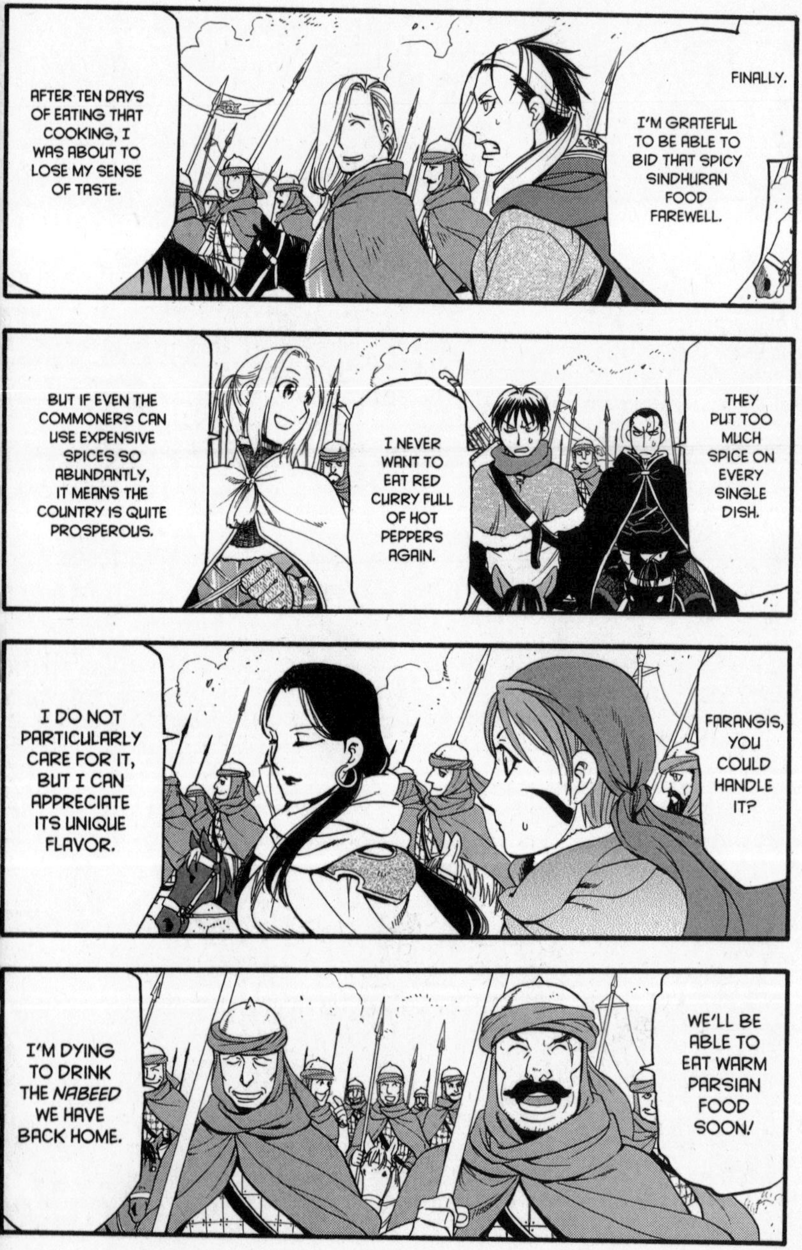
FINALLY.
I'M GRATEFUL TO BE ABLE TO BID THAT SPICY SINDHURAN FOOD FAREWELL.
AFTER TEN DAYS OF EATING THAT COOKING, I WAS ABOUT TO LOSE MY SENSE OF TASTE.
THEY PUT TOO MUCH SPICE ON EVERY SINGLE DISH.
I NEVER WANT TO EAT RED CURRY FULL OF HOT PEPPERS AGAIN.
BUT IF EVEN THE COMMONERS CAN USE EXPENSIVE SPICES SO ABUNDANTLY, IT MEANS THE COUNTRY IS QUITE PROSPEROUS.
FARANGIS, YOU COULD HANDLE IT?
I DO NOT PARTICULARLY CARE FOR IT, BUT I CAN APPRECIATE ITS UNIQUE FLAVOR.
WE'LL BE ABLE TO EAT WARM PARSIAN FOOD SOON!
I'M DYING TO DRINK THE *NABEED* WE HAVE BACK HOME.

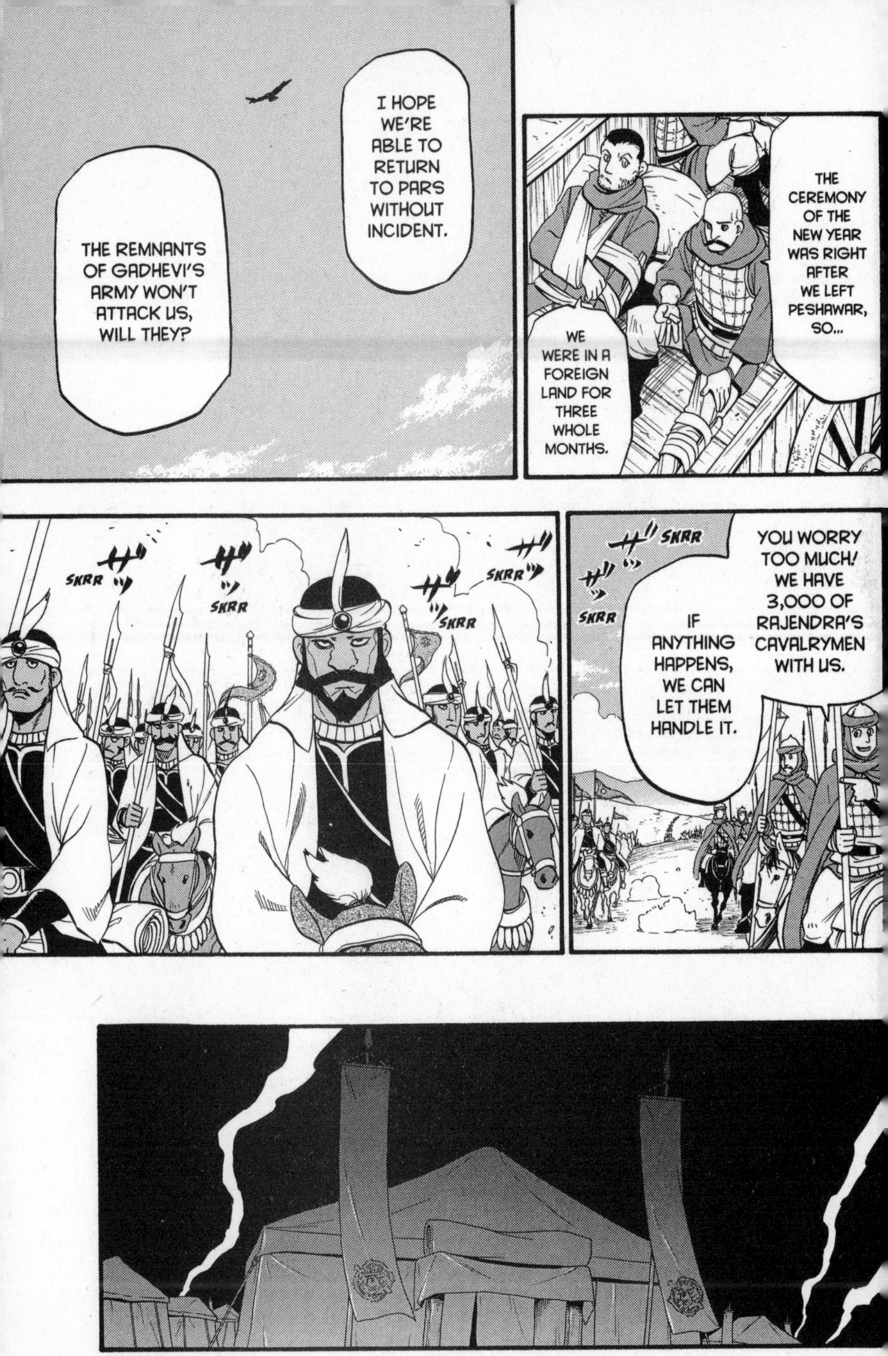
THE CEREMONY OF THE NEW YEAR WAS RIGHT AFTER WE LEFT PESHAWAR, SO...
WE WERE IN A FOREIGN LAND FOR THREE WHOLE MONTHS.
I HOPE WE'RE ABLE TO RETURN TO PARS WITHOUT INCIDENT.
THE REMNANTS OF GADHEVI'S ARMY WON'T ATTACK US, WILL THEY?
SKRR
SKRR
YOU WORRY TOO MUCH! WE HAVE 3,000 OF RAJENDRA'S CAVALRYMEN WITH US.
IF ANYTHING HAPPENS, WE CAN LET THEM HANDLE IT.
SKRR
SKRR
SKRR
SKRR
SKRR

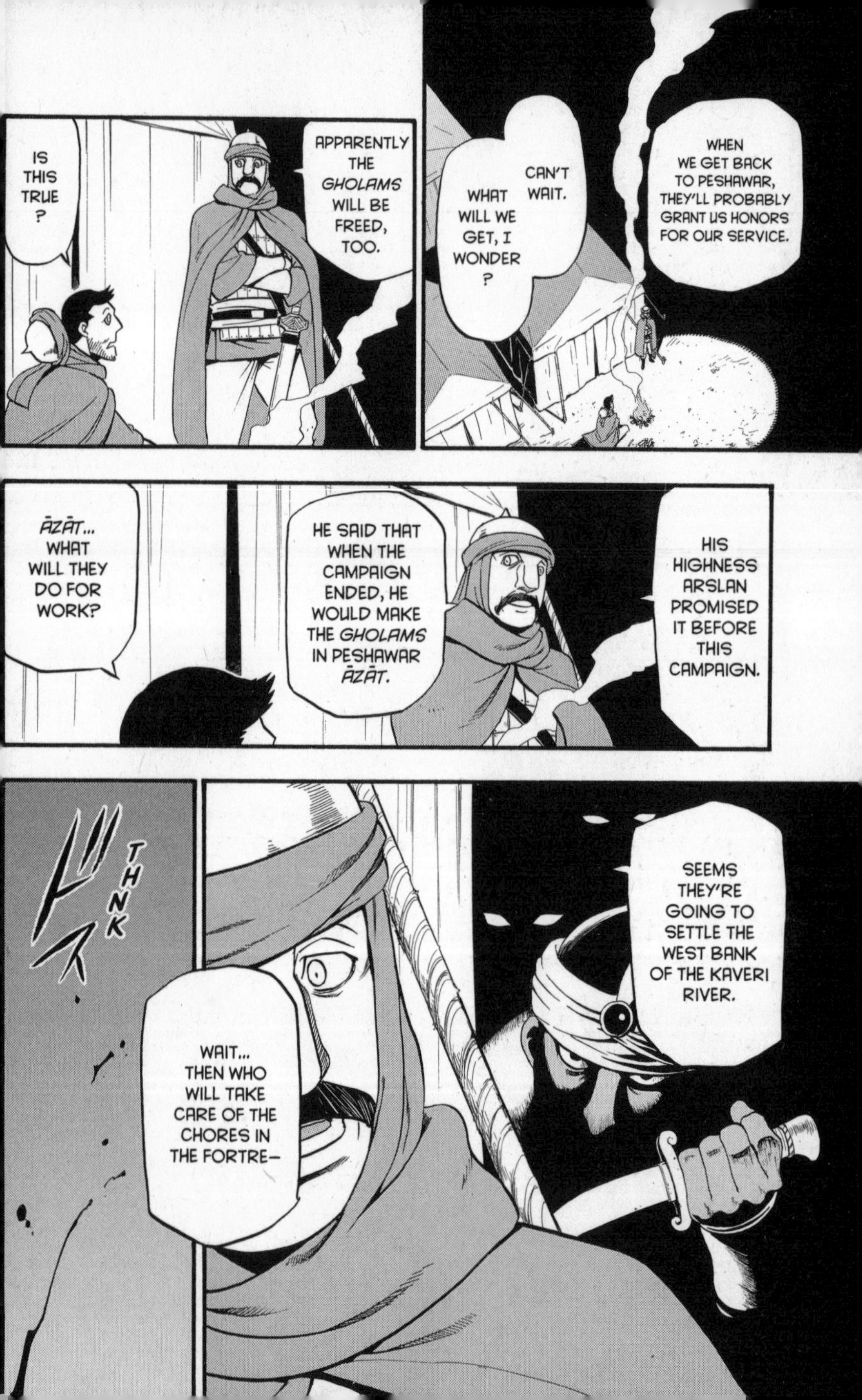
WHEN WE GET BACK TO PESHAWAR, THEY'LL PROBABLY GRANT US HONORS FOR OUR SERVICE.
CAN'T WAIT.
WHAT WILL WE GET, I WONDER?
APPARENTLY THE *GHOLAMS* WILL BE FREED, TOO.
IS THIS TRUE?
HIS HIGHNESS ARSLAN PROMISED IT BEFORE THIS CAMPAIGN.
HE SAID THAT WHEN THE CAMPAIGN ENDED, HE WOULD MAKE THE *GHOLAMS* IN PESHAWAR *ĀZĀT*.
ĀZĀT... WHAT WILL THEY DO FOR WORK?
SEEMS THEY'RE GOING TO SETTLE THE WEST BANK OF THE KAVERI RIVER.
WAIT... THEN WHO WILL TAKE CARE OF THE CHORES IN THE FORTRE–
ドス
THNK

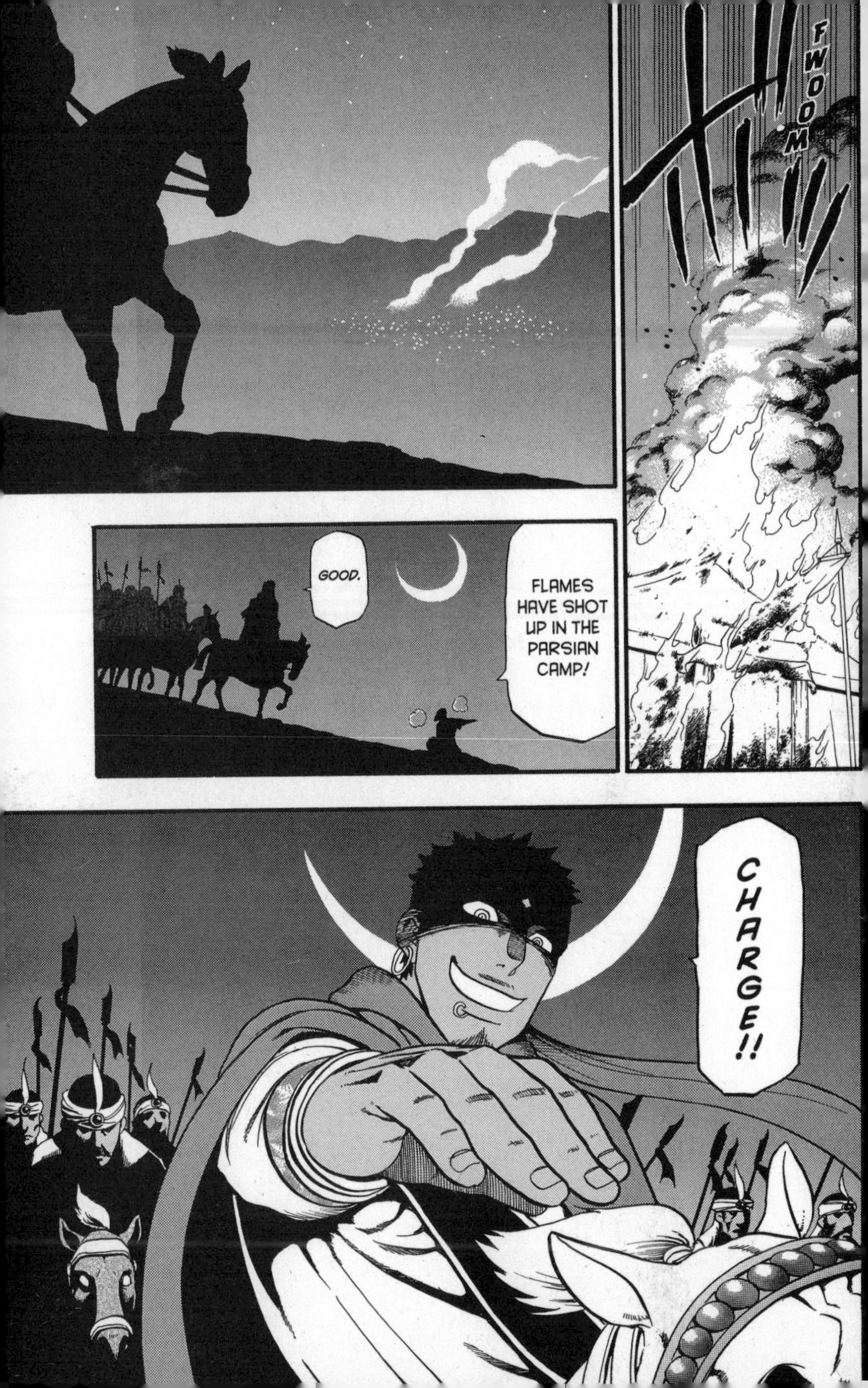
FWOOM
FLAMES HAVE SHOT UP IN THE PARSIAN CAMP!
GOOD.
CHARGE!!

THE HEROIC LEGEND OF
ARSLAN

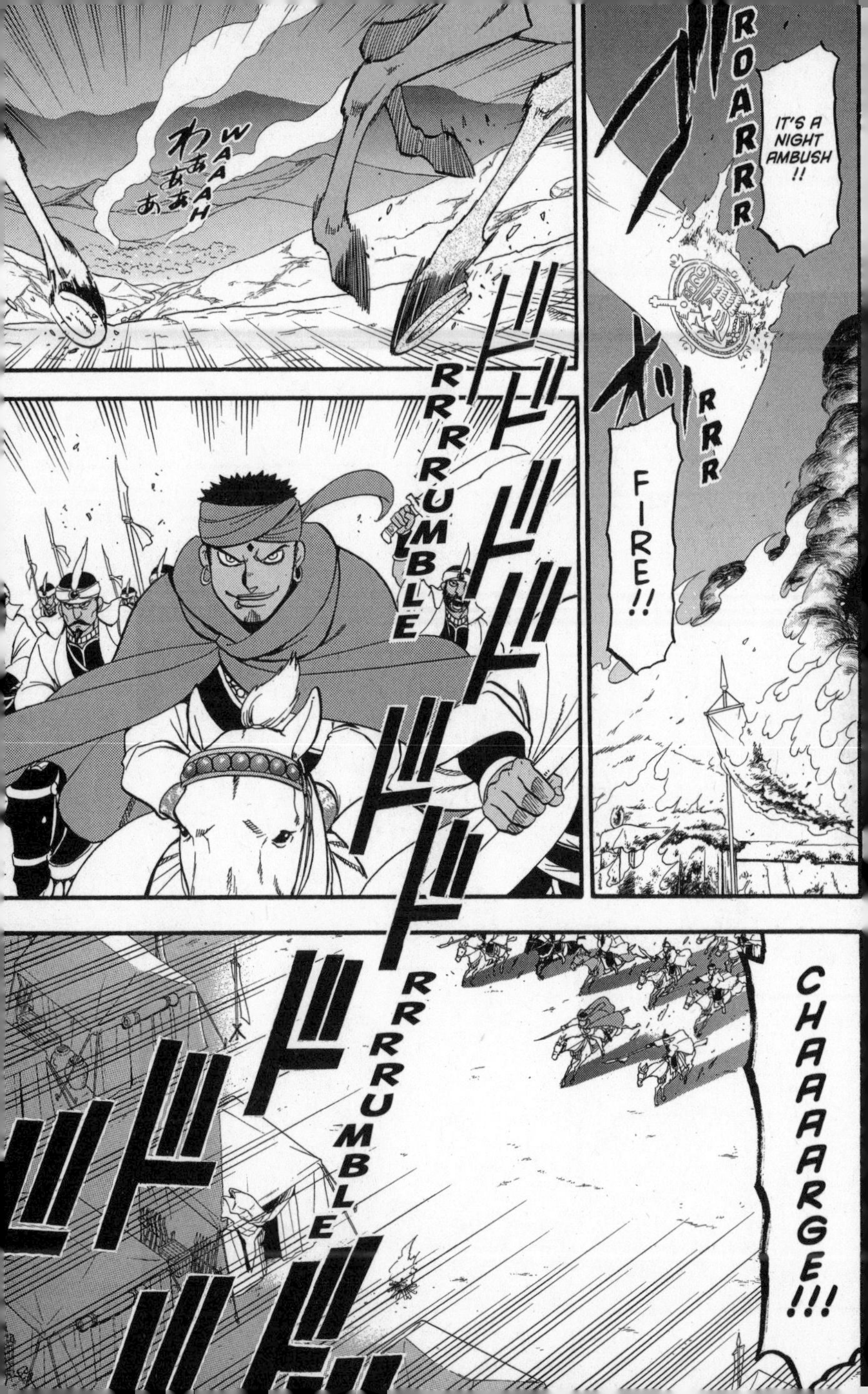
ROARRR
IT'S A NIGHT AMBUSH!!
RRR
FIRE!!
わあああ
WAAAH
RRRRUMBLE
CHAAAARGE!!!
RRRRUMBLE

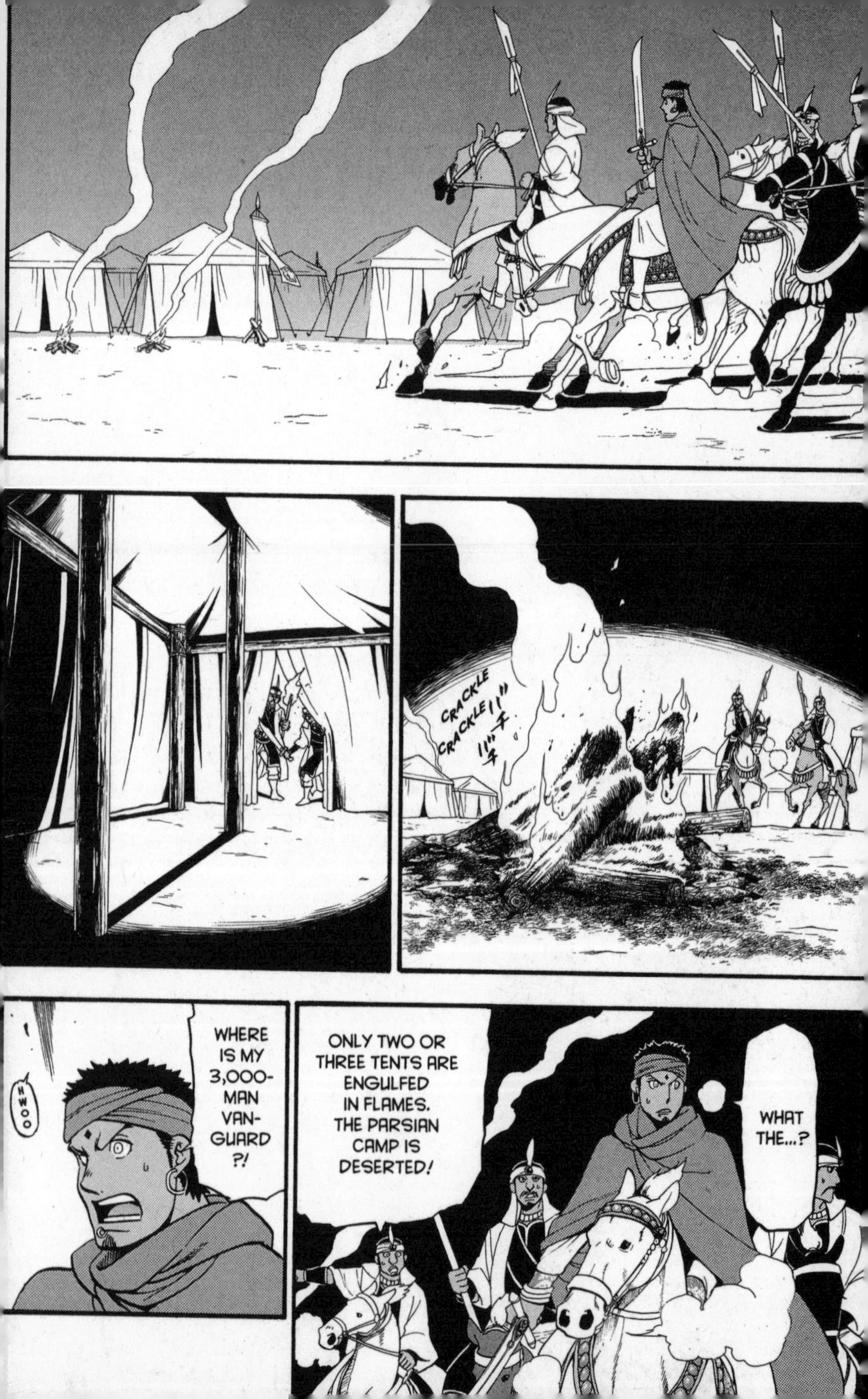
CRACKLE CRACKLE
パチ パチ
WHAT THE...?
ONLY TWO OR THREE TENTS ARE ENGULFED IN FLAMES. THE PARSIAN CAMP IS DESERTED!
WHERE IS MY 3,000-MAN VAN-GUARD ?!
HWOO

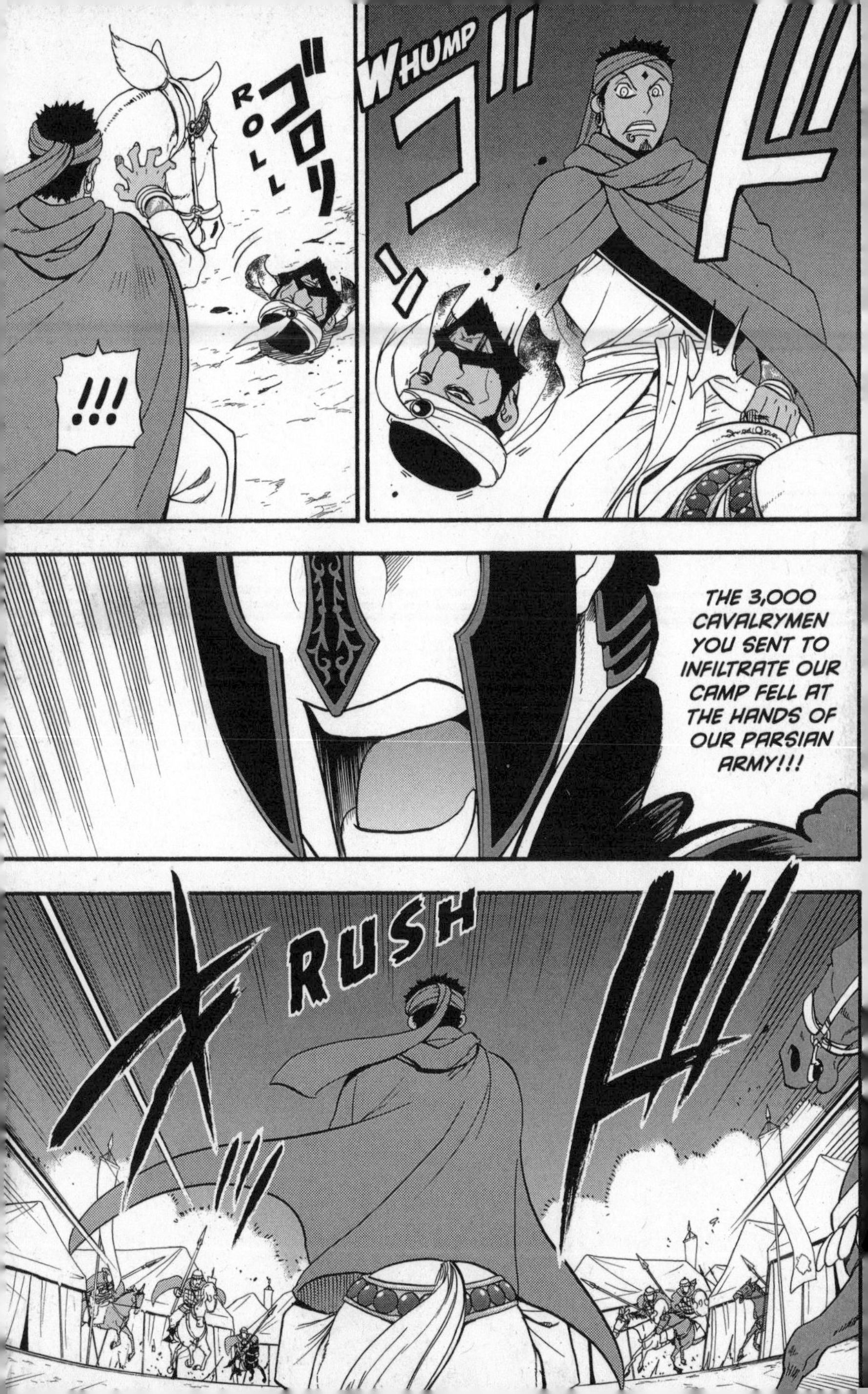
WHUMP
ROLL
ゴロリ
!!!
THE 3,000 CAVALRYMEN YOU SENT TO INFILTRATE OUR CAMP FELL AT THE HANDS OF OUR PARSIAN ARMY!!!
RUSH

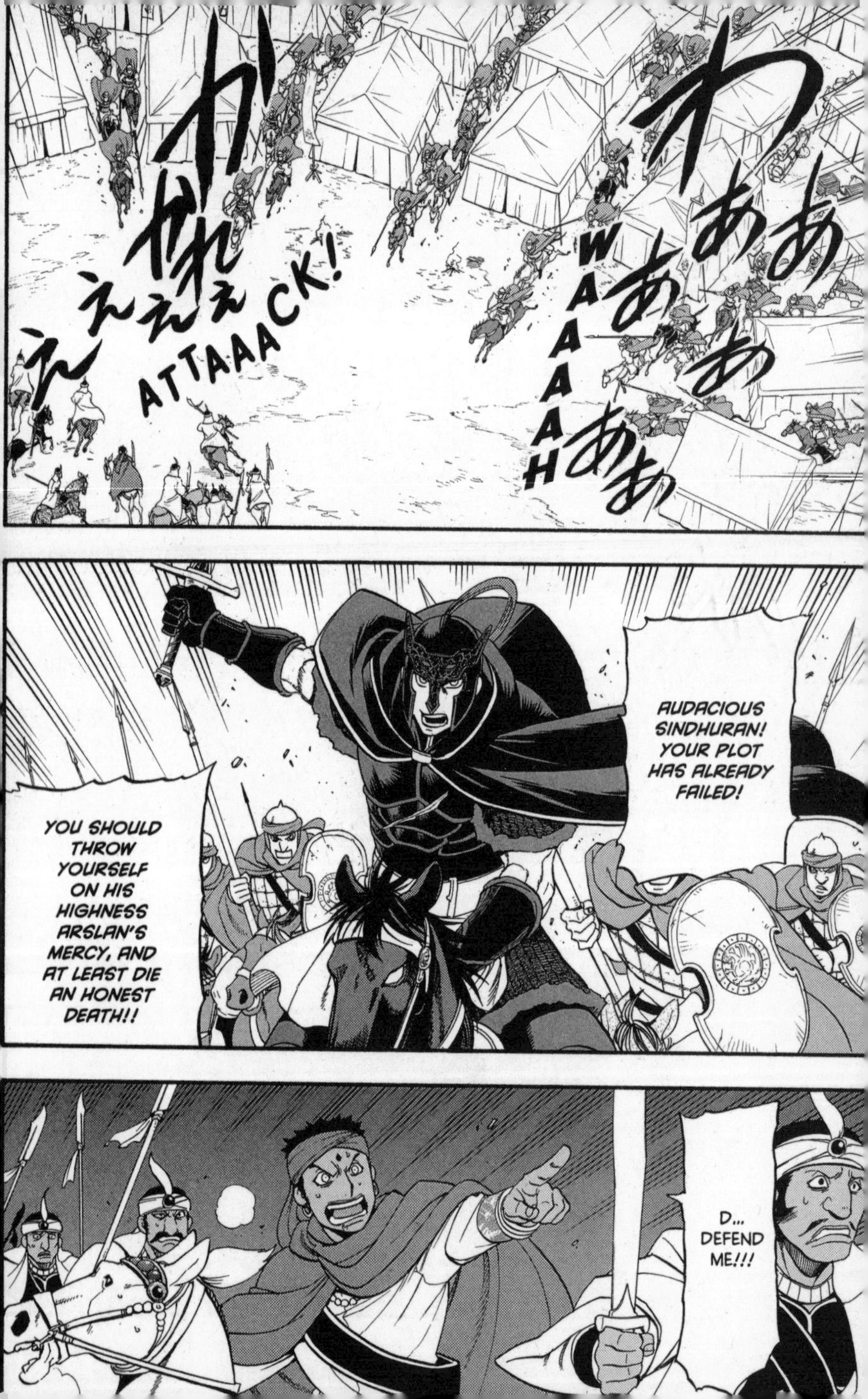
WAAAAAH
ATTAAACK!
AUDACIOUS SINDHURAN! YOUR PLOT HAS ALREADY FAILED!
YOU SHOULD THROW YOURSELF ON HIS HIGHNESS ARSLAN'S MERCY, AND AT LEAST DIE AN HONEST DEATH!!
D... DEFEND ME!!!

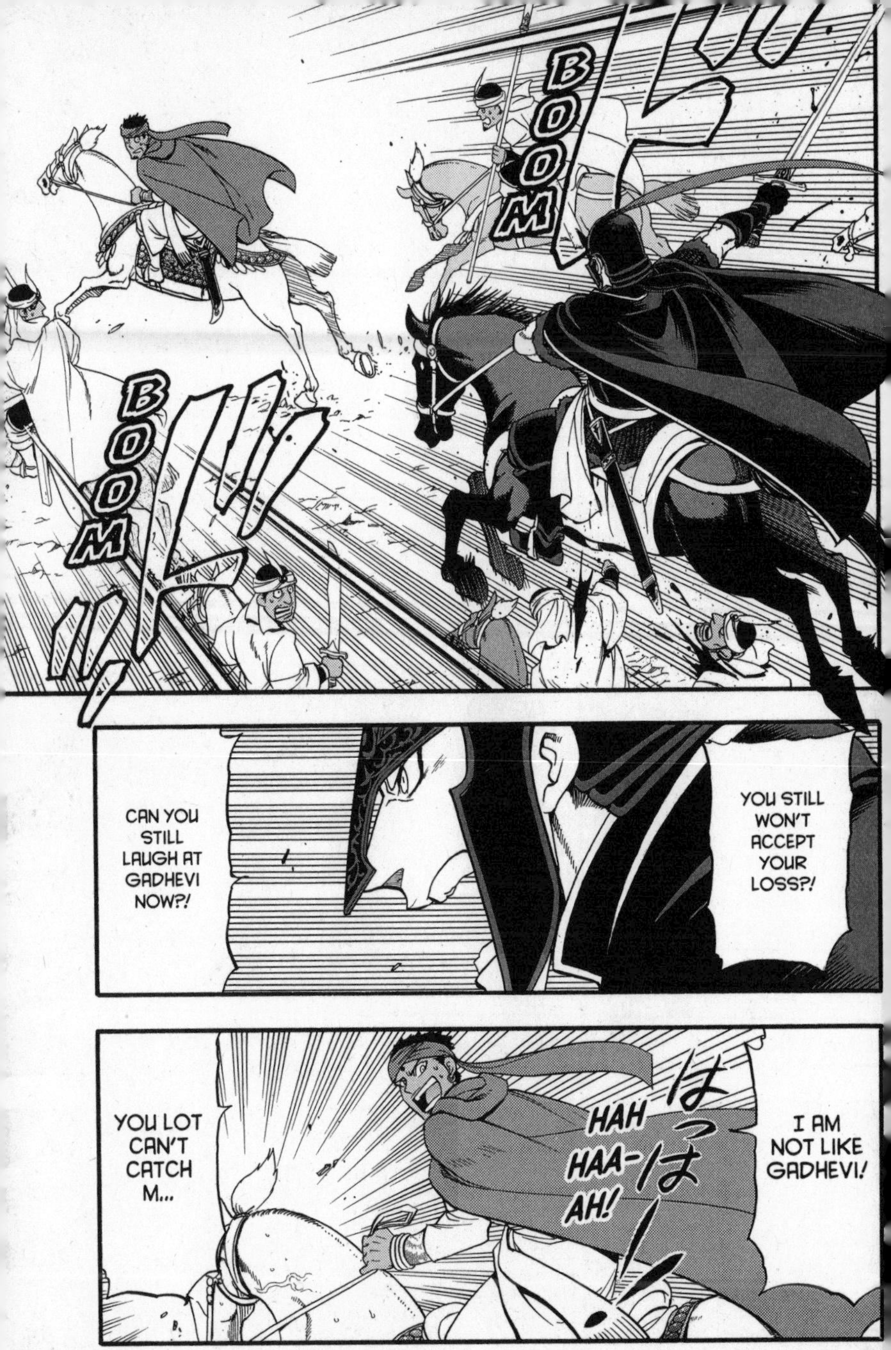
BOOM
BOOM
YOU STILL WON'T ACCEPT YOUR LOSS?!
CAN YOU STILL LAUGH AT GADHEVI NOW?!
I AM NOT LIKE GADHEVI!
はっは—!
HAH HAA-AH!
YOU LOT CAN'T CATCH M...

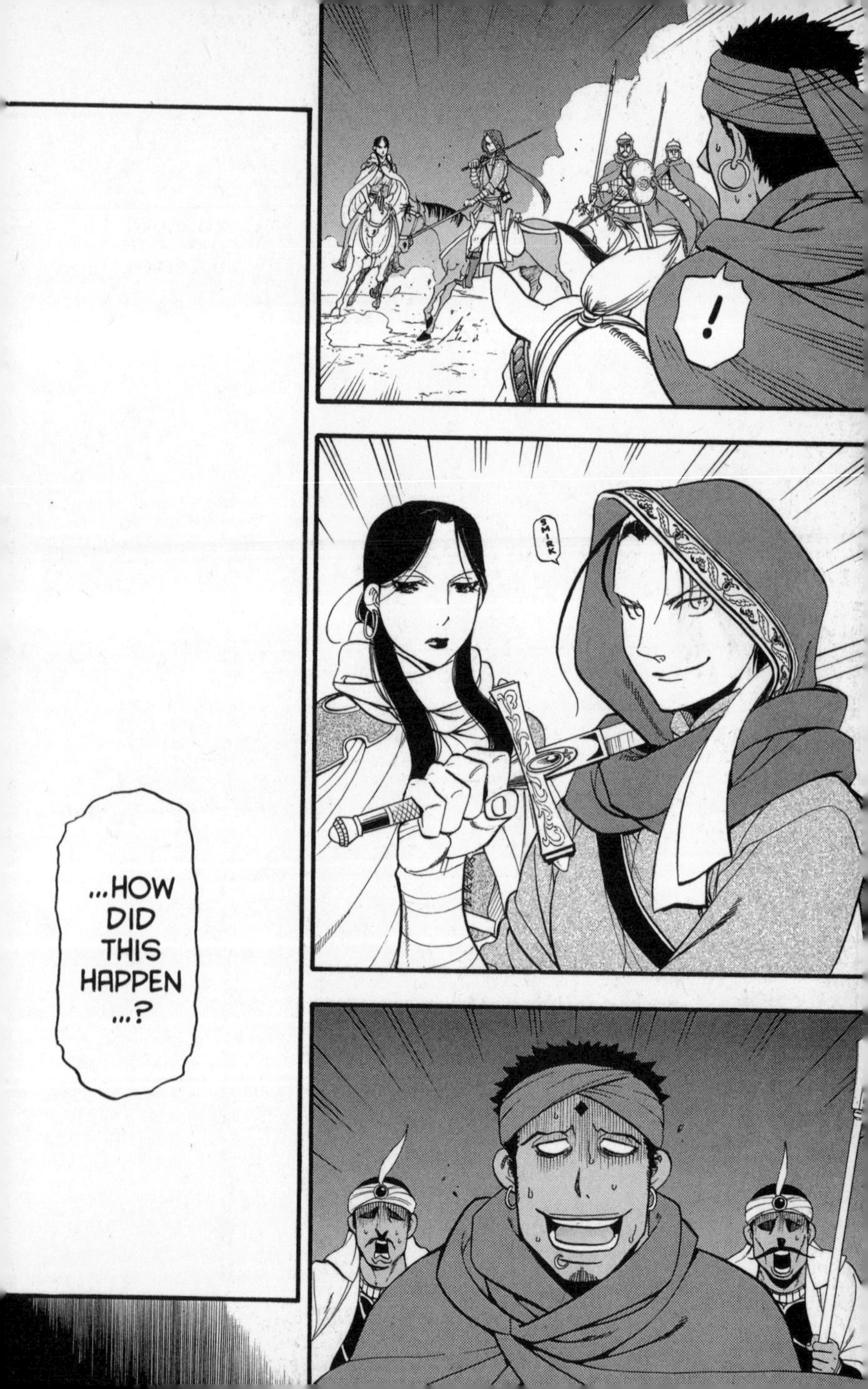
!
SMIRK
...HOW DID THIS HAPPEN ...?

HE SAID THAT WHEN THE CAMPAIGN ENDED, HE WOULD MAKE THE GHOLAMS IN PESHAWAR *ĀZĀT.*

APPARENTLY, THE *GHOLAMS* WILL BE FREED TOO.

ĀZĀT... WHAT WILL THEY DO FOR WORK?

TRULY ?

SEEMS THEY'RE GOING TO SETTLE THE WEST BANK OF THE KAVERI RIVER.

HIS HIGHNESS ARSLAN PROMISED IT BEFORE THIS CAMPAIGN.

AIT, , WAIT. N WHO TAKE ARE THE RES THE RTE...

Chapter 54: Return of the Warrior

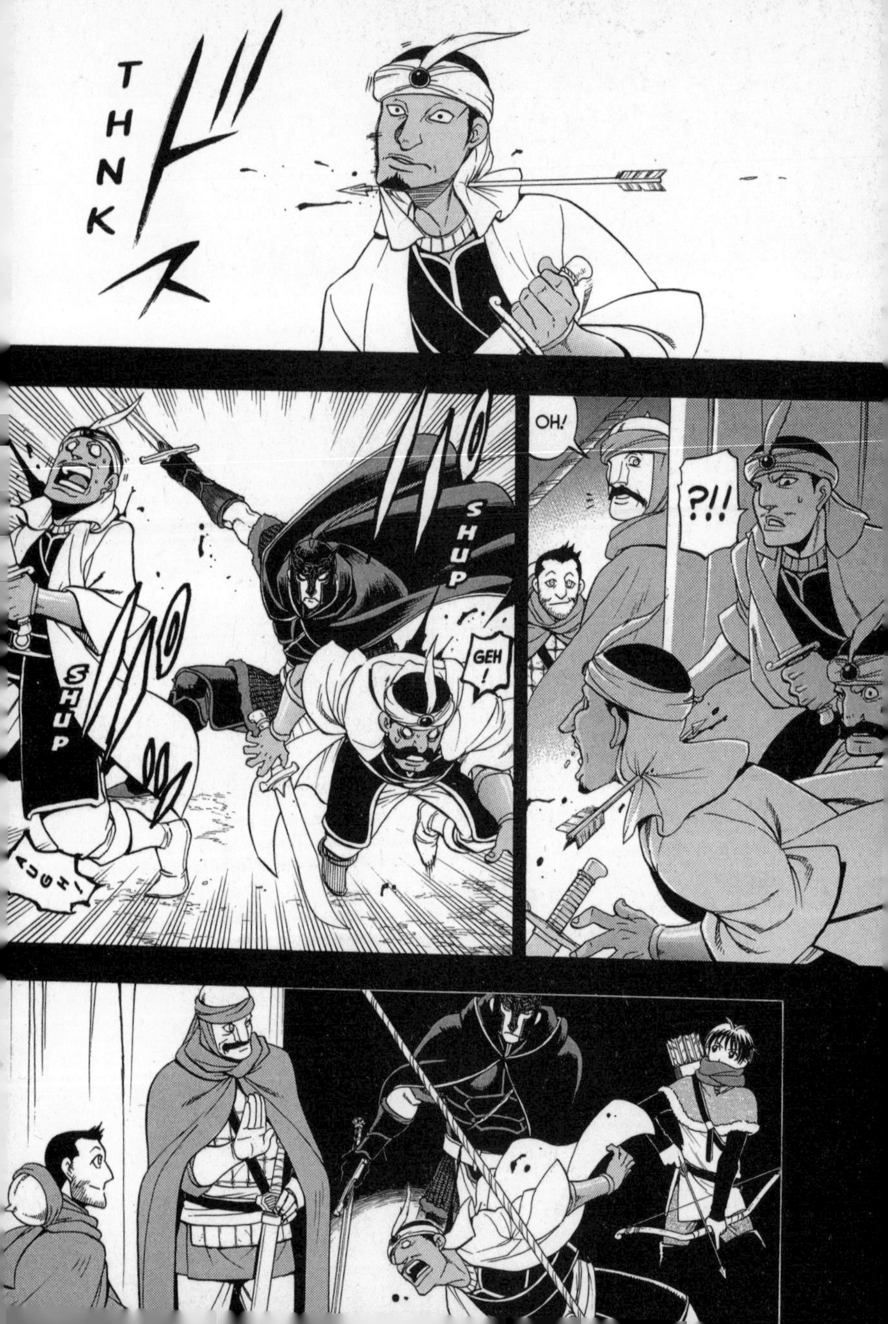
THNK
OH!
?!!
SHUP
GEH!
SHUP
AUGH!

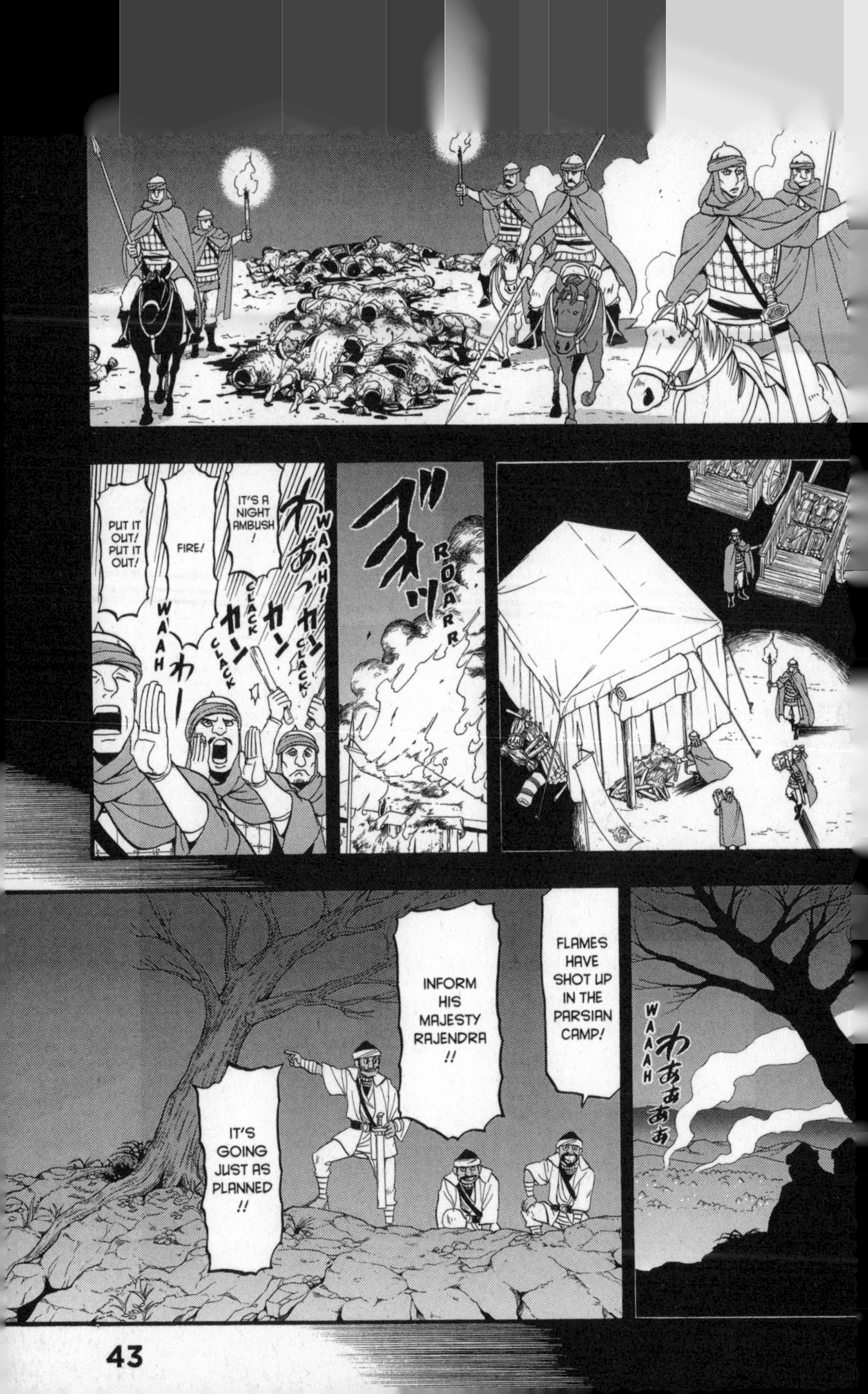
ゴオッ
ROARR
WAAAH!
わあっ
CLACK
カーン
CLACK
カーン
CLACK
カーン
IT'S A NIGHT AMBUSH!
FIRE!
PUT IT OUT! PUT IT OUT!
WAAH
わー
WAAAH
わあぁあ
FLAMES HAVE SHOT UP IN THE PARSIAN CAMP!
INFORM HIS MAJESTY RAJENDRA!!
IT'S GOING JUST AS PLANNED!!

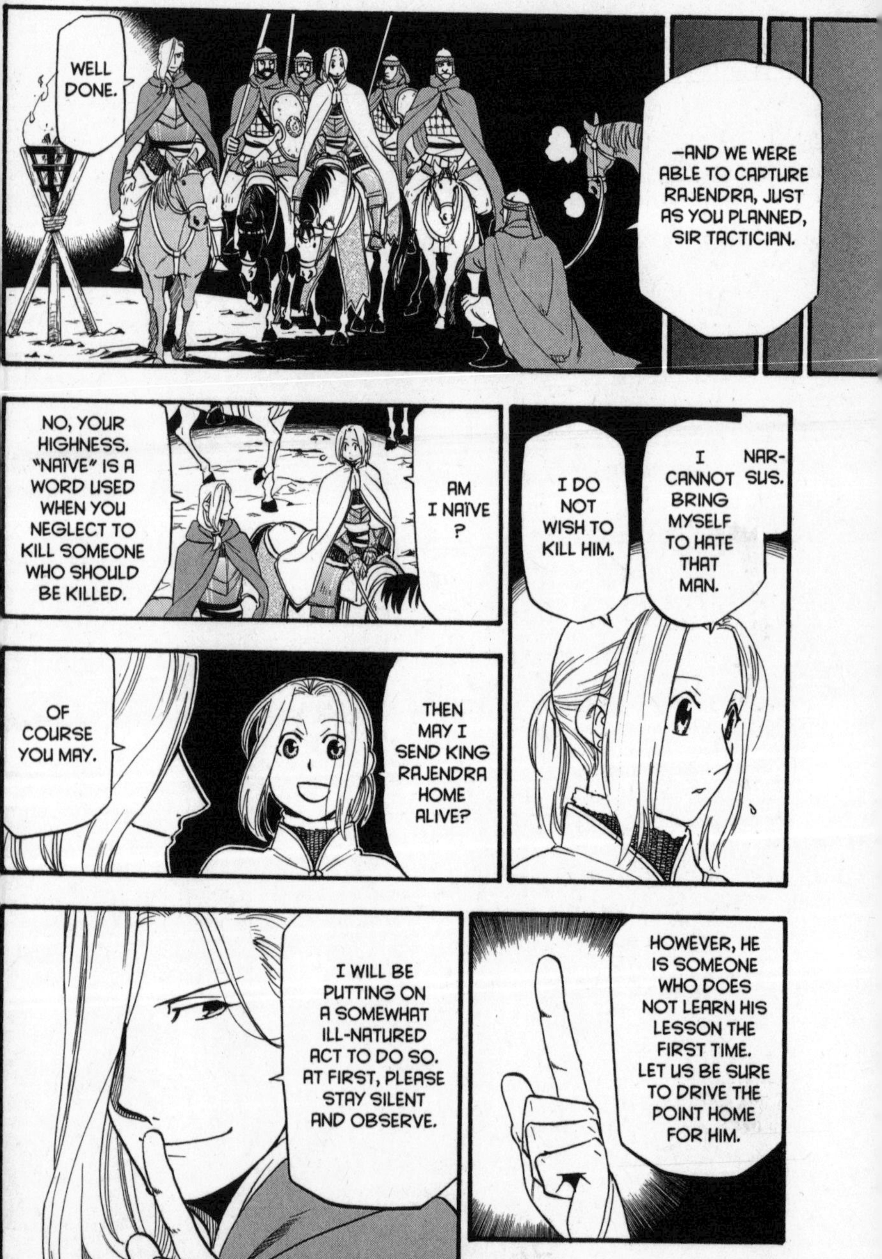
—AND WE WERE ABLE TO CAPTURE RAJENDRA, JUST AS YOU PLANNED, SIR TACTICIAN.
WELL DONE.
NARSUS.
I CANNOT BRING MYSELF TO HATE THAT MAN.
I DO NOT WISH TO KILL HIM.
AM I NAÏVE?
NO, YOUR HIGHNESS. "NAÏVE" IS A WORD USED WHEN YOU NEGLECT TO KILL SOMEONE WHO SHOULD BE KILLED.
THEN MAY I SEND KING RAJENDRA HOME ALIVE?
OF COURSE YOU MAY.
HOWEVER, HE IS SOMEONE WHO DOES NOT LEARN HIS LESSON THE FIRST TIME. LET US BE SURE TO DRIVE THE POINT HOME FOR HIM.
I WILL BE PUTTING ON A SOMEWHAT ILL-NATURED ACT TO DO SO. AT FIRST, PLEASE STAY SILENT AND OBSERVE.

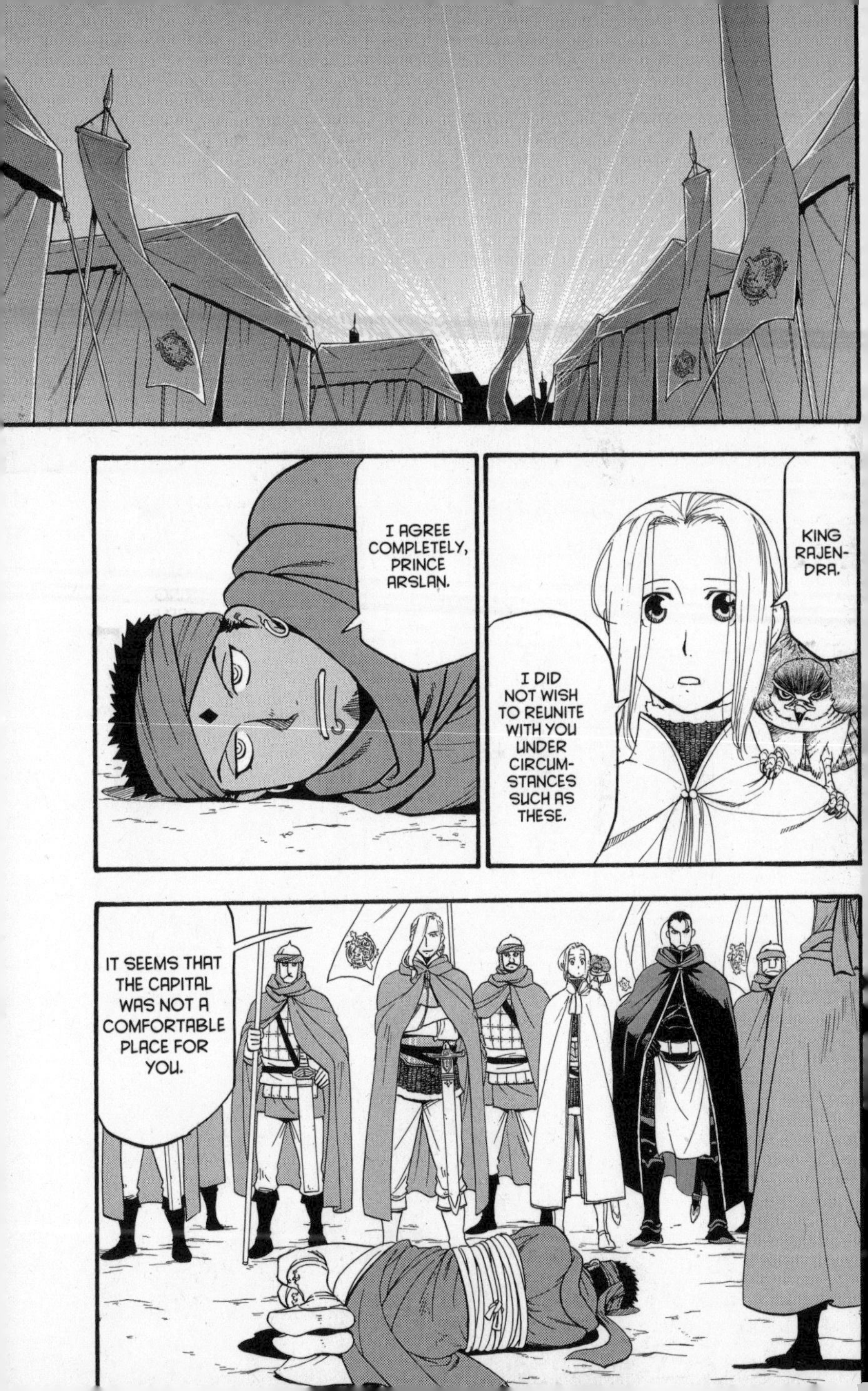
KING RAJEN-DRA.
I DID NOT WISH TO REUNITE WITH YOU UNDER CIRCUM-STANCES SUCH AS THESE.
I AGREE COMPLETELY, PRINCE ARSLAN.
IT SEEMS THAT THE CAPITAL WAS NOT A COMFORTABLE PLACE FOR YOU.

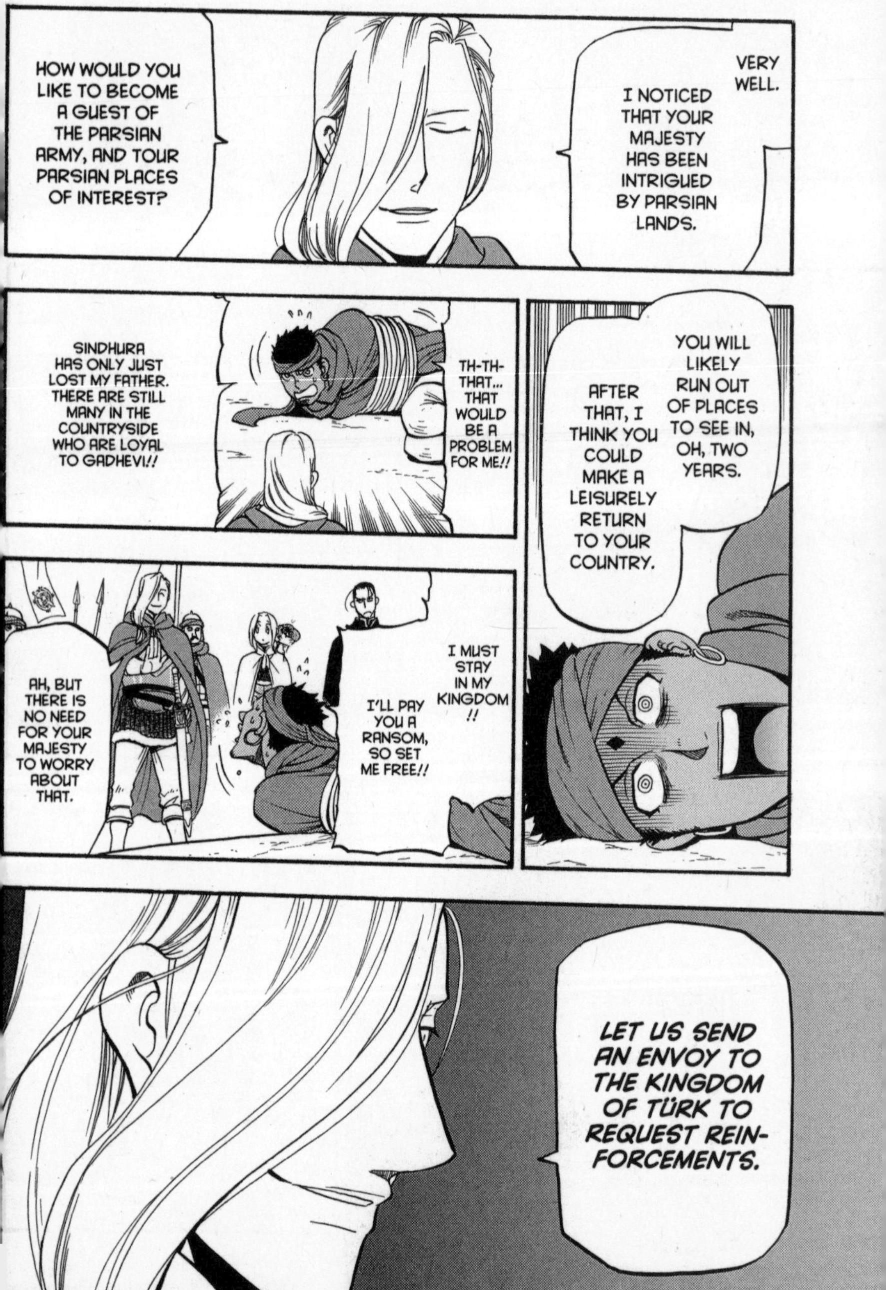
VERY WELL.
I NOTICED THAT YOUR MAJESTY HAS BEEN INTRIGUED BY PARSIAN LANDS.
HOW WOULD YOU LIKE TO BECOME A GUEST OF THE PARSIAN ARMY, AND TOUR PARSIAN PLACES OF INTEREST?
YOU WILL LIKELY RUN OUT OF PLACES TO SEE IN, OH, TWO YEARS.
AFTER THAT, I THINK YOU COULD MAKE A LEISURELY RETURN TO YOUR COUNTRY.
TH-TH-THAT... THAT WOULD BE A PROBLEM FOR ME!!
SINDHURA HAS ONLY JUST LOST MY FATHER. THERE ARE STILL MANY IN THE COUNTRYSIDE WHO ARE LOYAL TO GADHEVI!!
I MUST STAY IN MY KINGDOM!!
I'LL PAY YOU A RANSOM, SO SET ME FREE!!
AH, BUT THERE IS NO NEED FOR YOUR MAJESTY TO WORRY ABOUT THAT.
LET US SEND AN ENVOY TO THE KINGDOM OF TÜRK TO REQUEST REIN-FORCEMENTS.

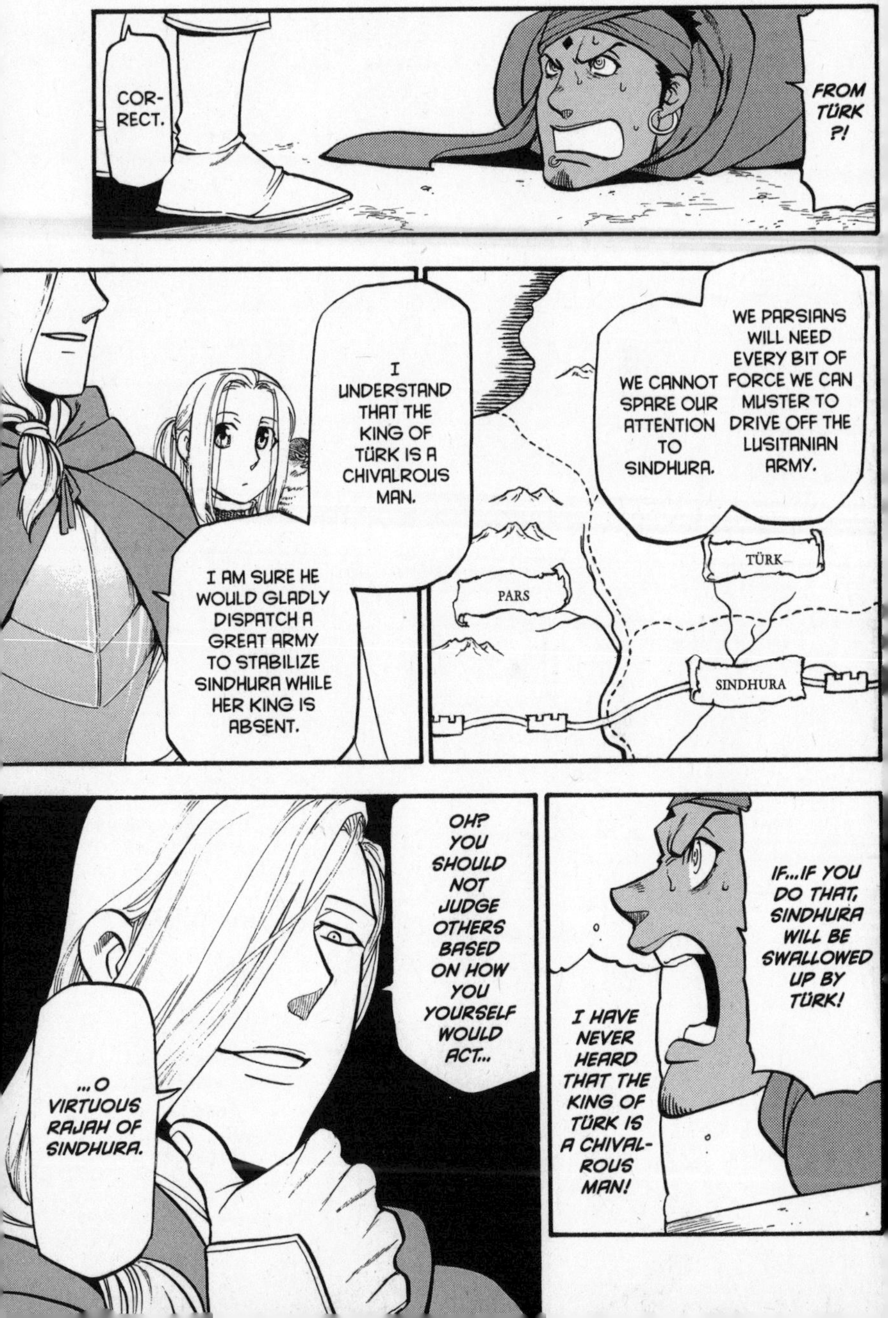
FROM TÜRK ?!
COR-RECT.
WE PARSIANS WILL NEED EVERY BIT OF FORCE WE CAN MUSTER TO DRIVE OFF THE LUSITANIAN ARMY.
WE CANNOT SPARE OUR ATTENTION TO SINDHURA.
TÜRK
PARS
SINDHURA
I UNDERSTAND THAT THE KING OF TÜRK IS A CHIVALROUS MAN.
I AM SURE HE WOULD GLADLY DISPATCH A GREAT ARMY TO STABILIZE SINDHURA WHILE HER KING IS ABSENT.
IF...IF YOU DO THAT, SINDHURA WILL BE SWALLOWED UP BY TÜRK!
I HAVE NEVER HEARD THAT THE KING OF TÜRK IS A CHIVAL-ROUS MAN!
OH? YOU SHOULD NOT JUDGE OTHERS BASED ON HOW YOU YOURSELF WOULD ACT...
...O VIRTUOUS RAJAH OF SINDHURA.

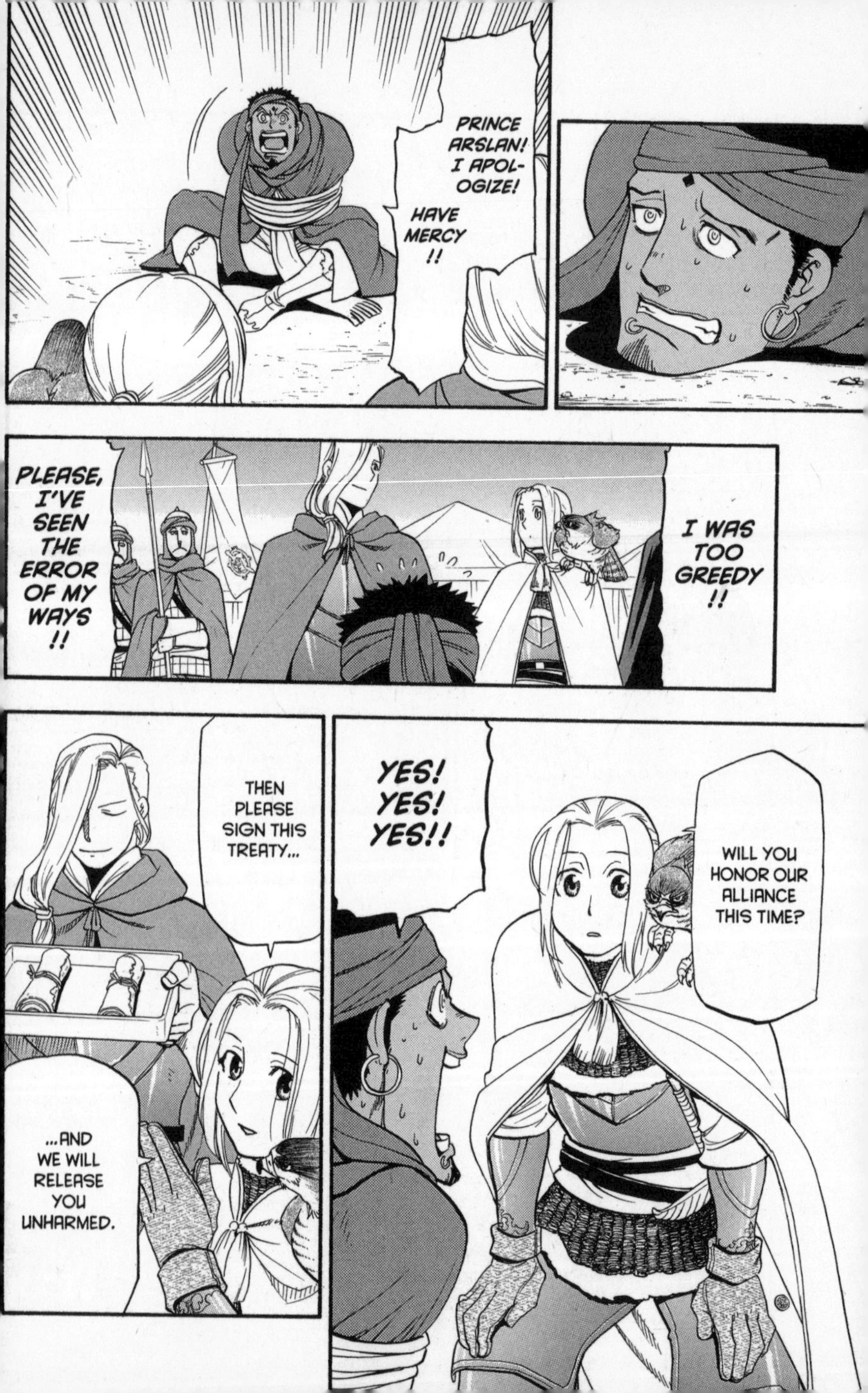
PRINCE ARSLAN! I APOLOGIZE!
HAVE MERCY !!
I WAS TOO GREEDY !!
PLEASE, I'VE SEEN THE ERROR OF MY WAYS !!
WILL YOU HONOR OUR ALLIANCE THIS TIME?
YES! YES! YES!!
THEN PLEASE SIGN THIS TREATY...
...AND WE WILL RELEASE YOU UNHARMED.

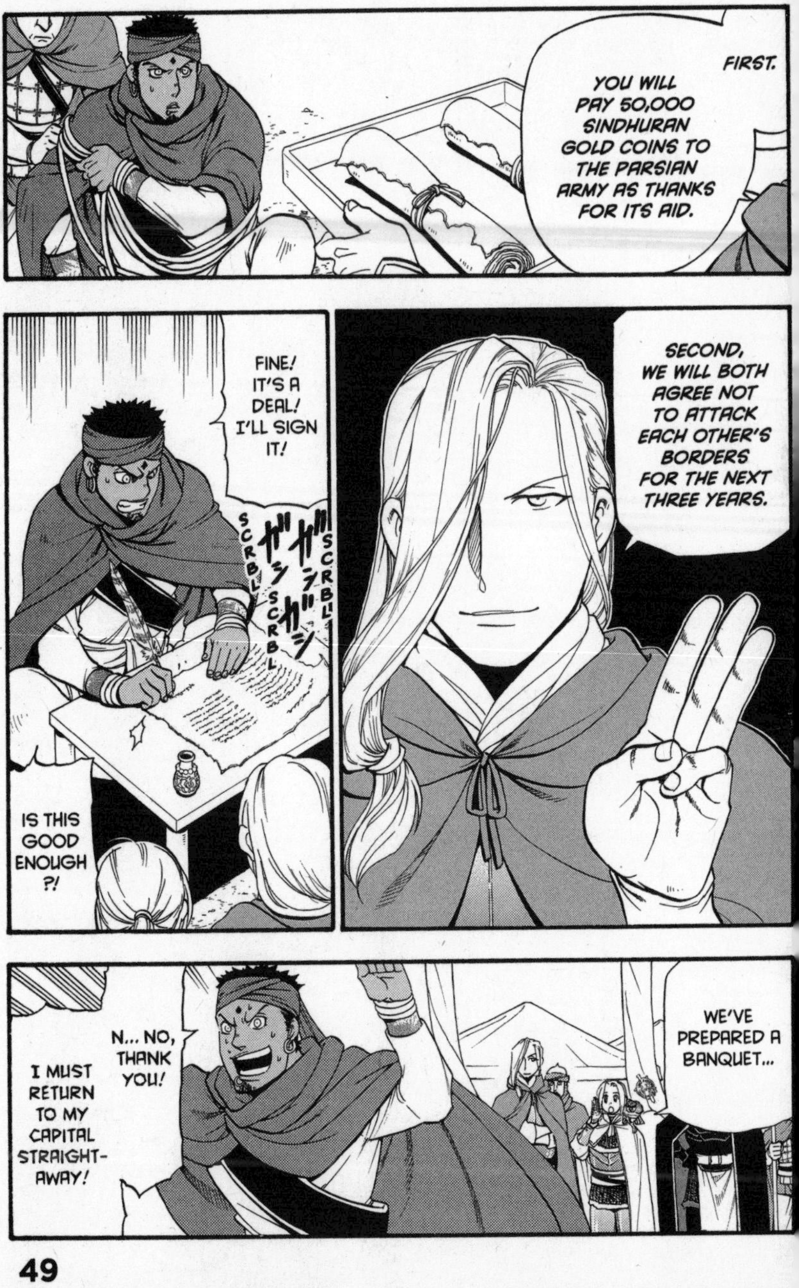
FIRST.
YOU WILL PAY 50,000 SINDHURAN GOLD COINS TO THE PARSIAN ARMY AS THANKS FOR ITS AID.
SECOND, WE WILL BOTH AGREE NOT TO ATTACK EACH OTHER'S BORDERS FOR THE NEXT THREE YEARS.
FINE! IT'S A DEAL! I'LL SIGN IT!
SCRBL
SCRBL
SCRBL
IS THIS GOOD ENOUGH?!
WE'VE PREPARED A BANQUET...
N... NO, THANK YOU!
I MUST RETURN TO MY CAPITAL STRAIGHTAWAY!

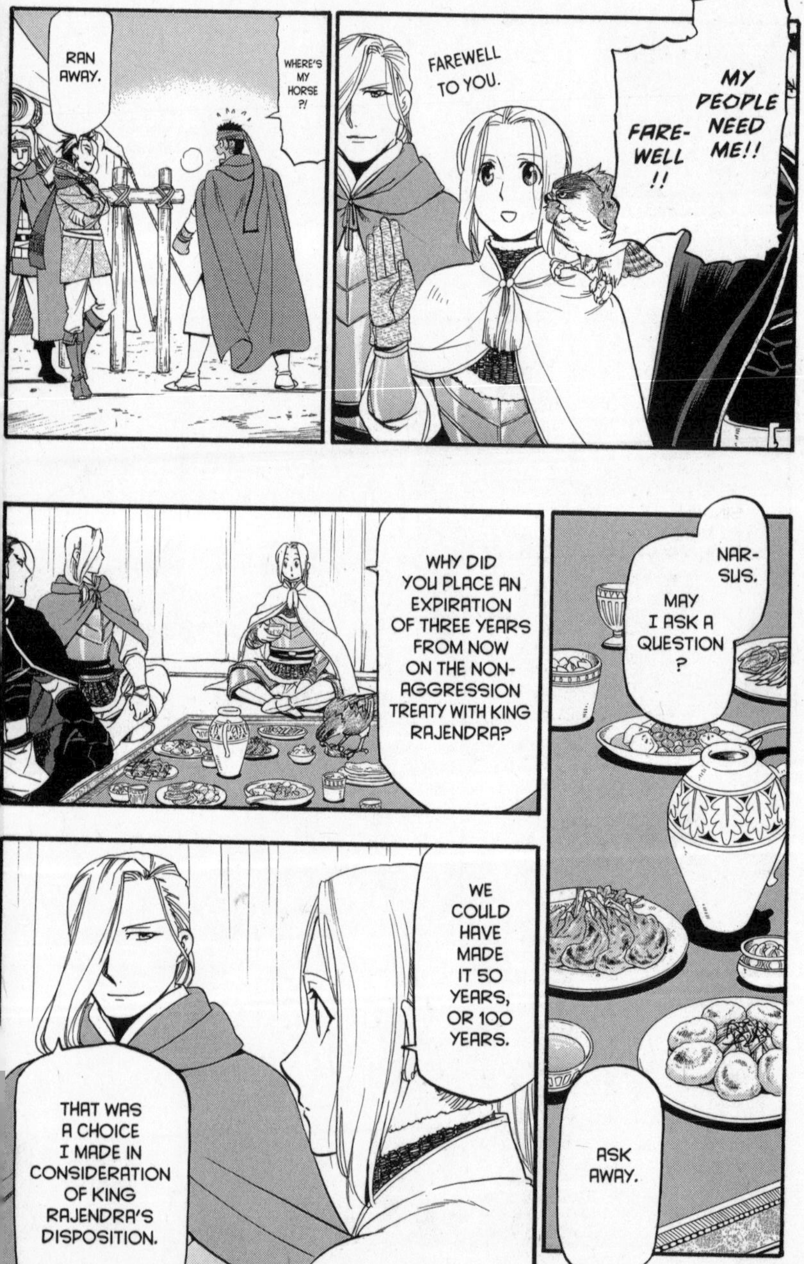
MY PEOPLE NEED ME!!
FARE-WELL!!
FAREWELL TO YOU.
WHERE'S MY HORSE?!
RAN AWAY.
NARSUS. MAY I ASK A QUESTION?
ASK AWAY.
WHY DID YOU PLACE AN EXPIRATION OF THREE YEARS FROM NOW ON THE NON-AGGRESSION TREATY WITH KING RAJENDRA?
WE COULD HAVE MADE IT 50 YEARS, OR 100 YEARS.
THAT WAS A CHOICE I MADE IN CONSIDERATION OF KING RAJENDRA'S DISPOSITION.

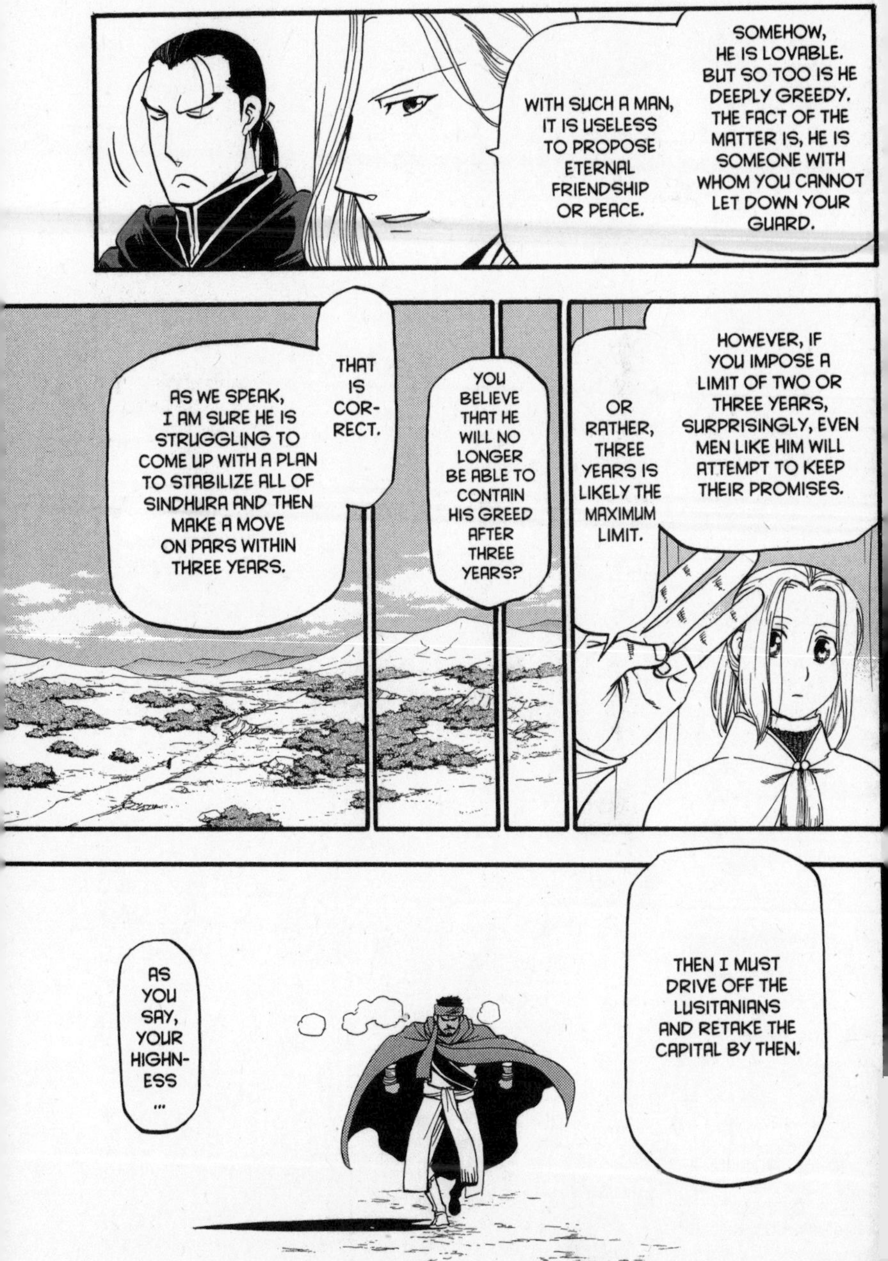
SOMEHOW, HE IS LOVABLE. BUT SO TOO IS HE DEEPLY GREEDY. THE FACT OF THE MATTER IS, HE IS SOMEONE WITH WHOM YOU CANNOT LET DOWN YOUR GUARD.
WITH SUCH A MAN, IT IS USELESS TO PROPOSE ETERNAL FRIENDSHIP OR PEACE.
HOWEVER, IF YOU IMPOSE A LIMIT OF TWO OR THREE YEARS, SURPRISINGLY, EVEN MEN LIKE HIM WILL ATTEMPT TO KEEP THEIR PROMISES.
OR RATHER, THREE YEARS IS LIKELY THE MAXIMUM LIMIT.
YOU BELIEVE THAT HE WILL NO LONGER BE ABLE TO CONTAIN HIS GREED AFTER THREE YEARS?
THAT IS COR-RECT.
AS WE SPEAK, I AM SURE HE IS STRUGGLING TO COME UP WITH A PLAN TO STABILIZE ALL OF SINDHURA AND THEN MAKE A MOVE ON PARS WITHIN THREE YEARS.
THEN I MUST DRIVE OFF THE LUSITANIANS AND RETAKE THE CAPITAL BY THEN.
AS YOU SAY, YOUR HIGHN-ESS ...

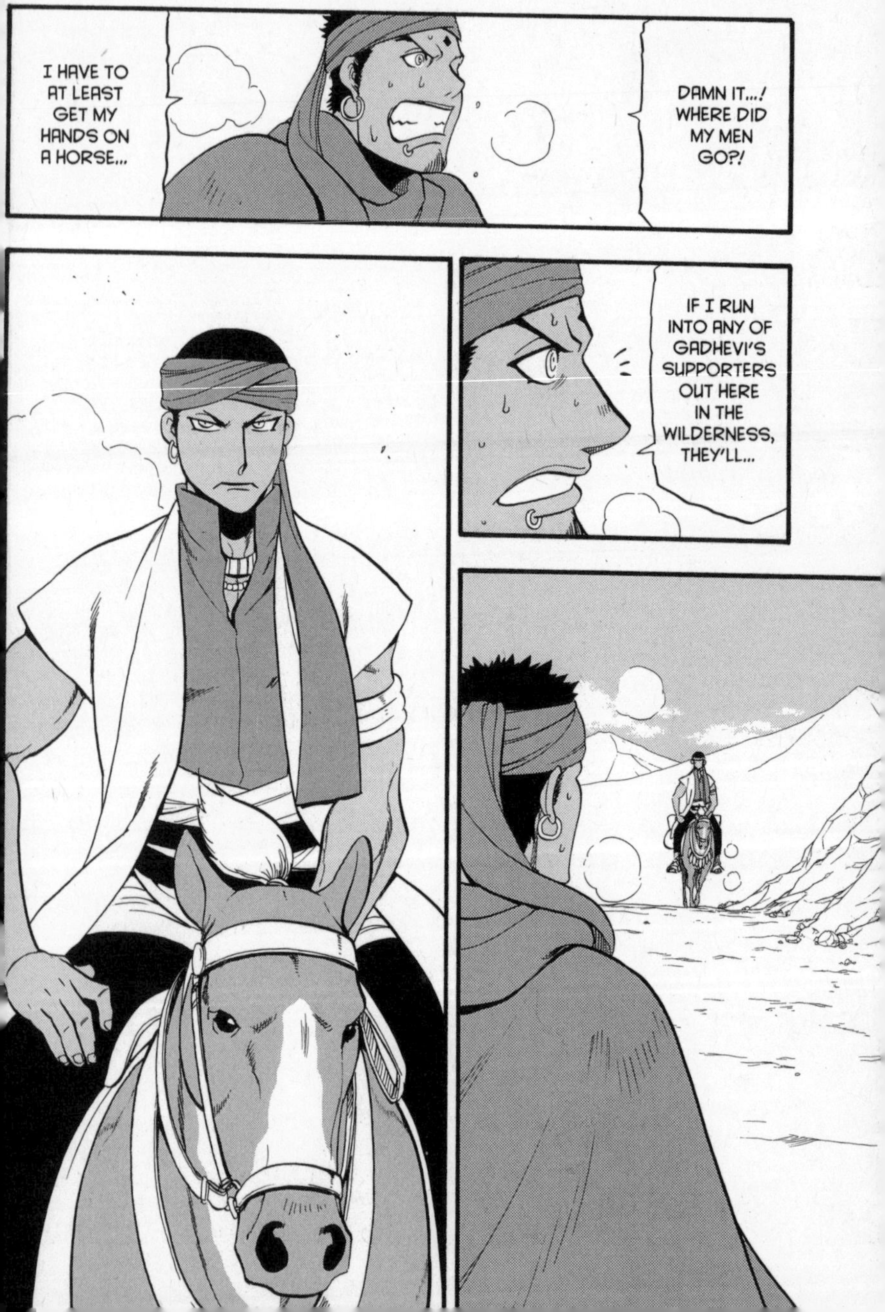
DAMN IT...! WHERE DID MY MEN GO?!
I HAVE TO AT LEAST GET MY HANDS ON A HORSE...
IF I RUN INTO ANY OF GADHEVI'S SUPPORTERS OUT HERE IN THE WILDERNESS, THEY'LL...

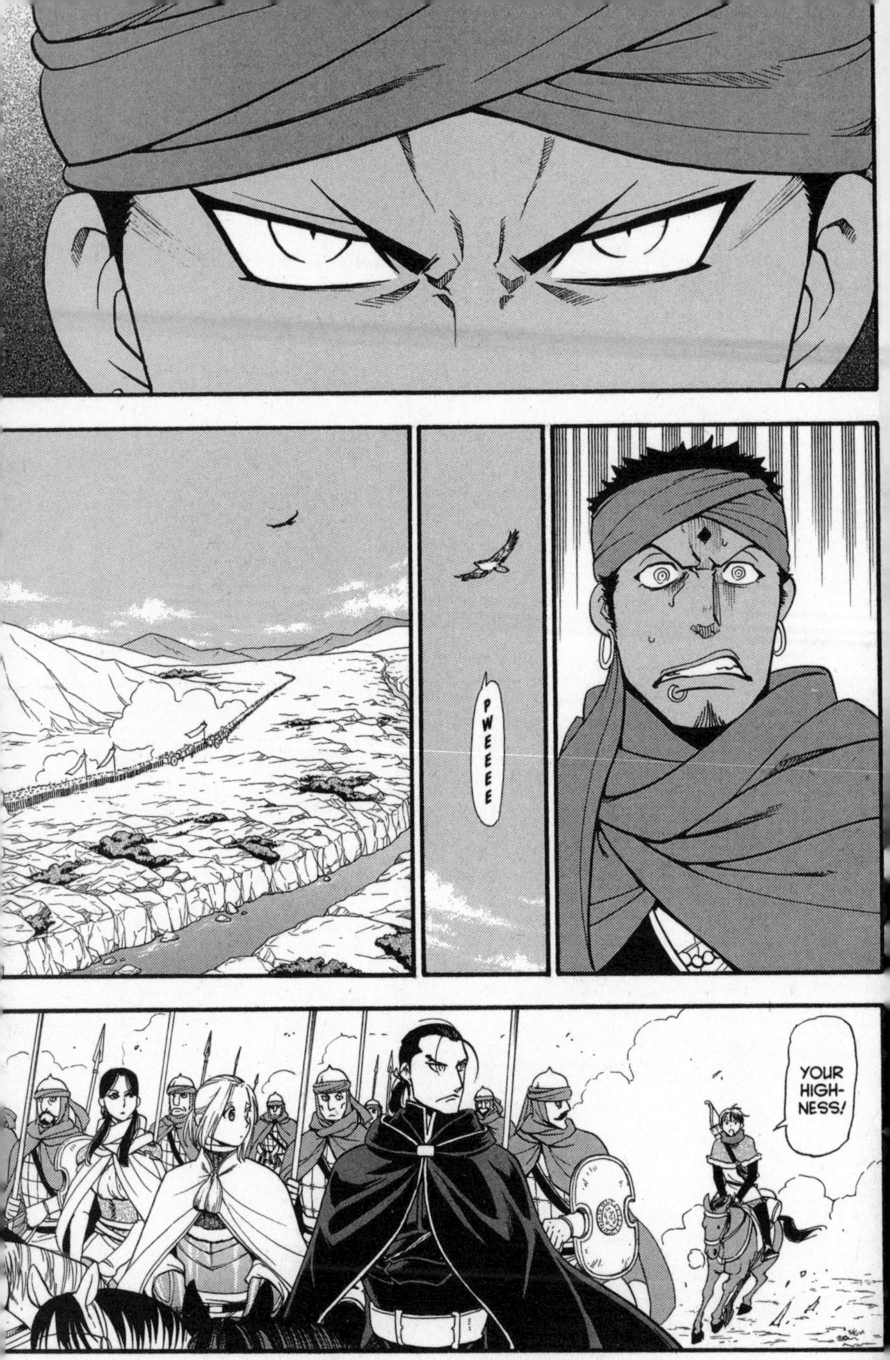
PWEEEE
YOUR HIGH-NESS!

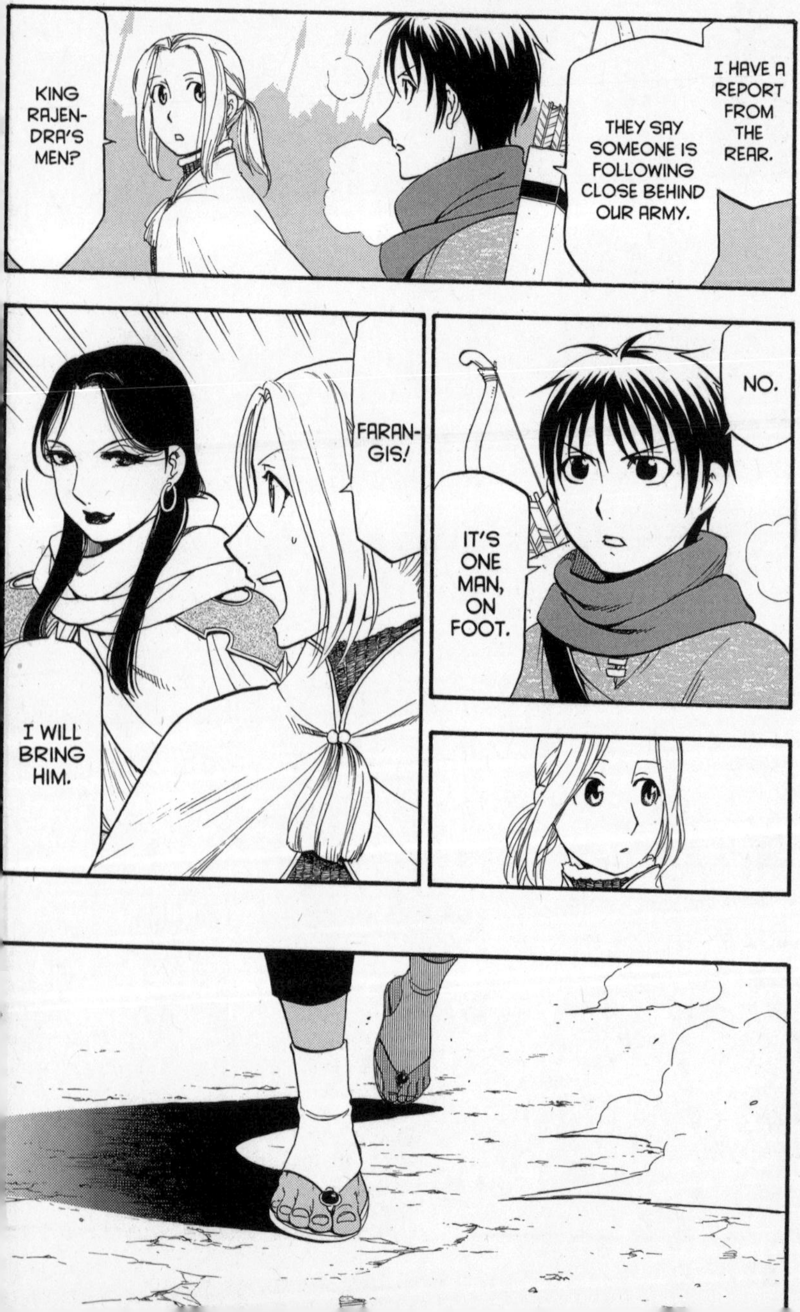
I HAVE A REPORT FROM THE REAR.
THEY SAY SOMEONE IS FOLLOWING CLOSE BEHIND OUR ARMY.
KING RAJENDRA'S MEN?
NO.
IT'S ONE MAN, ON FOOT.
FARANGIS!
I WILL BRING HIM.

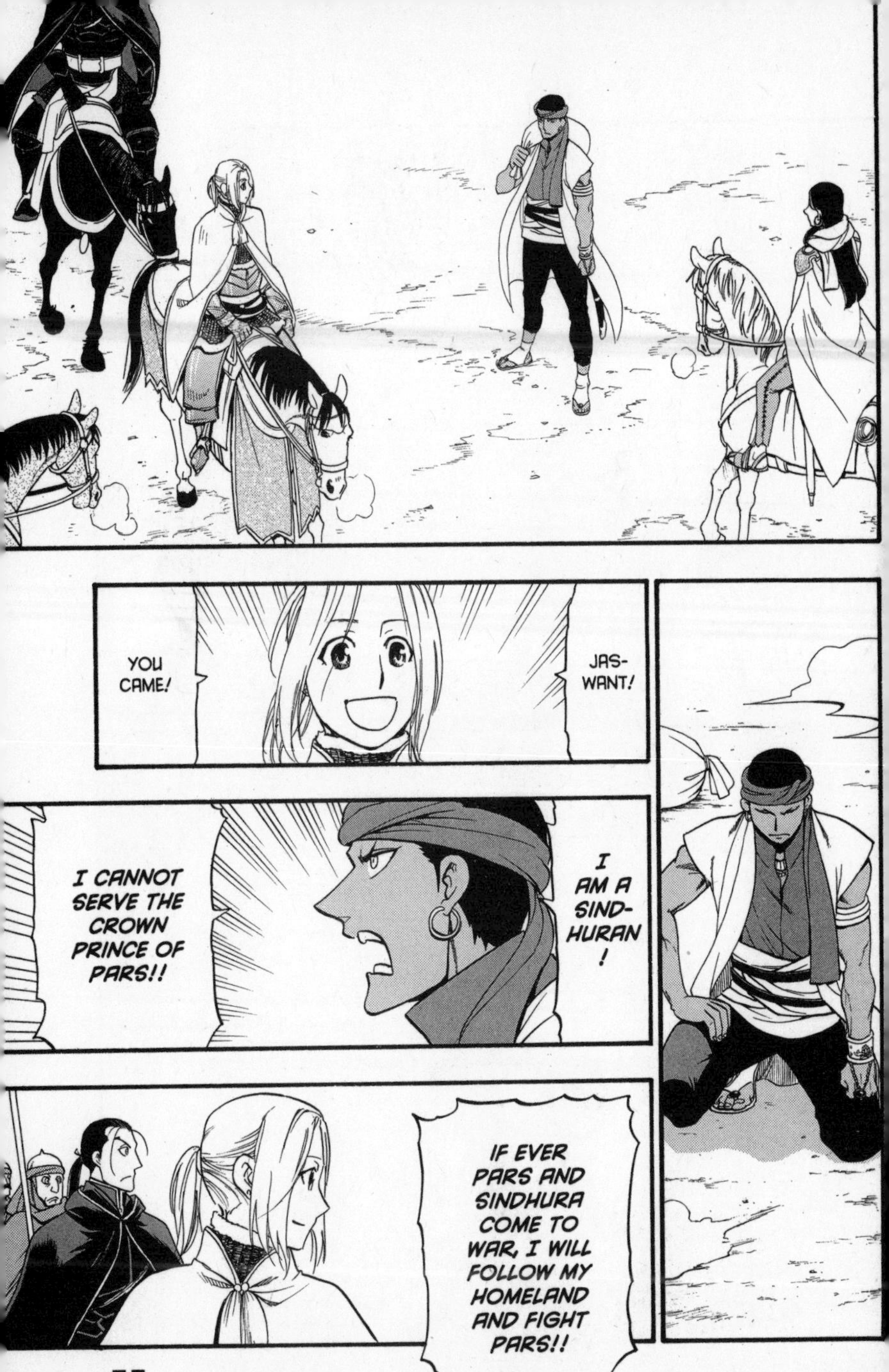
JAS-WANT!
YOU CAME!
I AM A SINDHURAN!
I CANNOT SERVE THE CROWN PRINCE OF PARS!!
IF EVER PARS AND SINDHURA COME TO WAR, I WILL FOLLOW MY HOMELAND AND FIGHT PARS!!

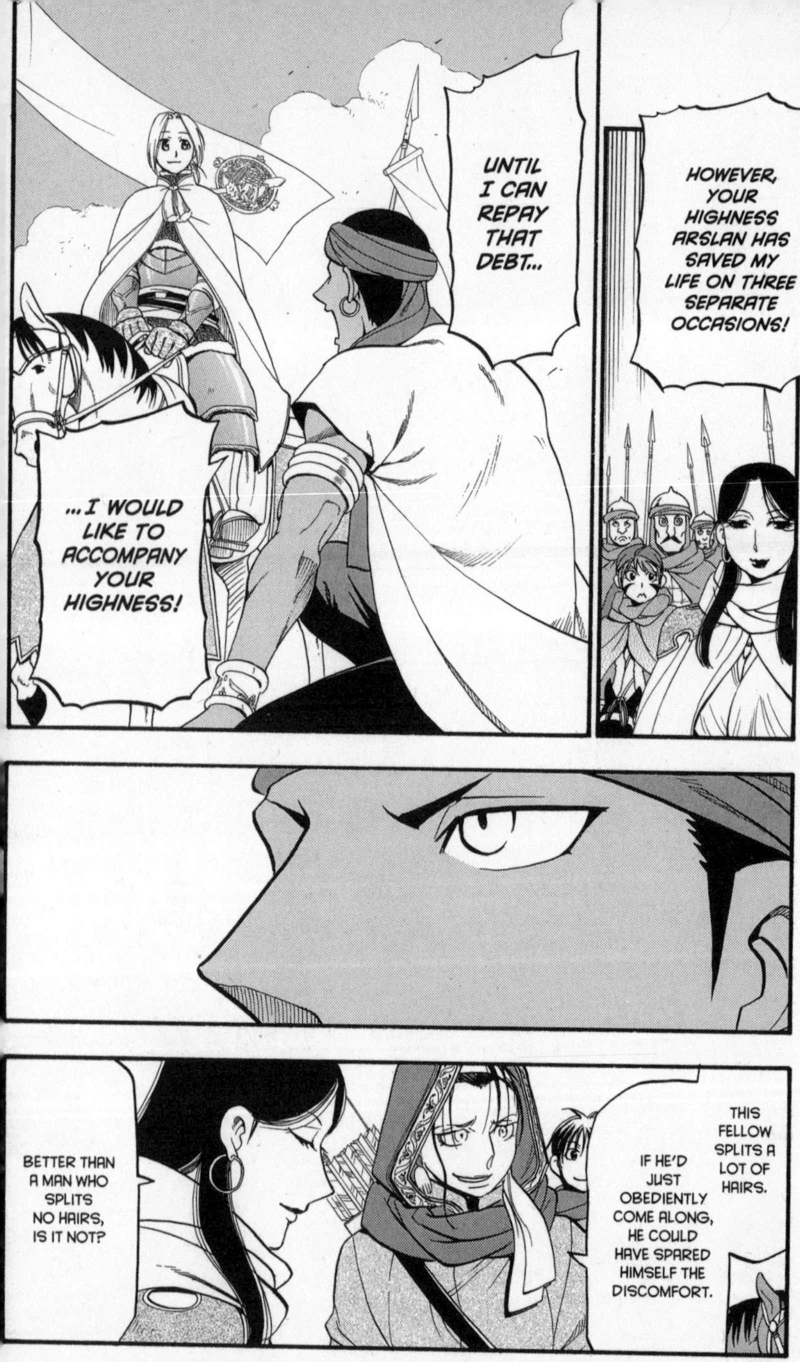
HOWEVER, YOUR HIGHNESS ARSLAN HAS SAVED MY LIFE ON THREE SEPARATE OCCASIONS!
UNTIL I CAN REPAY THAT DEBT...
...I WOULD LIKE TO ACCOMPANY YOUR HIGHNESS!
THIS FELLOW SPLITS A LOT OF HAIRS.
IF HE'D JUST OBEDIENTLY COME ALONG, HE COULD HAVE SPARED HIMSELF THE DISCOMFORT.
BETTER THAN A MAN WHO SPLITS NO HAIRS, IS IT NOT?

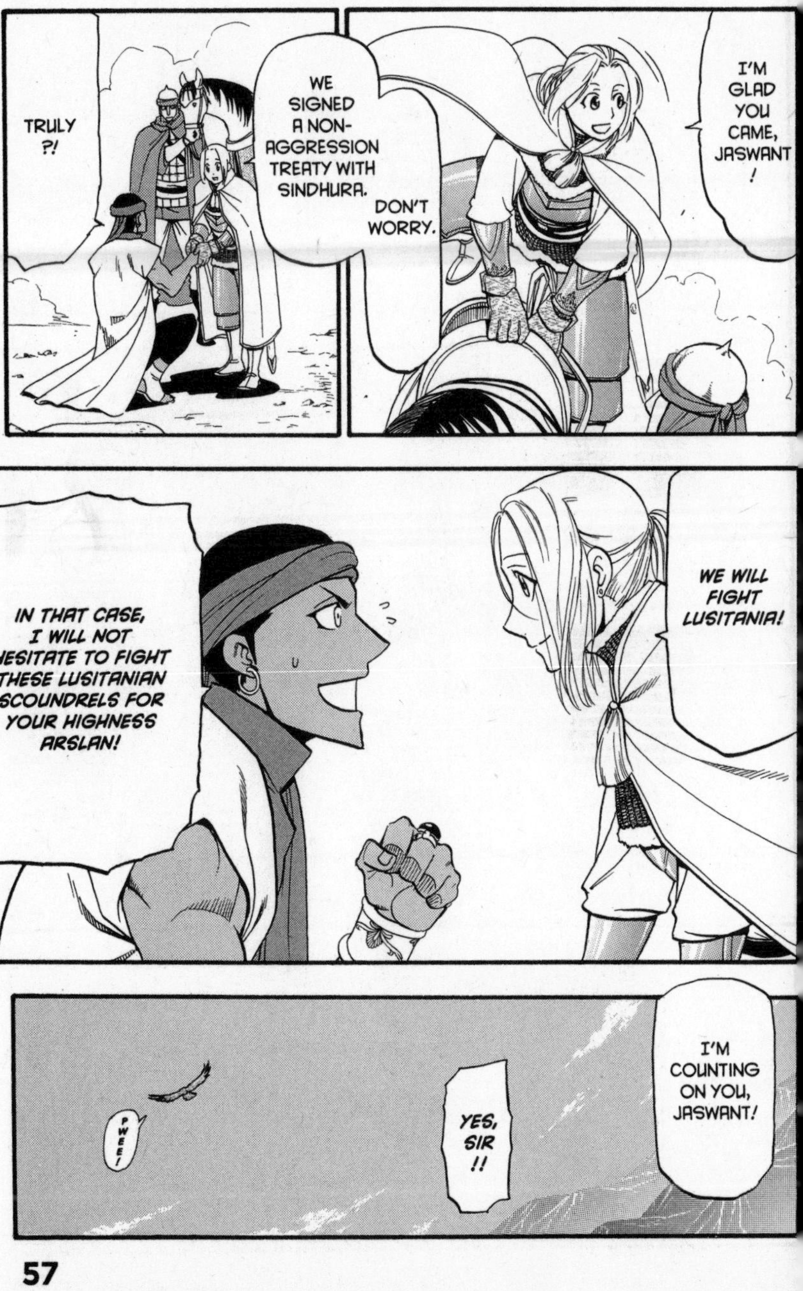

I'M GLAD YOU CAME, JASWANT!
WE SIGNED A NON-AGGRESSION TREATY WITH SINDHURA.
DON'T WORRY.
TRULY?!
WE WILL FIGHT LUSITANIA!
IN THAT CASE, I WILL NOT HESITATE TO FIGHT THESE LUSITANIAN SCOUNDRELS FOR YOUR HIGHNESS ARSLAN!
I'M COUNTING ON YOU, JASWANT!
YES, SIR!!
PWEE!

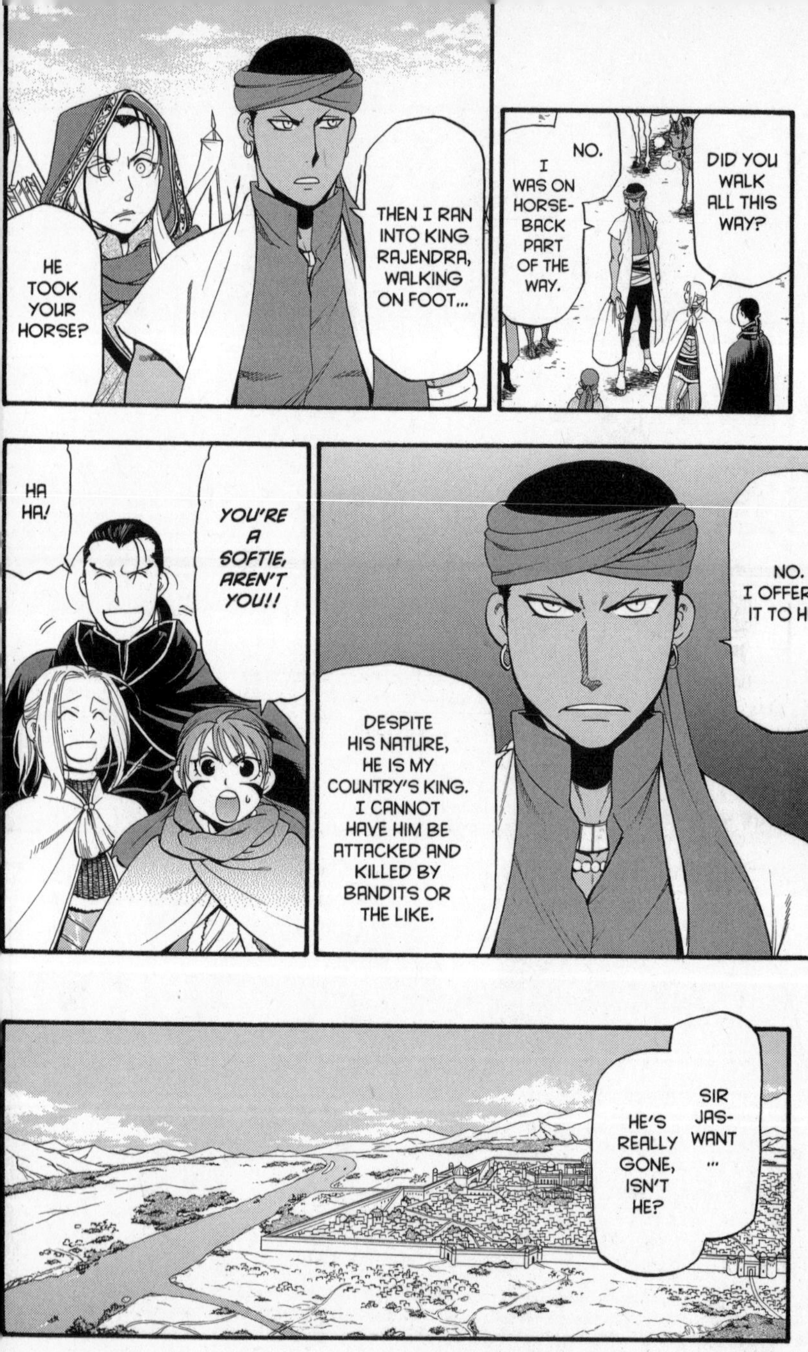
DID YOU WALK ALL THIS WAY?
NO.
I WAS ON HORSEBACK PART OF THE WAY.
THEN I RAN INTO KING RAJENDRA, WALKING ON FOOT...
HE TOOK YOUR HORSE?
NO. I OFFERED IT TO HIM.
DESPITE HIS NATURE, HE IS MY COUNTRY'S KING. I CANNOT HAVE HIM BE ATTACKED AND KILLED BY BANDITS OR THE LIKE.
YOU'RE A SOFTIE, AREN'T YOU!!
HA HA!
SIR JASWANT ...
HE'S REALLY GONE, ISN'T HE?

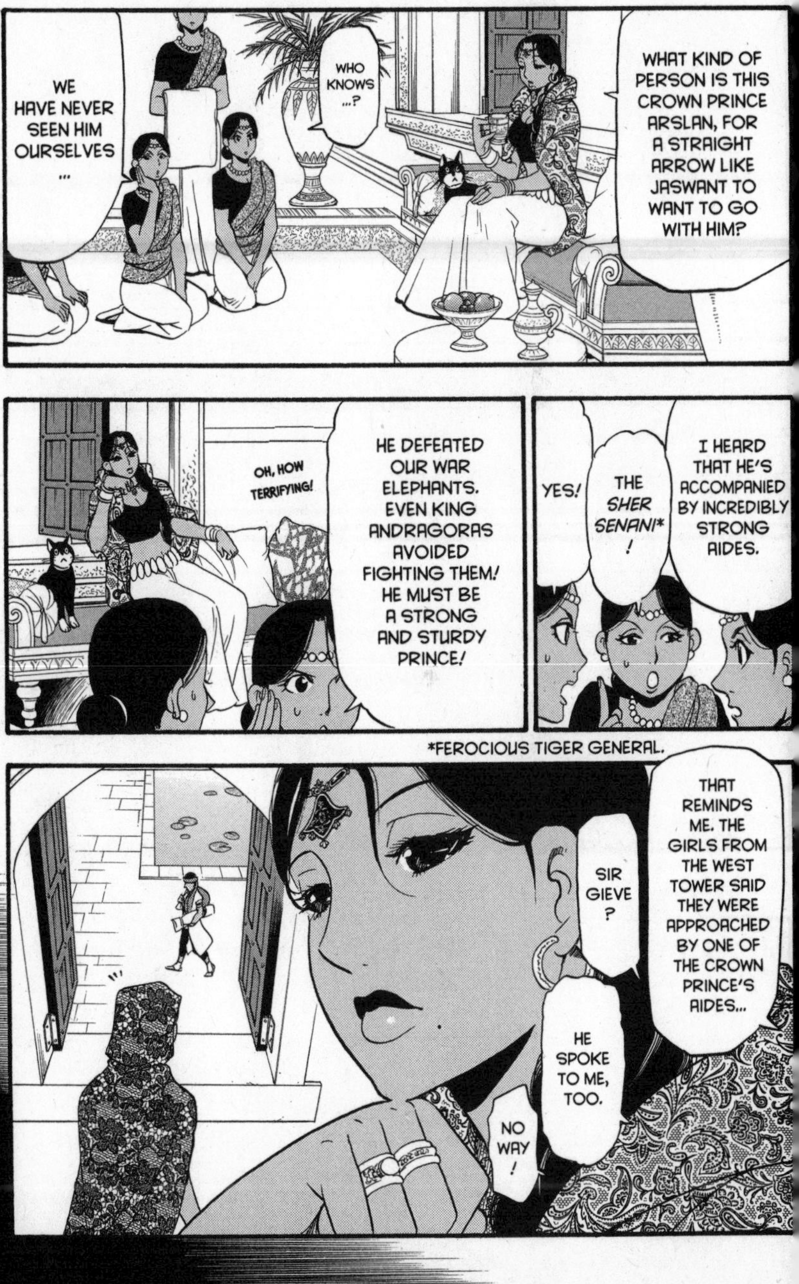
WHAT KIND OF PERSON IS THIS CROWN PRINCE ARSLAN, FOR A STRAIGHT ARROW LIKE JASWANT TO WANT TO GO WITH HIM?
WHO KNOWS ...?
WE HAVE NEVER SEEN HIM OURSELVES ...
I HEARD THAT HE'S ACCOMPANIED BY INCREDIBLY STRONG AIDES.
THE *SHER SENANI** !
YES!
HE DEFEATED OUR WAR ELEPHANTS. EVEN KING ANDRAGORAS AVOIDED FIGHTING THEM! HE MUST BE A STRONG AND STURDY PRINCE!
OH, HOW TERRIFYING!
*FEROCIOUS TIGER GENERAL.
THAT REMINDS ME. THE GIRLS FROM THE WEST TOWER SAID THEY WERE APPROACHED BY ONE OF THE CROWN PRINCE'S AIDES...
SIR GIEVE?
HE SPOKE TO ME, TOO.
NO WAY!

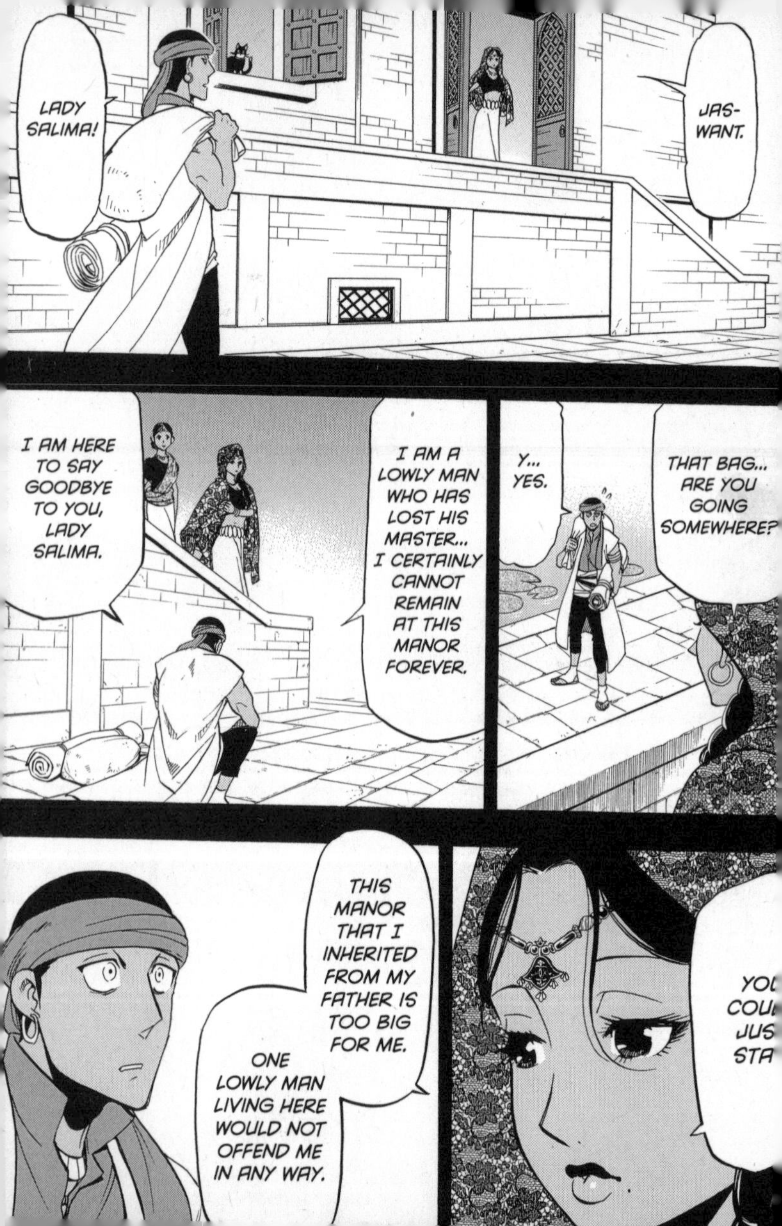
JAS-WANT.
LADY SALIMA!
THAT BAG... ARE YOU GOING SOMEWHERE?
Y... YES.
I AM A LOWLY MAN WHO HAS LOST HIS MASTER... I CERTAINLY CANNOT REMAIN AT THIS MANOR FOREVER.
I AM HERE TO SAY GOODBYE TO YOU, LADY SALIMA.
YOU COU JUS STA
THIS MANOR THAT I INHERITED FROM MY FATHER IS TOO BIG FOR ME.
ONE LOWLY MAN LIVING HERE WOULD NOT OFFEND ME IN ANY WAY.

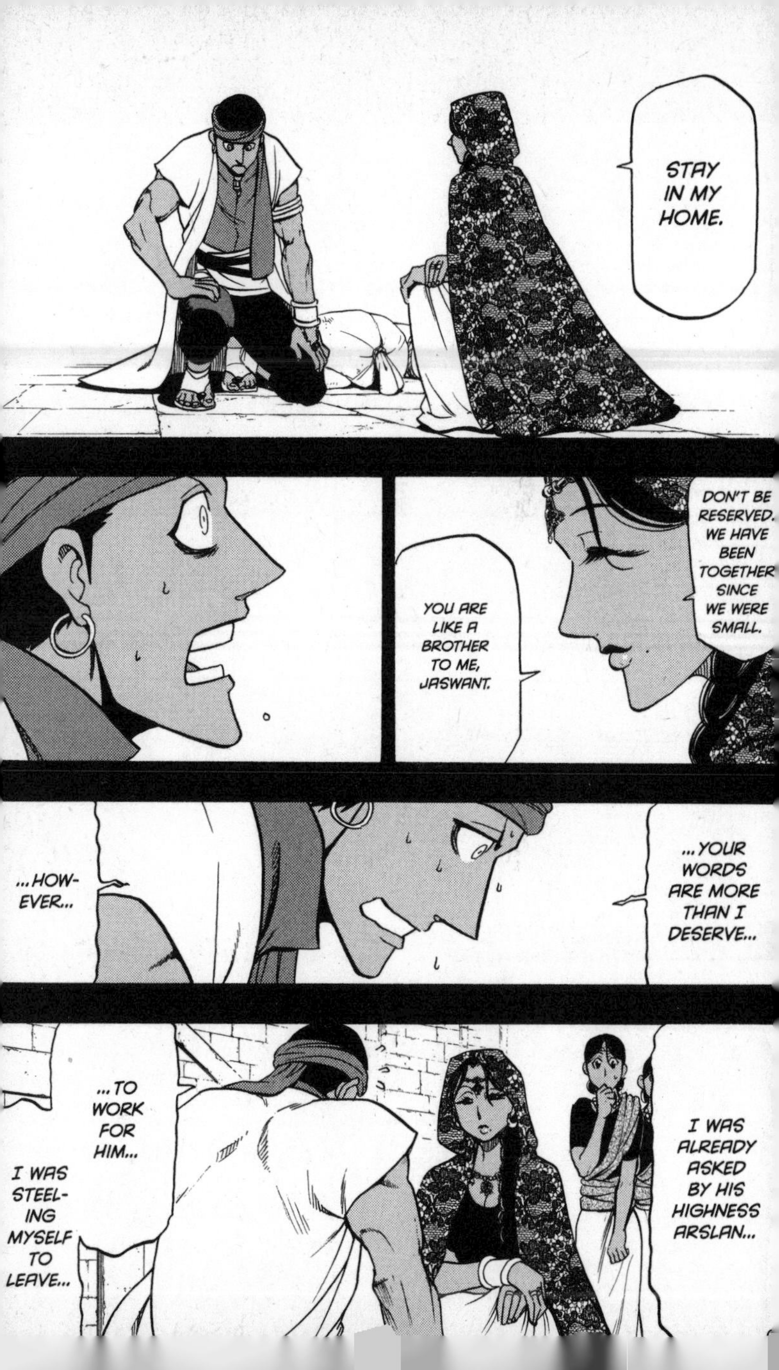
STAY IN MY HOME.
DON'T BE RESERVED. WE HAVE BEEN TOGETHER SINCE WE WERE SMALL.
YOU ARE LIKE A BROTHER TO ME, JASWANT.
...YOUR WORDS ARE MORE THAN I DESERVE...
...HOW-EVER...
I WAS ALREADY ASKED BY HIS HIGHNESS ARSLAN...
...TO WORK FOR HIM...
I WAS STEEL-ING MYSELF TO LEAVE...

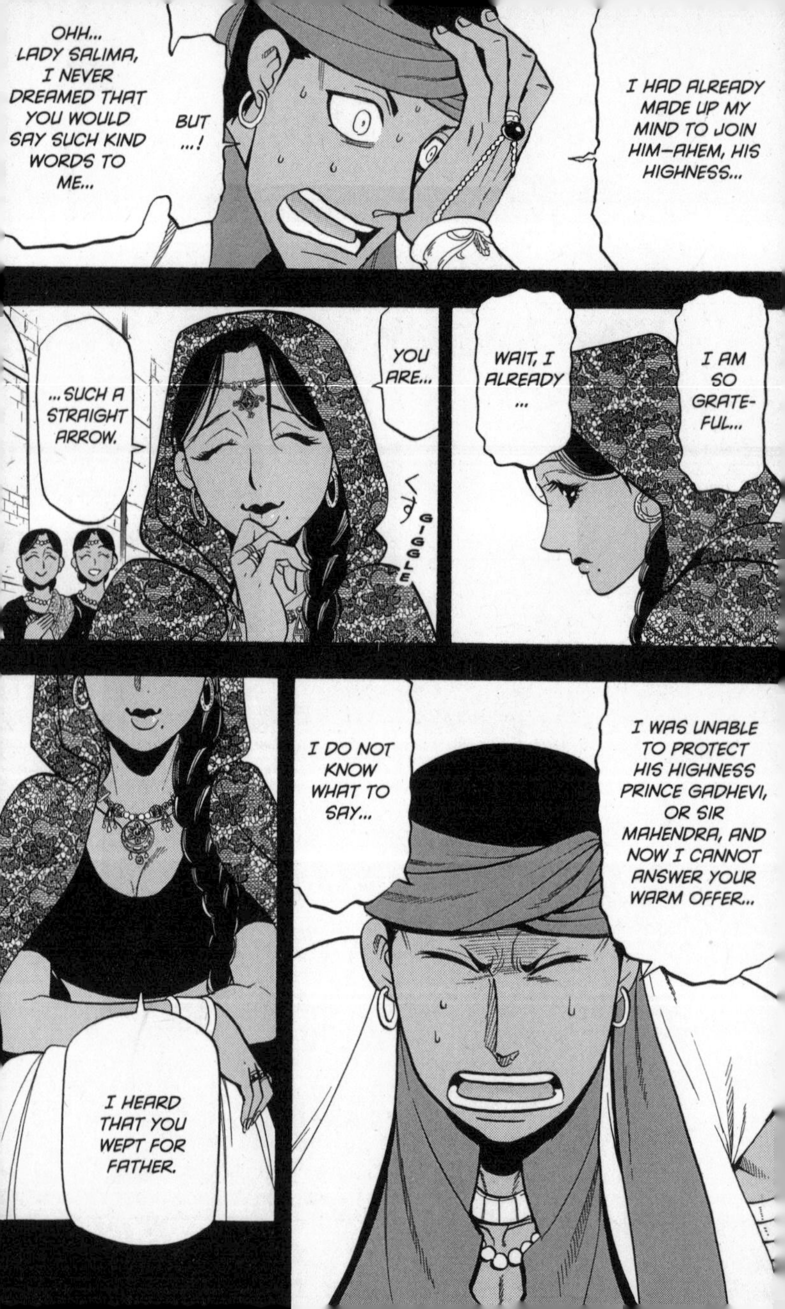
I HAD ALREADY MADE UP MY MIND TO JOIN HIM—AHEM, HIS HIGHNESS...
OHH... LADY SALIMA, I NEVER DREAMED THAT YOU WOULD SAY SUCH KIND WORDS TO ME...
BUT ...!
I AM SO GRATE-FUL...
WAIT, I ALREADY ...
YOU ARE...
...SUCH A STRAIGHT ARROW.
くす GIGGLE
I WAS UNABLE TO PROTECT HIS HIGHNESS PRINCE GADHEVI, OR SIR MAHENDRA, AND NOW I CANNOT ANSWER YOUR WARM OFFER...
I DO NOT KNOW WHAT TO SAY...
I HEARD THAT YOU WEPT FOR FATHER.

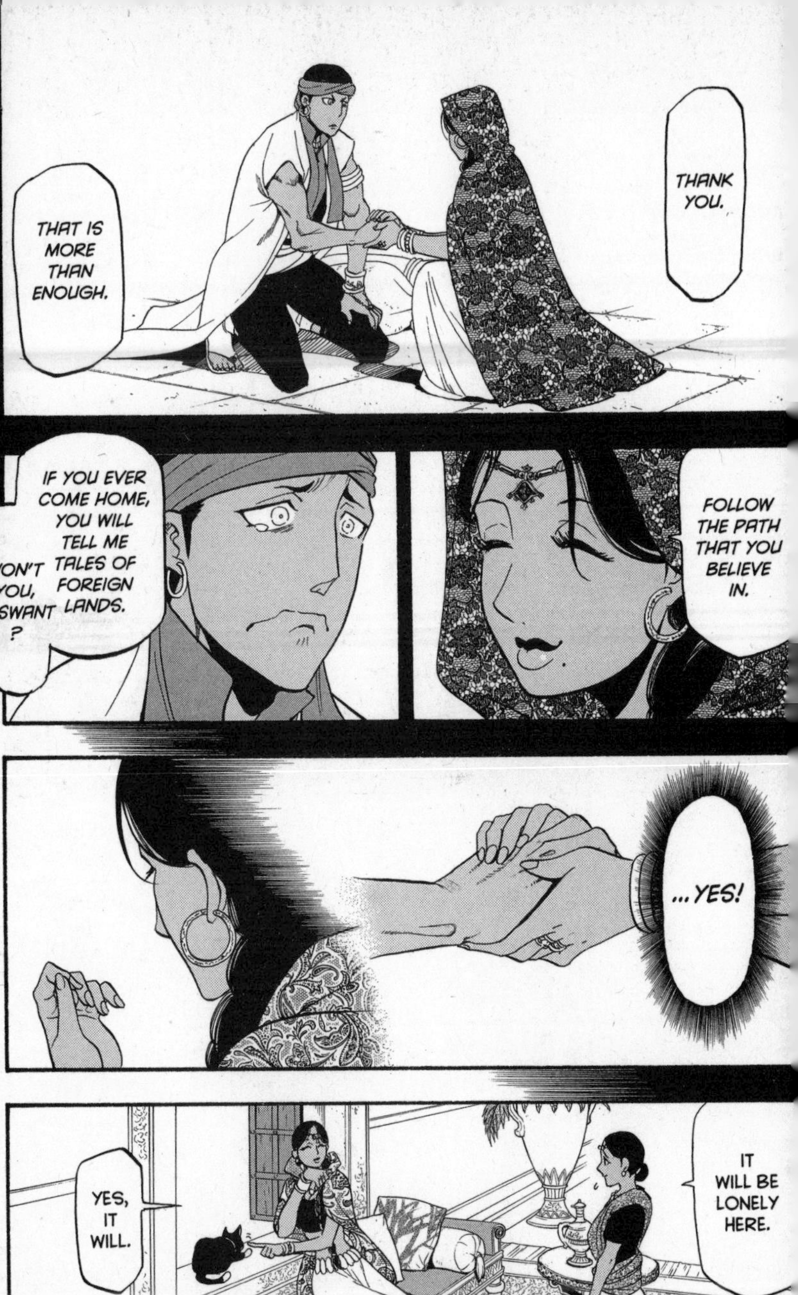
THANK YOU.
THAT IS MORE THAN ENOUGH.
FOLLOW THE PATH THAT YOU BELIEVE IN.
IF YOU EVER COME HOME, YOU WILL TELL ME TALES OF FOREIGN LANDS. WON'T YOU, JASWANT?
...YES!
IT WILL BE LONELY HERE.
YES, IT WILL.

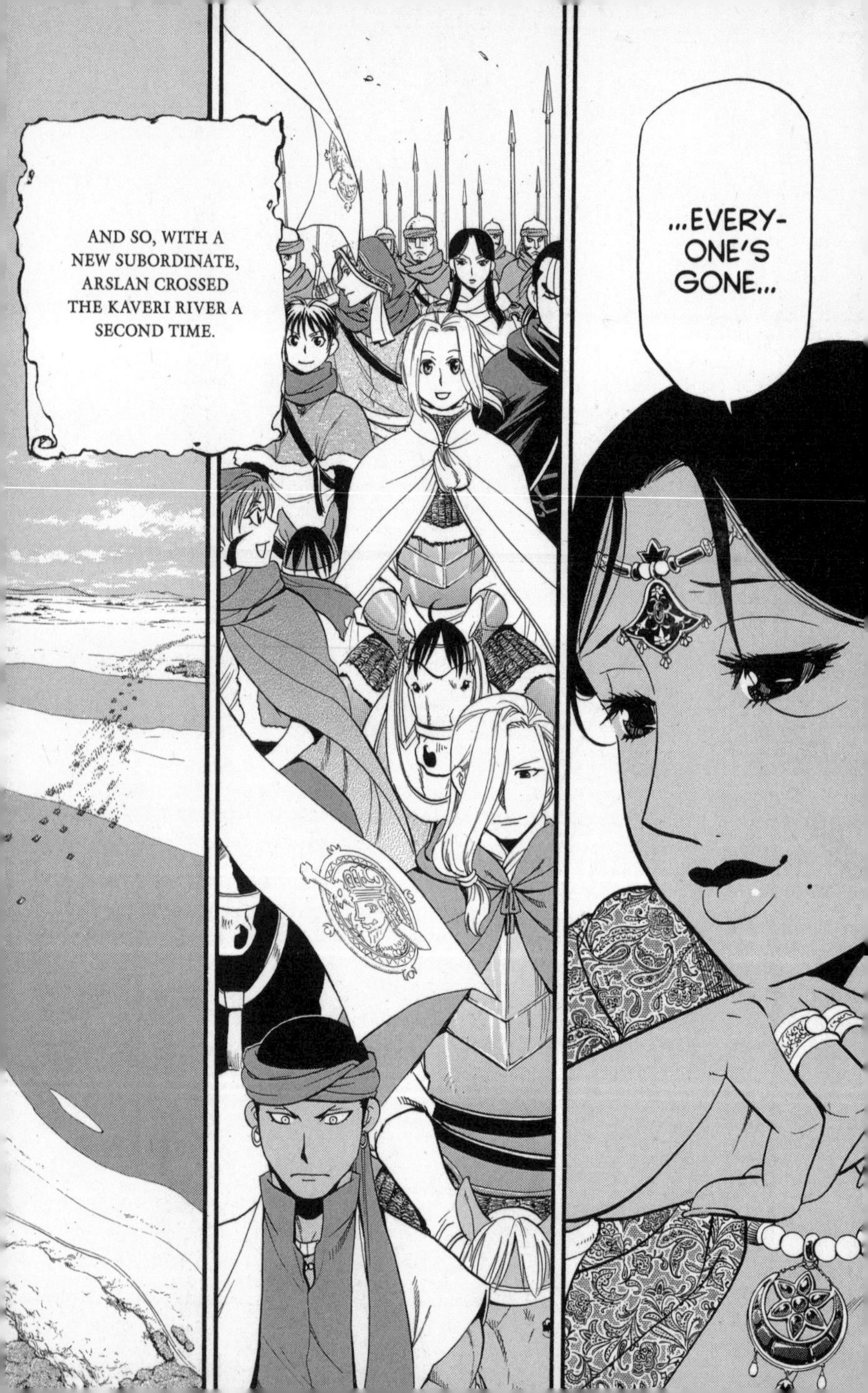
...EVERY-ONE'S GONE...
AND SO, WITH A NEW SUBORDINATE, ARSLAN CROSSED THE KAVERI RIVER A SECOND TIME.

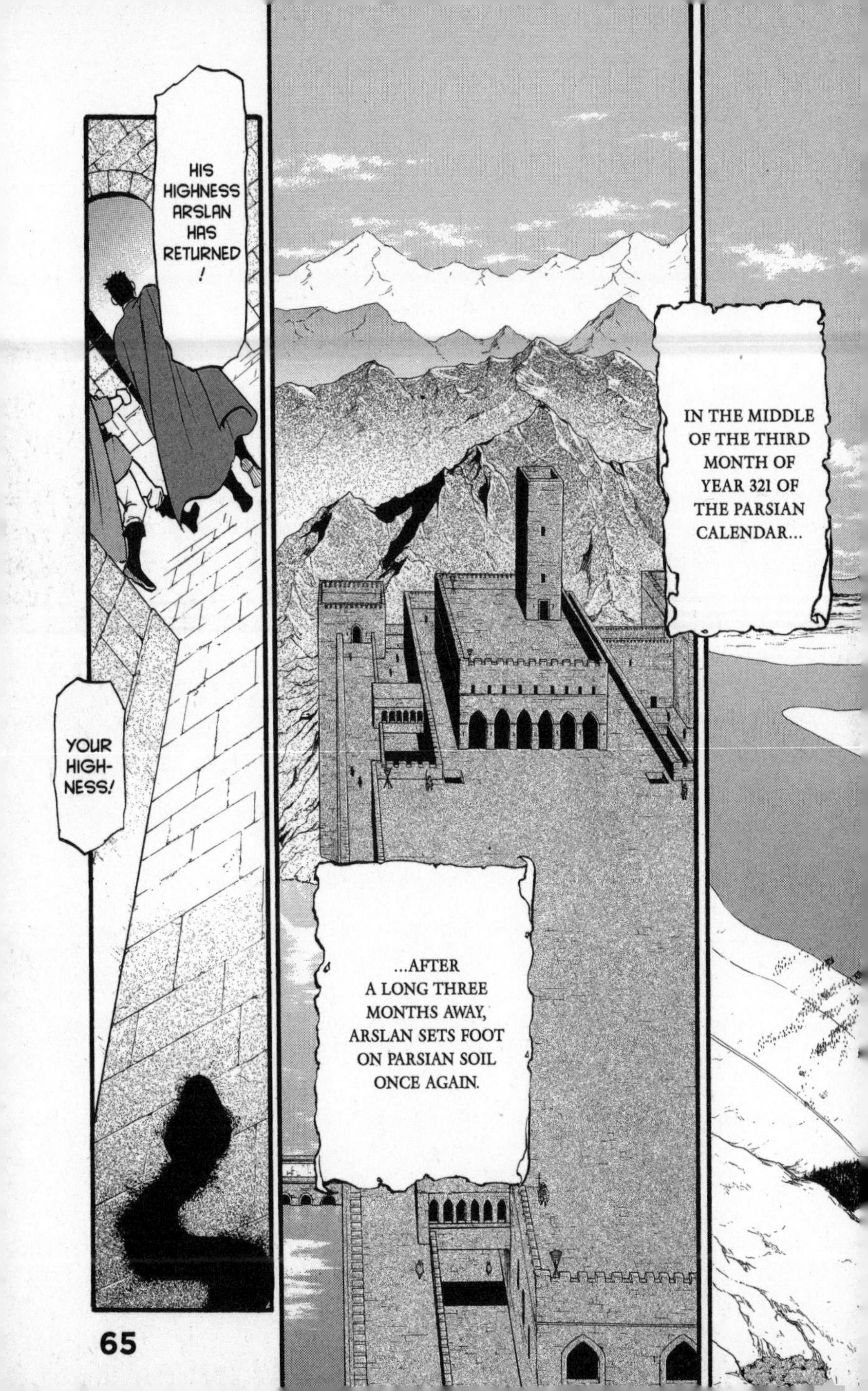
IN THE MIDDLE OF THE THIRD MONTH OF YEAR 321 OF THE PARSIAN CALENDAR...
...AFTER A LONG THREE MONTHS AWAY, ARSLAN SETS FOOT ON PARSIAN SOIL ONCE AGAIN.
HIS HIGHNESS ARSLAN HAS RETURNED!
YOUR HIGHNESS!

Chapter 55: Location of the Secret Letter

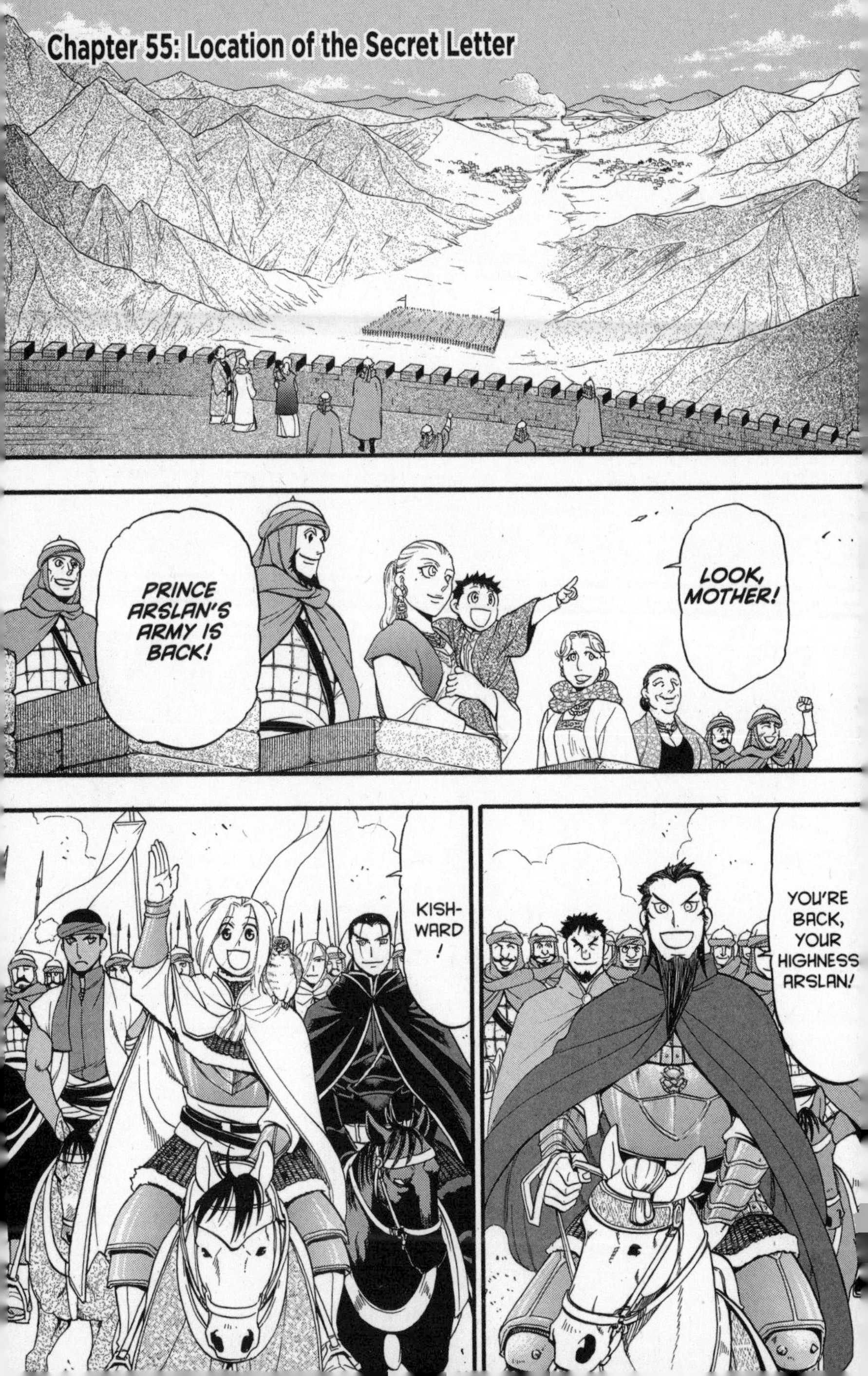

LOOK, MOTHER!
PRINCE ARSLAN'S ARMY IS BACK!
YOU'RE BACK, YOUR HIGHNESS ARSLAN!
KISHWARD!

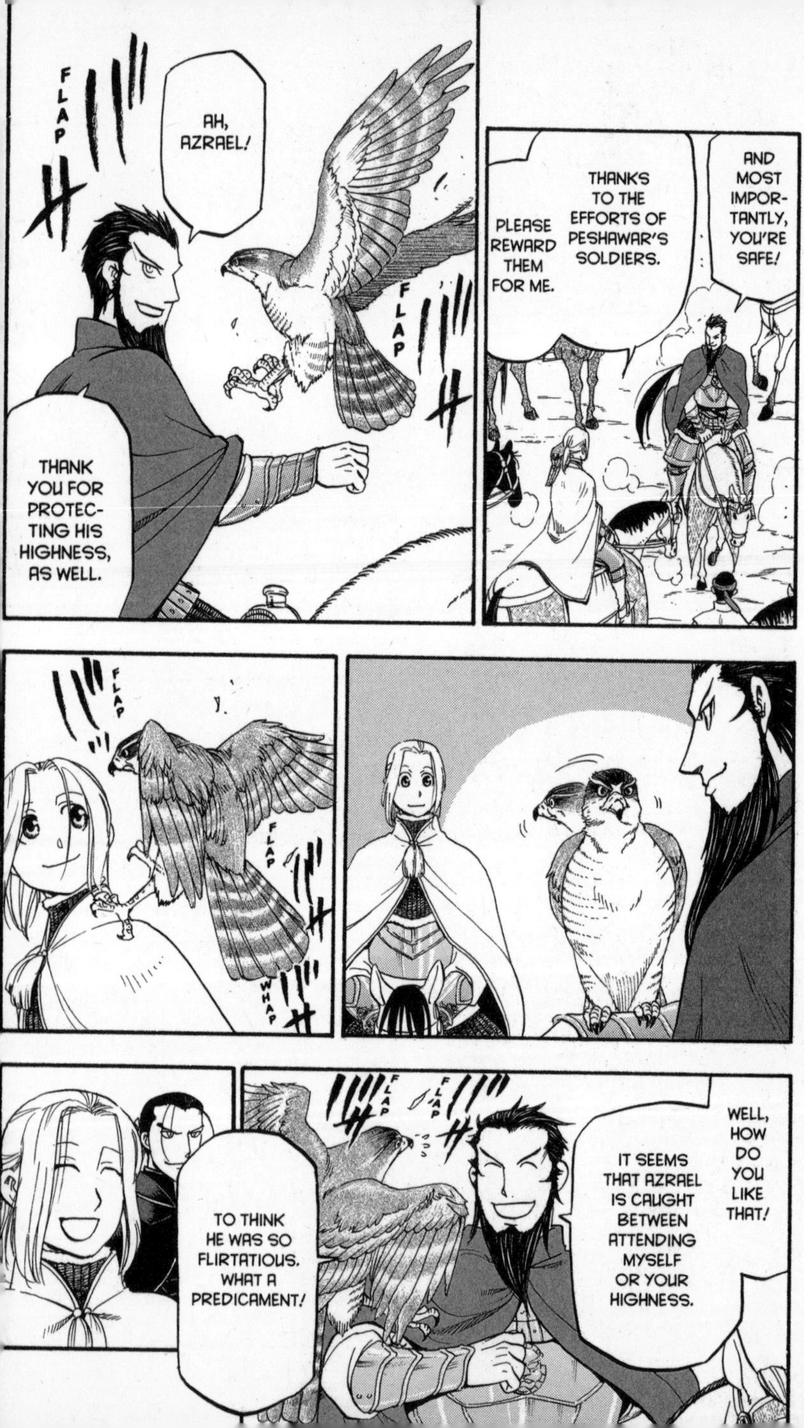
AND MOST IMPORTANTLY, YOU'RE SAFE!
THANKS TO THE EFFORTS OF PESHAWAR'S SOLDIERS.
PLEASE REWARD THEM FOR ME.
AH, AZRAEL!
FLAP
FLAP
THANK YOU FOR PROTECTING HIS HIGHNESS, AS WELL.
FLAP
FLAP
WHAP
WELL, HOW DO YOU LIKE THAT!
IT SEEMS THAT AZRAEL IS CAUGHT BETWEEN ATTENDING MYSELF OR YOUR HIGHNESS.
FLAP
FLAP
TO THINK HE WAS SO FLIRTATIOUS. WHAT A PREDICAMENT!

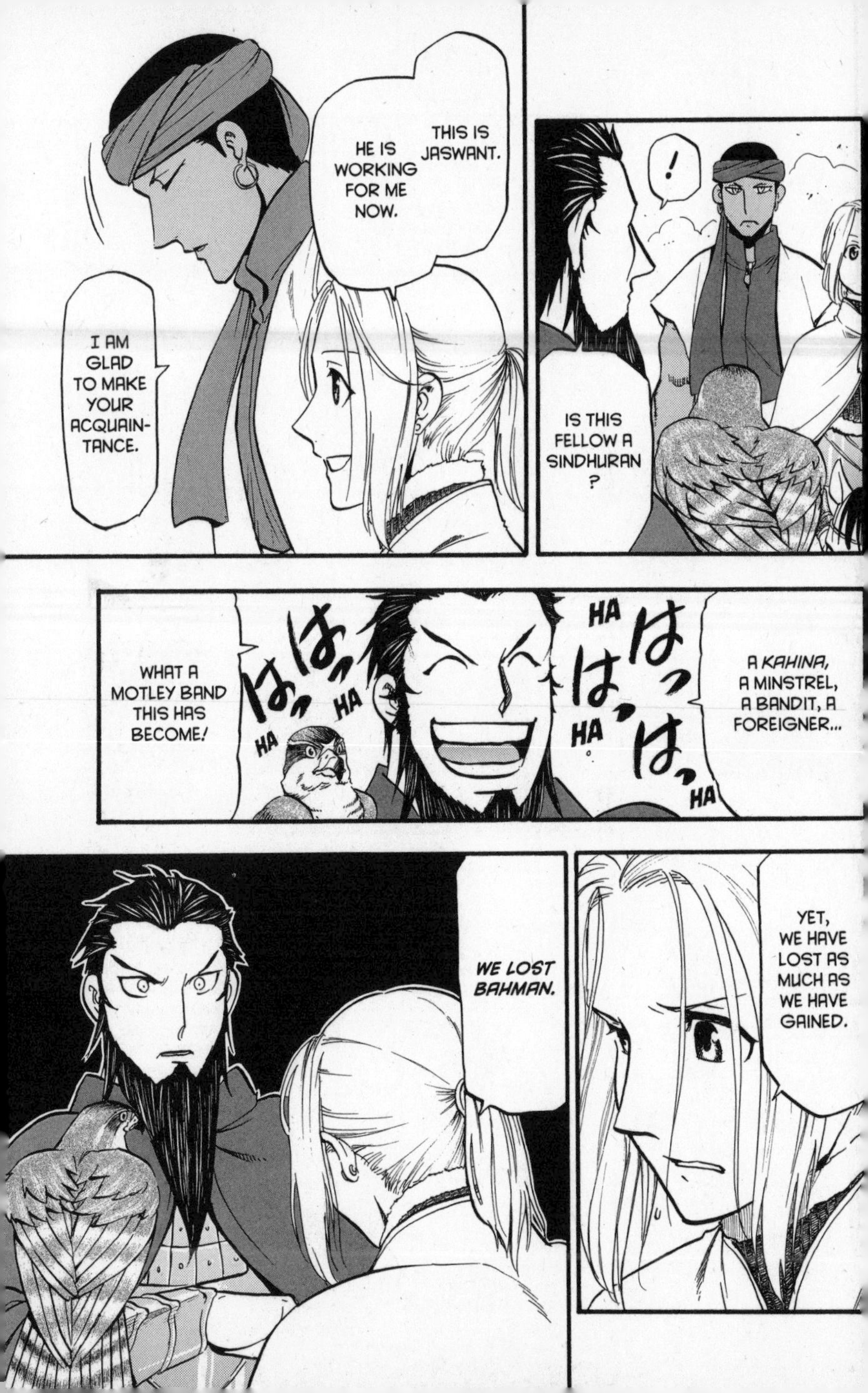
!
IS THIS FELLOW A SINDHURAN?
THIS IS JASWANT.
HE IS WORKING FOR ME NOW.
I AM GLAD TO MAKE YOUR ACQUAINTANCE.
A *KAHINA*, A MINSTREL, A BANDIT, A FOREIGNER...
はっはっ
HA HA HA
はっはっ
HA HA
WHAT A MOTLEY BAND THIS HAS BECOME!
YET, WE HAVE LOST AS MUCH AS WE HAVE GAINED.
WE LOST BAHMAN.

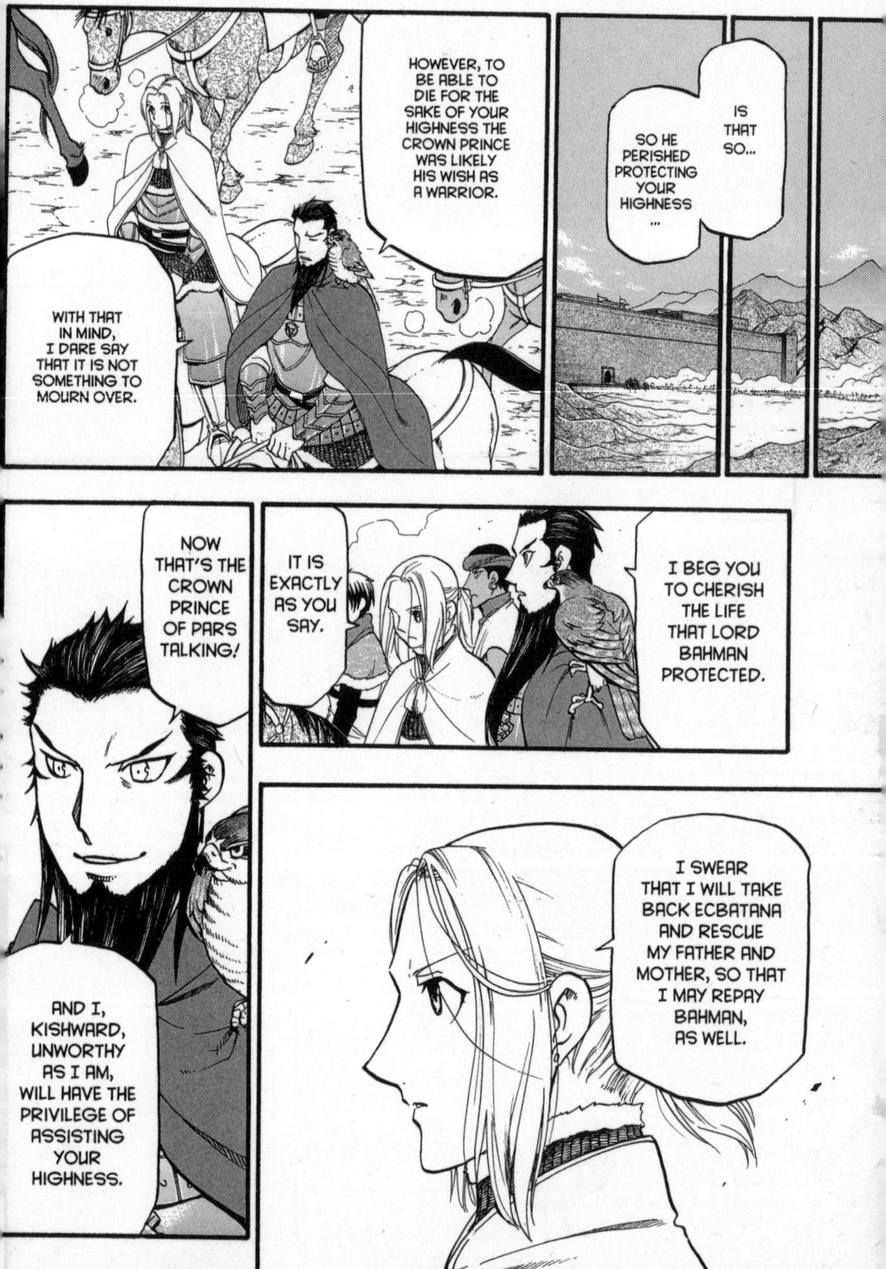
IS THAT SO...
SO HE PERISHED PROTECTING YOUR HIGHNESS...
HOWEVER, TO BE ABLE TO DIE FOR THE SAKE OF YOUR HIGHNESS THE CROWN PRINCE WAS LIKELY HIS WISH AS A WARRIOR.
WITH THAT IN MIND, I DARE SAY THAT IT IS NOT SOMETHING TO MOURN OVER.
I BEG YOU TO CHERISH THE LIFE THAT LORD BAHMAN PROTECTED.
IT IS EXACTLY AS YOU SAY.
I SWEAR THAT I WILL TAKE BACK ECBATANA AND RESCUE MY FATHER AND MOTHER, SO THAT I MAY REPAY BAHMAN, AS WELL.
NOW THAT'S THE CROWN PRINCE OF PARS TALKING!
AND I, KISHWARD, UNWORTHY AS I AM, WILL HAVE THE PRIVILEGE OF ASSISTING YOUR HIGHNESS.

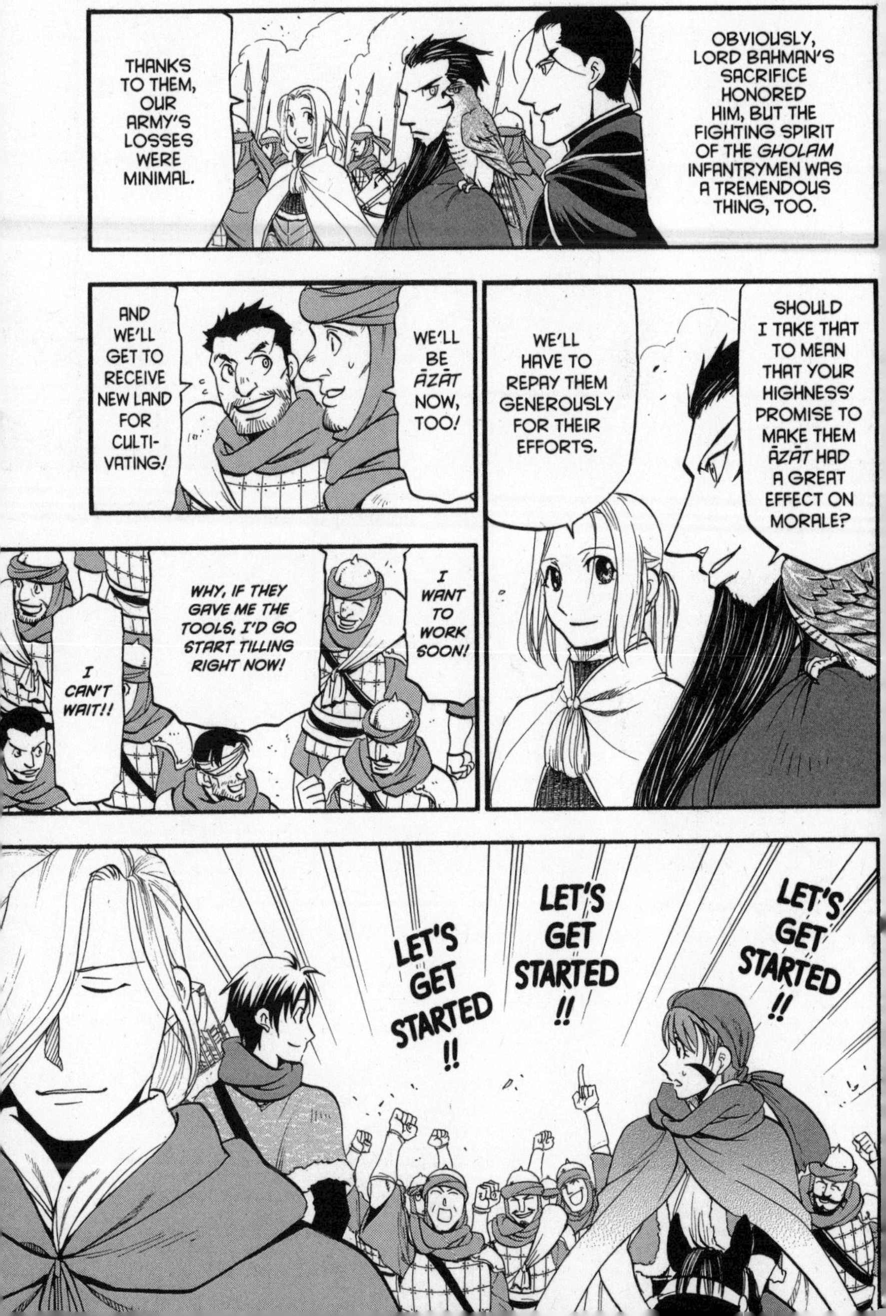

OBVIOUSLY, LORD BAHMAN'S SACRIFICE HONORED HIM, BUT THE FIGHTING SPIRIT OF THE *GHOLAM* INFANTRYMEN WAS A TREMENDOUS THING, TOO.
THANKS TO THEM, OUR ARMY'S LOSSES WERE MINIMAL.
SHOULD I TAKE THAT TO MEAN THAT YOUR HIGHNESS' PROMISE TO MAKE THEM *ĀZĀT* HAD A GREAT EFFECT ON MORALE?
WE'LL HAVE TO REPAY THEM GENEROUSLY FOR THEIR EFFORTS.
WE'LL BE *ĀZĀT* NOW, TOO!
AND WE'LL GET TO RECEIVE NEW LAND FOR CULTI-VATING!
I WANT TO WORK SOON!
WHY, IF THEY GAVE ME THE TOOLS, I'D GO START TILLING RIGHT NOW!
I CAN'T WAIT!!
LET'S GET STARTED!!
LET'S GET STARTED!!
LET'S GET STARTED!!

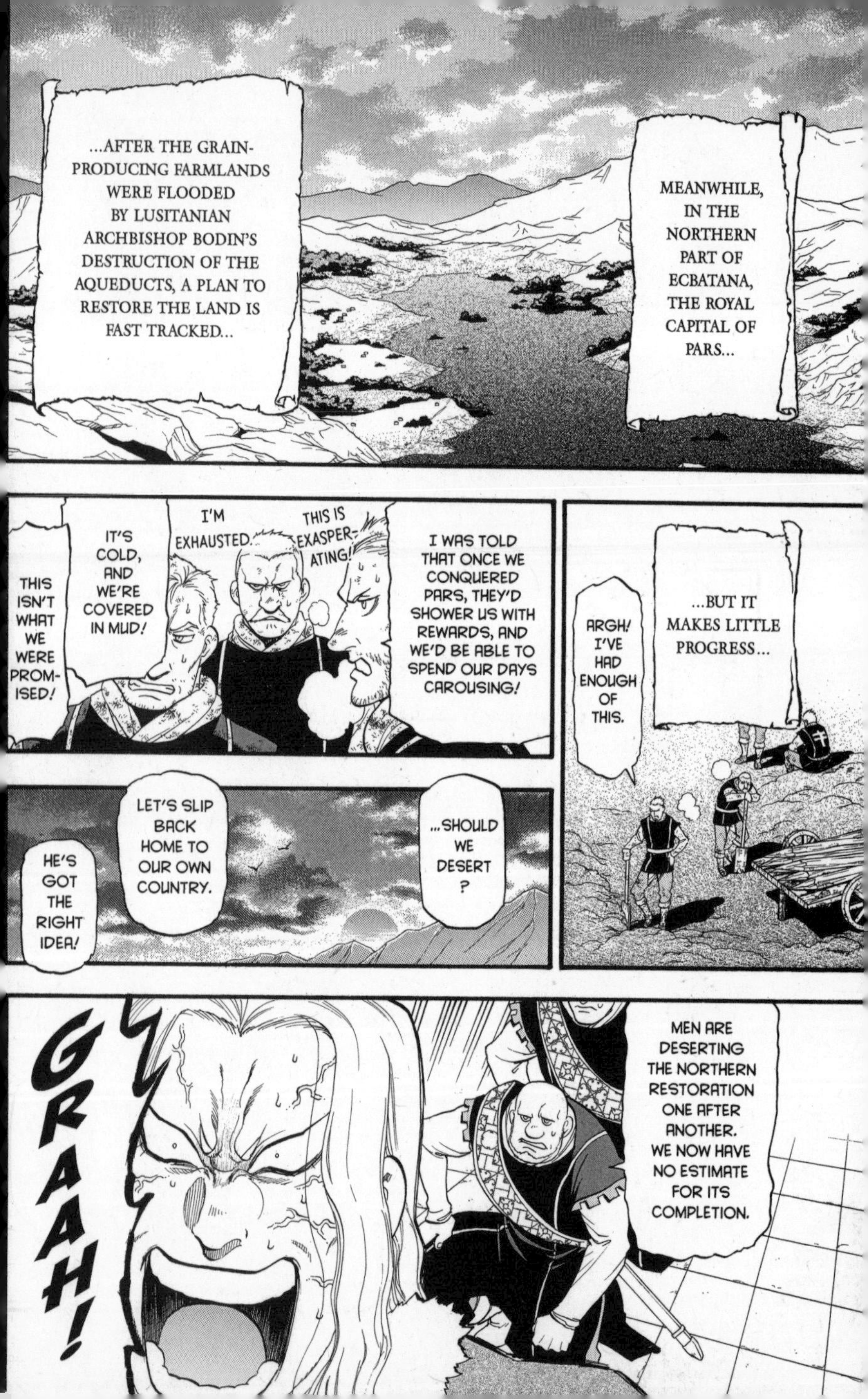
MEANWHILE, IN THE NORTHERN PART OF ECBATANA, THE ROYAL CAPITAL OF PARS...
...AFTER THE GRAIN-PRODUCING FARMLANDS WERE FLOODED BY LUSITANIAN ARCHBISHOP BODIN'S DESTRUCTION OF THE AQUEDUCTS, A PLAN TO RESTORE THE LAND IS FAST TRACKED...
...BUT IT MAKES LITTLE PROGRESS...
ARGH! I'VE HAD ENOUGH OF THIS.
I WAS TOLD THAT ONCE WE CONQUERED PARS, THEY'D SHOWER US WITH REWARDS, AND WE'D BE ABLE TO SPEND OUR DAYS CAROUSING!
THIS IS EXASPERATING!
I'M EXHAUSTED.
IT'S COLD, AND WE'RE COVERED IN MUD!
THIS ISN'T WHAT WE WERE PROMISED!
...SHOULD WE DESERT?
LET'S SLIP BACK HOME TO OUR OWN COUNTRY.
HE'S GOT THE RIGHT IDEA!
MEN ARE DESERTING THE NORTHERN RESTORATION ONE AFTER ANOTHER. WE NOW HAVE NO ESTIMATE FOR ITS COMPLETION.
GRAAH!

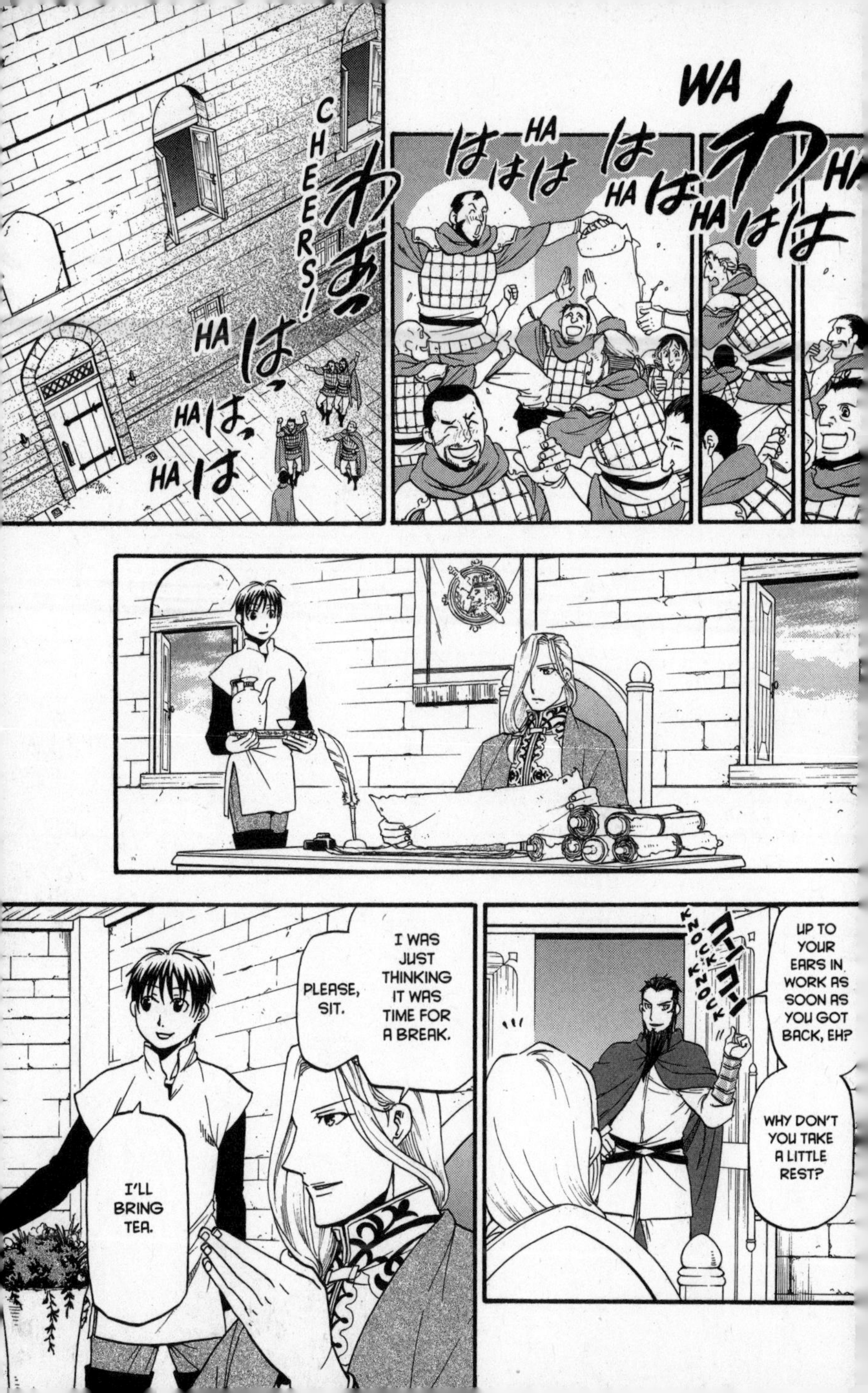
WA わ
HA ははは
HA は
HA は
HA はは
CHEERS! わあっ
HA はっ
HA はっ
HA は
KNOCK KNOCK コンコン
UP TO YOUR EARS IN WORK AS SOON AS YOU GOT BACK, EH?
WHY DON'T YOU TAKE A LITTLE REST?
I WAS JUST THINKING IT WAS TIME FOR A BREAK.
PLEASE, SIT.
I'LL BRING TEA.

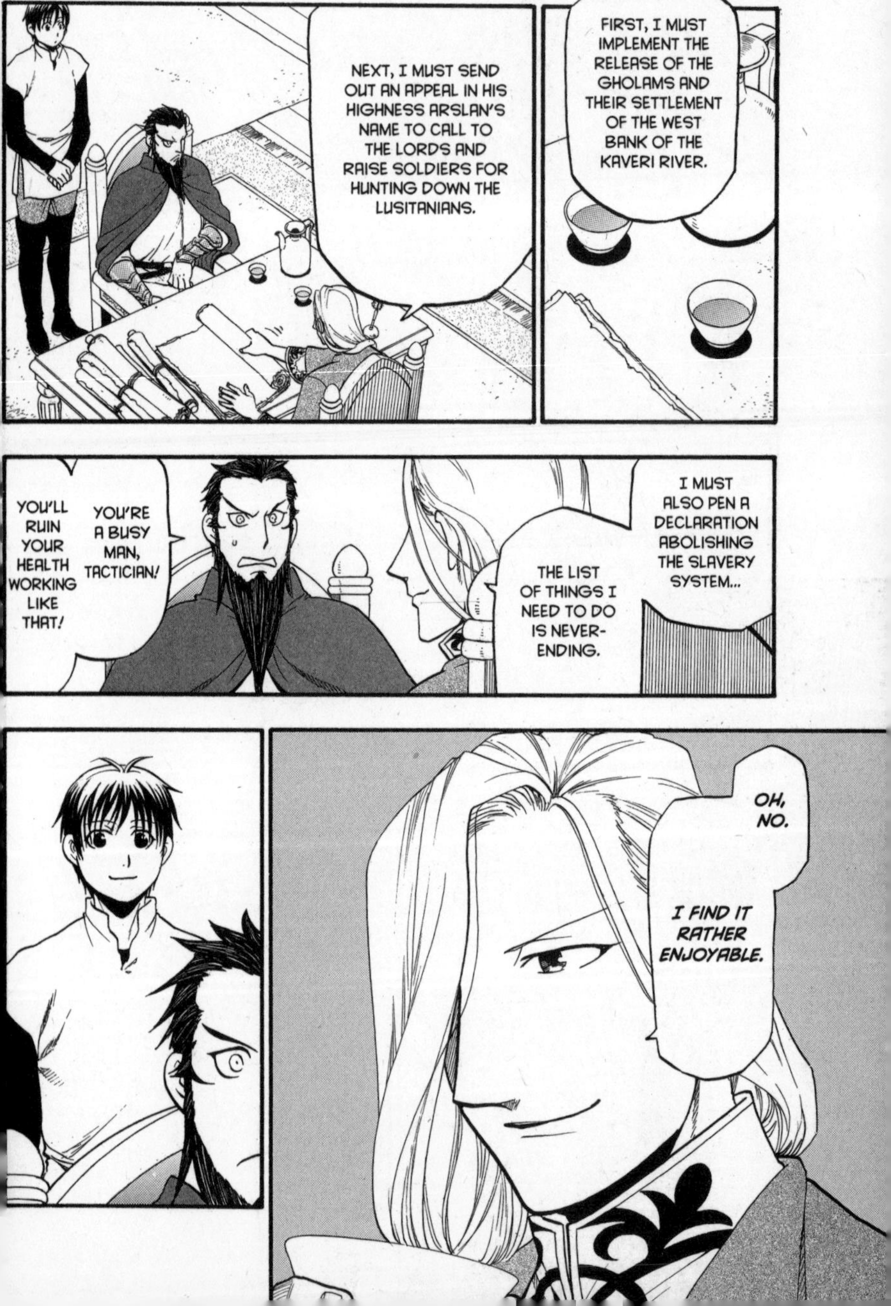
FIRST, I MUST IMPLEMENT THE RELEASE OF THE GHOLAMS AND THEIR SETTLEMENT OF THE WEST BANK OF THE KAVERI RIVER.
NEXT, I MUST SEND OUT AN APPEAL IN HIS HIGHNESS ARSLAN'S NAME TO CALL TO THE LORDS AND RAISE SOLDIERS FOR HUNTING DOWN THE LUSITANIANS.
I MUST ALSO PEN A DECLARATION ABOLISHING THE SLAVERY SYSTEM...
THE LIST OF THINGS I NEED TO DO IS NEVER-ENDING.
YOU'RE A BUSY MAN, TACTICIAN!
YOU'LL RUIN YOUR HEALTH WORKING LIKE THAT!
OH, NO.
I FIND IT RATHER ENJOYABLE.

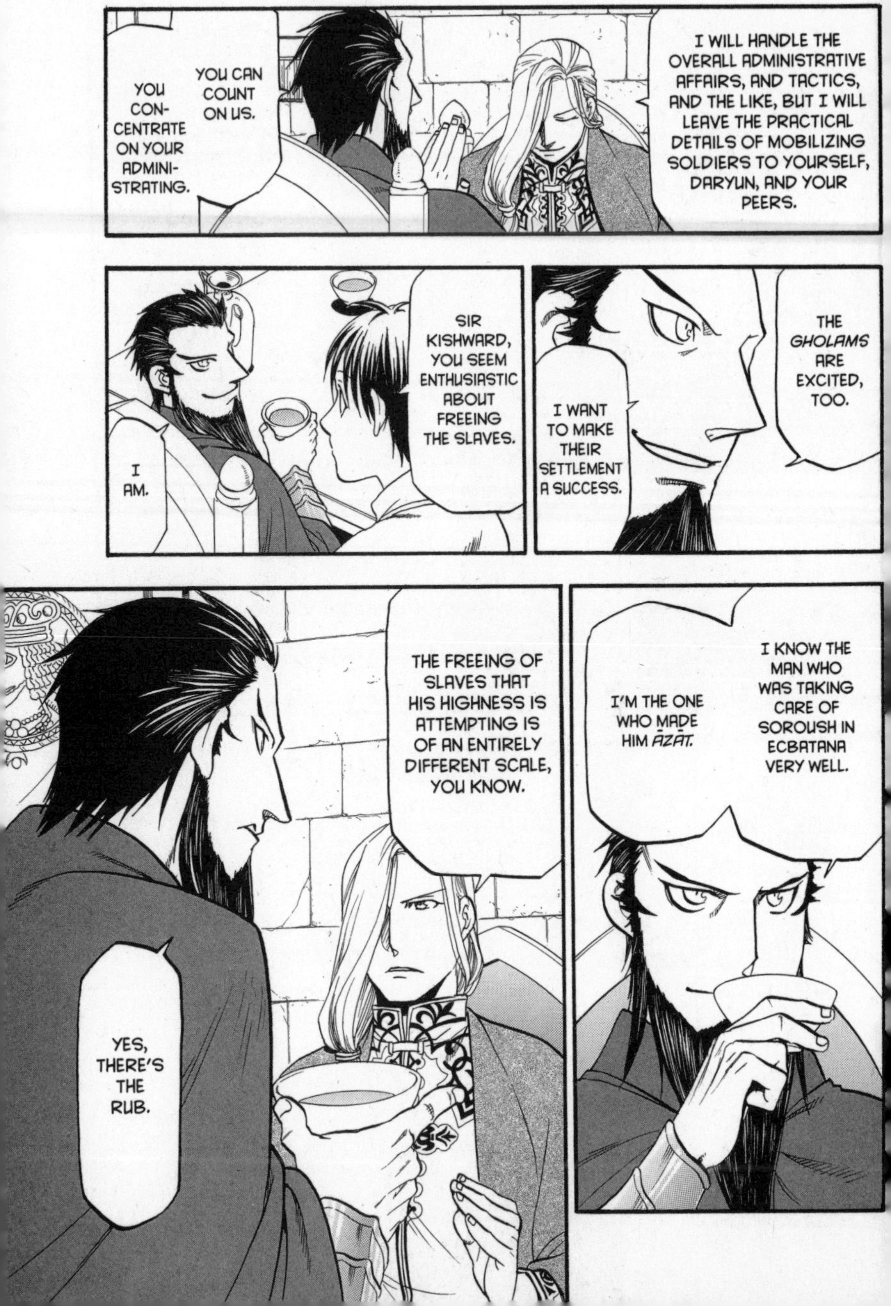
I WILL HANDLE THE OVERALL ADMINISTRATIVE AFFAIRS, AND TACTICS, AND THE LIKE, BUT I WILL LEAVE THE PRACTICAL DETAILS OF MOBILIZING SOLDIERS TO YOURSELF, DARYUN, AND YOUR PEERS.
YOU CAN COUNT ON US.
YOU CONCENTRATE ON YOUR ADMINISTRATING.
THE *GHOLAMS* ARE EXCITED, TOO.
I WANT TO MAKE THEIR SETTLEMENT A SUCCESS.
SIR KISHWARD, YOU SEEM ENTHUSIASTIC ABOUT FREEING THE SLAVES.
I AM.
I KNOW THE MAN WHO WAS TAKING CARE OF SOROUSH IN ECBATANA VERY WELL.
I'M THE ONE WHO MADE HIM *ĀZĀT*.
THE FREEING OF SLAVES THAT HIS HIGHNESS IS ATTEMPTING IS OF AN ENTIRELY DIFFERENT SCALE, YOU KNOW.
YES, THERE'S THE RUB.

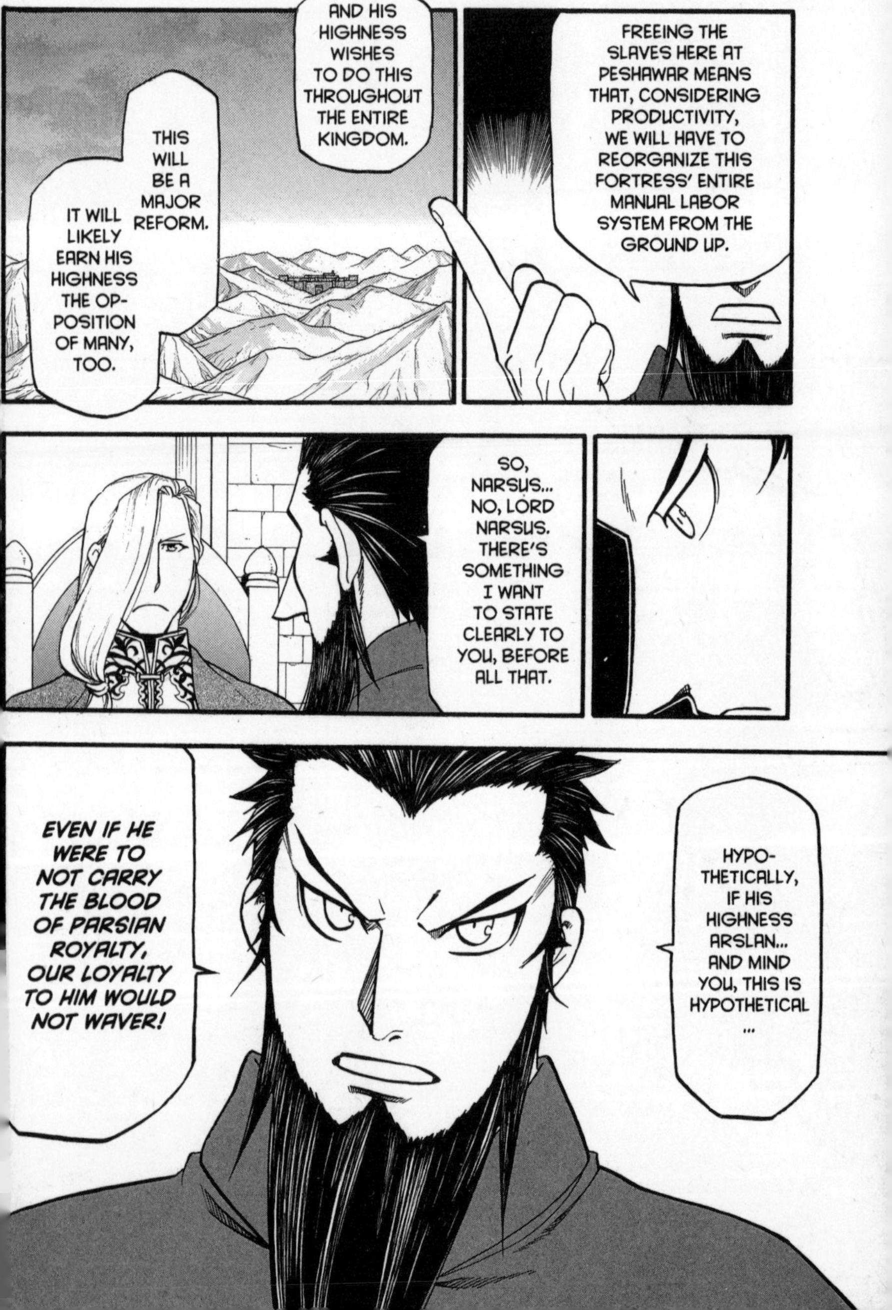
FREEING THE SLAVES HERE AT PESHAWAR MEANS THAT, CONSIDERING PRODUCTIVITY, WE WILL HAVE TO REORGANIZE THIS FORTRESS' ENTIRE MANUAL LABOR SYSTEM FROM THE GROUND UP.
AND HIS HIGHNESS WISHES TO DO THIS THROUGHOUT THE ENTIRE KINGDOM.
THIS WILL BE A MAJOR REFORM.
IT WILL LIKELY EARN HIS HIGHNESS THE OP-POSITION OF MANY, TOO.
SO, NARSUS... NO, LORD NARSUS. THERE'S SOMETHING I WANT TO STATE CLEARLY TO YOU, BEFORE ALL THAT.
HYPO-THETICALLY, IF HIS HIGHNESS ARSLAN... AND MIND YOU, THIS IS HYPOTHETICAL...
EVEN IF HE WERE TO NOT CARRY THE BLOOD OF PARSIAN ROYALTY, OUR LOYALTY TO HIM WOULD NOT WAVER!

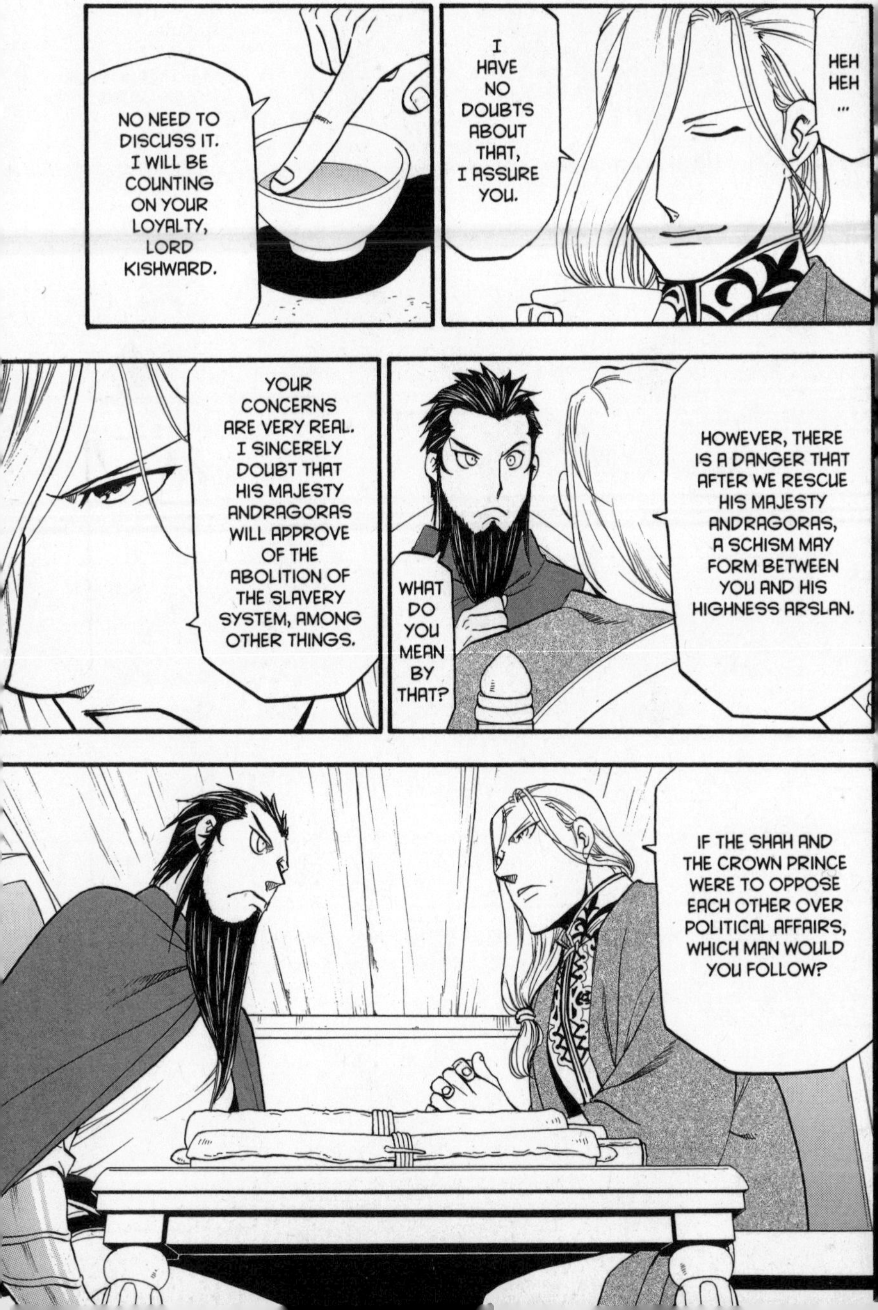
HEH HEH ...
I HAVE NO DOUBTS ABOUT THAT, I ASSURE YOU.
NO NEED TO DISCUSS IT. I WILL BE COUNTING ON YOUR LOYALTY, LORD KISHWARD.
HOWEVER, THERE IS A DANGER THAT AFTER WE RESCUE HIS MAJESTY ANDRAGORAS, A SCHISM MAY FORM BETWEEN YOU AND HIS HIGHNESS ARSLAN.
WHAT DO YOU MEAN BY THAT?
YOUR CONCERNS ARE VERY REAL. I SINCERELY DOUBT THAT HIS MAJESTY ANDRAGORAS WILL APPROVE OF THE ABOLITION OF THE SLAVERY SYSTEM, AMONG OTHER THINGS.
IF THE SHAH AND THE CROWN PRINCE WERE TO OPPOSE EACH OTHER OVER POLITICAL AFFAIRS, WHICH MAN WOULD YOU FOLLOW?

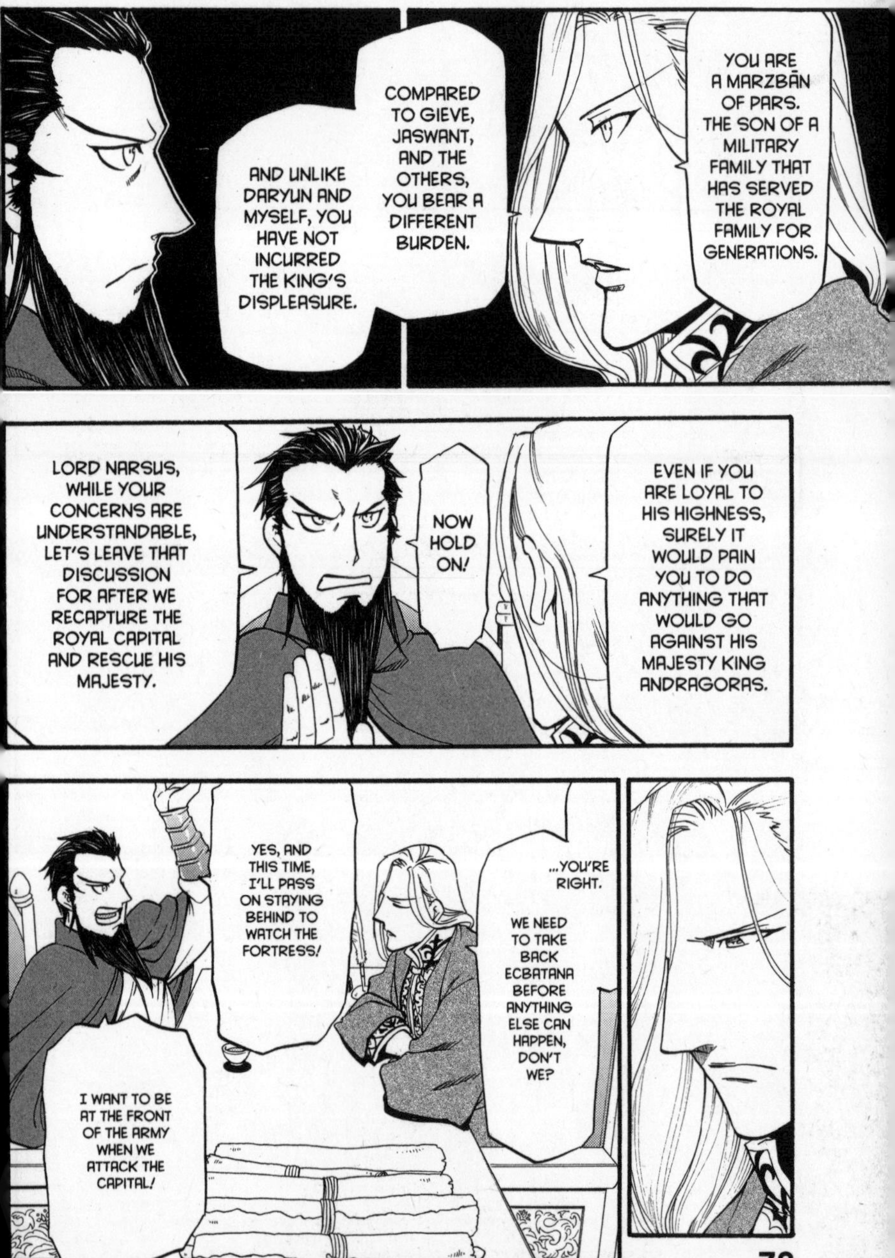
YOU ARE A MARZBĀN OF PARS. THE SON OF A MILITARY FAMILY THAT HAS SERVED THE ROYAL FAMILY FOR GENERATIONS.
COMPARED TO GIEVE, JASWANT, AND THE OTHERS, YOU BEAR A DIFFERENT BURDEN.
AND UNLIKE DARYUN AND MYSELF, YOU HAVE NOT INCURRED THE KING'S DISPLEASURE.
EVEN IF YOU ARE LOYAL TO HIS HIGHNESS, SURELY IT WOULD PAIN YOU TO DO ANYTHING THAT WOULD GO AGAINST HIS MAJESTY KING ANDRAGORAS.
NOW HOLD ON!
LORD NARSUS, WHILE YOUR CONCERNS ARE UNDERSTANDABLE, LET'S LEAVE THAT DISCUSSION FOR AFTER WE RECAPTURE THE ROYAL CAPITAL AND RESCUE HIS MAJESTY.
...YOU'RE RIGHT.
WE NEED TO TAKE BACK ECBATANA BEFORE ANYTHING ELSE CAN HAPPEN, DON'T WE?
YES, AND THIS TIME, I'LL PASS ON STAYING BEHIND TO WATCH THE FORTRESS!
I WANT TO BE AT THE FRONT OF THE ARMY WHEN WE ATTACK THE CAPITAL!

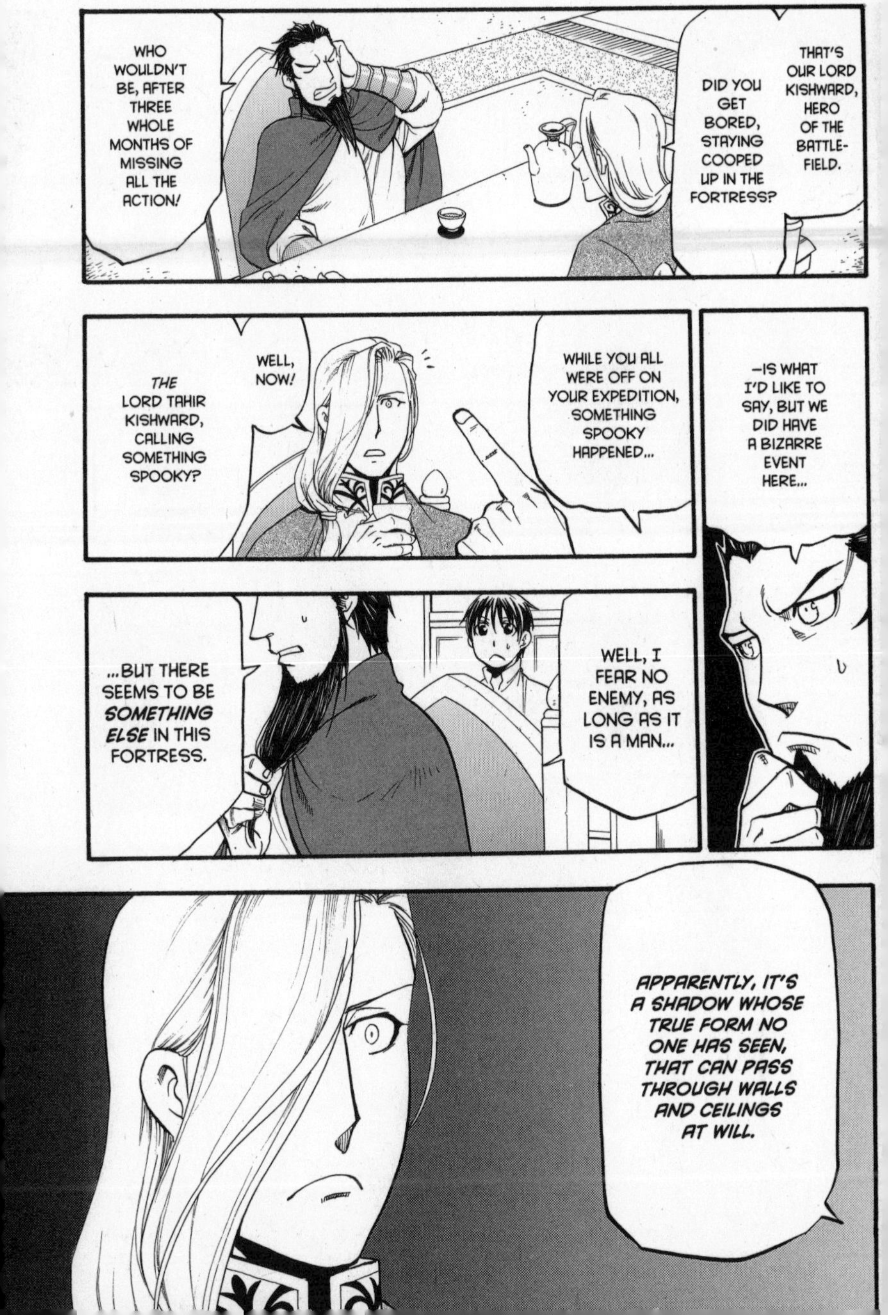
THAT'S OUR LORD KISHWARD, HERO OF THE BATTLE-FIELD.
DID YOU GET BORED, STAYING COOPED UP IN THE FORTRESS?
WHO WOULDN'T BE, AFTER THREE WHOLE MONTHS OF MISSING ALL THE ACTION!
—IS WHAT I'D LIKE TO SAY, BUT WE DID HAVE A BIZARRE EVENT HERE...
WHILE YOU ALL WERE OFF ON YOUR EXPEDITION, SOMETHING SPOOKY HAPPENED...
WELL, NOW!
THE LORD TAHIR KISHWARD, CALLING SOMETHING SPOOKY?
WELL, I FEAR NO ENEMY, AS LONG AS IT IS A MAN...
...BUT THERE SEEMS TO BE ***SOMETHING ELSE*** IN THIS FORTRESS.
APPARENTLY, IT'S A SHADOW WHOSE TRUE FORM NO ONE HAS SEEN, THAT CAN PASS THROUGH WALLS AND CEILINGS AT WILL.

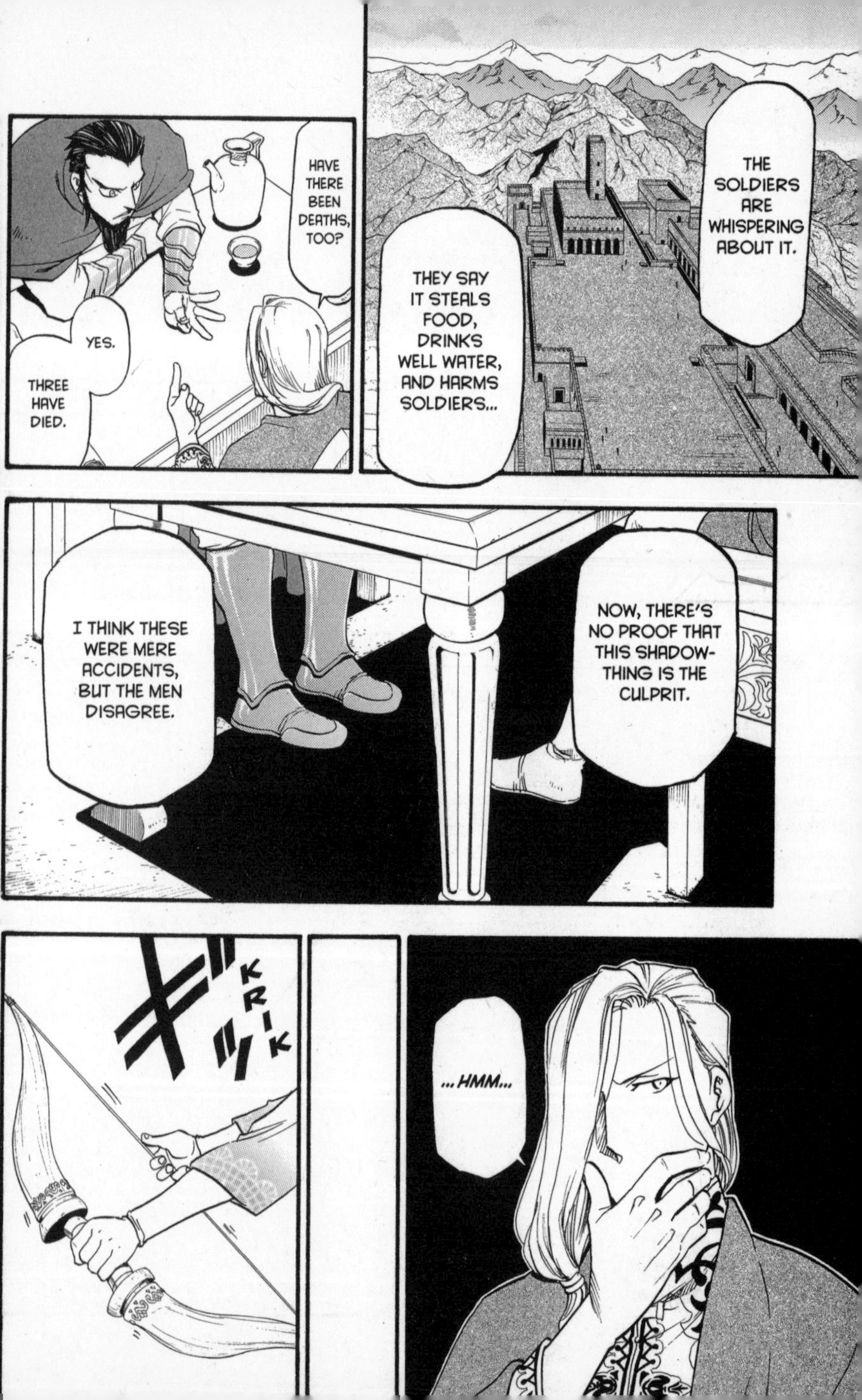
THE SOLDIERS ARE WHISPERING ABOUT IT.
THEY SAY IT STEALS FOOD, DRINKS WELL WATER, AND HARMS SOLDIERS...
HAVE THERE BEEN DEATHS, TOO?
YES.
THREE HAVE DIED.
NOW, THERE'S NO PROOF THAT THIS SHADOW-THING IS THE CULPRIT.
I THINK THESE WERE MERE ACCIDENTS, BUT THE MEN DISAGREE.
...HMM...
KRIK

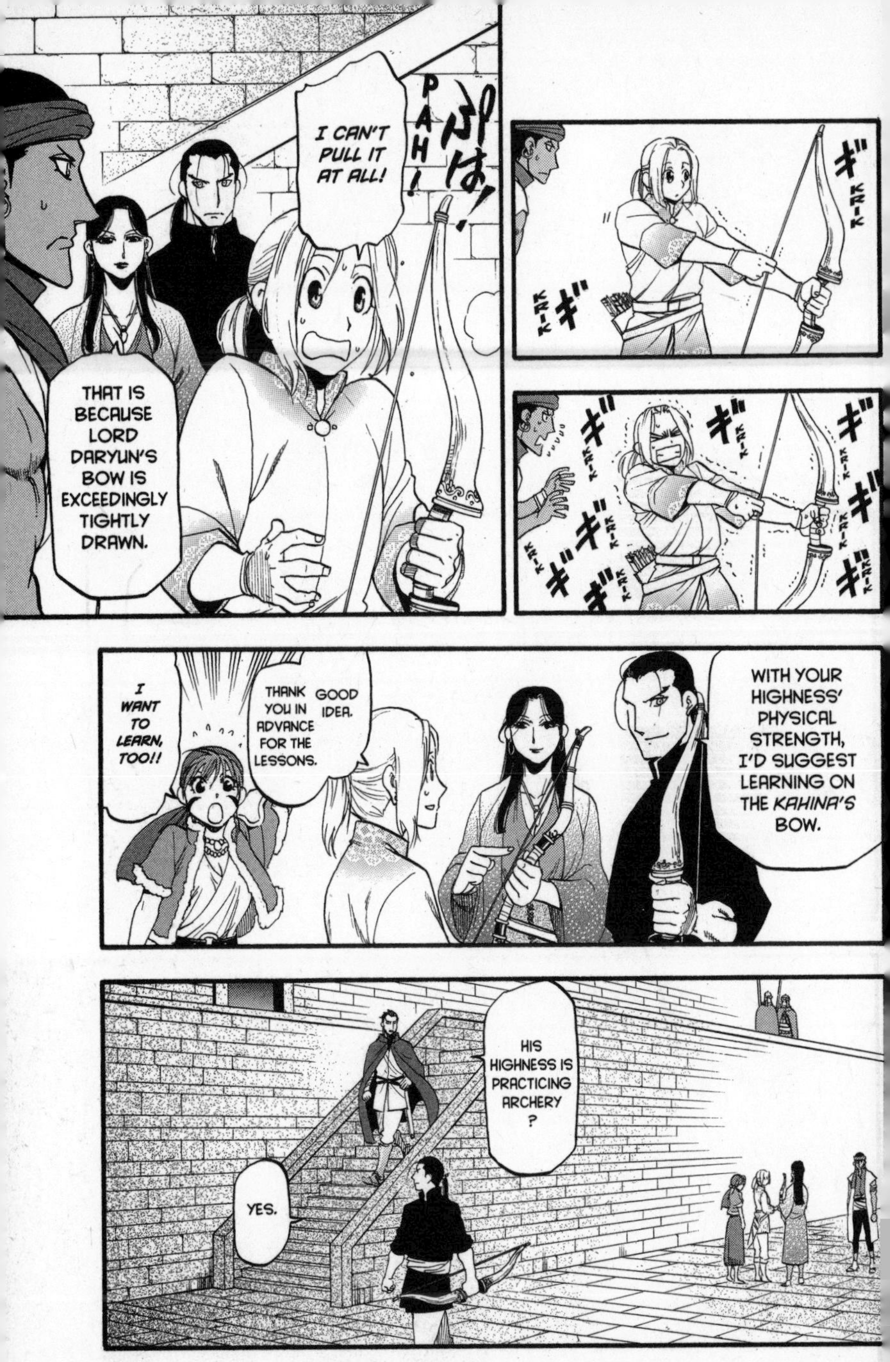

ギ KRIK
ギ KRIK
ギ KRIK
ギ KRIK
ギ KRIK
ギ KRIK
ギ KRIK
ギ KRIK
ギ KRIK
ぷは! PAH!
I CAN'T PULL IT AT ALL!
THAT IS BECAUSE LORD DARYUN'S BOW IS EXCEEDINGLY TIGHTLY DRAWN.
WITH YOUR HIGHNESS' PHYSICAL STRENGTH, I'D SUGGEST LEARNING ON THE KAHINA'S BOW.
GOOD IDEA.
THANK YOU IN ADVANCE FOR THE LESSONS.
I WANT TO LEARN, TOO!!
HIS HIGHNESS IS PRACTICING ARCHERY?
YES.

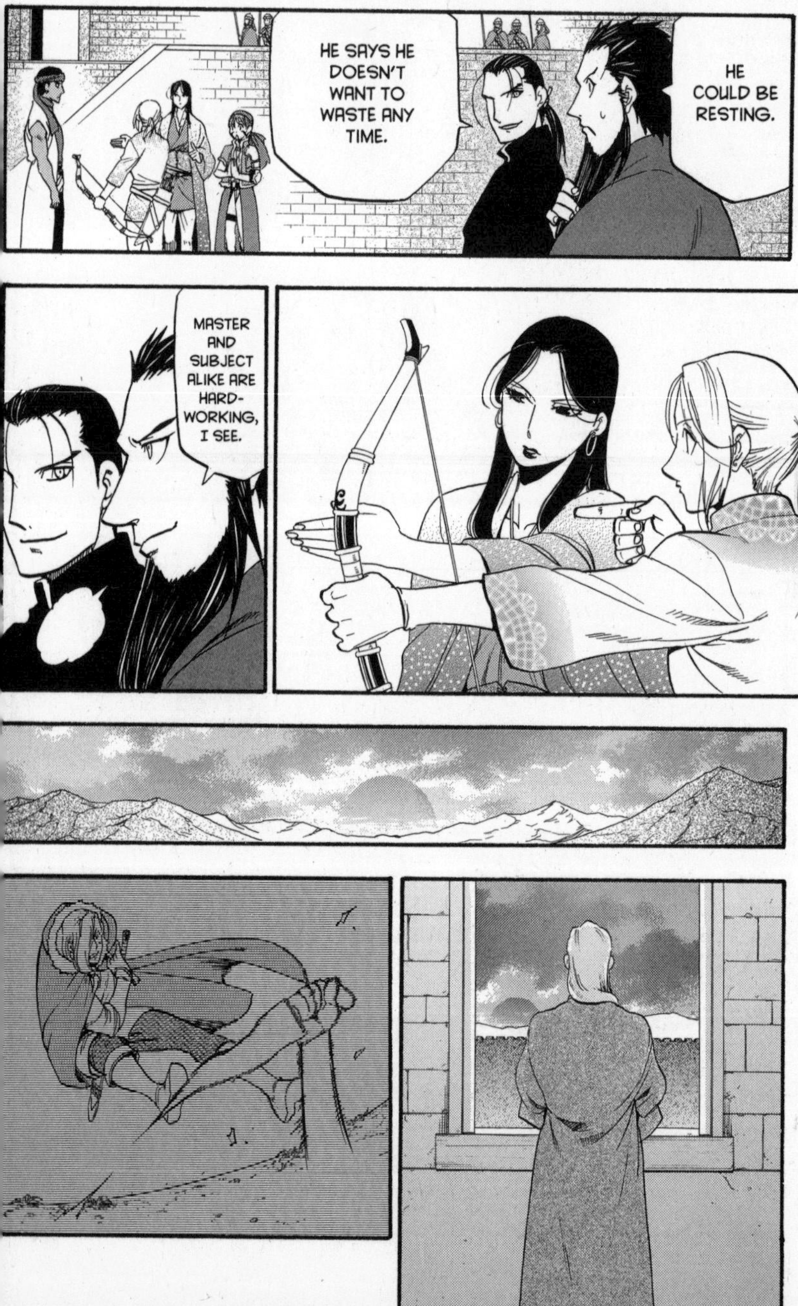
HE COULD BE RESTING.
HE SAYS HE DOESN'T WANT TO WASTE ANY TIME.
MASTER AND SUBJECT ALIKE ARE HARD-WORKING, I SEE.

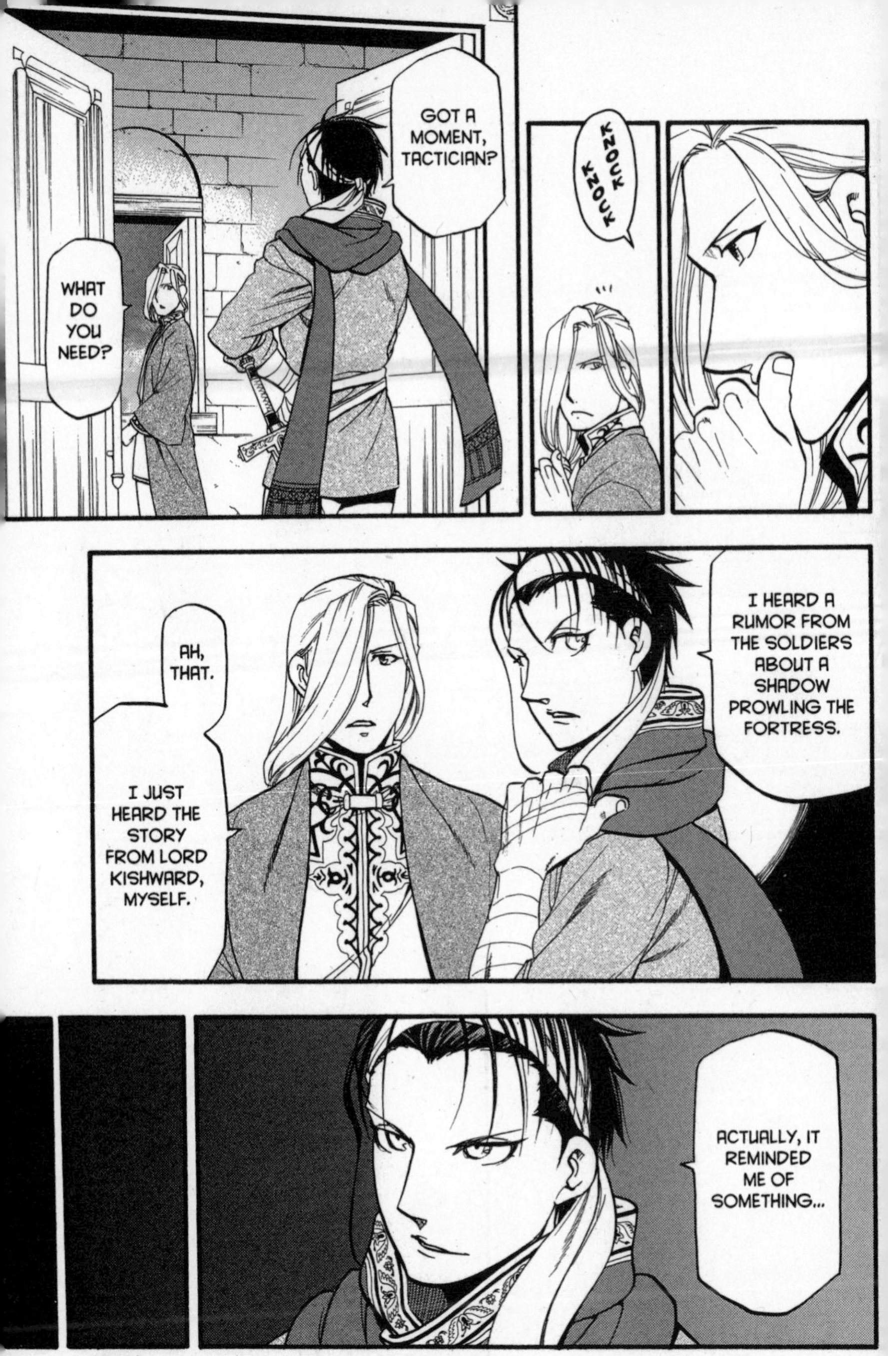
KNOCK KNOCK
GOT A MOMENT, TACTICIAN?
WHAT DO YOU NEED?
I HEARD A RUMOR FROM THE SOLDIERS ABOUT A SHADOW PROWLING THE FORTRESS.
AH, THAT.
I JUST HEARD THE STORY FROM LORD KISHWARD, MYSELF.
ACTUALLY, IT REMINDED ME OF SOMETHING...

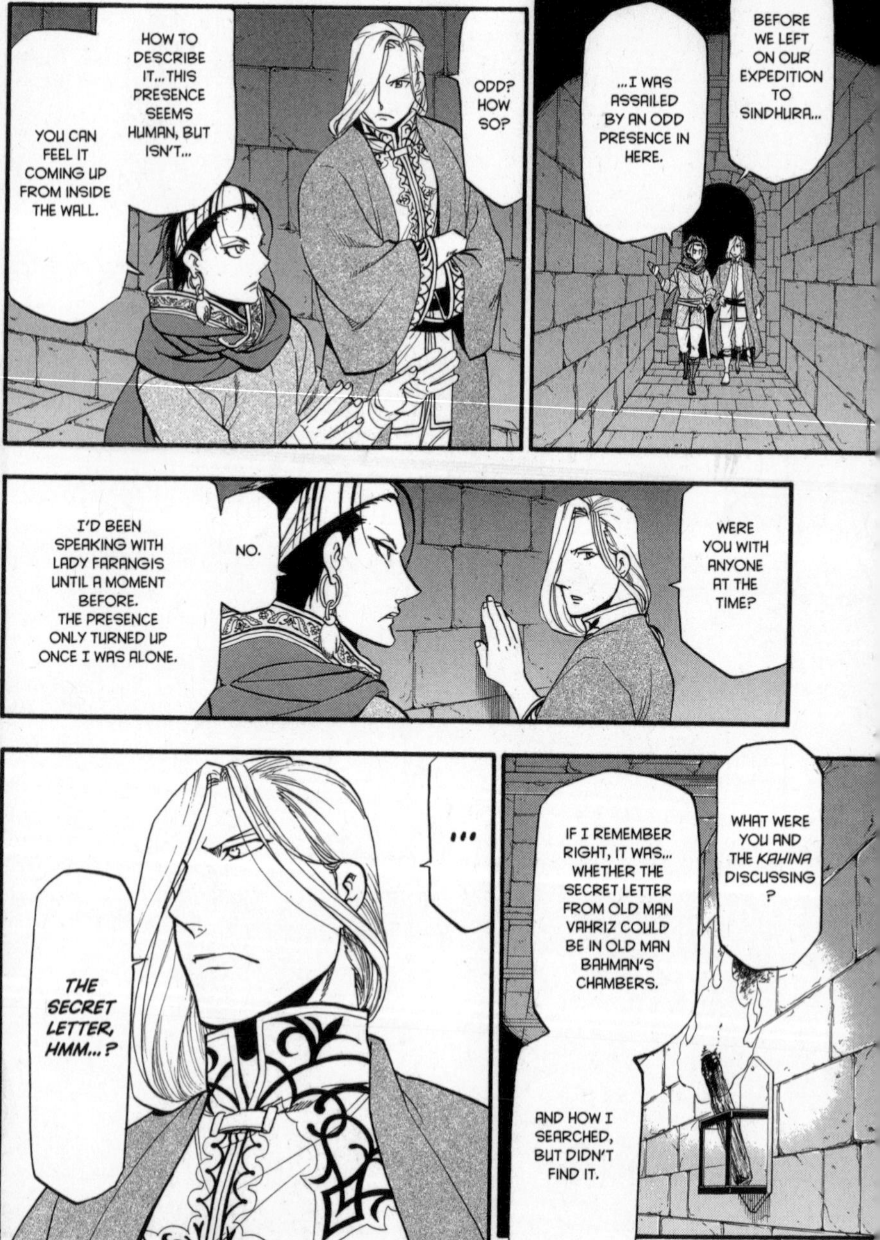

BEFORE WE LEFT ON OUR EXPEDITION TO SINDHURA...
...I WAS ASSAILED BY AN ODD PRESENCE IN HERE.
ODD? HOW SO?
HOW TO DESCRIBE IT... THIS PRESENCE SEEMS HUMAN, BUT ISN'T...
YOU CAN FEEL IT COMING UP FROM INSIDE THE WALL.
WERE YOU WITH ANYONE AT THE TIME?
NO.
I'D BEEN SPEAKING WITH LADY FARANGIS UNTIL A MOMENT BEFORE. THE PRESENCE ONLY TURNED UP ONCE I WAS ALONE.
WHAT WERE YOU AND THE *KAHINA* DISCUSSING?
IF I REMEMBER RIGHT, IT WAS... WHETHER THE SECRET LETTER FROM OLD MAN VAHRIZ COULD BE IN OLD MAN BAHMAN'S CHAMBERS.
AND HOW I SEARCHED, BUT DIDN'T FIND IT.
...
THE SECRET LETTER, HMM...?

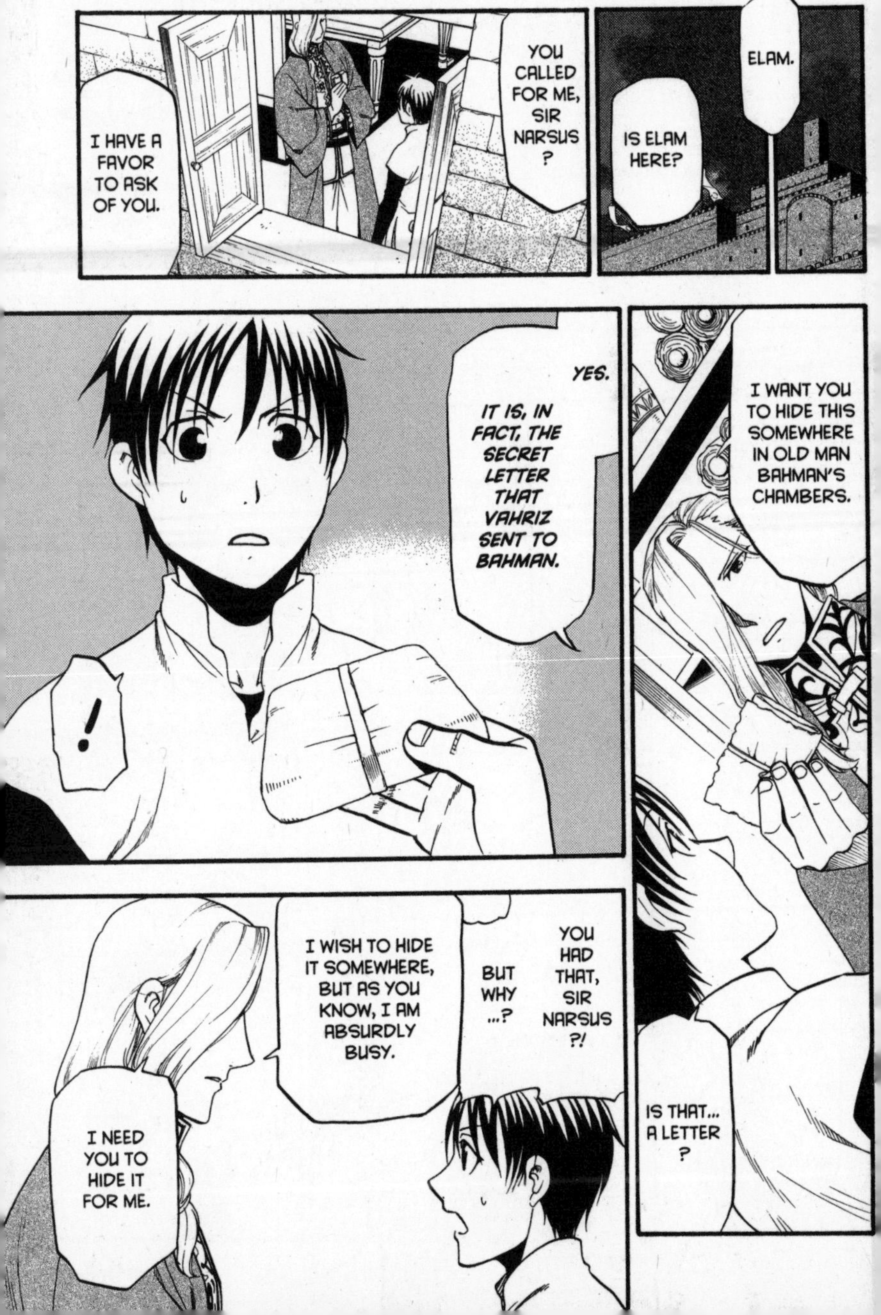
ELAM.
IS ELAM HERE?
YOU CALLED FOR ME, SIR NARSUS?
I HAVE A FAVOR TO ASK OF YOU.
I WANT YOU TO HIDE THIS SOMEWHERE IN OLD MAN BAHMAN'S CHAMBERS.
IS THAT... A LETTER?
YES.
IT IS, IN FACT, THE SECRET LETTER THAT VAHRIZ SENT TO BAHMAN.
!
YOU HAD THAT, SIR NARSUS?!
BUT WHY...?
I WISH TO HIDE IT SOMEWHERE, BUT AS YOU KNOW, I AM ABSURDLY BUSY.
I NEED YOU TO HIDE IT FOR ME.

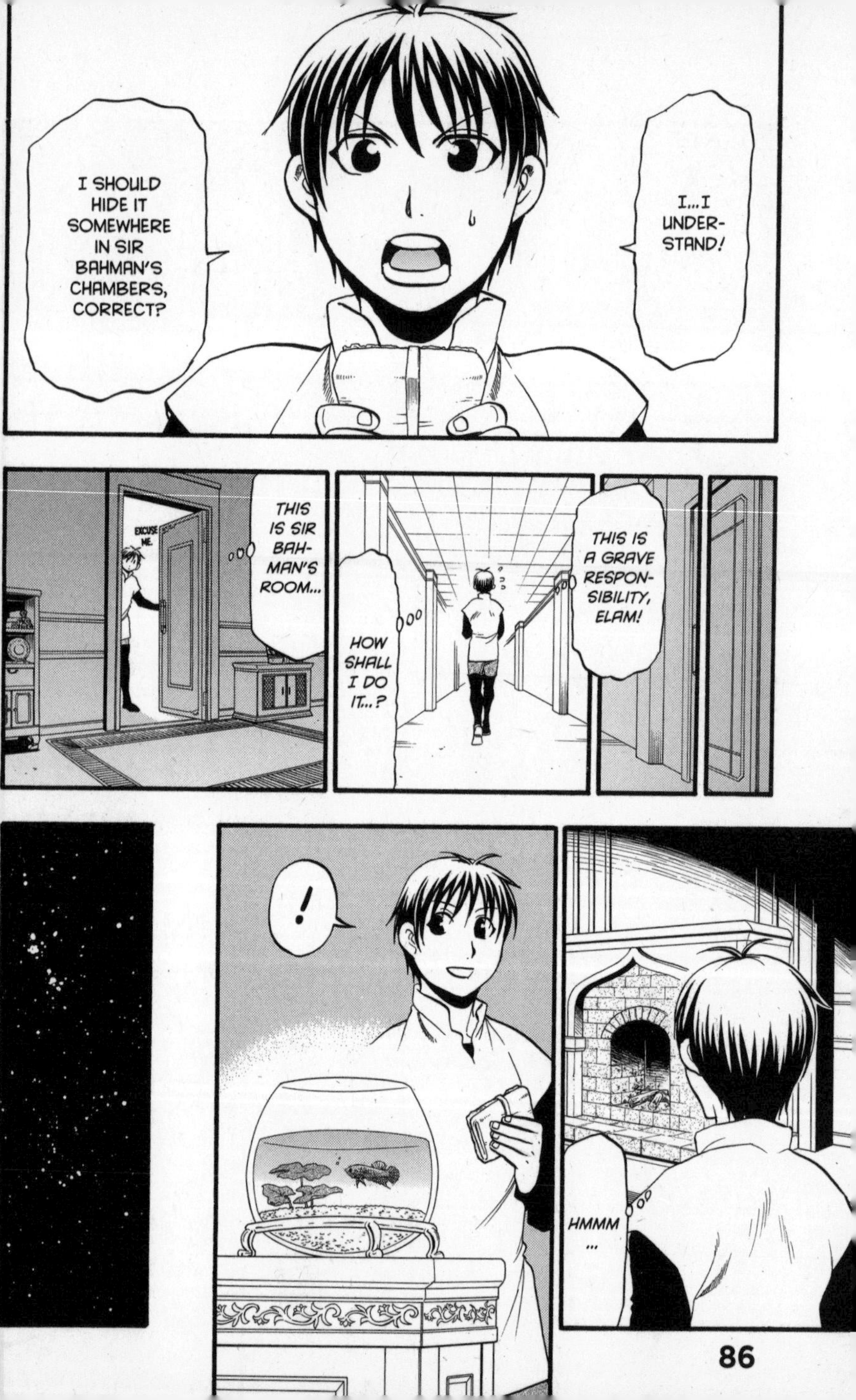
I...I UNDERSTAND!
I SHOULD HIDE IT SOMEWHERE IN SIR BAHMAN'S CHAMBERS, CORRECT?
THIS IS A GRAVE RESPONSIBILITY, ELAM!
HOW SHALL I DO IT...?
THIS IS SIR BAHMAN'S ROOM...
EXCUSE ME.
HMMM ...
!

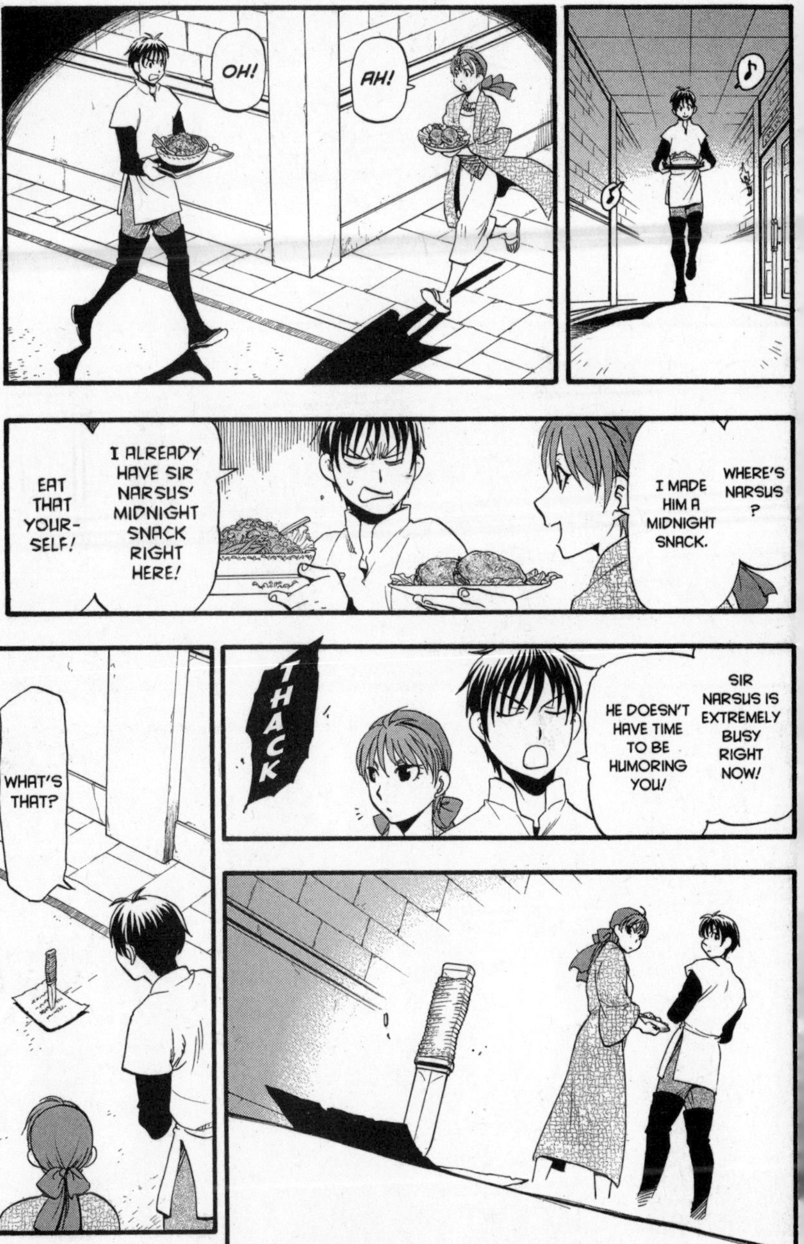
♪
♪
AH!
OH!
WHERE'S NARSUS?
I MADE HIM A MIDNIGHT SNACK.
I ALREADY HAVE SIR NARSUS' MIDNIGHT SNACK RIGHT HERE!
EAT THAT YOURSELF!
SIR NARSUS IS EXTREMELY BUSY RIGHT NOW!
HE DOESN'T HAVE TIME TO BE HUMORING YOU!
THACK
WHAT'S THAT?

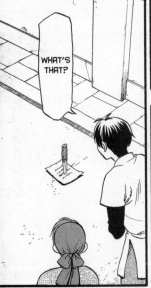

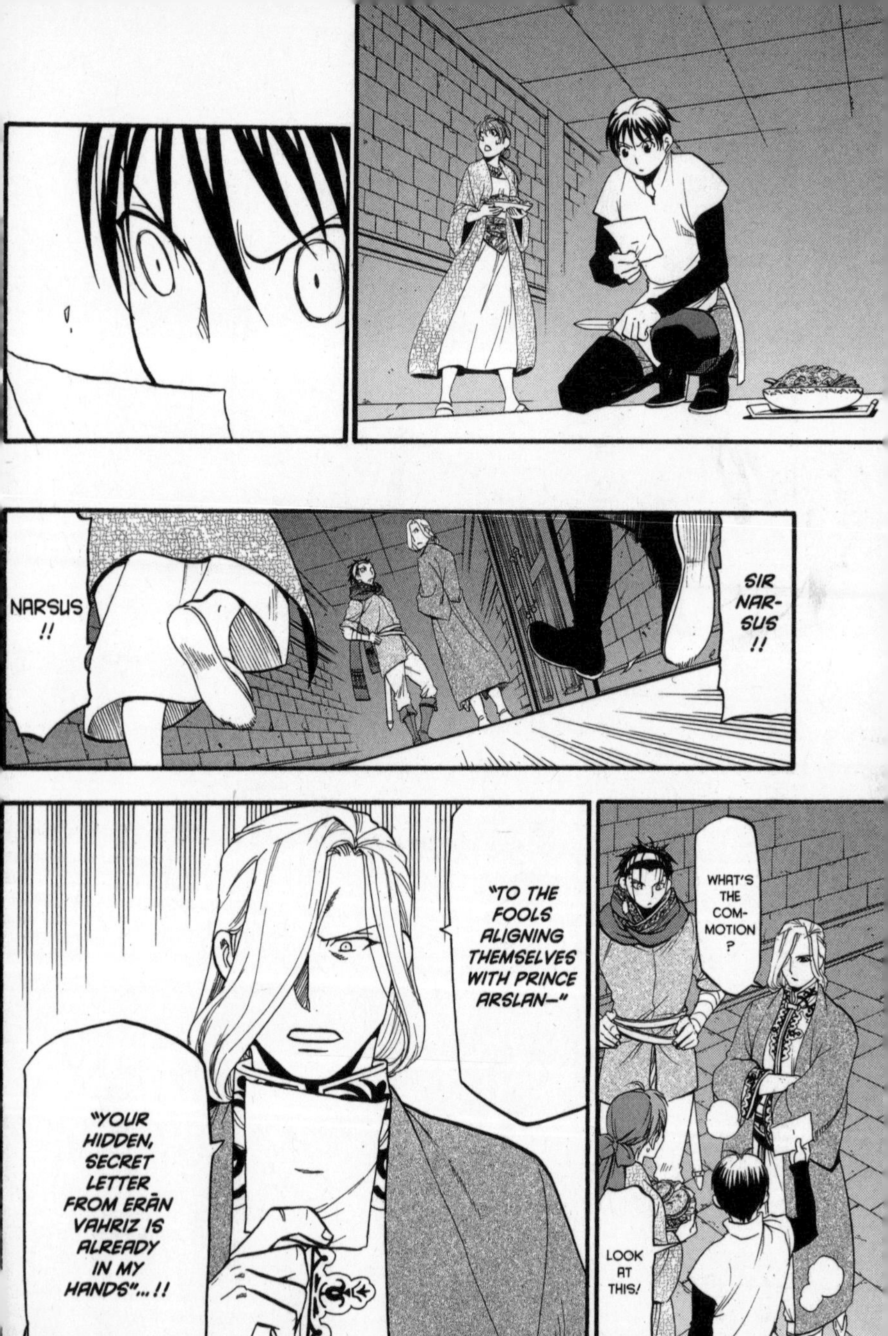
SIR NARSUS !!
NARSUS !!
WHAT'S THE COMMOTION?
LOOK AT THIS!
"TO THE FOOLS ALIGNING THEMSELVES WITH PRINCE ARSLAN—"
"YOUR HIDDEN, SECRET LETTER FROM ERĀN VAHRIZ IS ALREADY IN MY HANDS"...!!

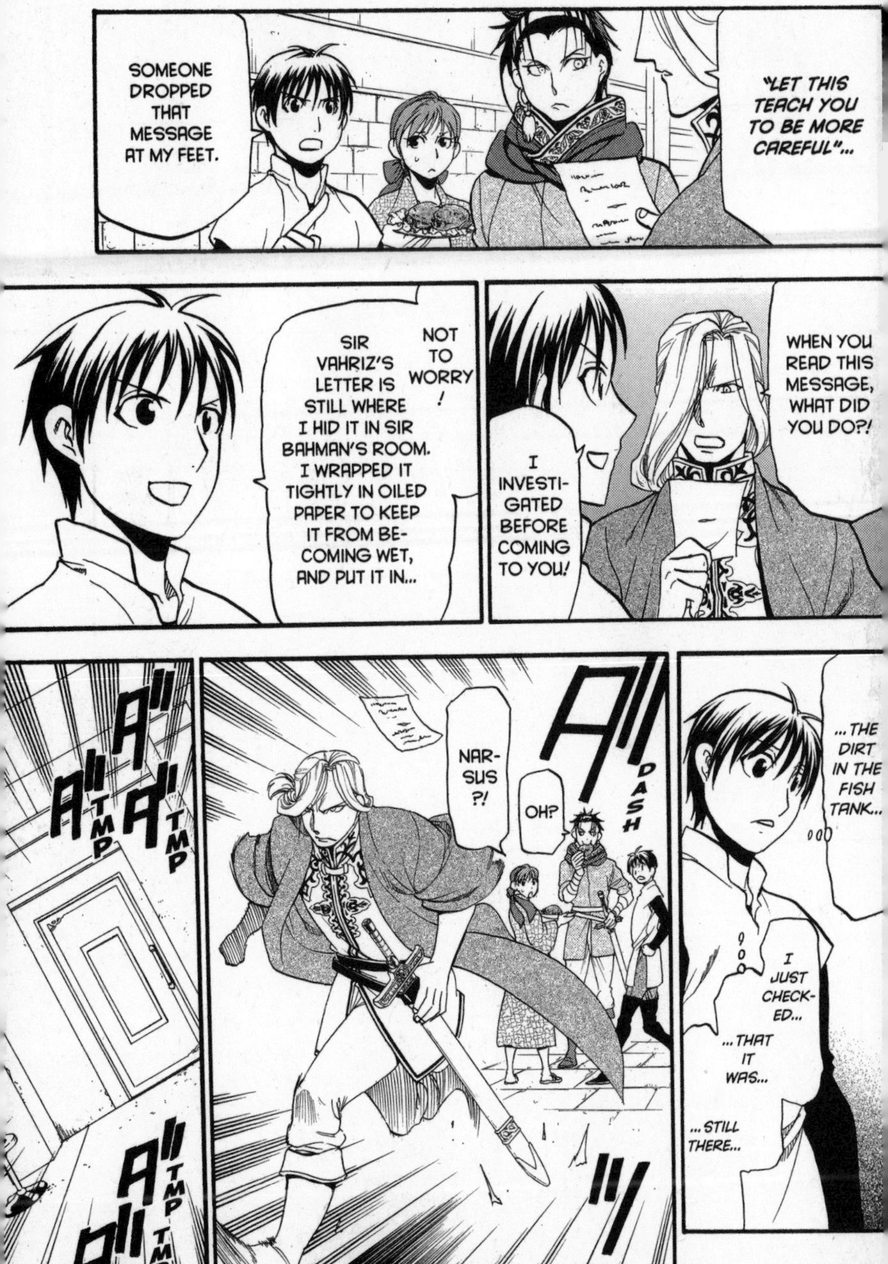
"LET THIS TEACH YOU TO BE MORE CAREFUL"...
SOMEONE DROPPED THAT MESSAGE AT MY FEET.
WHEN YOU READ THIS MESSAGE, WHAT DID YOU DO?!
I INVESTIGATED BEFORE COMING TO YOU!
NOT TO WORRY!
SIR VAHRIZ'S LETTER IS STILL WHERE I HID IT IN SIR BAHMAN'S ROOM. I WRAPPED IT TIGHTLY IN OILED PAPER TO KEEP IT FROM BECOMING WET, AND PUT IT IN...
...THE DIRT IN THE FISH TANK...
I JUST CHECKED...
...THAT IT WAS...
...STILL THERE...
A
DASH
OH?
NARSUS?!
A
A
A
TMP
TMP
A
A
TMP TMP
TMP

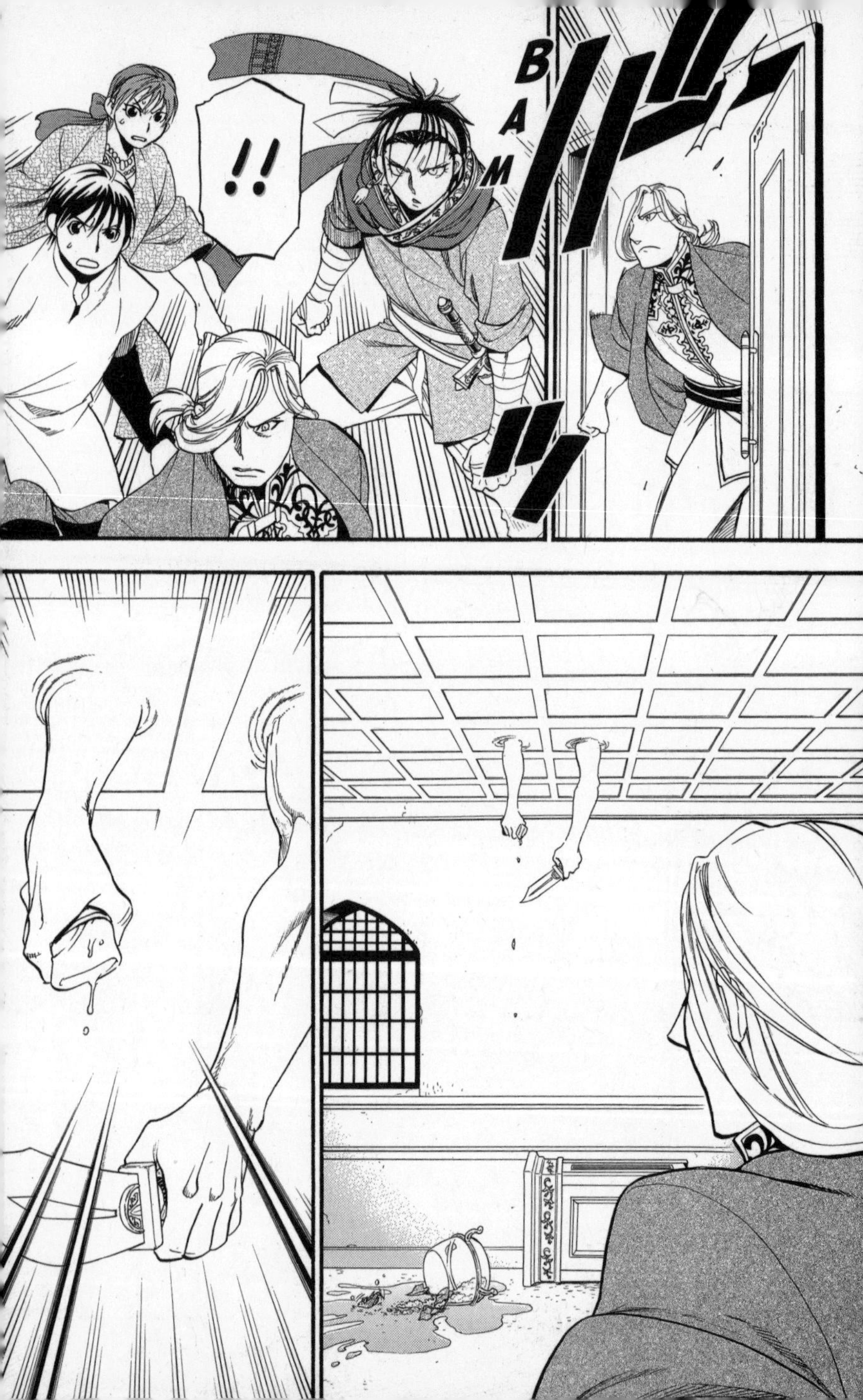
BAM
!!

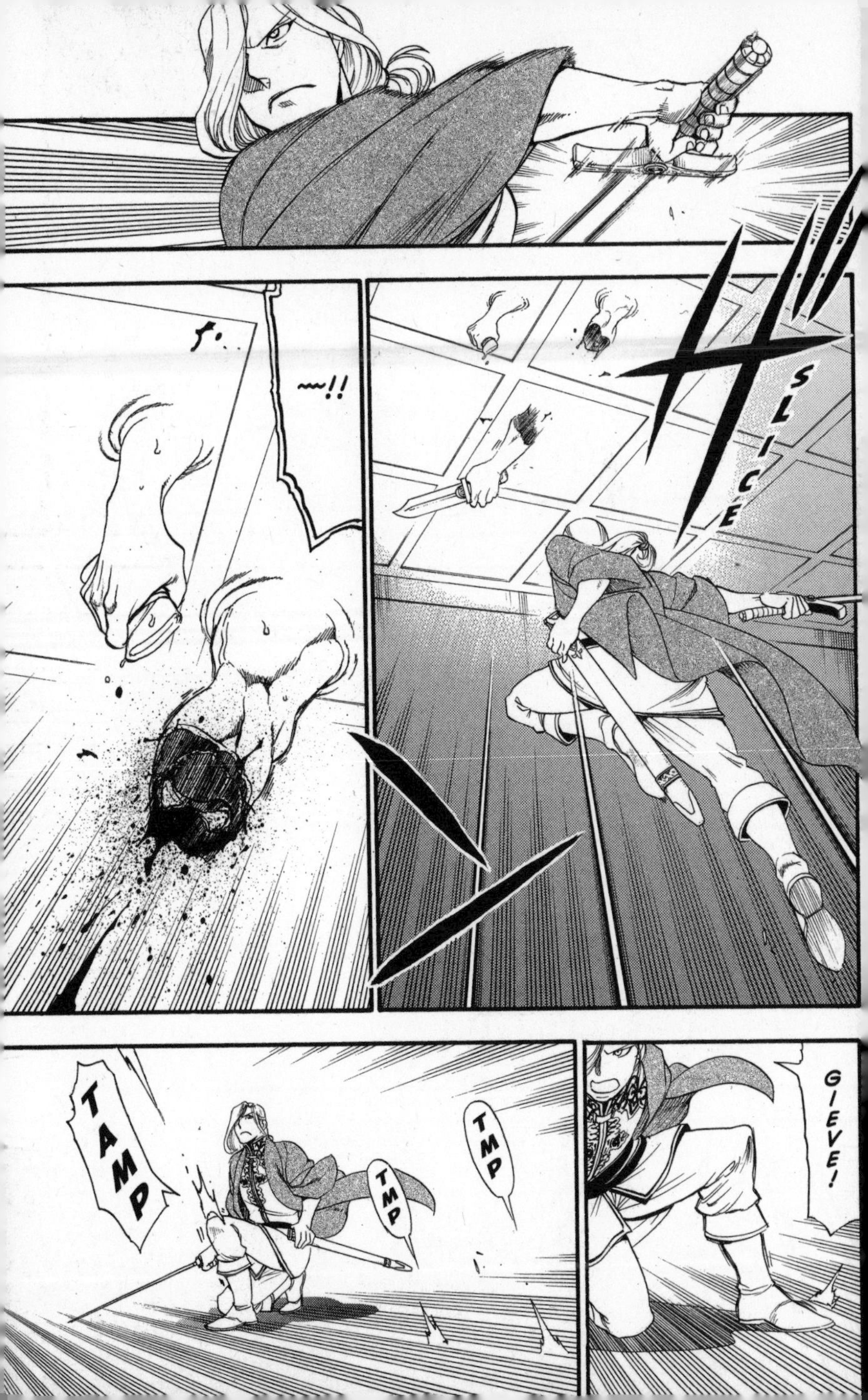
SLICE
~~!!
GIEVE!
TMP
TMP
TAMP

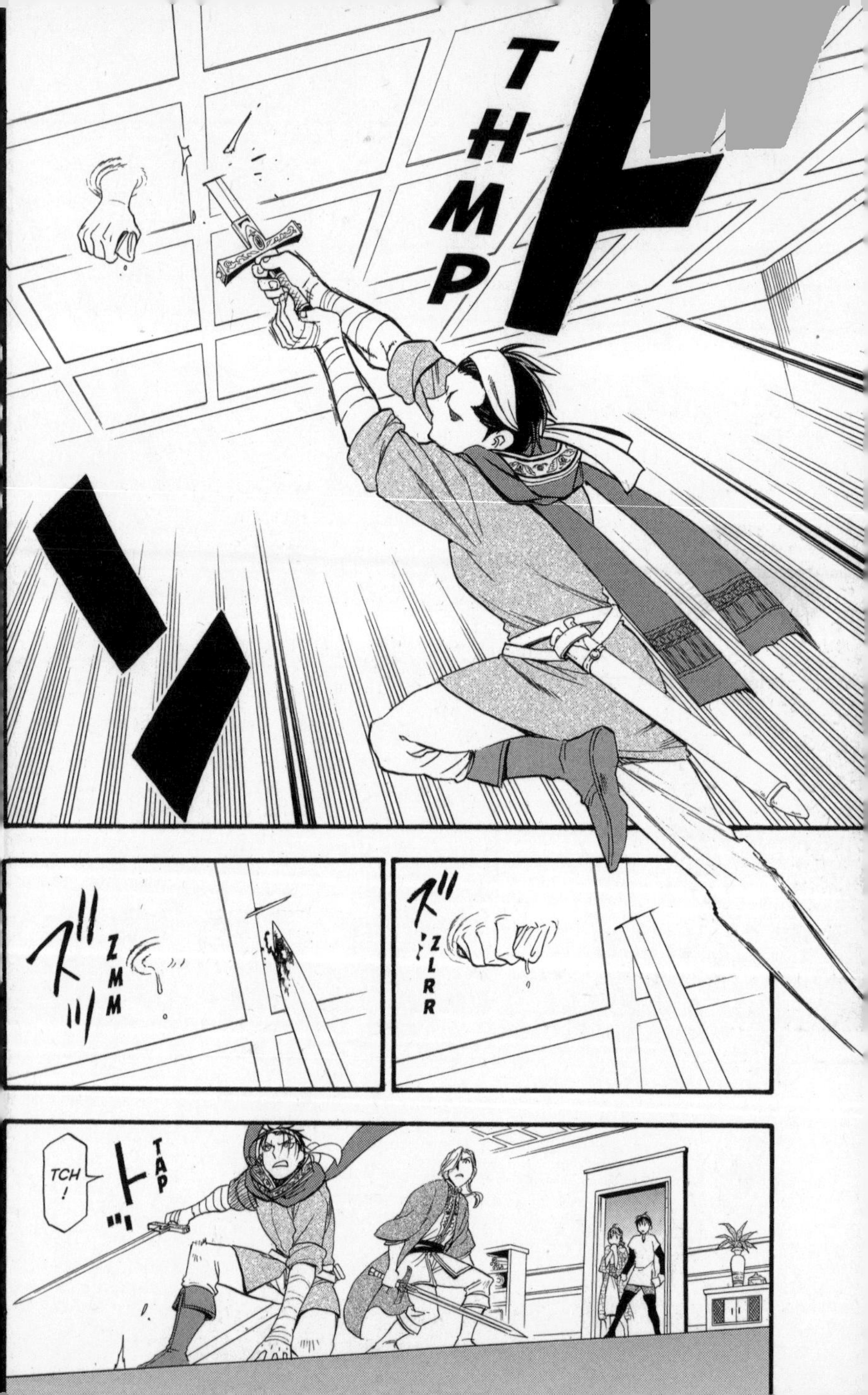
THMP
ZLRR
ZMM
TCH!
TAP

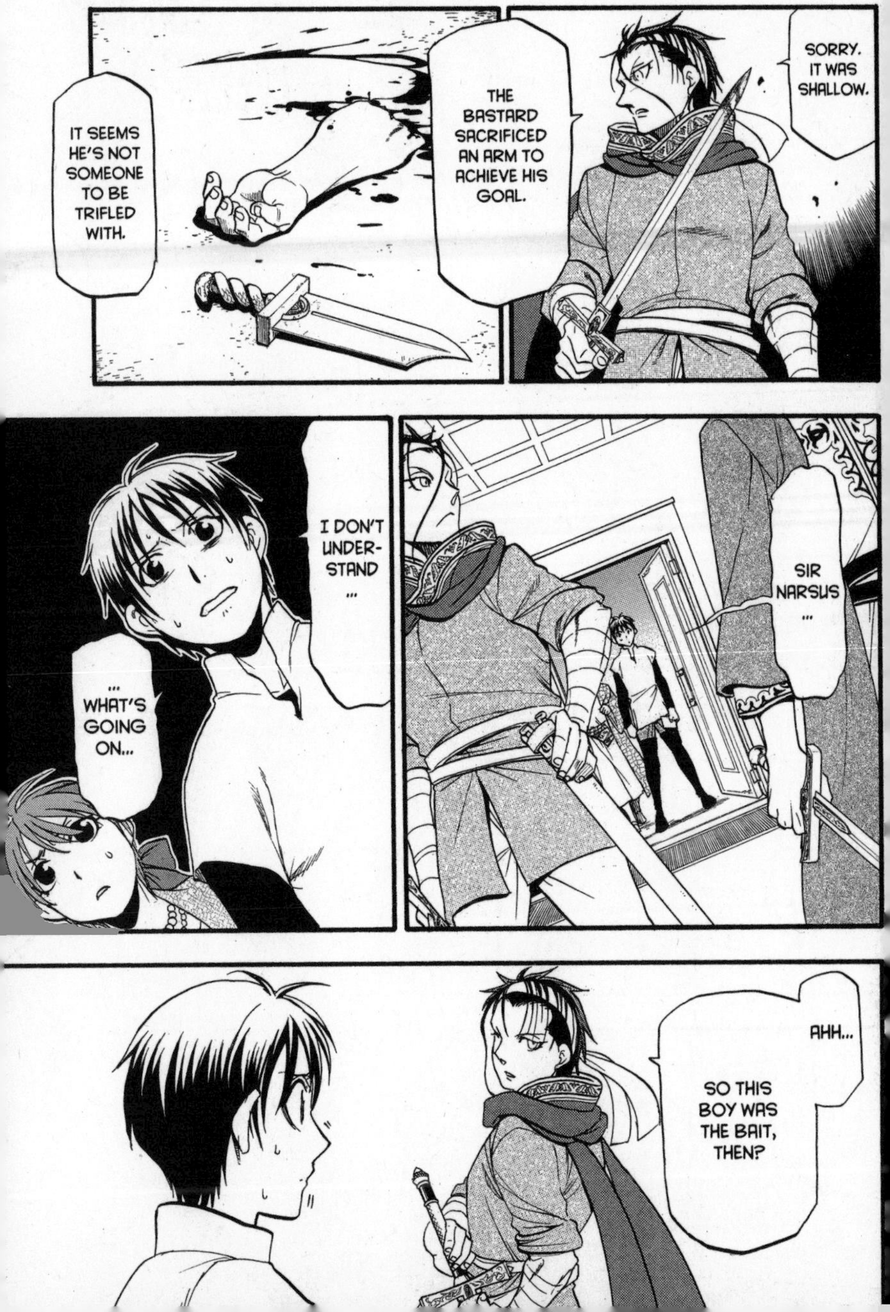
SORRY. IT WAS SHALLOW.
THE BASTARD SACRIFICED AN ARM TO ACHIEVE HIS GOAL.
IT SEEMS HE'S NOT SOMEONE TO BE TRIFLED WITH.
SIR NARSUS ...
I DON'T UNDER-STAND ...
... WHAT'S GOING ON...
AHH...
SO THIS BOY WAS THE BAIT, THEN?

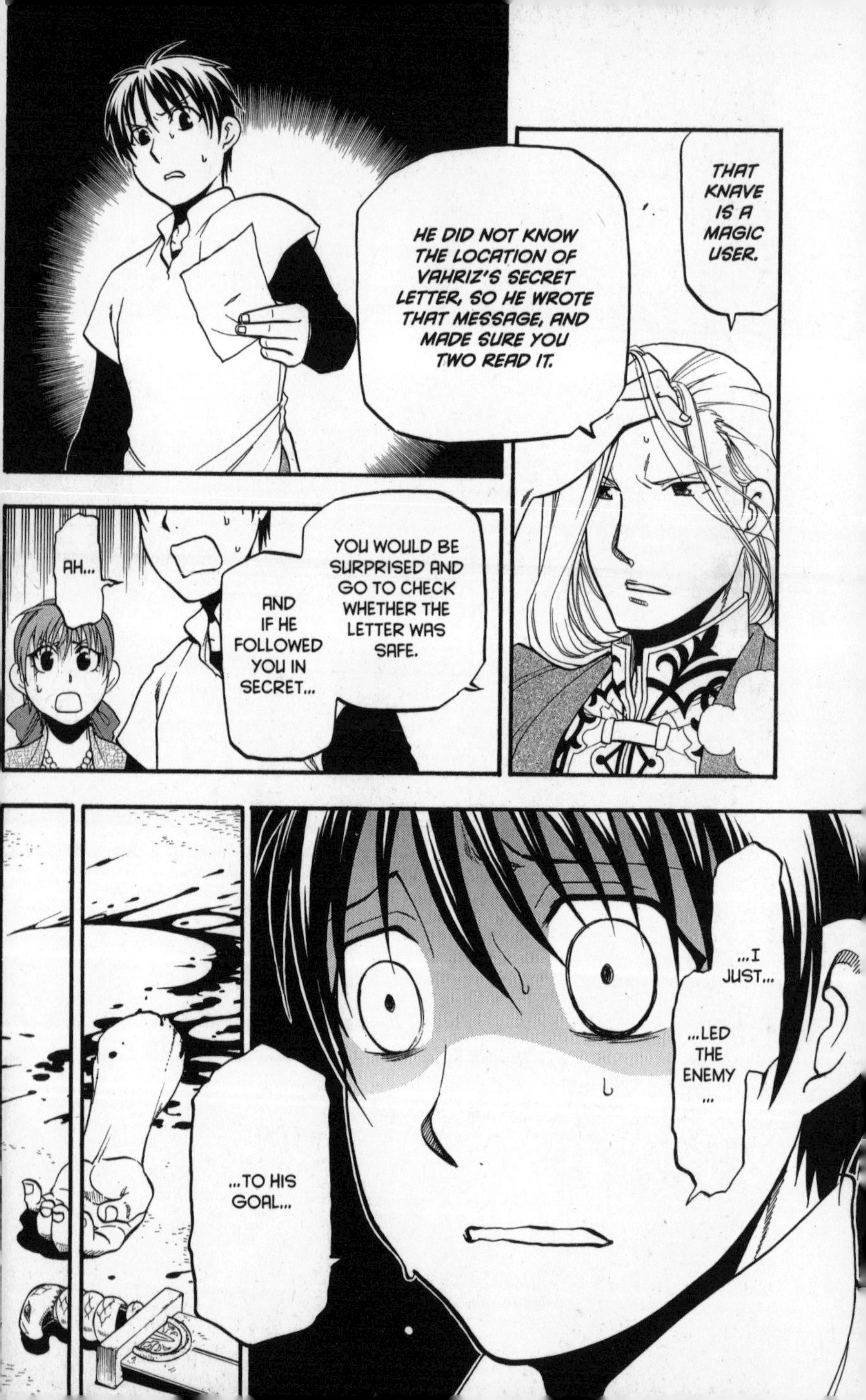
THAT KNAVE IS A MAGIC USER.
HE DID NOT KNOW THE LOCATION OF VAHRIZ'S SECRET LETTER, SO HE WROTE THAT MESSAGE, AND MADE SURE YOU TWO READ IT.
YOU WOULD BE SURPRISED AND GO TO CHECK WHETHER THE LETTER WAS SAFE.
AND IF HE FOLLOWED YOU IN SECRET...
AH...
...I JUST...
...LED THE ENEMY...
...TO HIS GOAL...

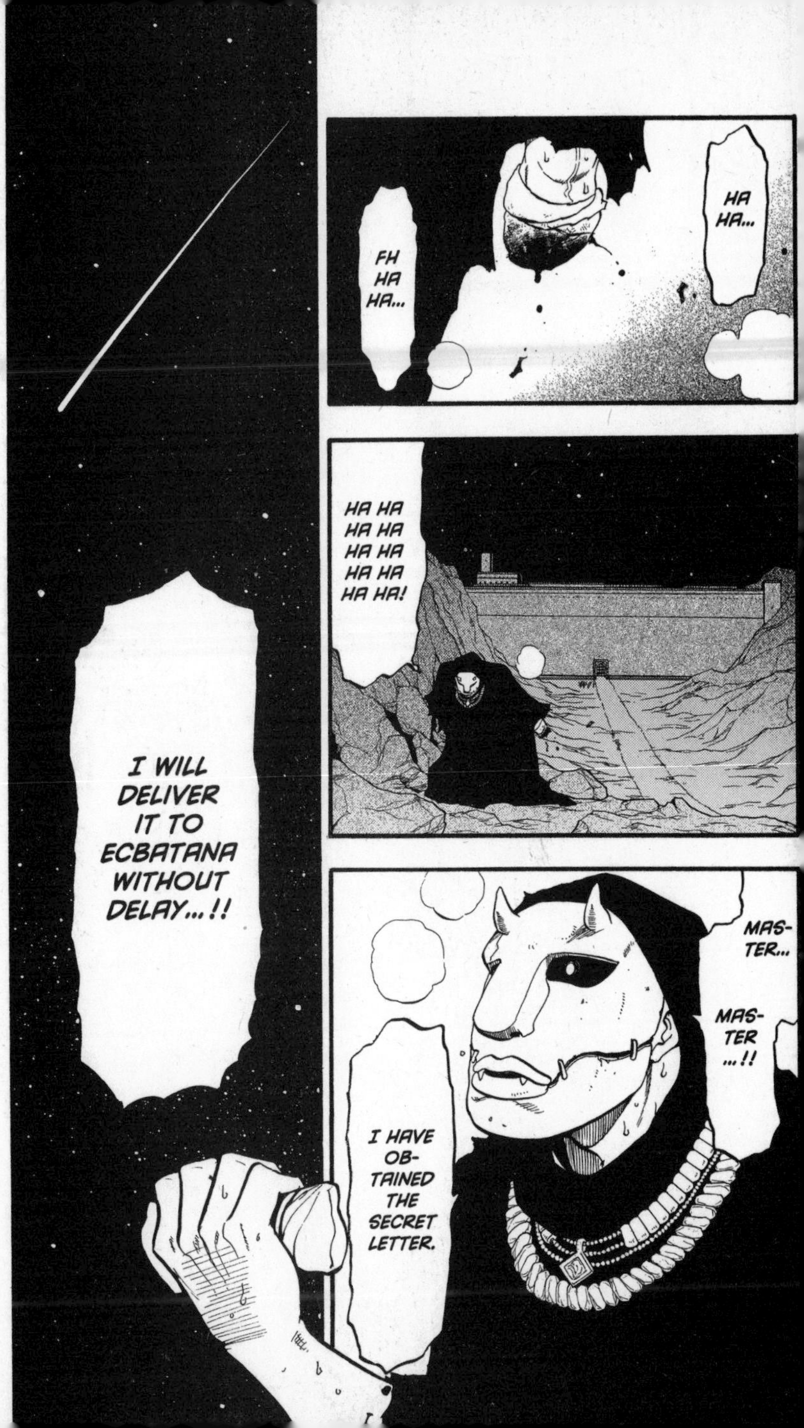
HA HA...
FH HA HA...
HA HA HA HA HA HA HA HA HA HA!
MAS-TER...
MAS-TER ...!!
I HAVE OB-TAINED THE SECRET LETTER.
I WILL DELIVER IT TO ECBATANA WITHOUT DELAY...!!

THE HEROIC LEGEND OF
ARSLAN

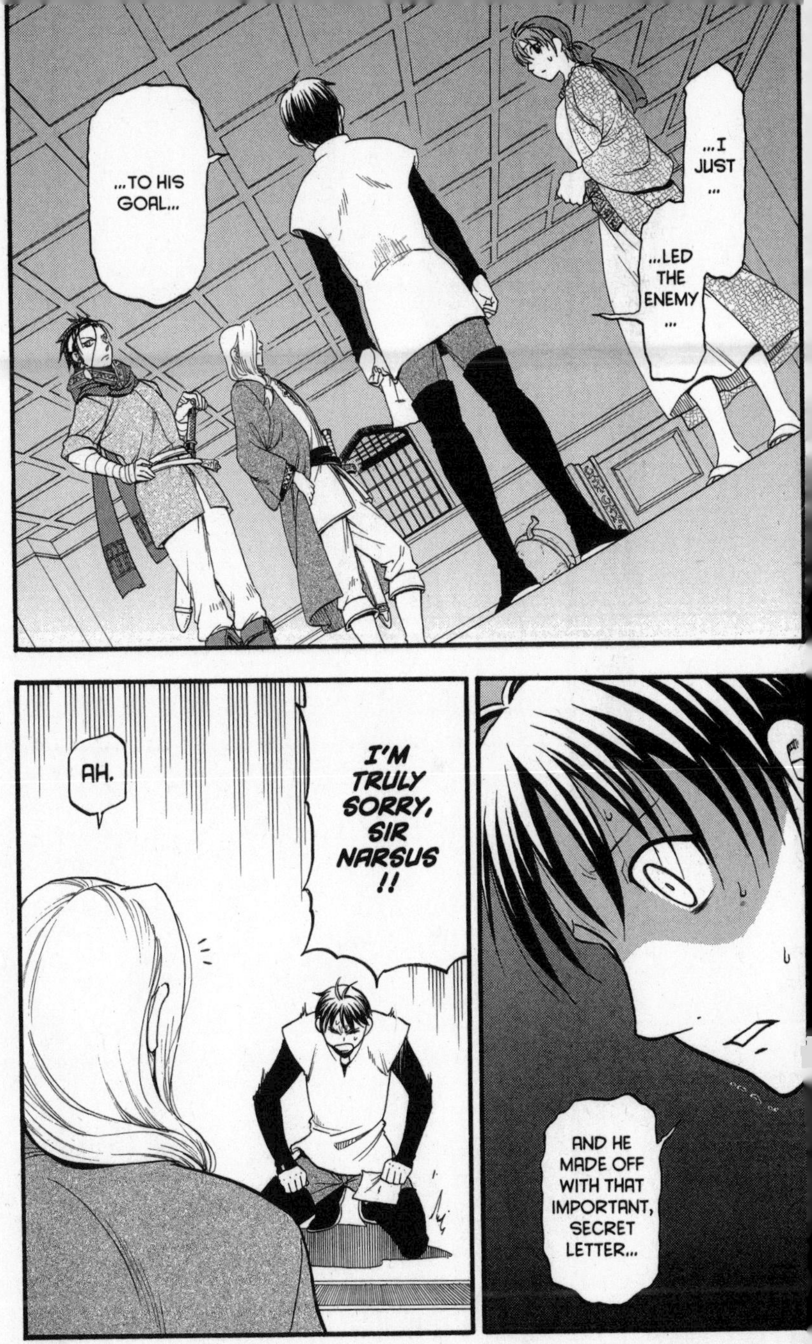
...I JUST ...
...LED THE ENEMY ...
...TO HIS GOAL...
AND HE MADE OFF WITH THAT IMPORTANT, SECRET LETTER...
I'M TRULY SORRY, SIR NARSUS !!
AH.

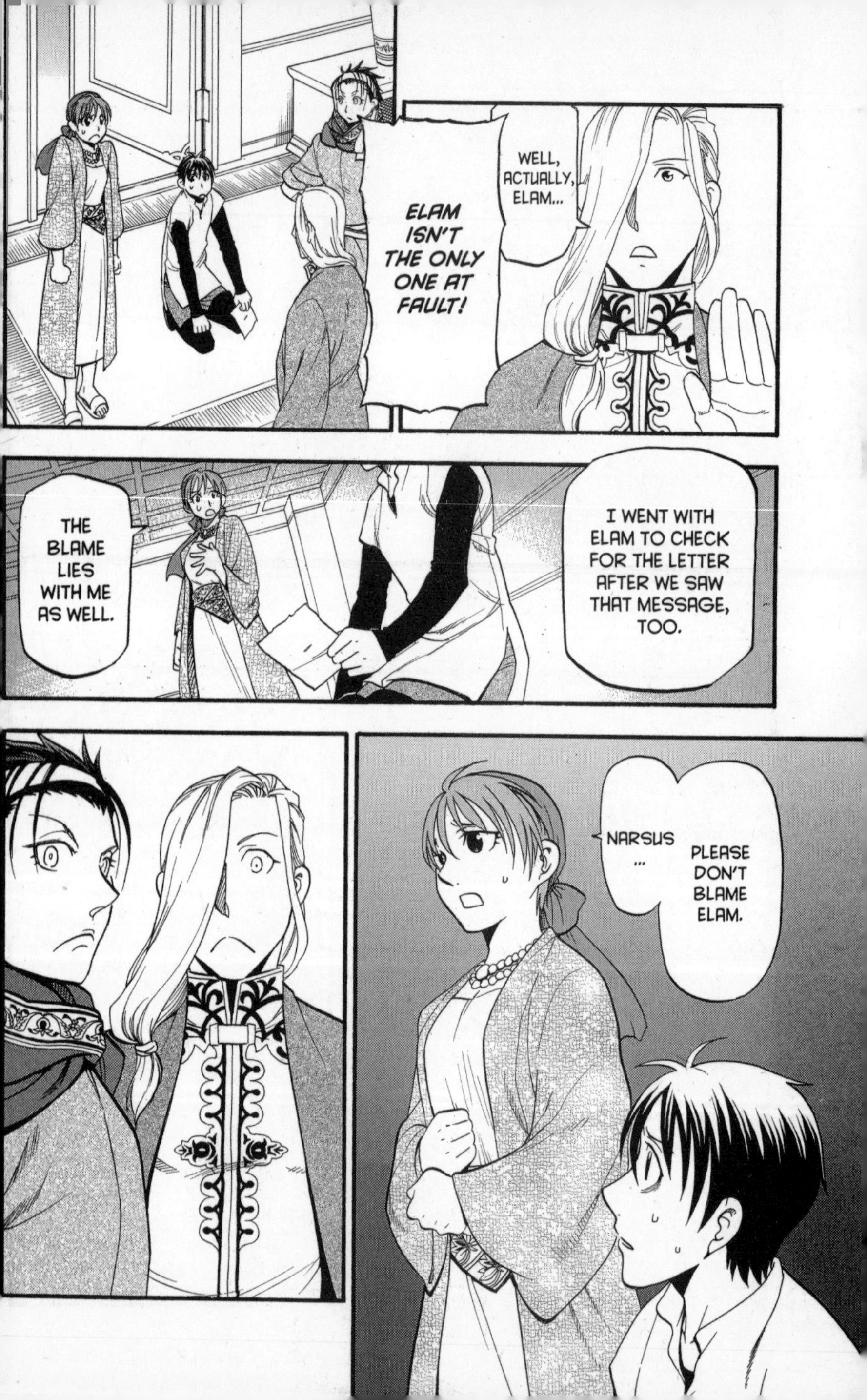
WELL, ACTUALLY, ELAM...
ELAM ISN'T THE ONLY ONE AT FAULT!
I WENT WITH ELAM TO CHECK FOR THE LETTER AFTER WE SAW THAT MESSAGE, TOO.
THE BLAME LIES WITH ME AS WELL.
NARSUS...
PLEASE DON'T BLAME ELAM.

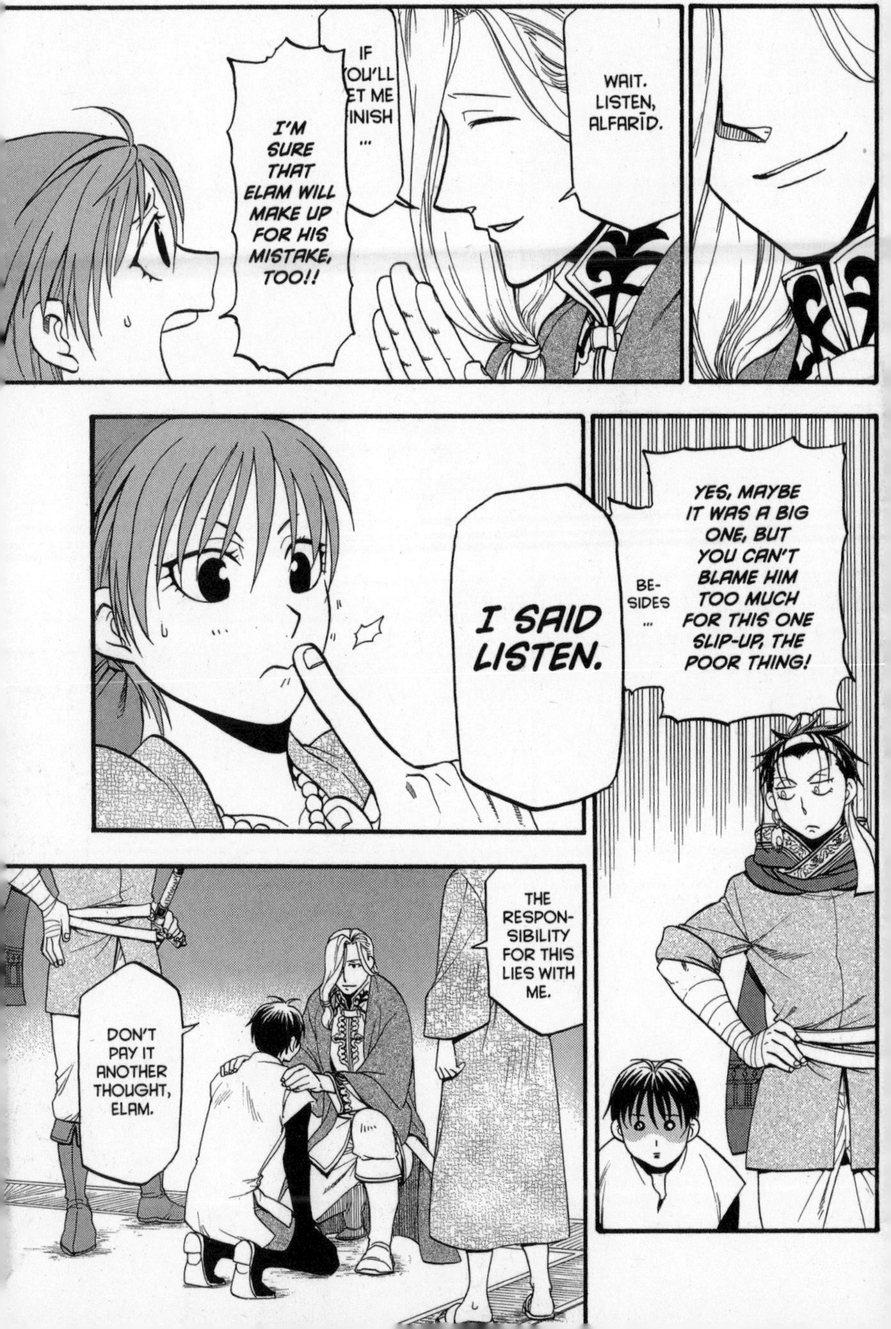
WAIT. LISTEN, ALFARĪD.
IF OU'LL ET ME INISH ...
I'M SURE THAT ELAM WILL MAKE UP FOR HIS MISTAKE, TOO!!
YES, MAYBE IT WAS A BIG ONE, BUT YOU CAN'T BLAME HIM TOO MUCH FOR THIS ONE SLIP-UP, THE POOR THING!
BE-SIDES ...
I SAID LISTEN.
THE RESPON-SIBILITY FOR THIS LIES WITH ME.
DON'T PAY IT ANOTHER THOUGHT, ELAM.

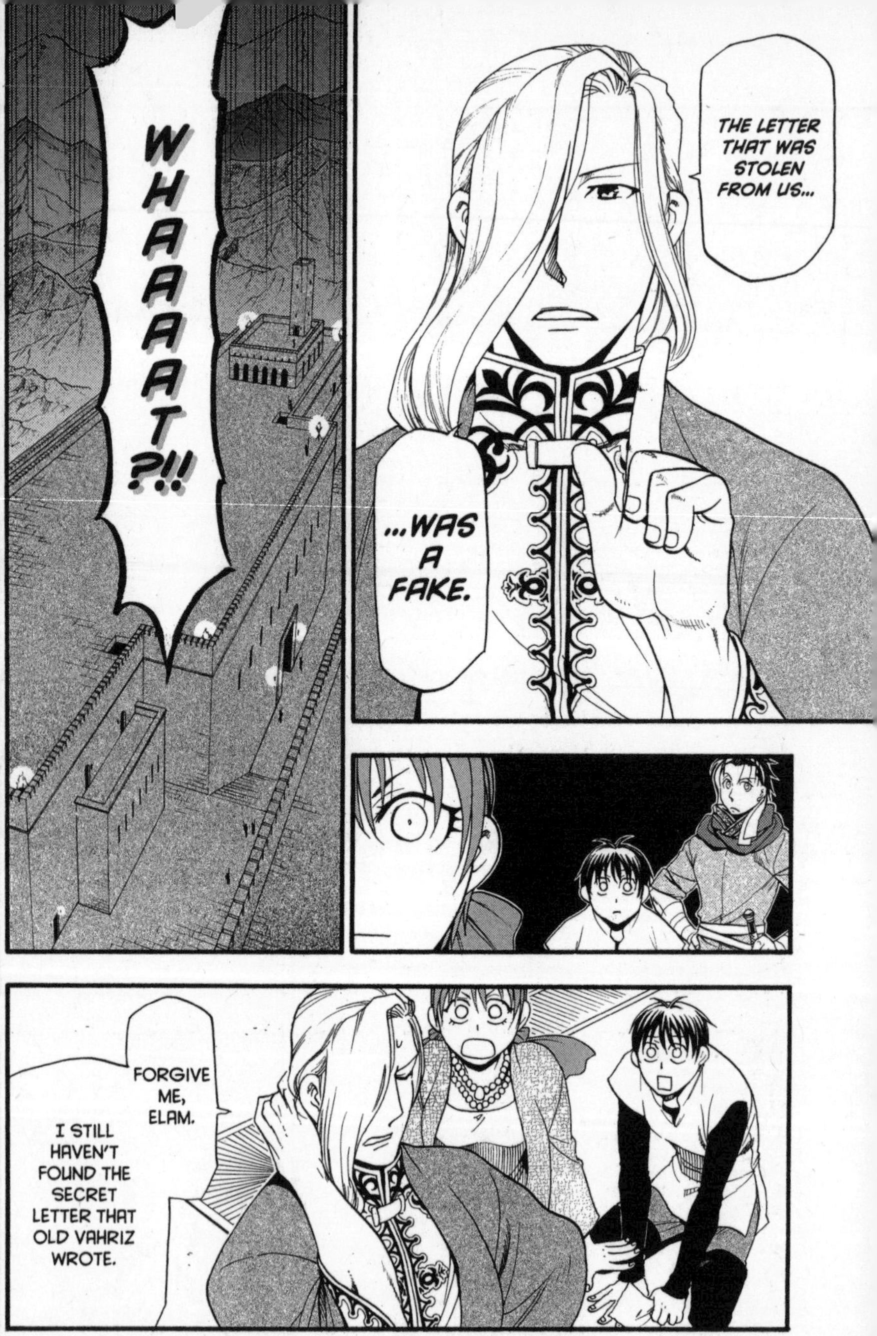
THE LETTER THAT WAS STOLEN FROM US...
...WAS A FAKE.
WHAAAAAT?!!
FORGIVE ME, ELAM.
I STILL HAVEN'T FOUND THE SECRET LETTER THAT OLD VAHRIZ WROTE.

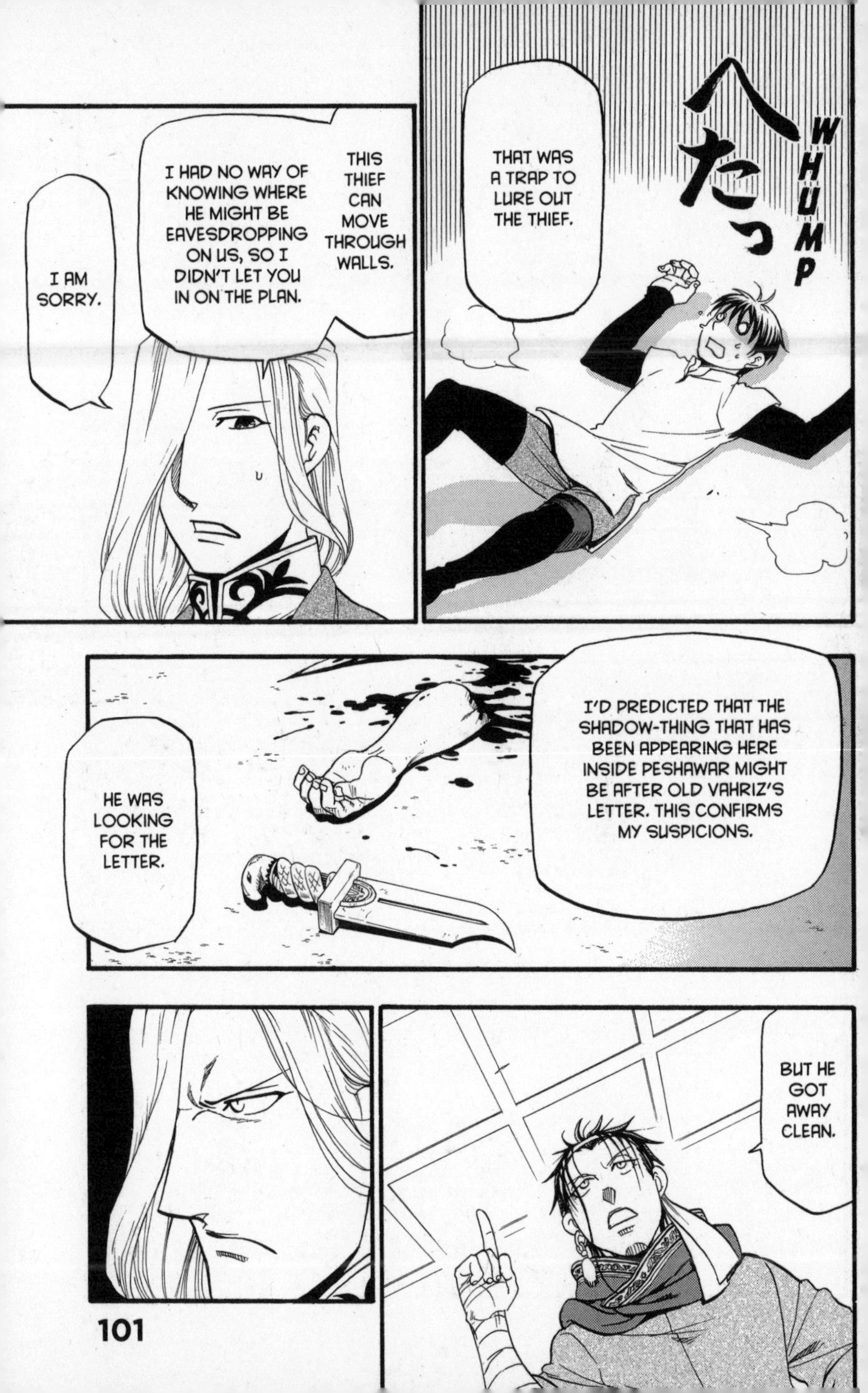

へたっ
WHUMP
THAT WAS A TRAP TO LURE OUT THE THIEF.
THIS THIEF CAN MOVE THROUGH WALLS.
I HAD NO WAY OF KNOWING WHERE HE MIGHT BE EAVESDROPPING ON US, SO I DIDN'T LET YOU IN ON THE PLAN.
I AM SORRY.
I'D PREDICTED THAT THE SHADOW-THING THAT HAS BEEN APPEARING HERE INSIDE PESHAWAR MIGHT BE AFTER OLD VAHRIZ'S LETTER. THIS CONFIRMS MY SUSPICIONS.
HE WAS LOOKING FOR THE LETTER.
BUT HE GOT AWAY CLEAN.

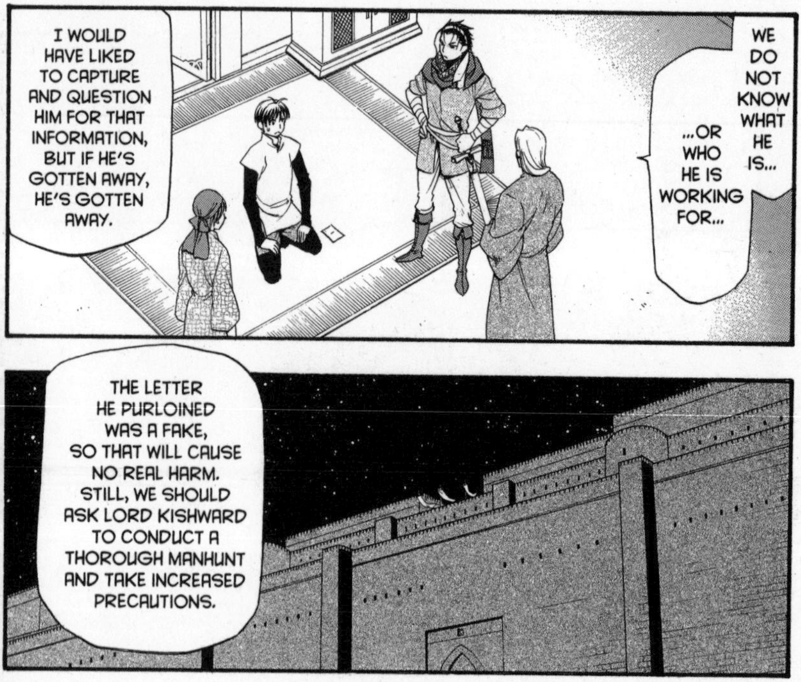
WE DO NOT KNOW WHAT HE IS...
...OR WHO HE IS WORKING FOR...
I WOULD HAVE LIKED TO CAPTURE AND QUESTION HIM FOR THAT INFORMATION, BUT IF HE'S GOTTEN AWAY, HE'S GOTTEN AWAY.
THE LETTER HE PURLOINED WAS A FAKE, SO THAT WILL CAUSE NO REAL HARM. STILL, WE SHOULD ASK LORD KISHWARD TO CONDUCT A THOROUGH MANHUNT AND TAKE INCREASED PRECAUTIONS.

Chapter 56: Pool of Blood

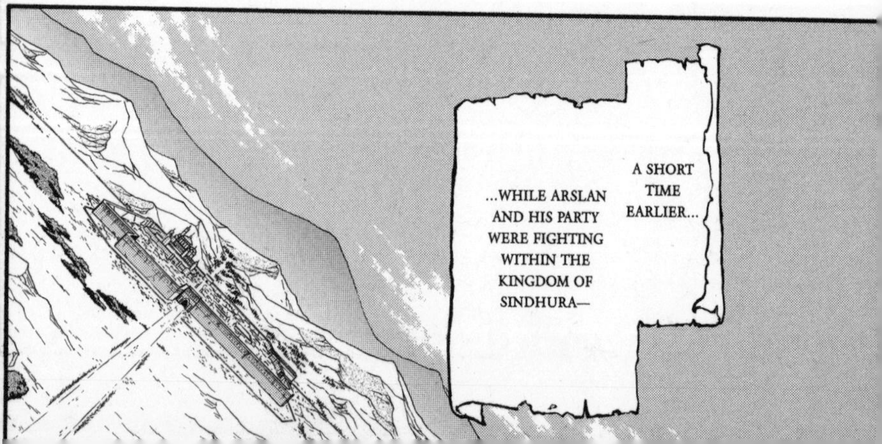
A SHORT TIME EARLIER...
...WHILE ARSLAN AND HIS PARTY WERE FIGHTING WITHIN THE KINGDOM OF SINDHURA—

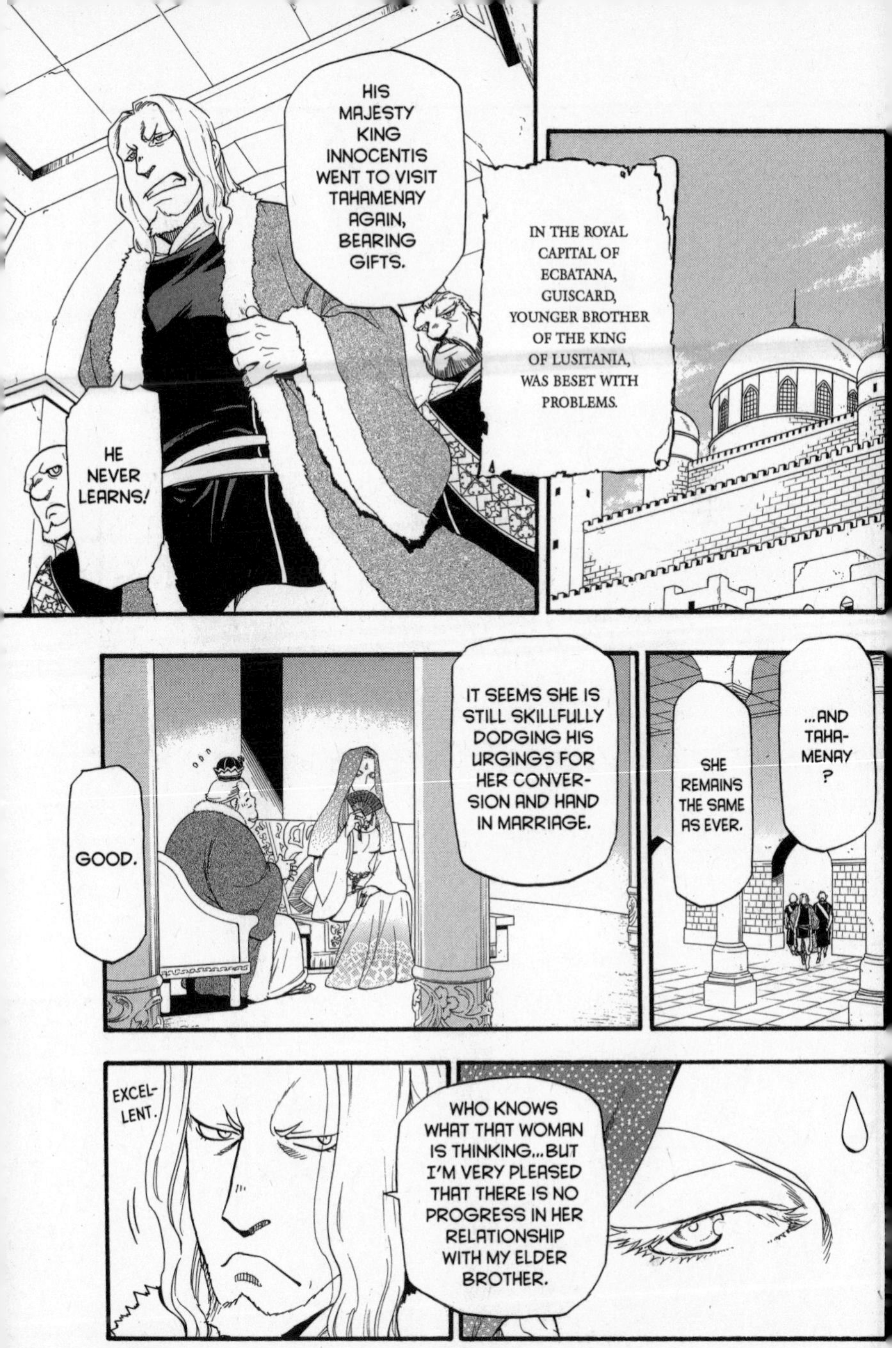
IN THE ROYAL CAPITAL OF ECBATANA, GUISCARD, YOUNGER BROTHER OF THE KING OF LUSITANIA, WAS BESET WITH PROBLEMS.
HIS MAJESTY KING INNOCENTIS WENT TO VISIT TAHAMENAY AGAIN, BEARING GIFTS.
HE NEVER LEARNS!
...AND TAHA-MENAY?
SHE REMAINS THE SAME AS EVER.
IT SEEMS SHE IS STILL SKILLFULLY DODGING HIS URGINGS FOR HER CONVER-SION AND HAND IN MARRIAGE.
GOOD.
EXCEL-LENT.
WHO KNOWS WHAT THAT WOMAN IS THINKING...BUT I'M VERY PLEASED THAT THERE IS NO PROGRESS IN HER RELATIONSHIP WITH MY ELDER BROTHER.

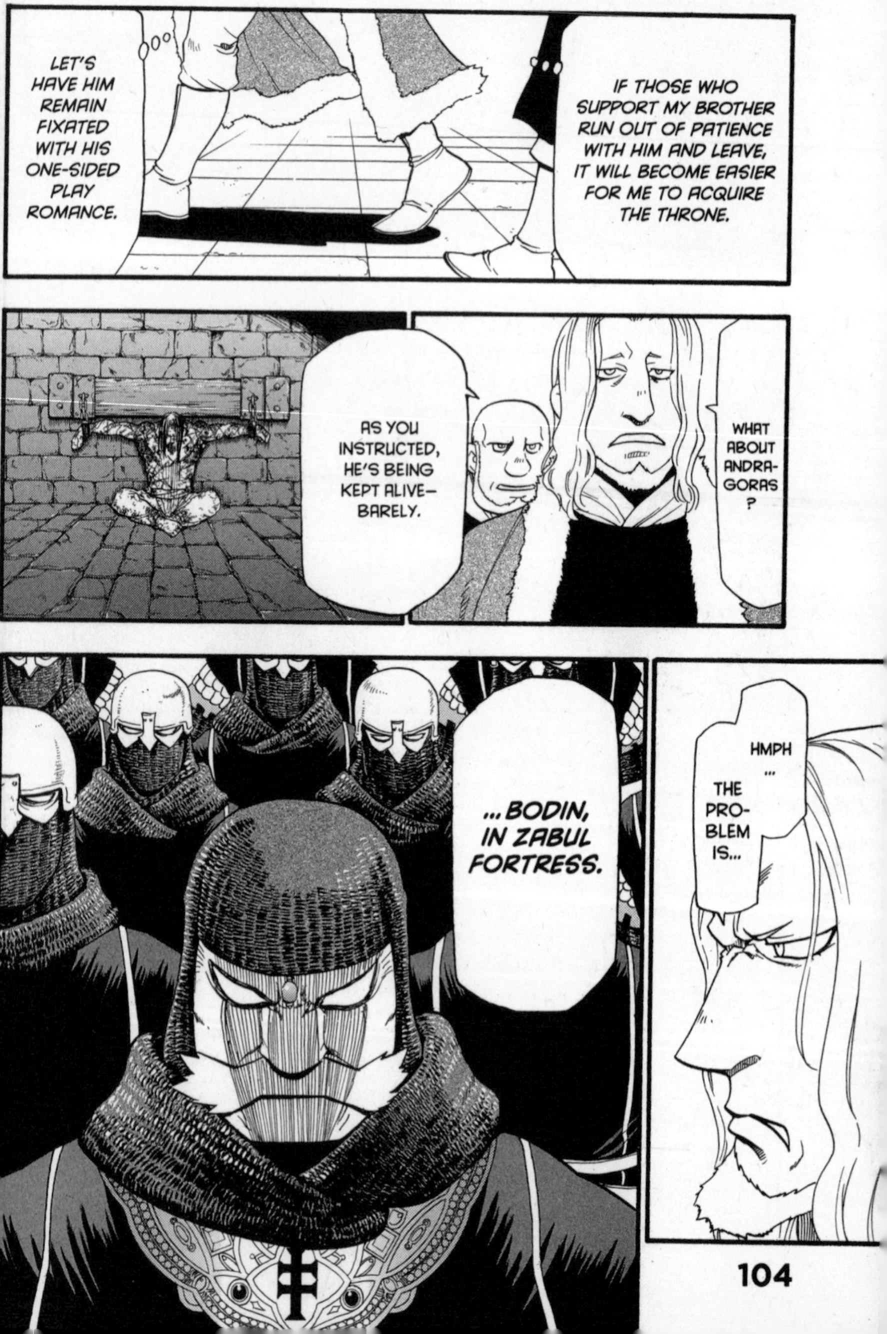
IF THOSE WHO SUPPORT MY BROTHER RUN OUT OF PATIENCE WITH HIM AND LEAVE, IT WILL BECOME EASIER FOR ME TO ACQUIRE THE THRONE.
LET'S HAVE HIM REMAIN FIXATED WITH HIS ONE-SIDED PLAY ROMANCE.
WHAT ABOUT ANDRAGORAS?
AS YOU INSTRUCTED, HE'S BEING KEPT ALIVE—BARELY.
HMPH... THE PROBLEM IS...
...BODIN, IN ZABUL FORTRESS.

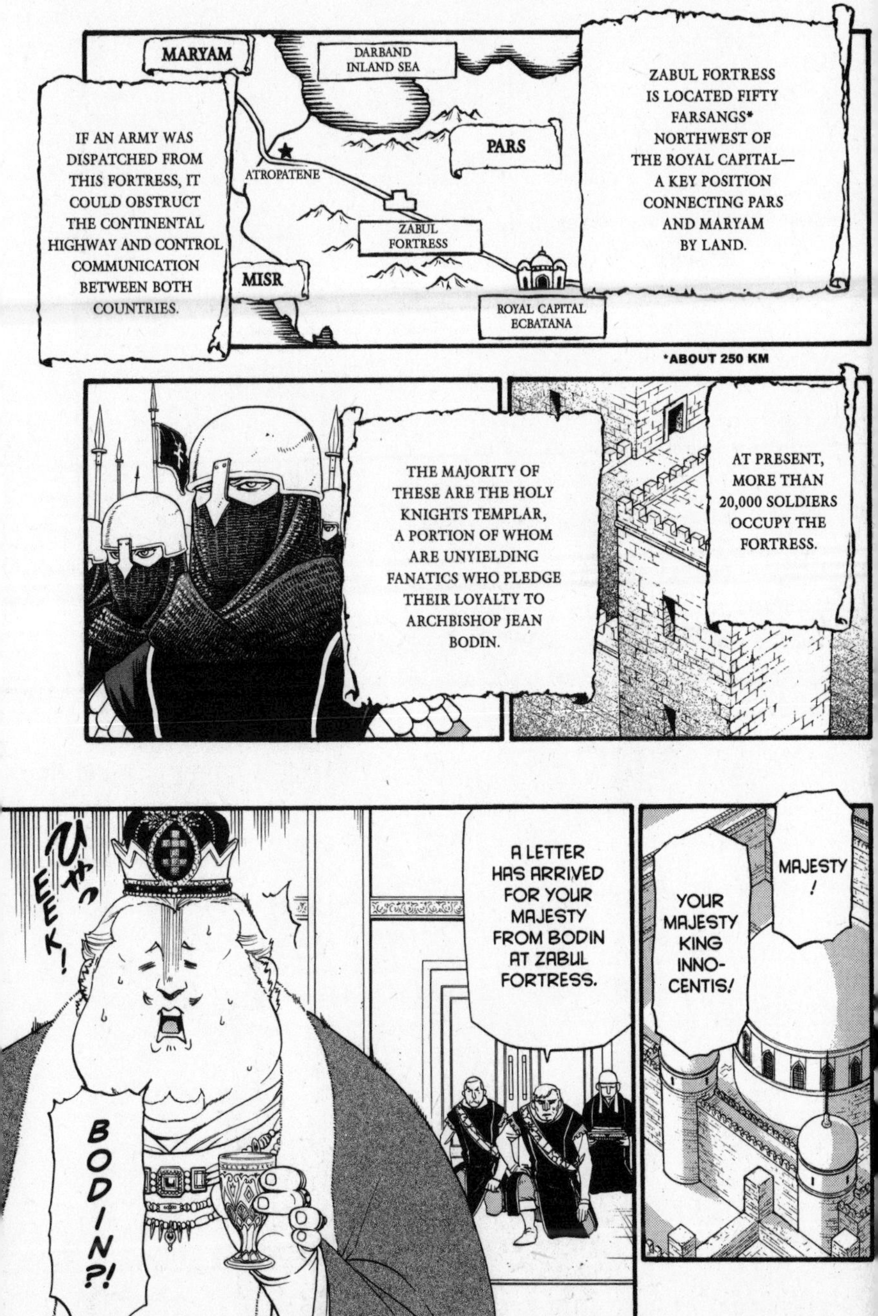
ZABUL FORTRESS IS LOCATED FIFTY FARSANGS* NORTHWEST OF THE ROYAL CAPITAL—A KEY POSITION CONNECTING PARS AND MARYAM BY LAND.
DARBAND INLAND SEA
MARYAM
PARS
ATROPATENE
ZABUL FORTRESS
ROYAL CAPITAL ECBATANA
MISR
IF AN ARMY WAS DISPATCHED FROM THIS FORTRESS, IT COULD OBSTRUCT THE CONTINENTAL HIGHWAY AND CONTROL COMMUNICATION BETWEEN BOTH COUNTRIES.
*ABOUT 250 KM
AT PRESENT, MORE THAN 20,000 SOLDIERS OCCUPY THE FORTRESS.
THE MAJORITY OF THESE ARE THE HOLY KNIGHTS TEMPLAR, A PORTION OF WHOM ARE UNYIELDING FANATICS WHO PLEDGE THEIR LOYALTY TO ARCHBISHOP JEAN BODIN.
MAJESTY!
YOUR MAJESTY KING INNOCENTIS!
A LETTER HAS ARRIVED FOR YOUR MAJESTY FROM BODIN AT ZABUL FORTRESS.
EEK!
BODIN?!

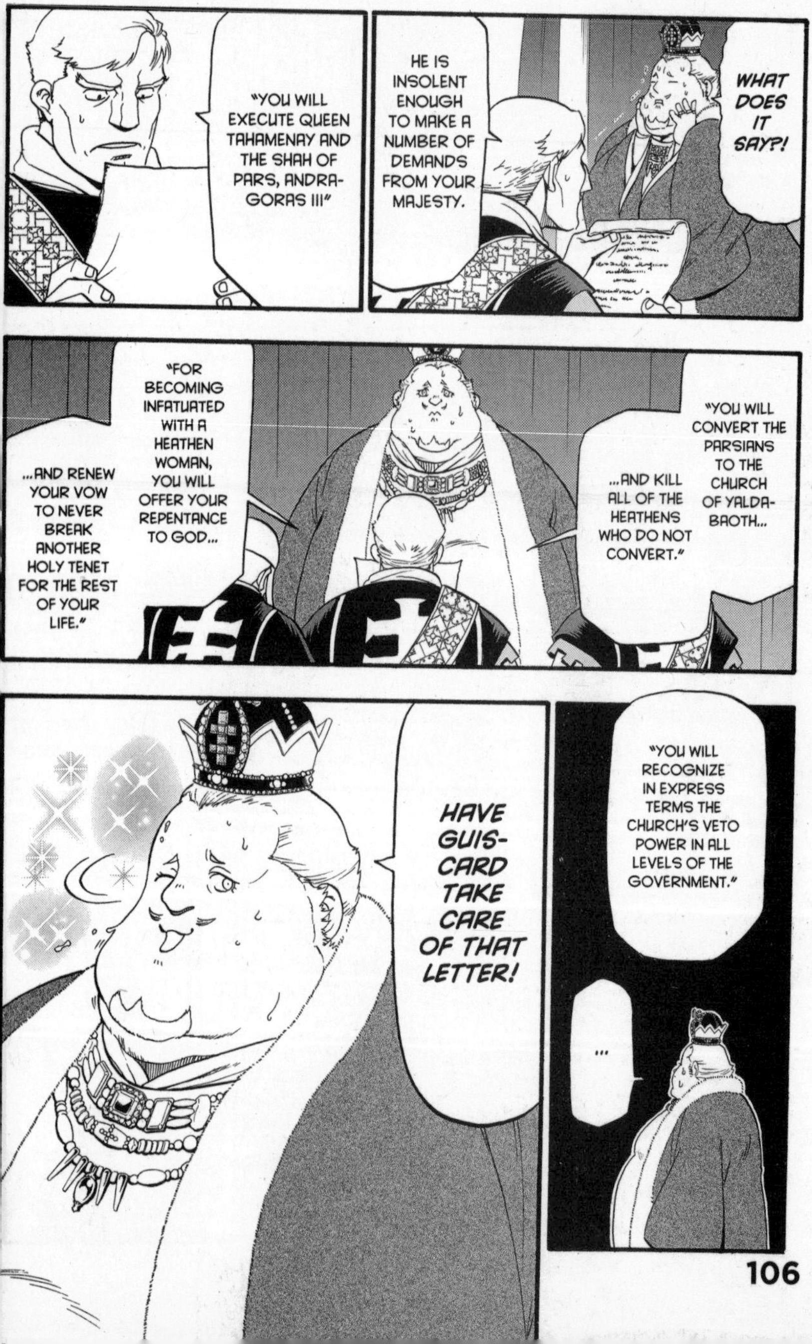
WHAT DOES IT SAY?!
HE IS INSOLENT ENOUGH TO MAKE A NUMBER OF DEMANDS FROM YOUR MAJESTY.
"YOU WILL EXECUTE QUEEN TAHAMENAY AND THE SHAH OF PARS, ANDRA-GORAS III"
"YOU WILL CONVERT THE PARSIANS TO THE CHURCH OF YALDA-BAOTH...
...AND KILL ALL OF THE HEATHENS WHO DO NOT CONVERT."
"FOR BECOMING INFATUATED WITH A HEATHEN WOMAN, YOU WILL OFFER YOUR REPENTANCE TO GOD...
...AND RENEW YOUR VOW TO NEVER BREAK ANOTHER HOLY TENET FOR THE REST OF YOUR LIFE."
"YOU WILL RECOGNIZE IN EXPRESS TERMS THE CHURCH'S VETO POWER IN ALL LEVELS OF THE GOVERNMENT."
...
HAVE GUIS-CARD TAKE CARE OF THAT LETTER!

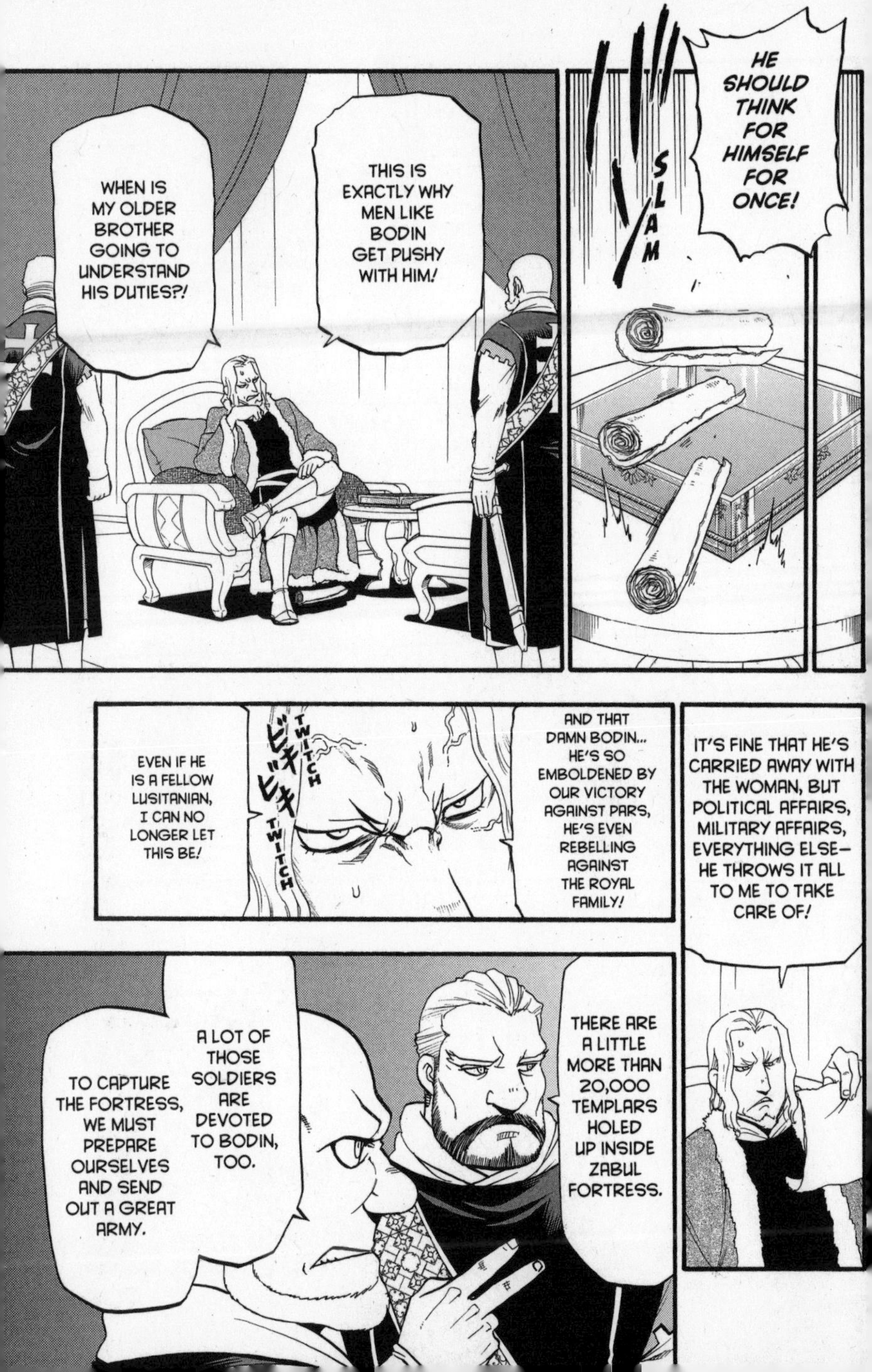
SLAM
HE SHOULD THINK FOR HIMSELF FOR ONCE!
THIS IS EXACTLY WHY MEN LIKE BODIN GET PUSHY WITH HIM!
WHEN IS MY OLDER BROTHER GOING TO UNDERSTAND HIS DUTIES?!
IT'S FINE THAT HE'S CARRIED AWAY WITH THE WOMAN, BUT POLITICAL AFFAIRS, MILITARY AFFAIRS, EVERYTHING ELSE—HE THROWS IT ALL TO ME TO TAKE CARE OF!
AND THAT DAMN BODIN... HE'S SO EMBOLDENED BY OUR VICTORY AGAINST PARS, HE'S EVEN REBELLING AGAINST THE ROYAL FAMILY!
TWITCH TWITCH
EVEN IF HE IS A FELLOW LUSITANIAN, I CAN NO LONGER LET THIS BE!
THERE ARE A LITTLE MORE THAN 20,000 TEMPLARS HOLED UP INSIDE ZABUL FORTRESS.
A LOT OF THOSE SOLDIERS ARE DEVOTED TO BODIN, TOO.
TO CAPTURE THE FORTRESS, WE MUST PREPARE OURSELVES AND SEND OUT A GREAT ARMY.

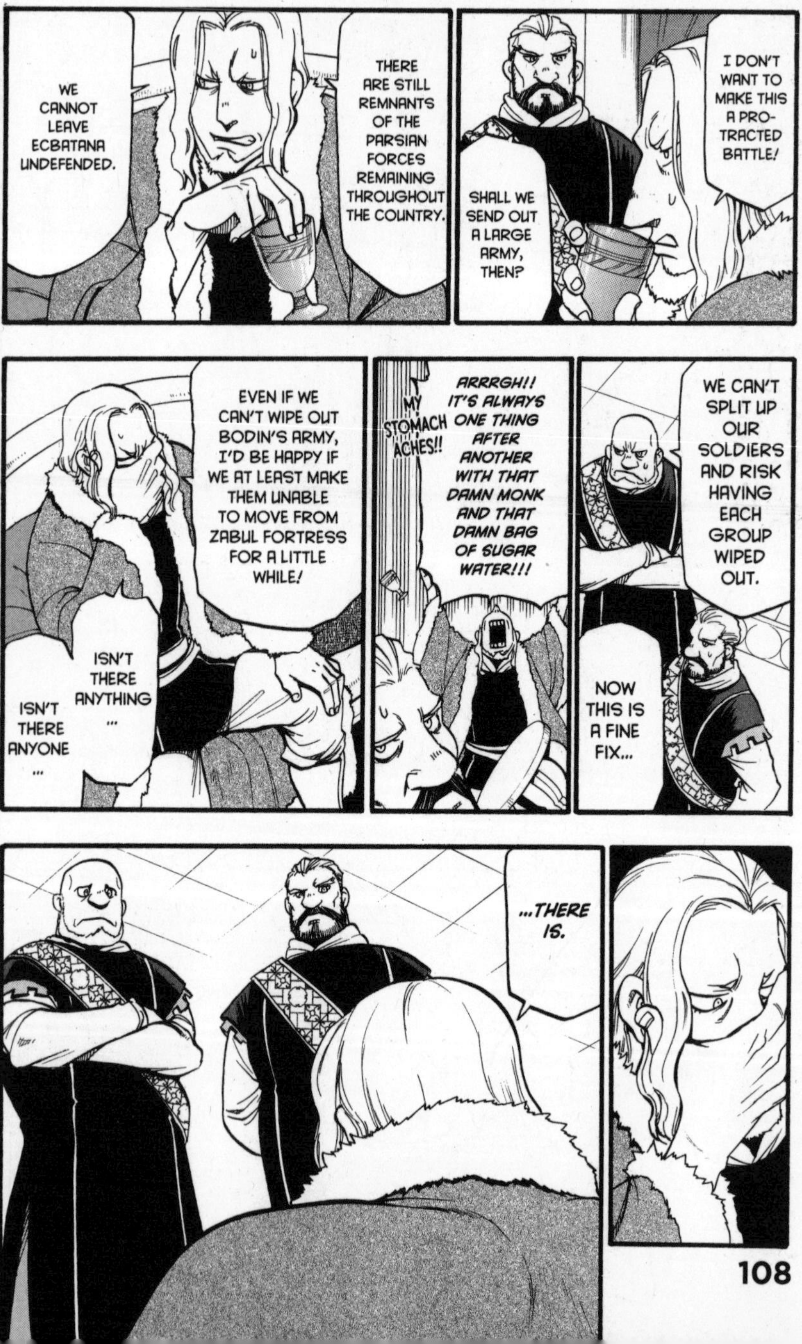
I DON'T WANT TO MAKE THIS A PRO-TRACTED BATTLE!
SHALL WE SEND OUT A LARGE ARMY, THEN?
THERE ARE STILL REMNANTS OF THE PARSIAN FORCES REMAINING THROUGHOUT THE COUNTRY.
WE CANNOT LEAVE ECBATANA UNDEFENDED.
WE CAN'T SPLIT UP OUR SOLDIERS AND RISK HAVING EACH GROUP WIPED OUT.
NOW THIS IS A FINE FIX...
ARRRGH!! IT'S ALWAYS ONE THING AFTER ANOTHER WITH THAT DAMN MONK AND THAT DAMN BAG OF SUGAR WATER!!!
MY STOMACH ACHES!!
EVEN IF WE CAN'T WIPE OUT BODIN'S ARMY, I'D BE HAPPY IF WE AT LEAST MAKE THEM UNABLE TO MOVE FROM ZABUL FORTRESS FOR A LITTLE WHILE!
ISN'T THERE ANYTHING ...
ISN'T THERE ANYONE ...
...THERE IS.

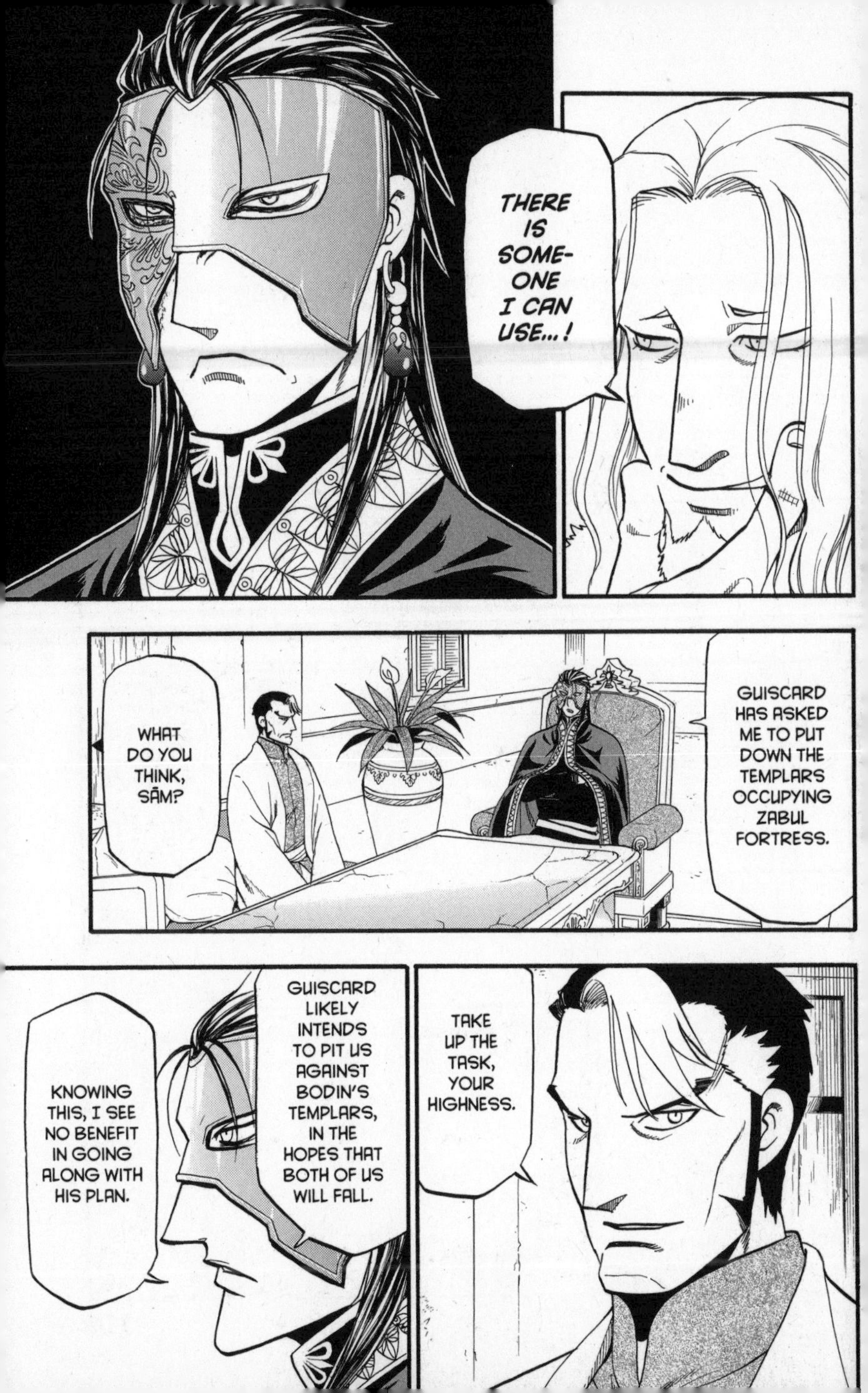
THERE IS SOME-ONE I CAN USE...!
GUISCARD HAS ASKED ME TO PUT DOWN THE TEMPLARS OCCUPYING ZABUL FORTRESS.
WHAT DO YOU THINK, SĀM?
TAKE UP THE TASK, YOUR HIGHNESS.
GUISCARD LIKELY INTENDS TO PIT US AGAINST BODIN'S TEMPLARS, IN THE HOPES THAT BOTH OF US WILL FALL.
KNOWING THIS, I SEE NO BENEFIT IN GOING ALONG WITH HIS PLAN.

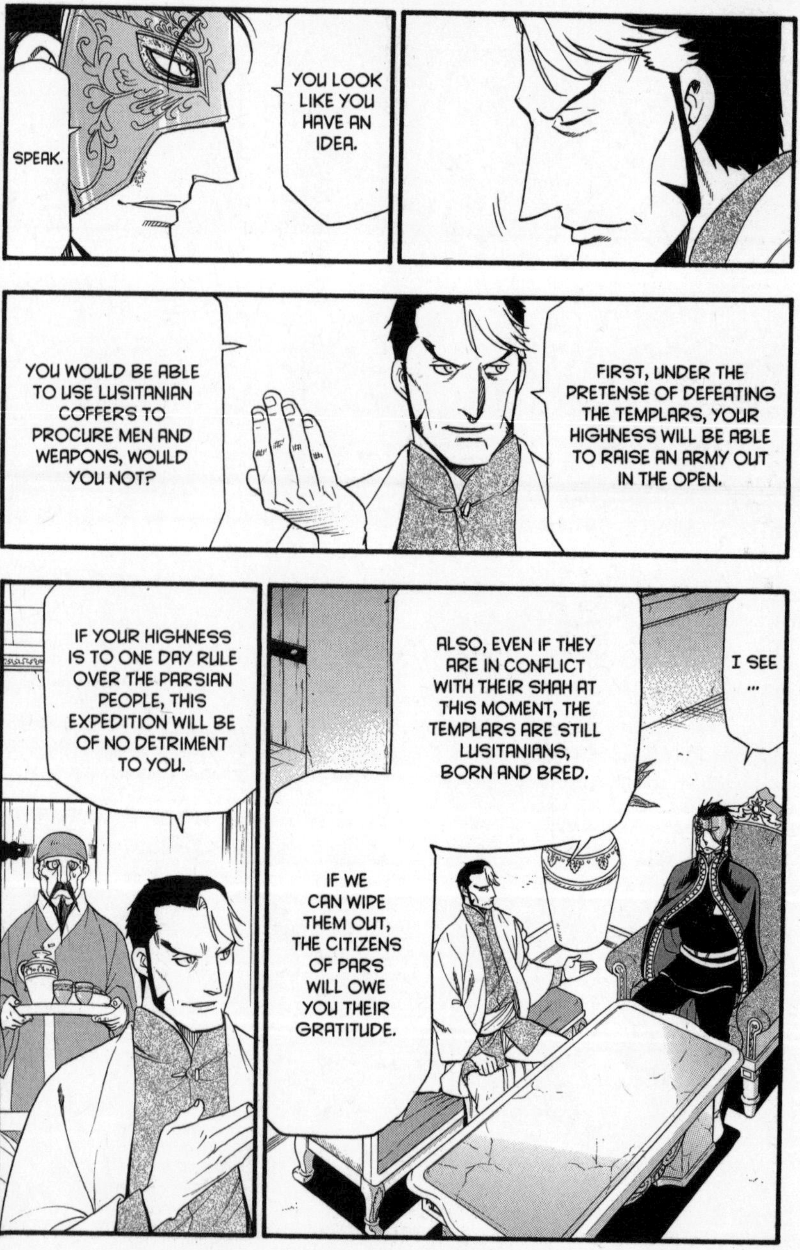
YOU LOOK LIKE YOU HAVE AN IDEA.
SPEAK.
FIRST, UNDER THE PRETENSE OF DEFEATING THE TEMPLARS, YOUR HIGHNESS WILL BE ABLE TO RAISE AN ARMY OUT IN THE OPEN.
YOU WOULD BE ABLE TO USE LUSITANIAN COFFERS TO PROCURE MEN AND WEAPONS, WOULD YOU NOT?
I SEE ...
ALSO, EVEN IF THEY ARE IN CONFLICT WITH THEIR SHAH AT THIS MOMENT, THE TEMPLARS ARE STILL LUSITANIANS, BORN AND BRED.
IF WE CAN WIPE THEM OUT, THE CITIZENS OF PARS WILL OWE YOU THEIR GRATITUDE.
IF YOUR HIGHNESS IS TO ONE DAY RULE OVER THE PARSIAN PEOPLE, THIS EXPEDITION WILL BE OF NO DETRIMENT TO YOU.

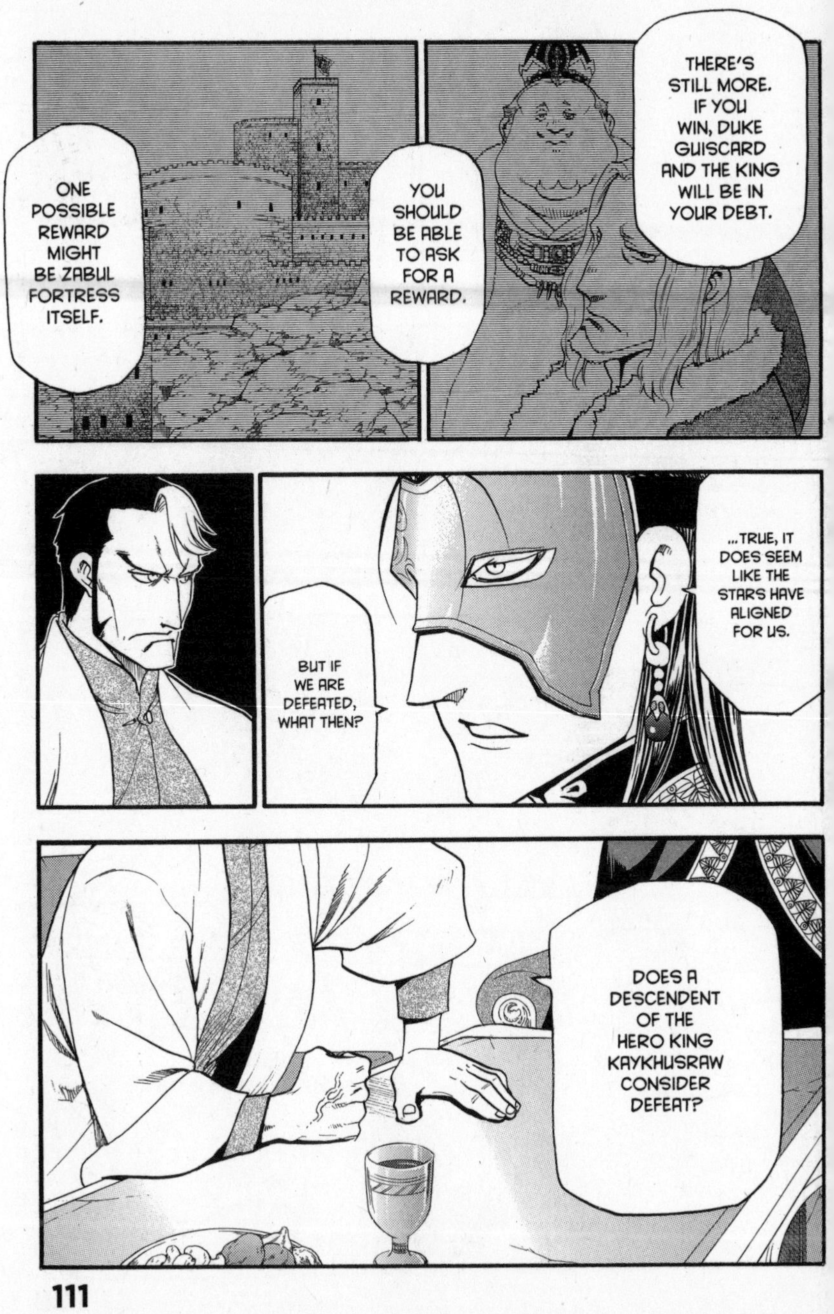
THERE'S STILL MORE. IF YOU WIN, DUKE GUISCARD AND THE KING WILL BE IN YOUR DEBT.
YOU SHOULD BE ABLE TO ASK FOR A REWARD.
ONE POSSIBLE REWARD MIGHT BE ZABUL FORTRESS ITSELF.
...TRUE, IT DOES SEEM LIKE THE STARS HAVE ALIGNED FOR US.
BUT IF WE ARE DEFEATED, WHAT THEN?
DOES A DESCENDENT OF THE HERO KING KAYKHUSRAW CONSIDER DEFEAT?

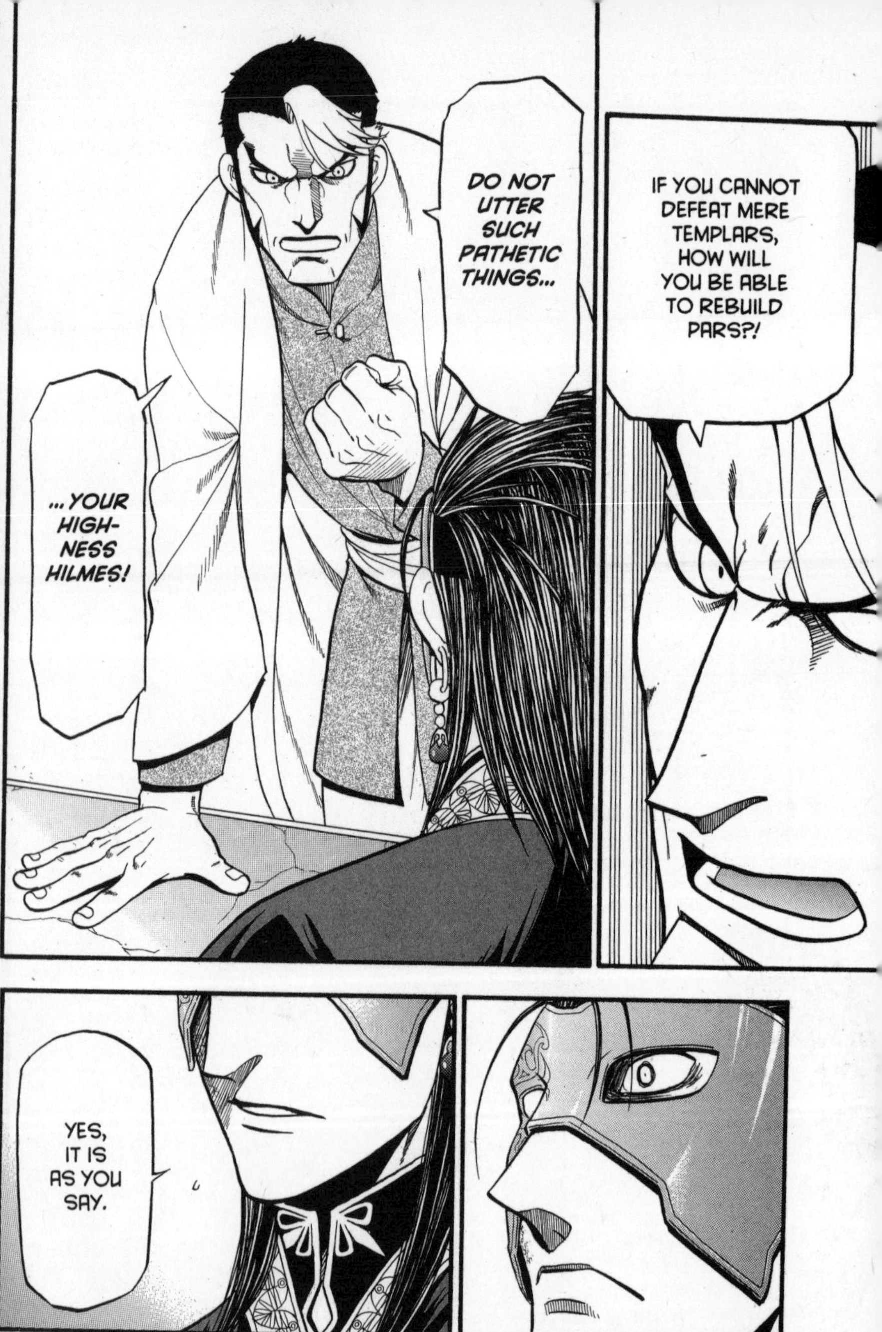
IF YOU CANNOT DEFEAT MERE TEMPLARS, HOW WILL YOU BE ABLE TO REBUILD PARS?!
DO NOT UTTER SUCH PATHETIC THINGS...
...YOUR HIGH-NESS HILMES!
YES, IT IS AS YOU SAY.

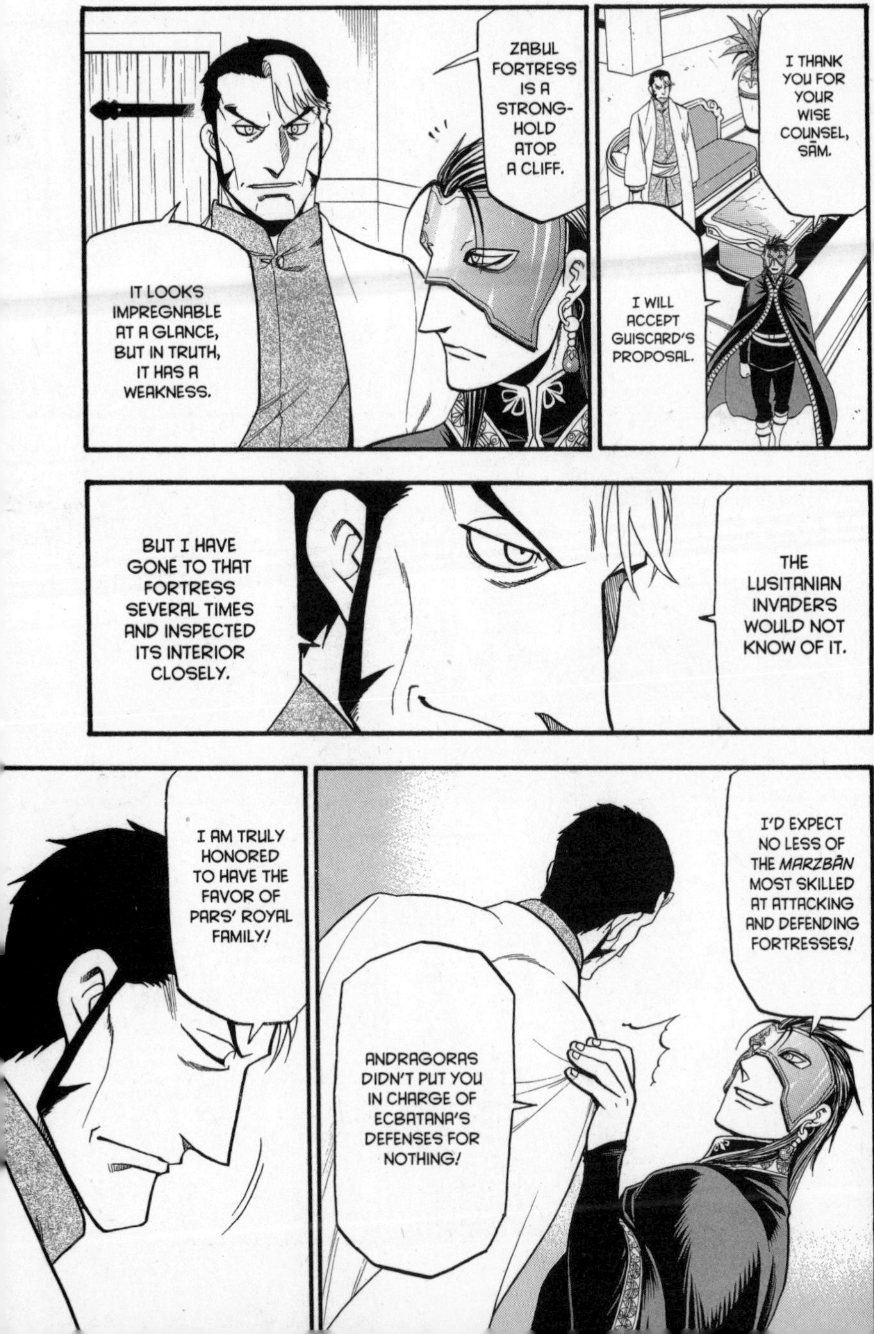
I THANK YOU FOR YOUR WISE COUNSEL, SĀM.
I WILL ACCEPT GUISCARD'S PROPOSAL.
ZABUL FORTRESS IS A STRONG-HOLD ATOP A CLIFF.
IT LOOKS IMPREGNABLE AT A GLANCE, BUT IN TRUTH, IT HAS A WEAKNESS.
THE LUSITANIAN INVADERS WOULD NOT KNOW OF IT.
BUT I HAVE GONE TO THAT FORTRESS SEVERAL TIMES AND INSPECTED ITS INTERIOR CLOSELY.
I'D EXPECT NO LESS OF THE *MARZBĀN* MOST SKILLED AT ATTACKING AND DEFENDING FORTRESSES!
ANDRAGORAS DIDN'T PUT YOU IN CHARGE OF ECBATANA'S DEFENSES FOR NOTHING!
I AM TRULY HONORED TO HAVE THE FAVOR OF PARS' ROYAL FAMILY!

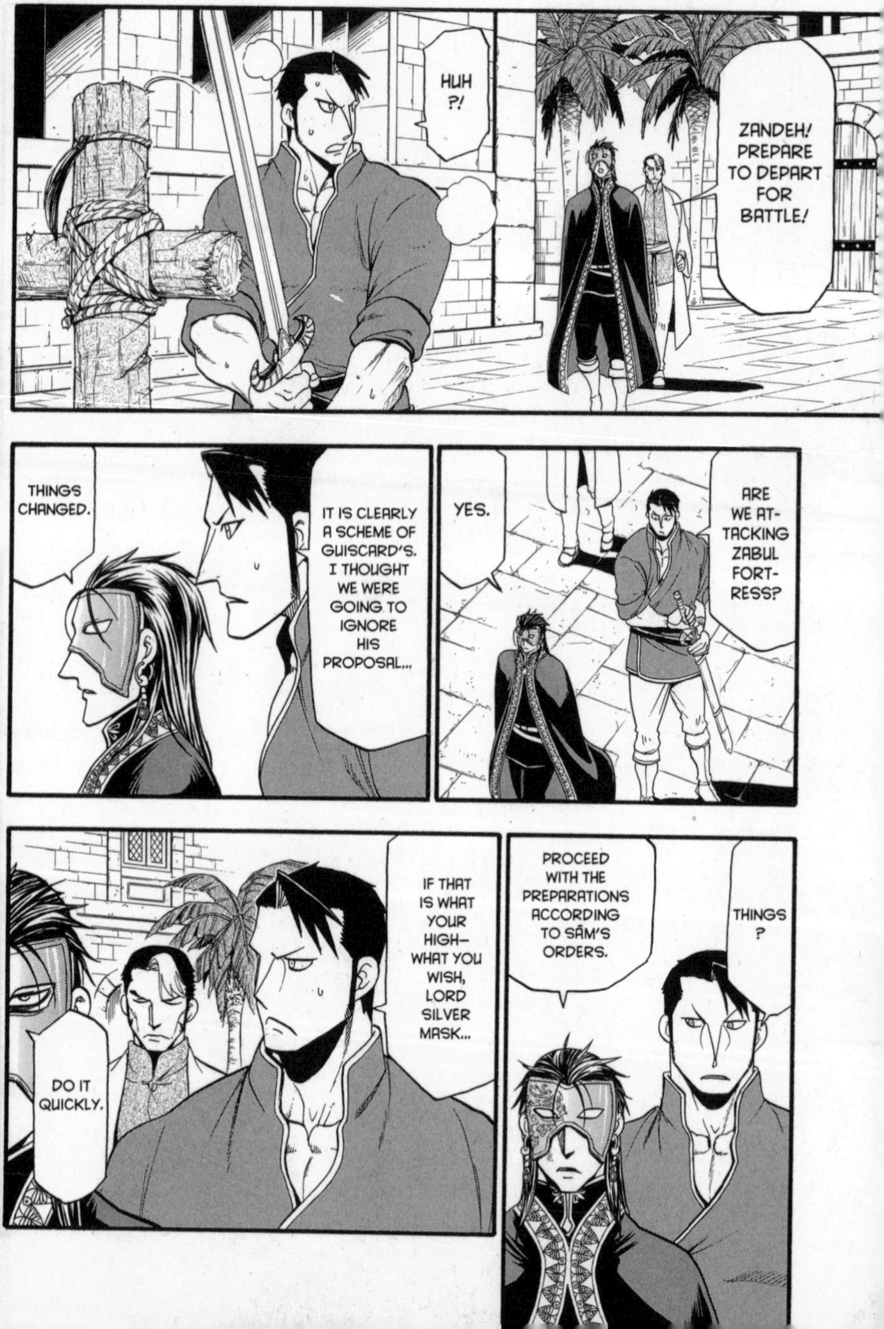
ZANDEH! PREPARE TO DEPART FOR BATTLE!
HUH ?!
ARE WE AT-TACKING ZABUL FORT-RESS?
YES.
IT IS CLEARLY A SCHEME OF GUISCARD'S. I THOUGHT WE WERE GOING TO IGNORE HIS PROPOSAL...
THINGS CHANGED.
THINGS ?
PROCEED WITH THE PREPARATIONS ACCORDING TO SĀM'S ORDERS.
IF THAT IS WHAT YOUR HIGH— WHAT YOU WISH, LORD SILVER MASK...
DO IT QUICKLY.

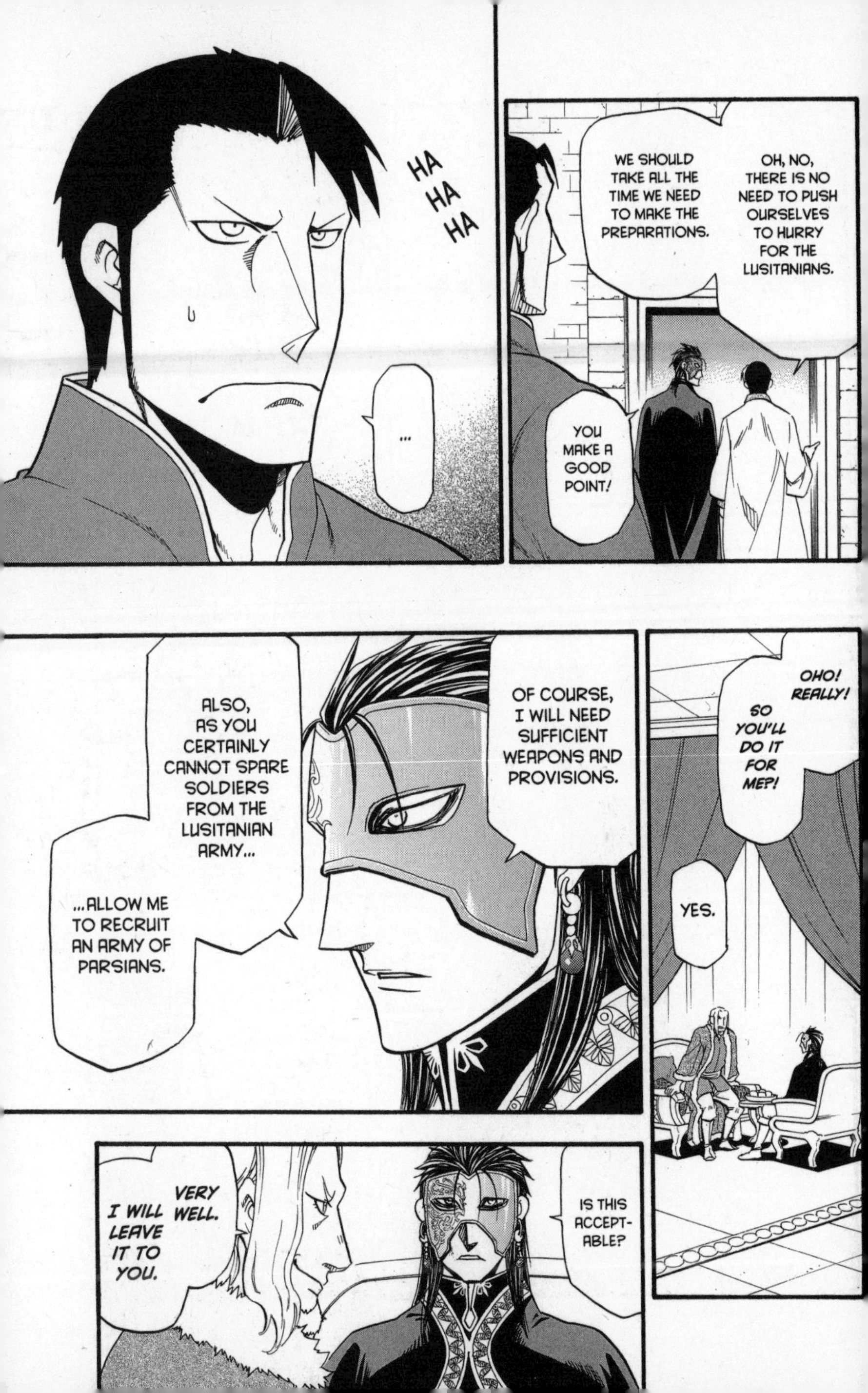
OH, NO, THERE IS NO NEED TO PUSH OURSELVES TO HURRY FOR THE LUSITANIANS.
WE SHOULD TAKE ALL THE TIME WE NEED TO MAKE THE PREPARATIONS.
YOU MAKE A GOOD POINT!
HA HA HA
...
OHO! REALLY!
SO YOU'LL DO IT FOR ME?!
YES.
OF COURSE, I WILL NEED SUFFICIENT WEAPONS AND PROVISIONS.
ALSO, AS YOU CERTAINLY CANNOT SPARE SOLDIERS FROM THE LUSITANIAN ARMY...
...ALLOW ME TO RECRUIT AN ARMY OF PARSIANS.
IS THIS ACCEPT-ABLE?
VERY WELL.
I WILL LEAVE IT TO YOU.

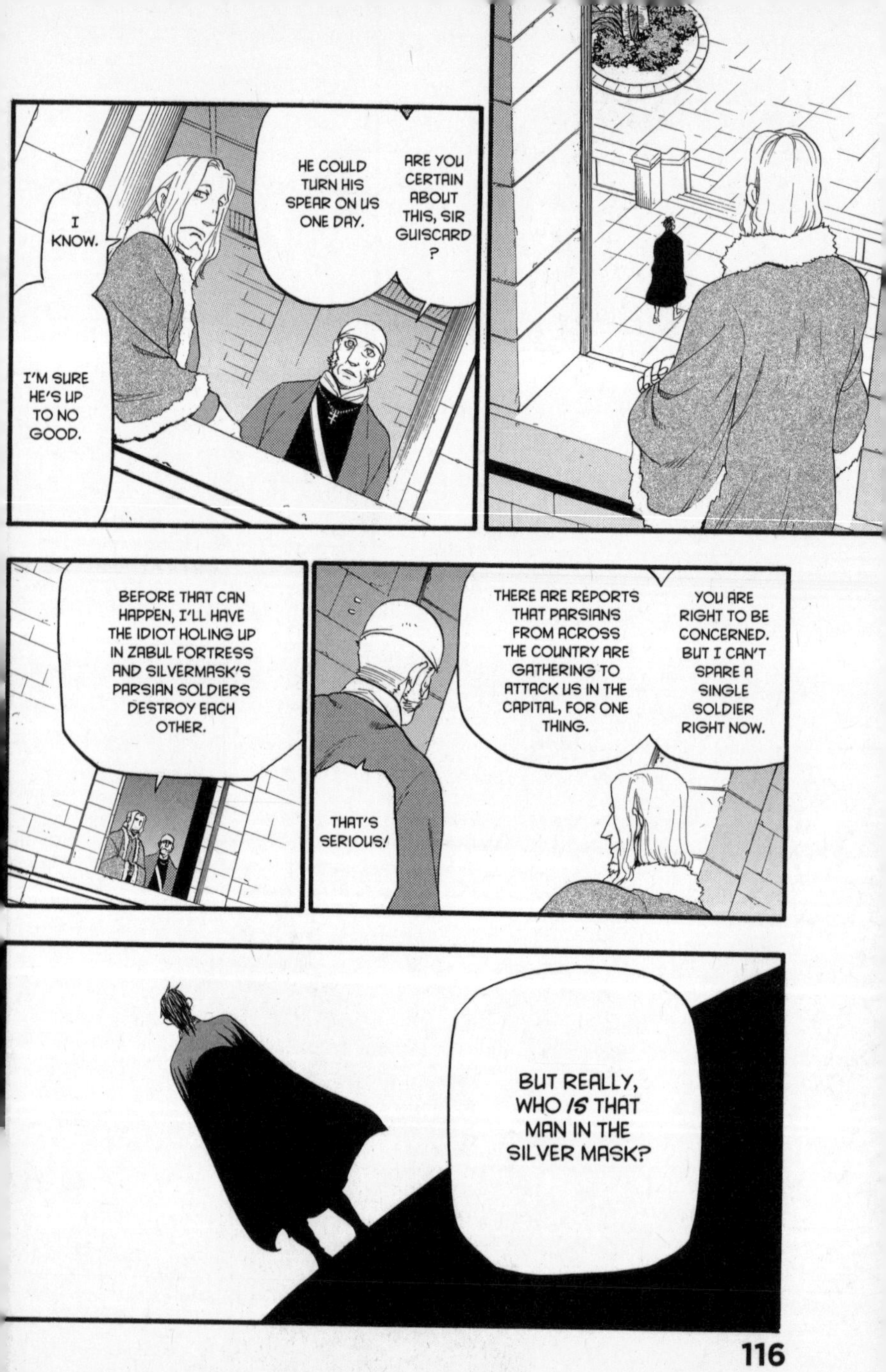
ARE YOU CERTAIN ABOUT THIS, SIR GUISCARD?
HE COULD TURN HIS SPEAR ON US ONE DAY.
I KNOW.
I'M SURE HE'S UP TO NO GOOD.
YOU ARE RIGHT TO BE CONCERNED. BUT I CAN'T SPARE A SINGLE SOLDIER RIGHT NOW.
THERE ARE REPORTS THAT PARSIANS FROM ACROSS THE COUNTRY ARE GATHERING TO ATTACK US IN THE CAPITAL, FOR ONE THING.
THAT'S SERIOUS!
BEFORE THAT CAN HAPPEN, I'LL HAVE THE IDIOT HOLING UP IN ZABUL FORTRESS AND SILVERMASK'S PARSIAN SOLDIERS DESTROY EACH OTHER.
BUT REALLY, WHO *IS* THAT MAN IN THE SILVER MASK?

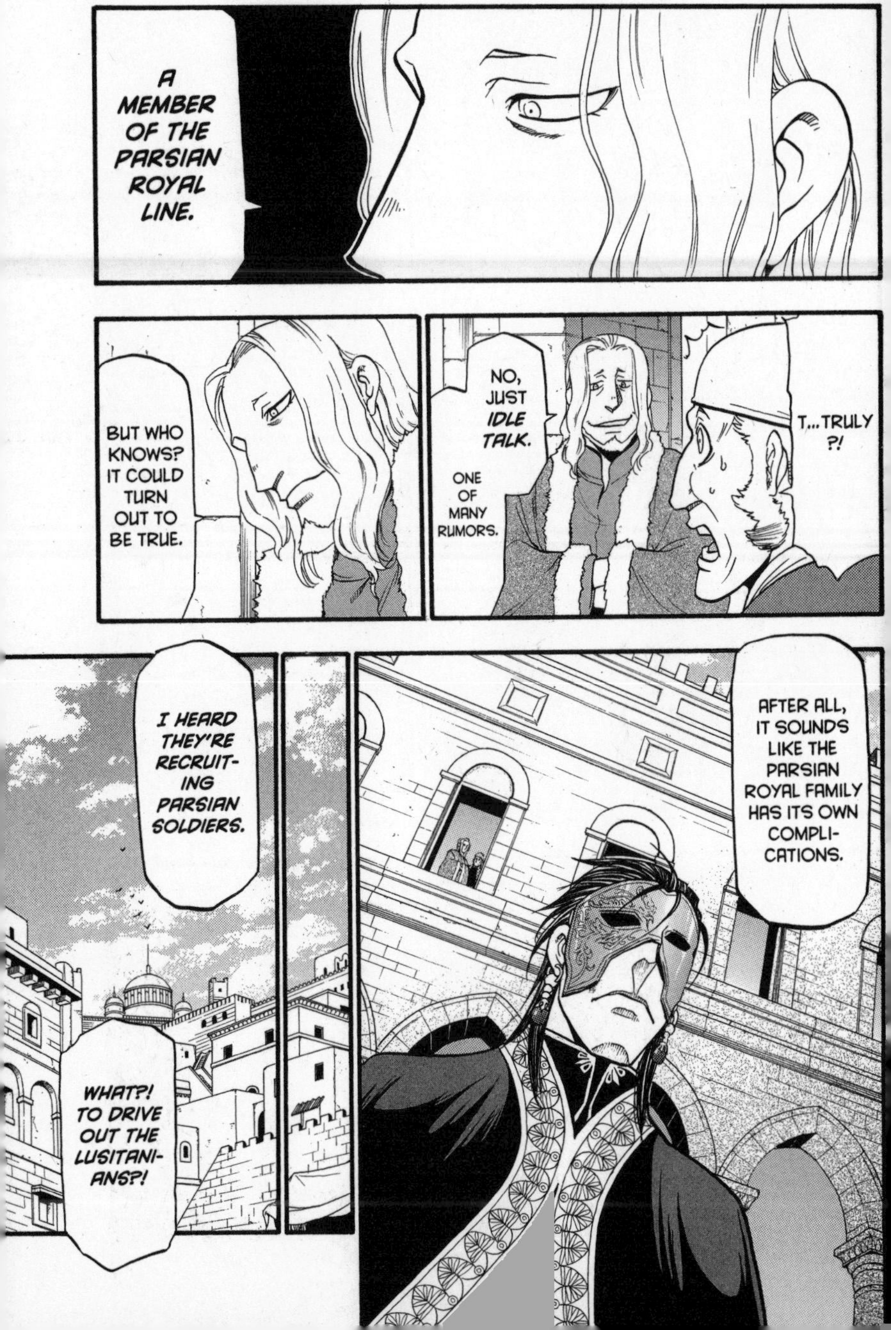
A MEMBER OF THE PARSIAN ROYAL LINE.
T...TRULY ?!
NO, JUST IDLE TALK.
ONE OF MANY RUMORS.
BUT WHO KNOWS? IT COULD TURN OUT TO BE TRUE.
AFTER ALL, IT SOUNDS LIKE THE PARSIAN ROYAL FAMILY HAS ITS OWN COMPLICATIONS.
I HEARD THEY'RE RECRUITING PARSIAN SOLDIERS.
WHAT?! TO DRIVE OUT THE LUSITANIANS?!

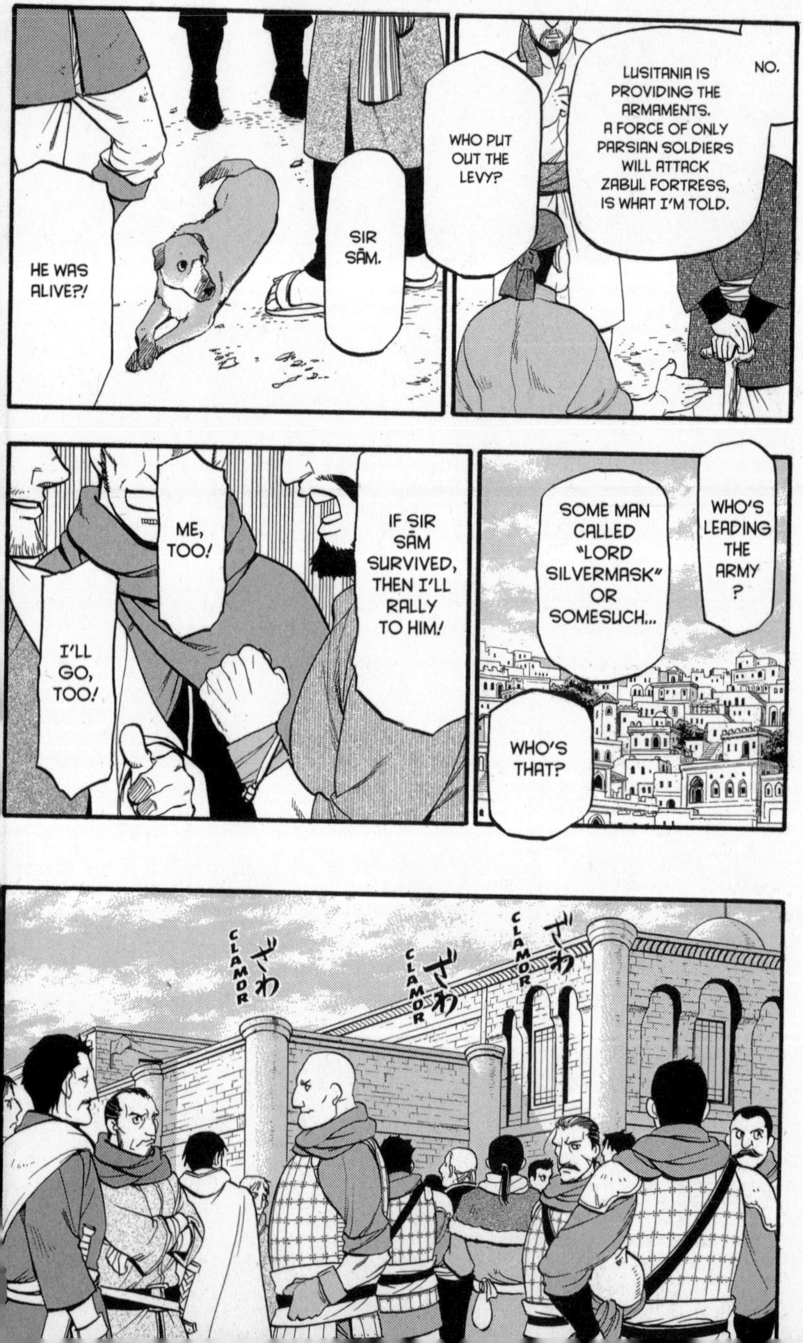
NO.
LUSITANIA IS PROVIDING THE ARMAMENTS. A FORCE OF ONLY PARSIAN SOLDIERS WILL ATTACK ZABUL FORTRESS, IS WHAT I'M TOLD.
WHO PUT OUT THE LEVY?
SIR SĀM.
HE WAS ALIVE?!
WHO'S LEADING THE ARMY?
SOME MAN CALLED "LORD SILVERMASK" OR SOMESUCH...
WHO'S THAT?
IF SIR SĀM SURVIVED, THEN I'LL RALLY TO HIM!
ME, TOO!
I'LL GO, TOO!
ざわ CLAMOR
ざわ CLAMOR
ざわ CLAMOR

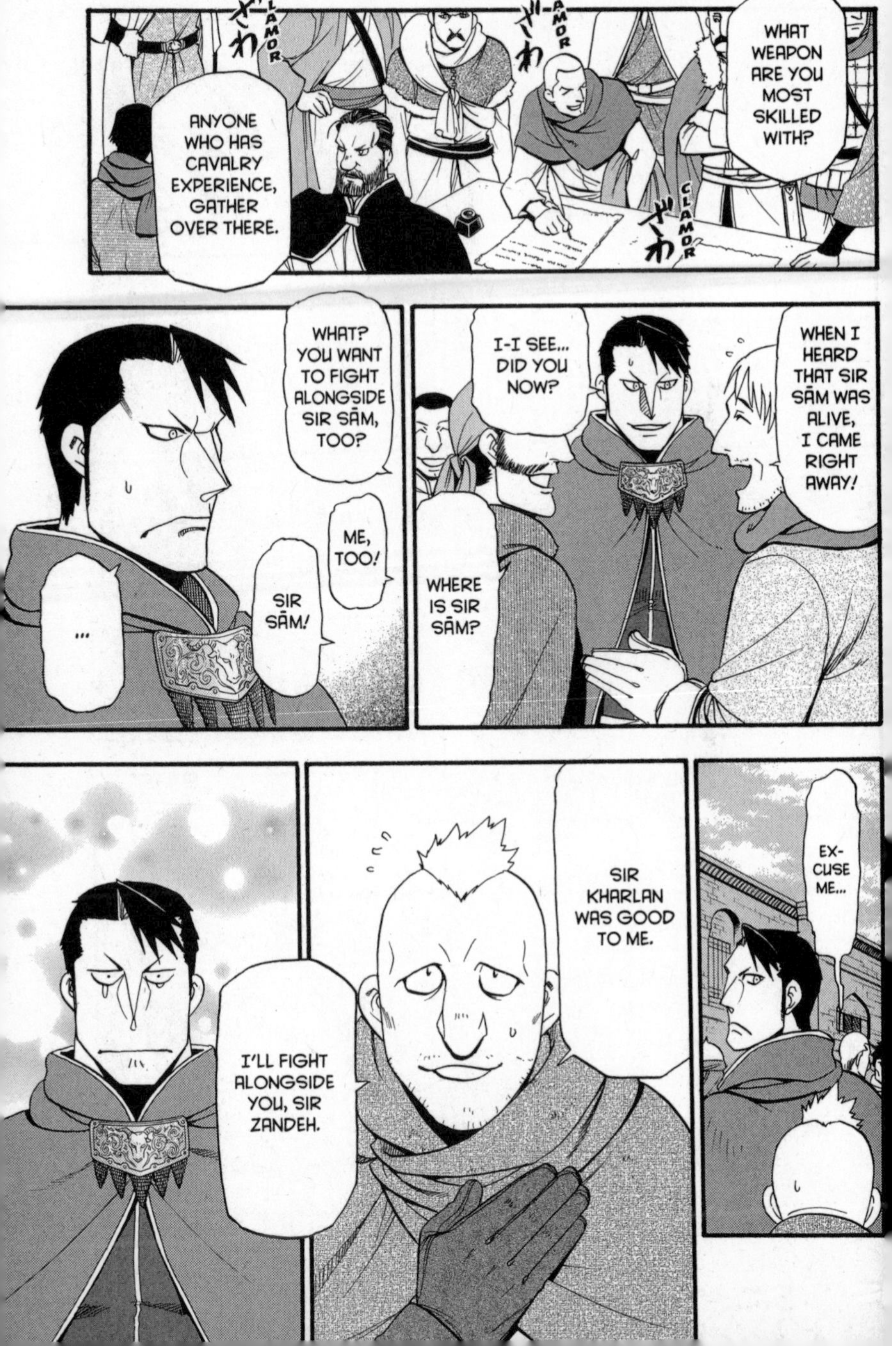
WHAT WEAPON ARE YOU MOST SKILLED WITH?
ざわ CLAMOR
ざわ CLAMOR
ざわ CLAMOR
ANYONE WHO HAS CAVALRY EXPERIENCE, GATHER OVER THERE.
WHEN I HEARD THAT SIR SĀM WAS ALIVE, I CAME RIGHT AWAY!
I-I SEE... DID YOU NOW?
WHERE IS SIR SĀM?
WHAT? YOU WANT TO FIGHT ALONGSIDE SIR SĀM, TOO?
ME, TOO!
SIR SĀM!
...
EX-CUSE ME...
SIR KHARLAN WAS GOOD TO ME.
I'LL FIGHT ALONGSIDE YOU, SIR ZANDEH.

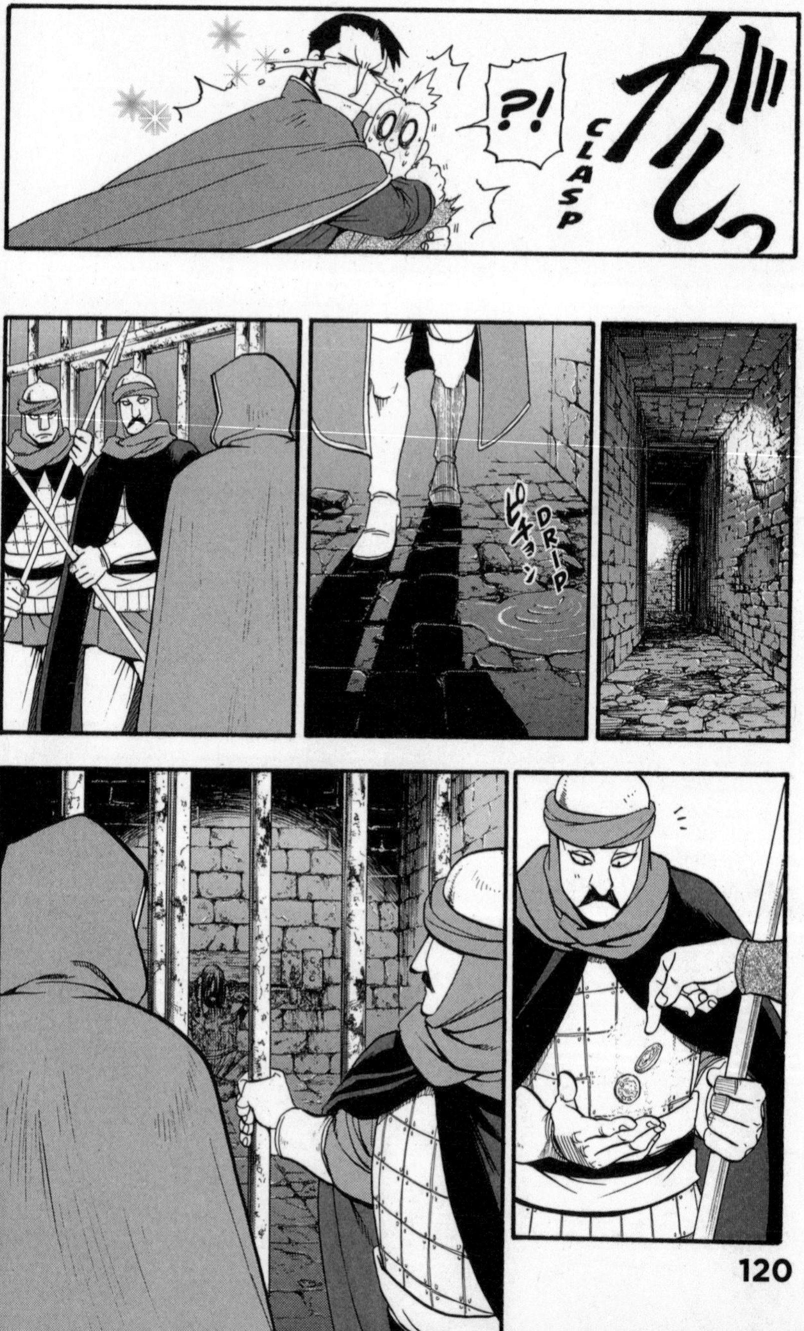
がしっ
CLASP
?!
ピチョン
DRIP

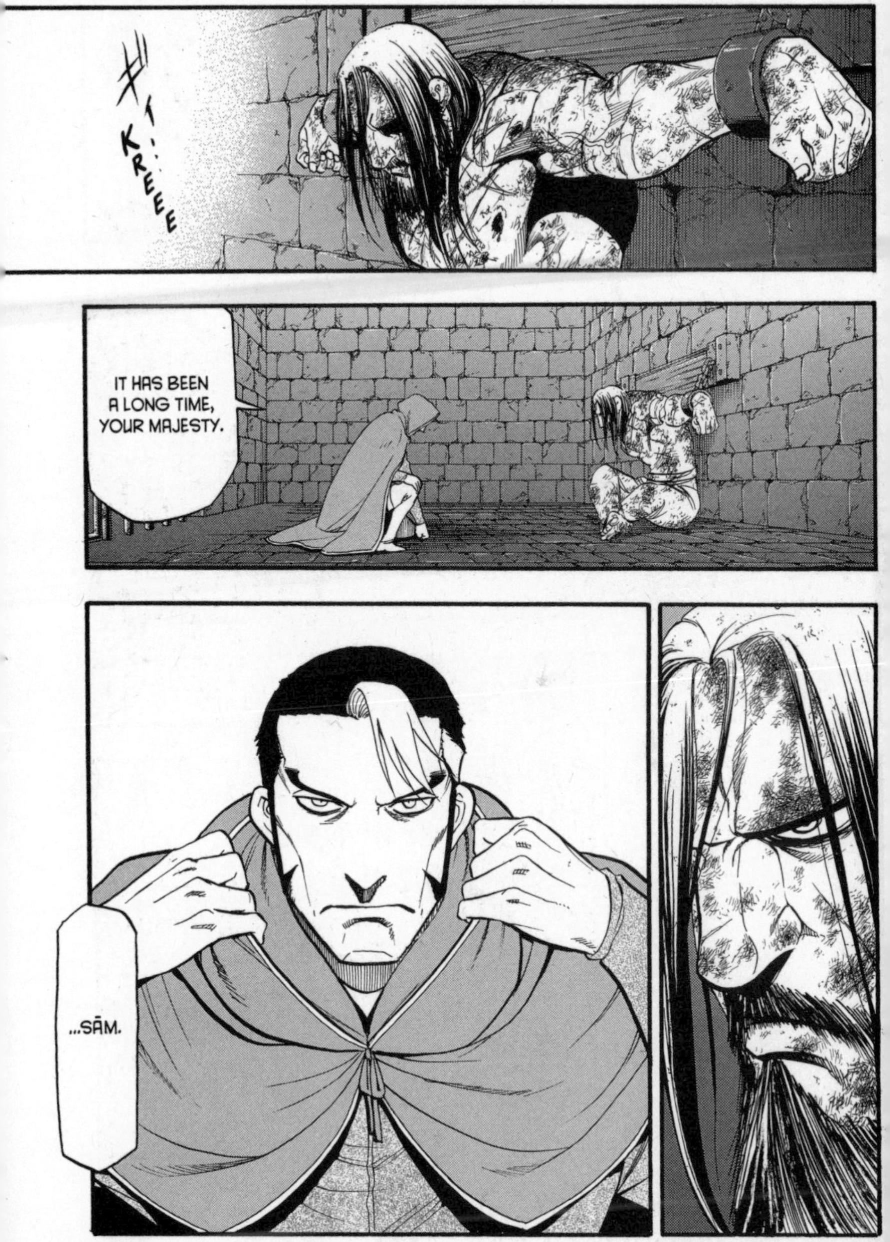
KREEE
IT HAS BEEN A LONG TIME, YOUR MAJESTY.
...SĀM.

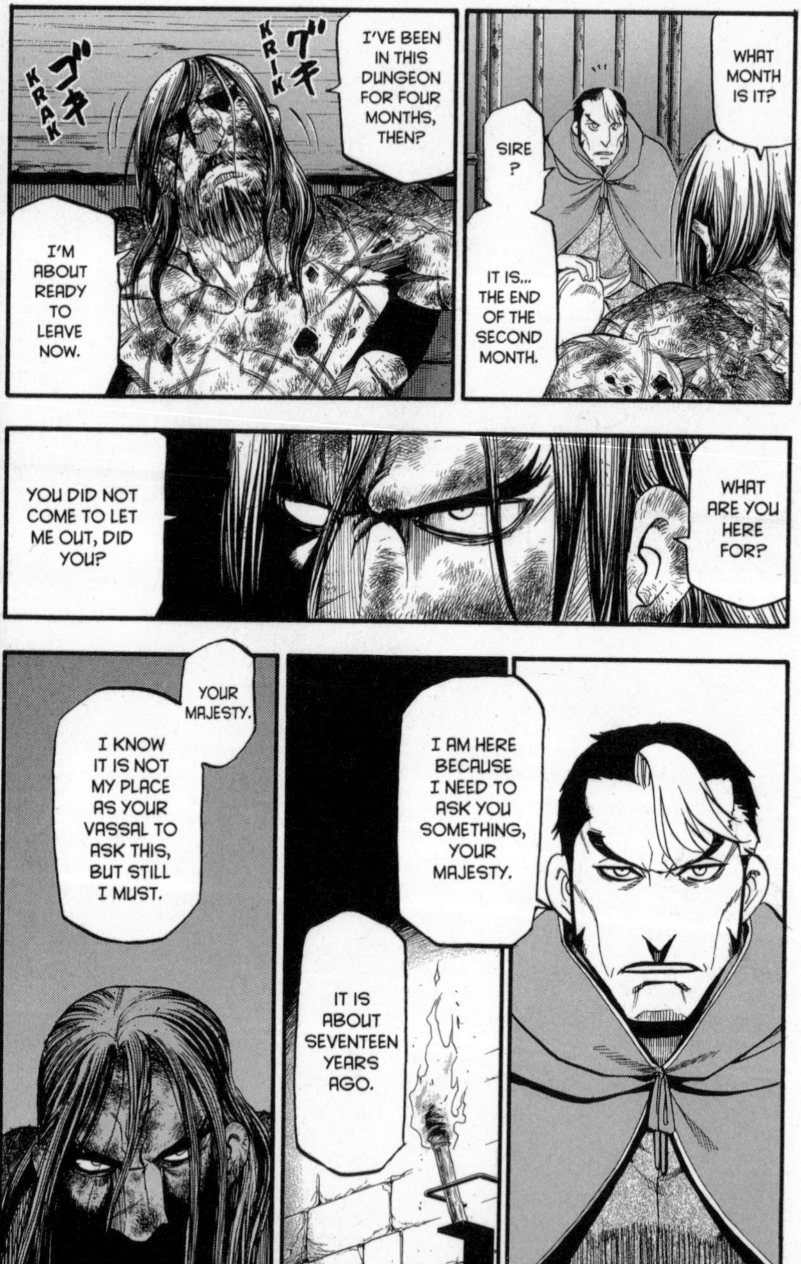
WHAT MONTH IS IT?
SIRE ?
IT IS... THE END OF THE SECOND MONTH.
I'VE BEEN IN THIS DUNGEON FOR FOUR MONTHS, THEN?
グキ KRIK
ゴキ KRAK
I'M ABOUT READY TO LEAVE NOW.
WHAT ARE YOU HERE FOR?
YOU DID NOT COME TO LET ME OUT, DID YOU?
I AM HERE BECAUSE I NEED TO ASK YOU SOMETHING, YOUR MAJESTY.
IT IS ABOUT SEVENTEEN YEARS AGO.
YOUR MAJESTY.
I KNOW IT IS NOT MY PLACE AS YOUR VASSAL TO ASK THIS, BUT STILL I MUST.

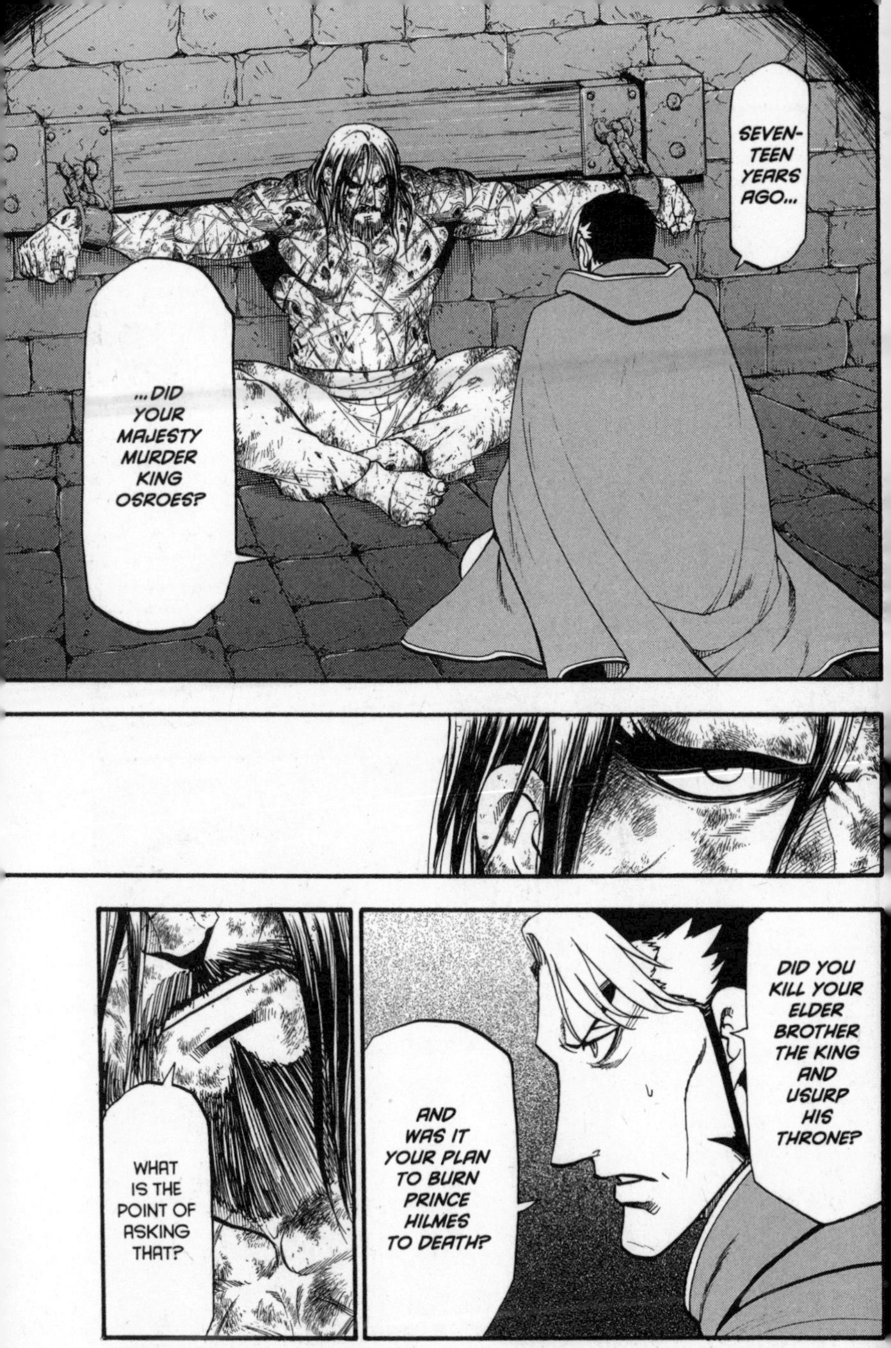
SEVEN-TEEN YEARS AGO...
...DID YOUR MAJESTY MURDER KING OSROES?
DID YOU KILL YOUR ELDER BROTHER THE KING AND USURP HIS THRONE?
AND WAS IT YOUR PLAN TO BURN PRINCE HILMES TO DEATH?
WHAT IS THE POINT OF ASKING THAT?

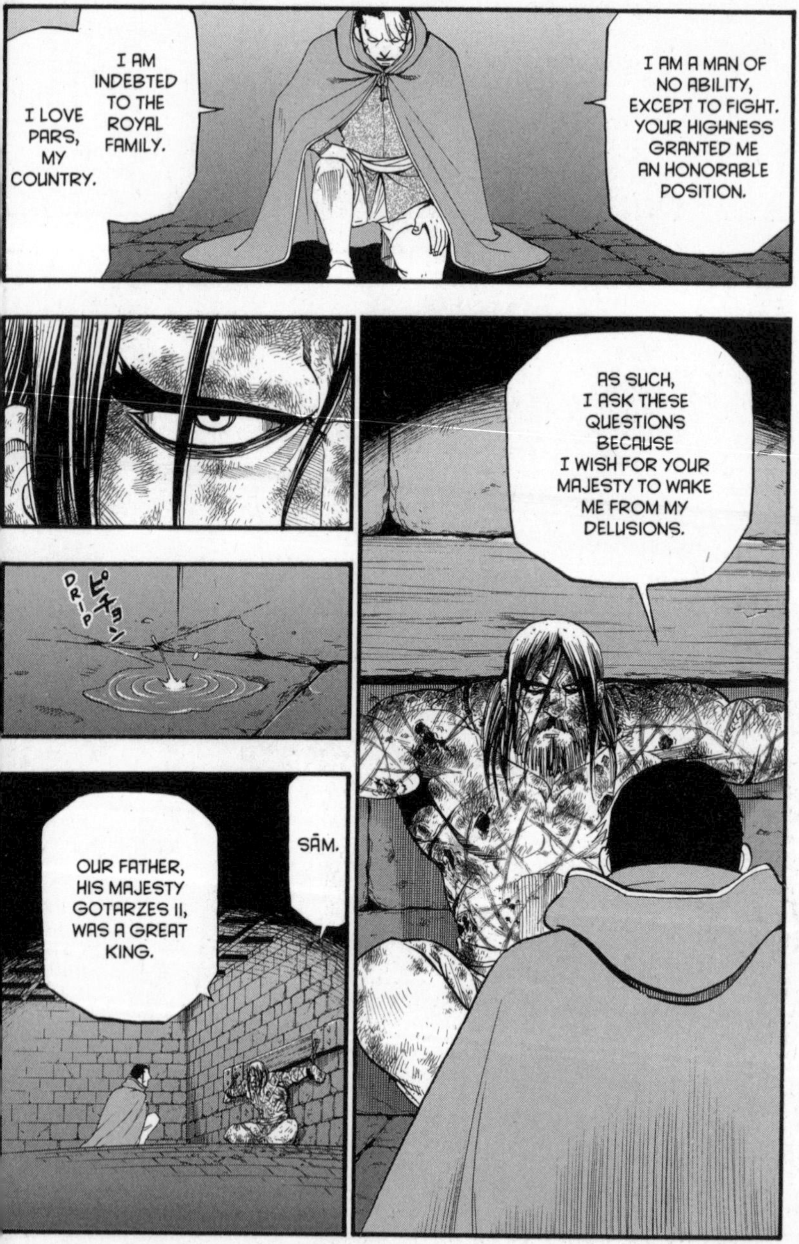
I AM A MAN OF NO ABILITY, EXCEPT TO FIGHT. YOUR HIGHNESS GRANTED ME AN HONORABLE POSITION.
I AM INDEBTED TO THE ROYAL FAMILY.
I LOVE PARS, MY COUNTRY.
AS SUCH, I ASK THESE QUESTIONS BECAUSE I WISH FOR YOUR MAJESTY TO WAKE ME FROM MY DELUSIONS.
ピチョン
DRIP
SĀM.
OUR FATHER, HIS MAJESTY GOTARZES II, WAS A GREAT KING.

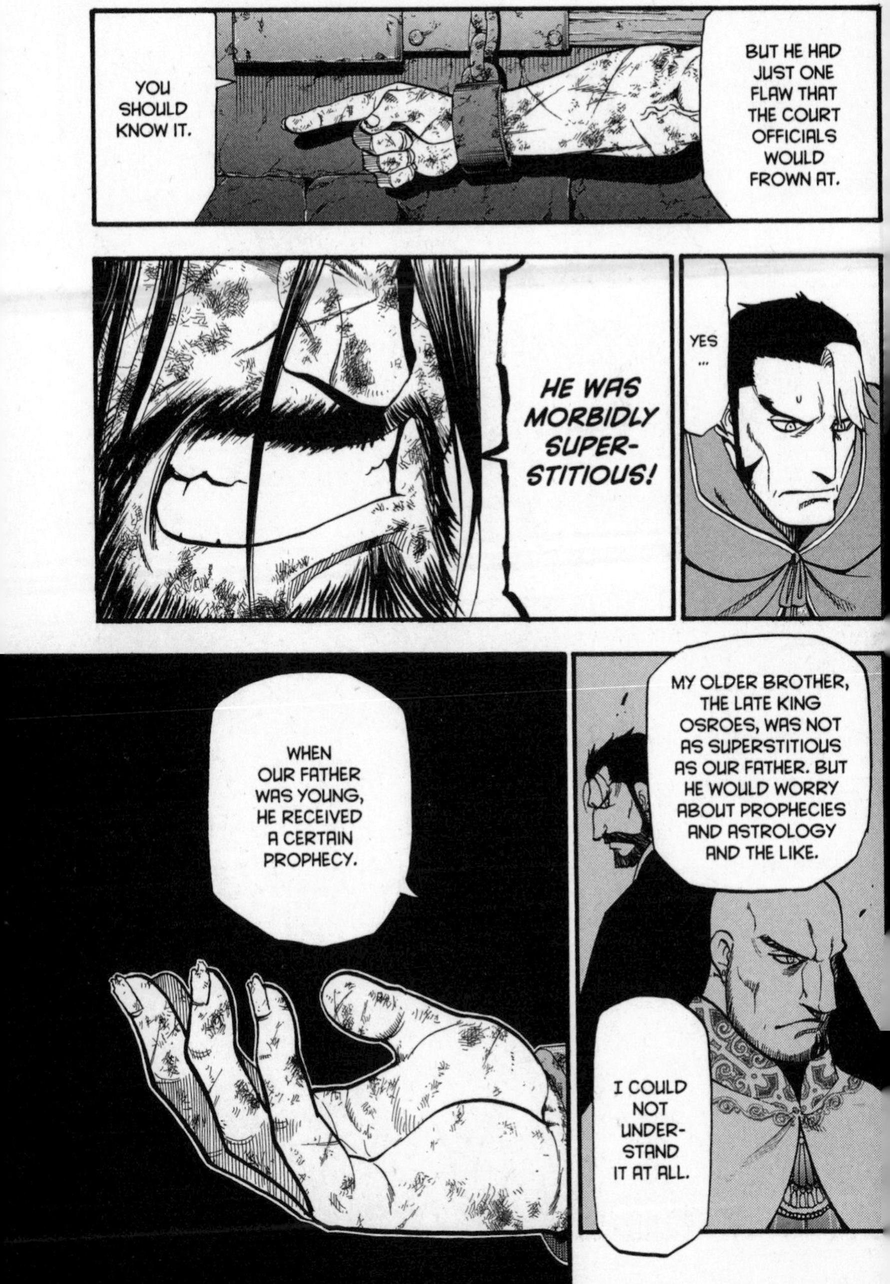
BUT HE HAD JUST ONE FLAW THAT THE COURT OFFICIALS WOULD FROWN AT.
YOU SHOULD KNOW IT.
YES ...
HE WAS MORBIDLY SUPER-STITIOUS!
MY OLDER BROTHER, THE LATE KING OSROES, WAS NOT AS SUPERSTITIOUS AS OUR FATHER. BUT HE WOULD WORRY ABOUT PROPHECIES AND ASTROLOGY AND THE LIKE.
I COULD NOT UNDER-STAND IT AT ALL.
WHEN OUR FATHER WAS YOUNG, HE RECEIVED A CERTAIN PROPHECY.

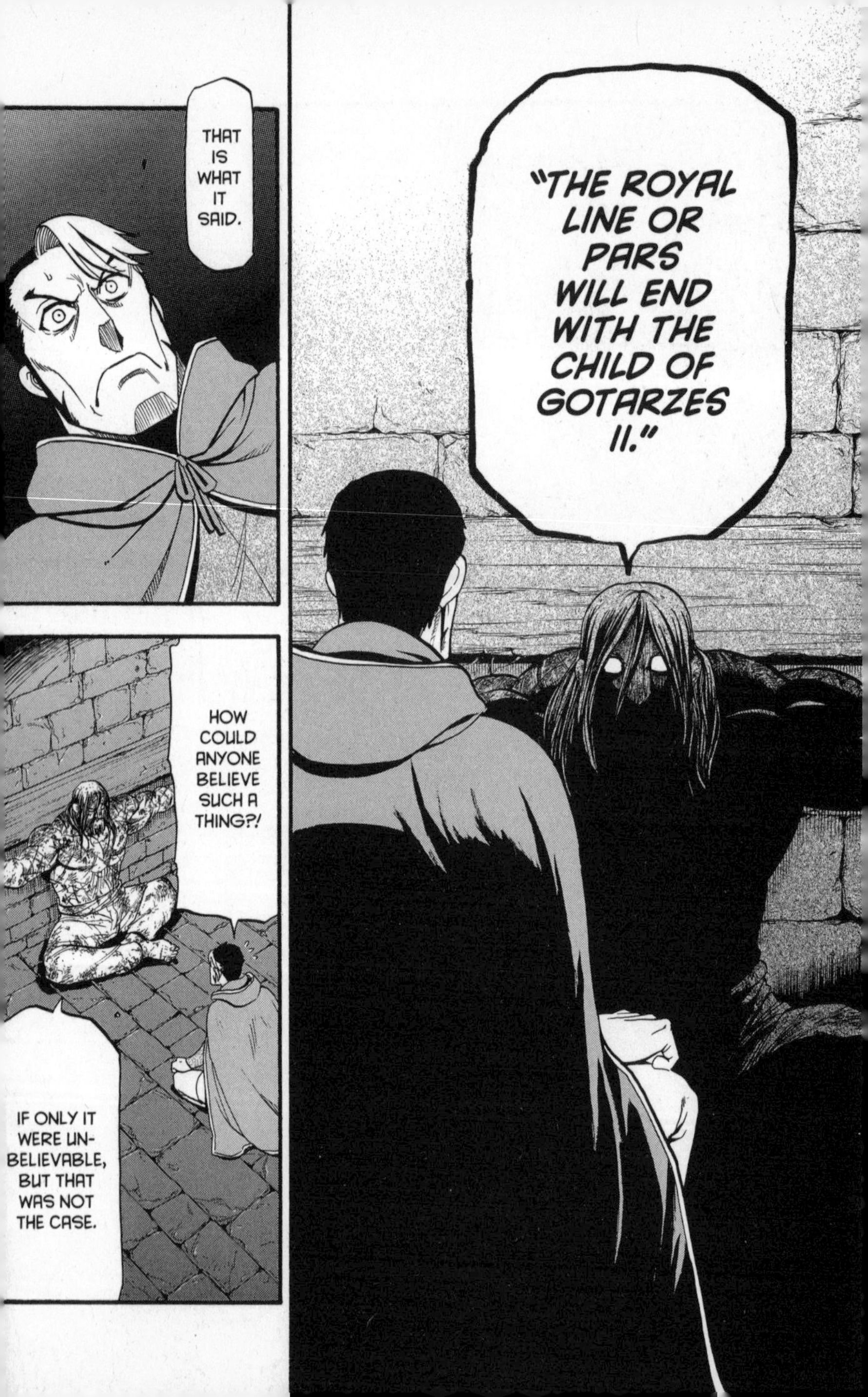
"THE ROYAL LINE OR PARS WILL END WITH THE CHILD OF GOTARZES II."
THAT IS WHAT IT SAID.
HOW COULD ANYONE BELIEVE SUCH A THING?!
IF ONLY IT WERE UN-BELIEVABLE, BUT THAT WAS NOT THE CASE.

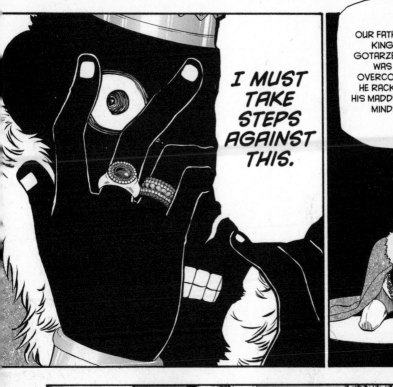

OUR FATHER, KING GOTARZES II, WAS OVERCOME. HE RACKED HIS MADDENED MIND.

I MUST TAKE STEPS AGAINST THIS.

...WHAT DID HIS MAJESTY THE GREAT KING GOTARZES DO...?

...SÂM.

THE OLDER THE ROYAL LINE, THE MORE THE BLOOD POOLS, AND THE MORE FILTH ACCUMULATES...

THE HEROIC LEGEND OF
ARSLAN

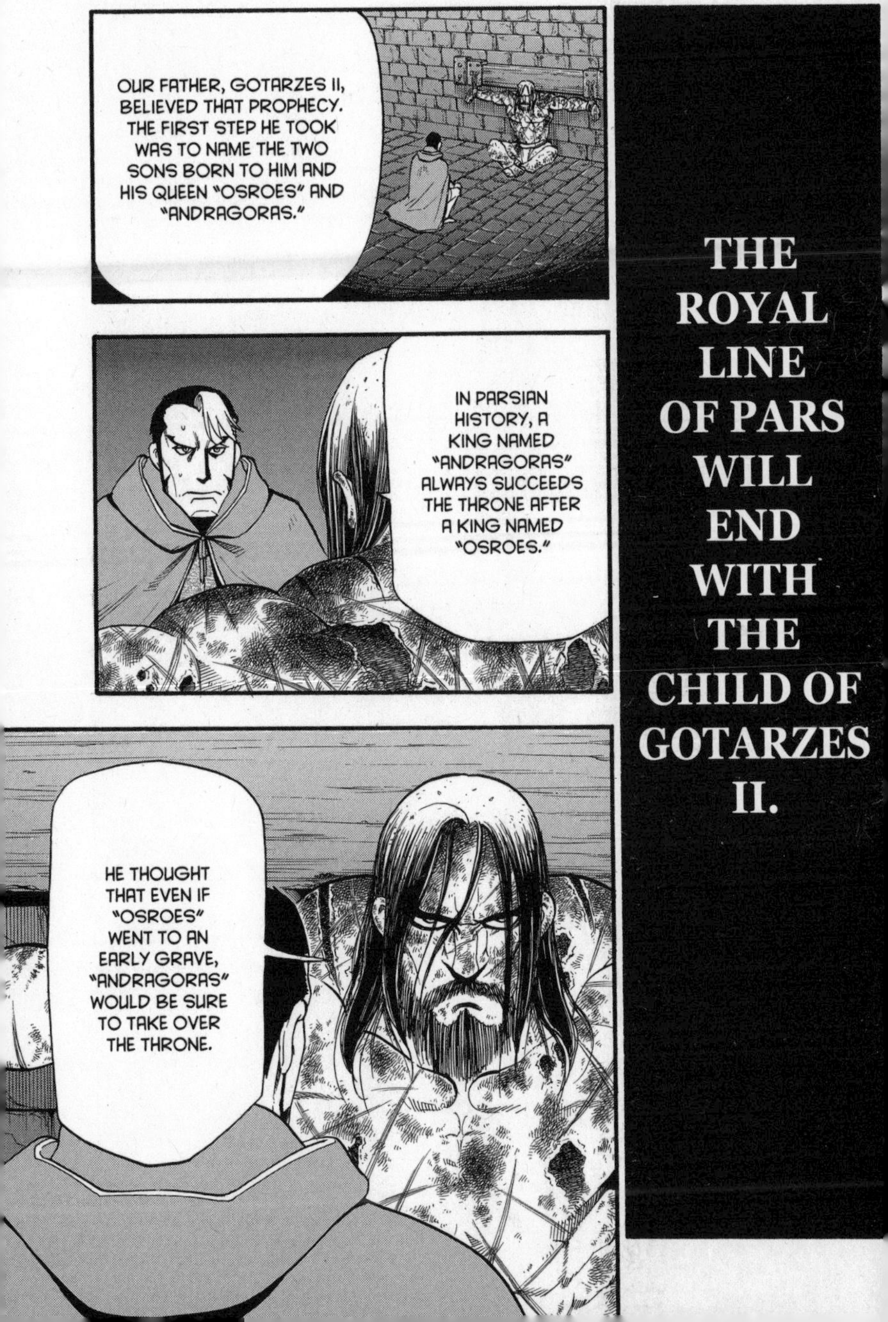
THE ROYAL LINE OF PARS WILL END WITH THE CHILD OF GOTARZES II.
OUR FATHER, GOTARZES II, BELIEVED THAT PROPHECY. THE FIRST STEP HE TOOK WAS TO NAME THE TWO SONS BORN TO HIM AND HIS QUEEN "OSROES" AND "ANDRAGORAS."
IN PARSIAN HISTORY, A KING NAMED "ANDRAGORAS" ALWAYS SUCCEEDS THE THRONE AFTER A KING NAMED "OSROES."
HE THOUGHT THAT EVEN IF "OSROES" WENT TO AN EARLY GRAVE, "ANDRAGORAS" WOULD BE SURE TO TAKE OVER THE THRONE.

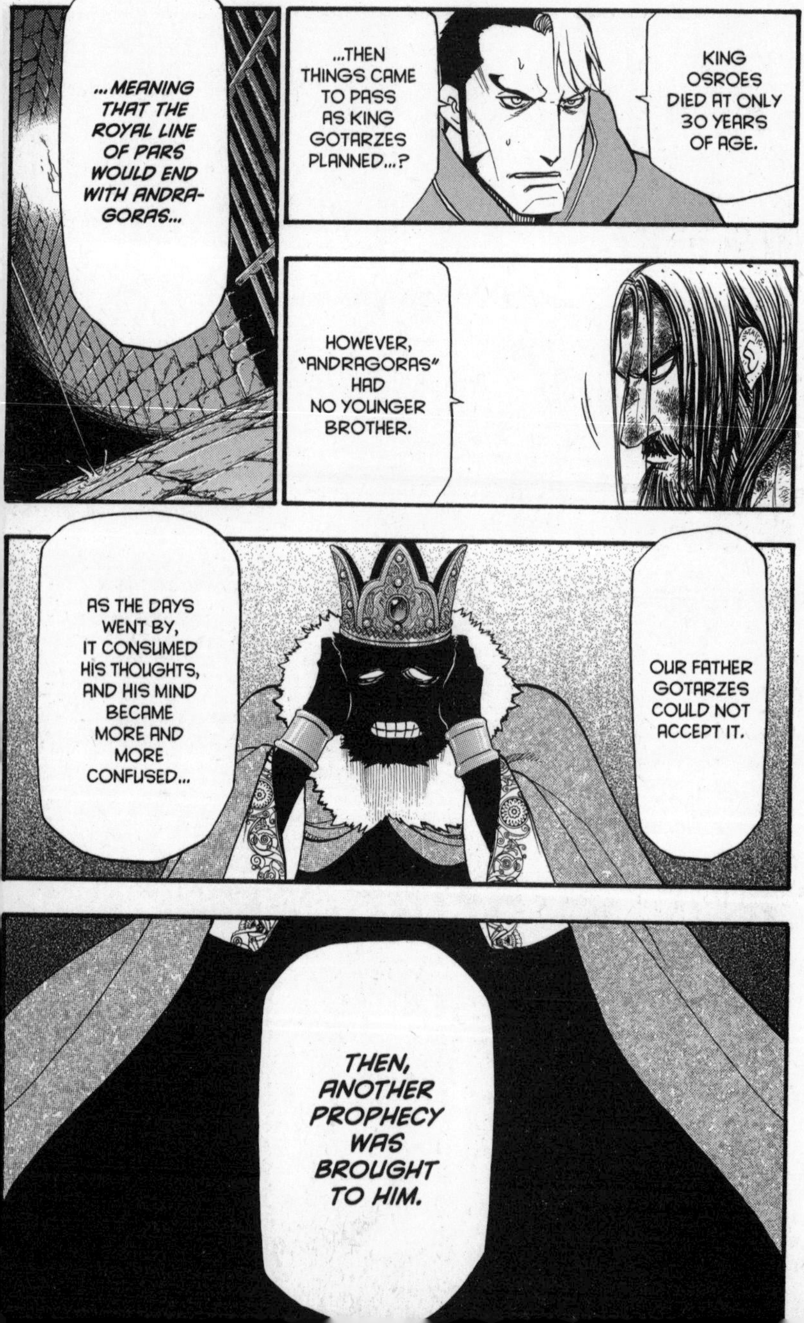
KING OSROES DIED AT ONLY 30 YEARS OF AGE.
...THEN THINGS CAME TO PASS AS KING GOTARZES PLANNED...?
HOWEVER, "ANDRAGORAS" HAD NO YOUNGER BROTHER.
...MEANING THAT THE ROYAL LINE OF PARS WOULD END WITH ANDRA-GORAS...
OUR FATHER GOTARZES COULD NOT ACCEPT IT.
AS THE DAYS WENT BY, IT CONSUMED HIS THOUGHTS, AND HIS MIND BECAME MORE AND MORE CONFUSED...
THEN, ANOTHER PROPHECY WAS BROUGHT TO HIM.

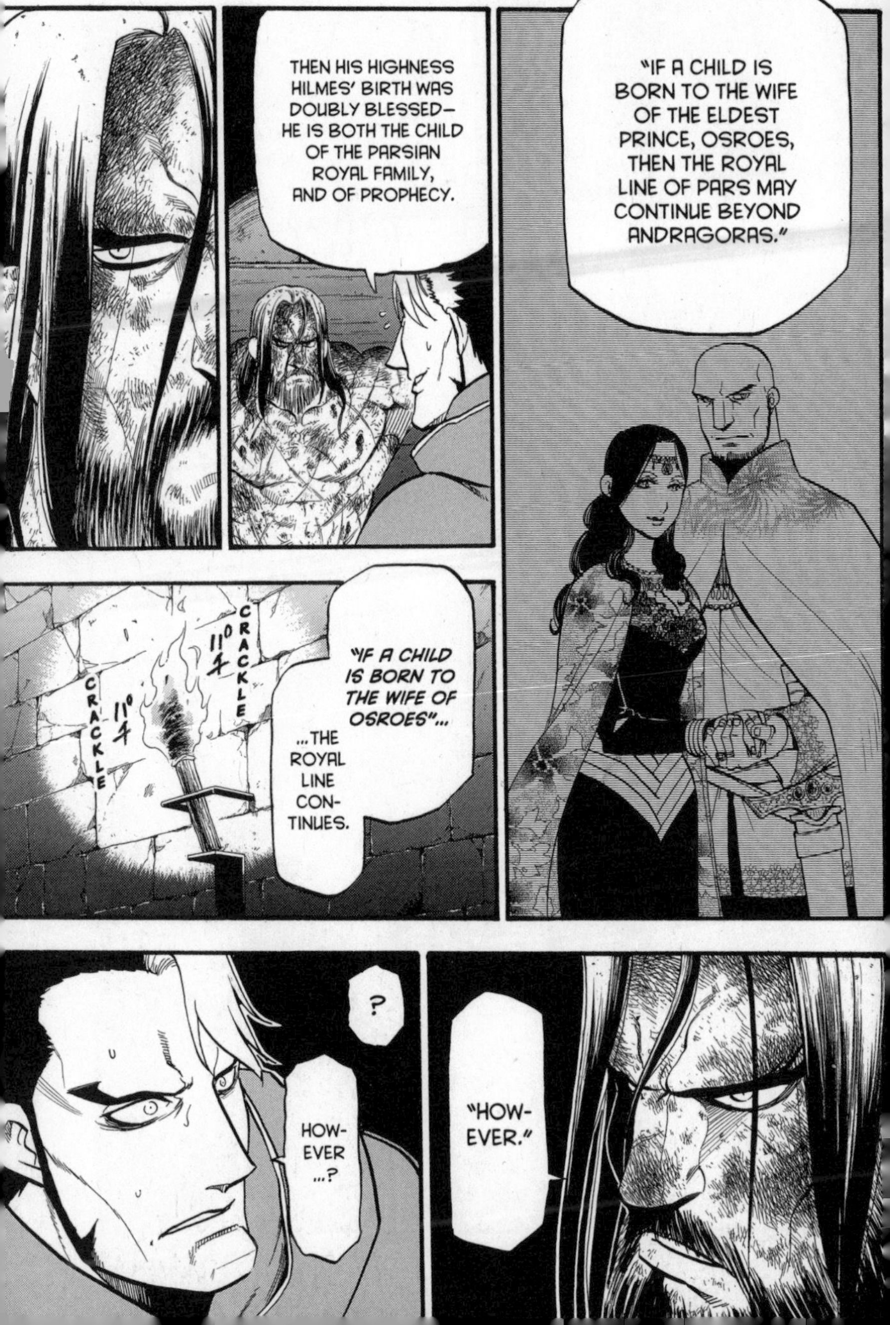
"IF A CHILD IS BORN TO THE WIFE OF THE ELDEST PRINCE, OSROES, THEN THE ROYAL LINE OF PARS MAY CONTINUE BEYOND ANDRAGORAS."
THEN HIS HIGHNESS HILMES' BIRTH WAS DOUBLY BLESSED—HE IS BOTH THE CHILD OF THE PARSIAN ROYAL FAMILY, AND OF PROPHECY.
"IF A CHILD IS BORN TO THE WIFE OF OSROES"...
...THE ROYAL LINE CON-TINUES.
CRACKLE
CRACKLE
"HOW-EVER."
?
HOW-EVER ...?

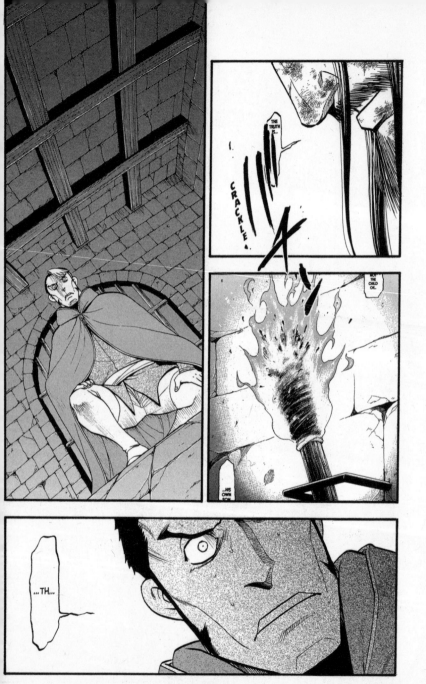

THE TRUTH IS

CRACKLE...

NOT THE CHILD OF...

...HIS OWN SON.

...TH...

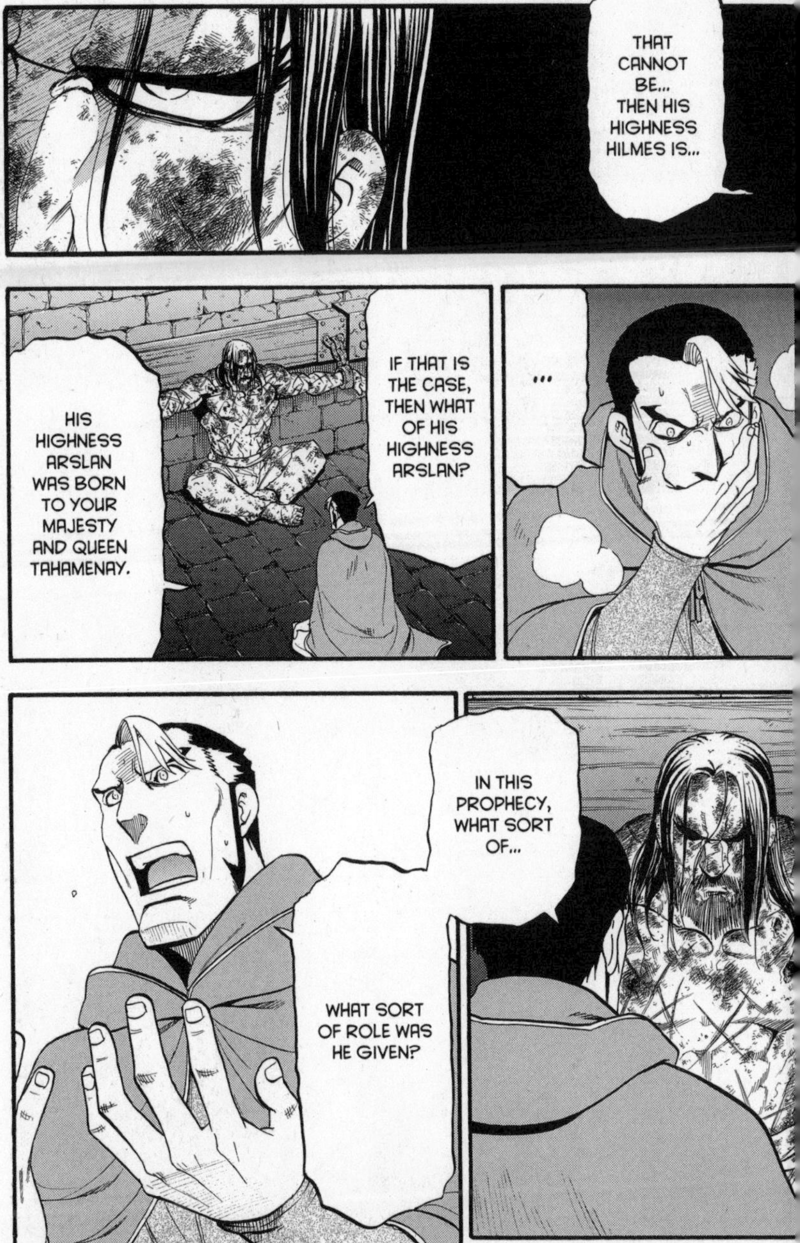
THAT CANNOT BE... THEN HIS HIGHNESS HILMES IS...
...
IF THAT IS THE CASE, THEN WHAT OF HIS HIGHNESS ARSLAN?
HIS HIGHNESS ARSLAN WAS BORN TO YOUR MAJESTY AND QUEEN TAHAMENAY.
IN THIS PROPHECY, WHAT SORT OF...
WHAT SORT OF ROLE WAS HE GIVEN?

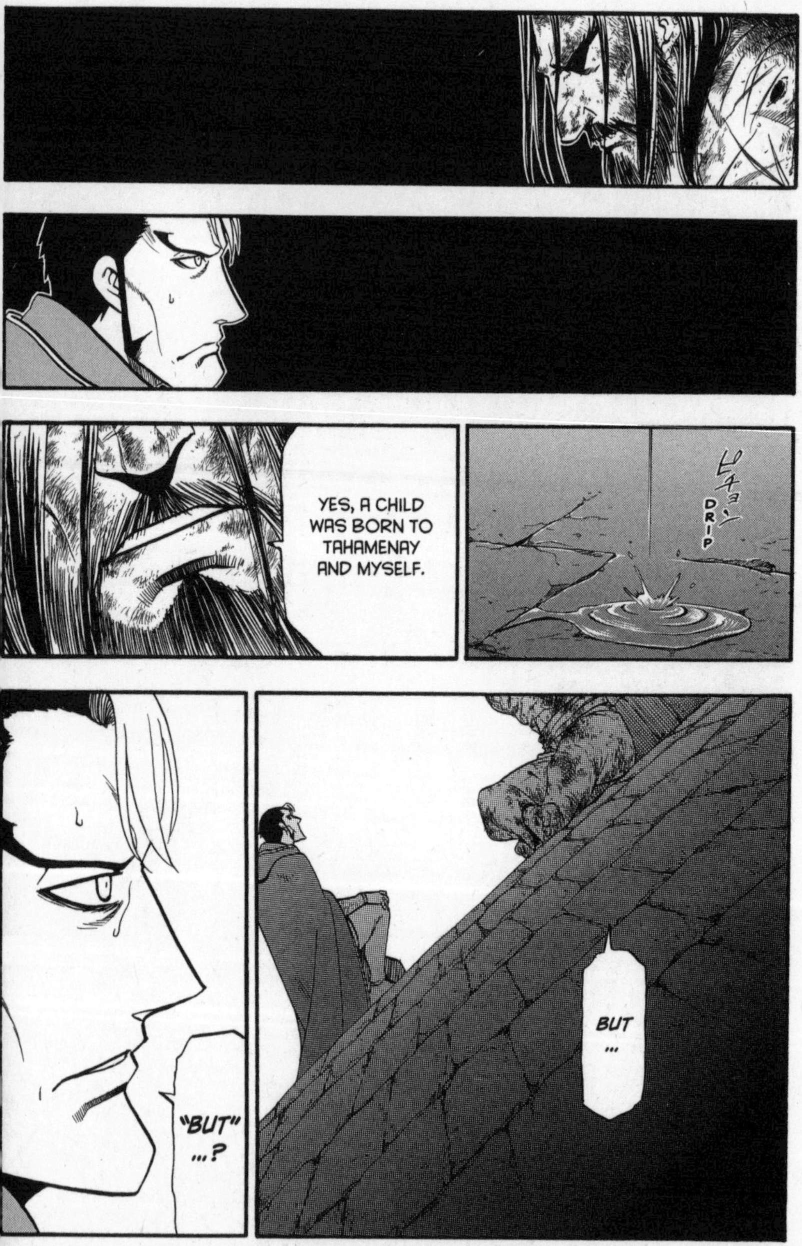
ピチョン
DRIP
YES, A CHILD WAS BORN TO TAHAMENAY AND MYSELF.
BUT ...
"BUT" ...?

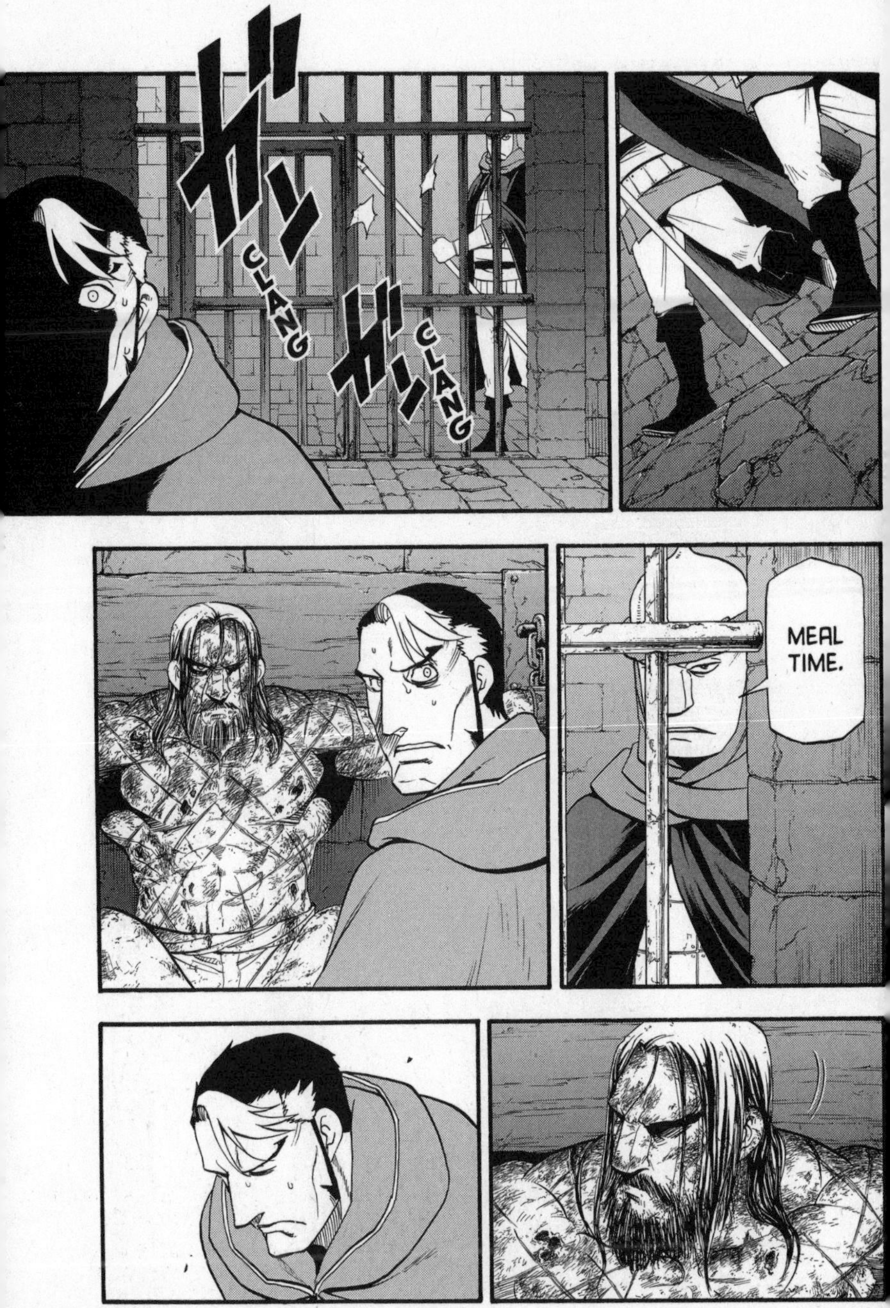
CLANG
CLANG
MEAL TIME.

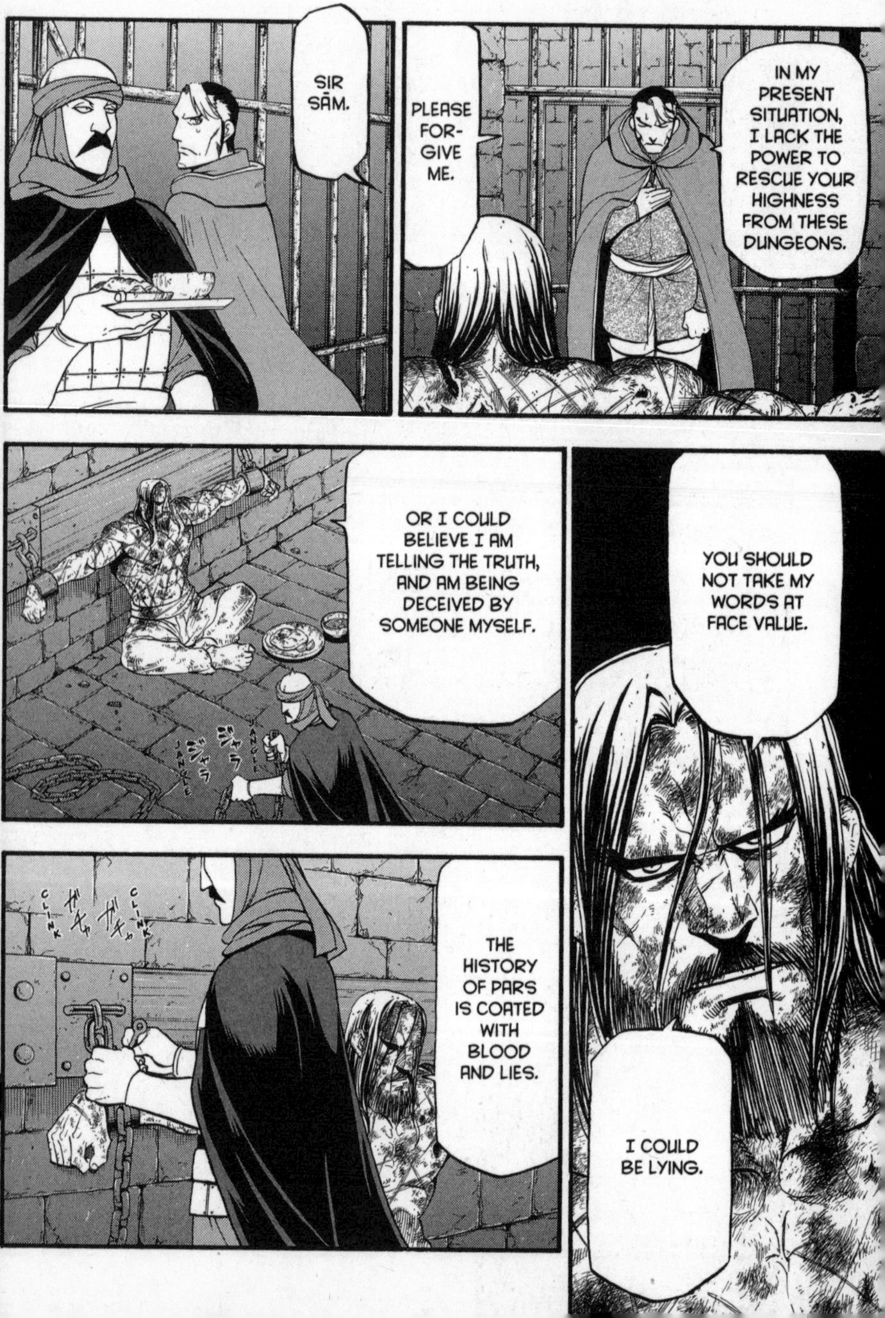
IN MY PRESENT SITUATION, I LACK THE POWER TO RESCUE YOUR HIGHNESS FROM THESE DUNGEONS.
PLEASE FOR-GIVE ME.
SIR SĀM.
YOU SHOULD NOT TAKE MY WORDS AT FACE VALUE.
I COULD BE LYING.
OR I COULD BELIEVE I AM TELLING THE TRUTH, AND AM BEING DECEIVED BY SOMEONE MYSELF.
ジャラ JANGLE
ジャラ JANGLE
ガチャ CLINK
ガチャ CLINK
THE HISTORY OF PARS IS COATED WITH BLOOD AND LIES.

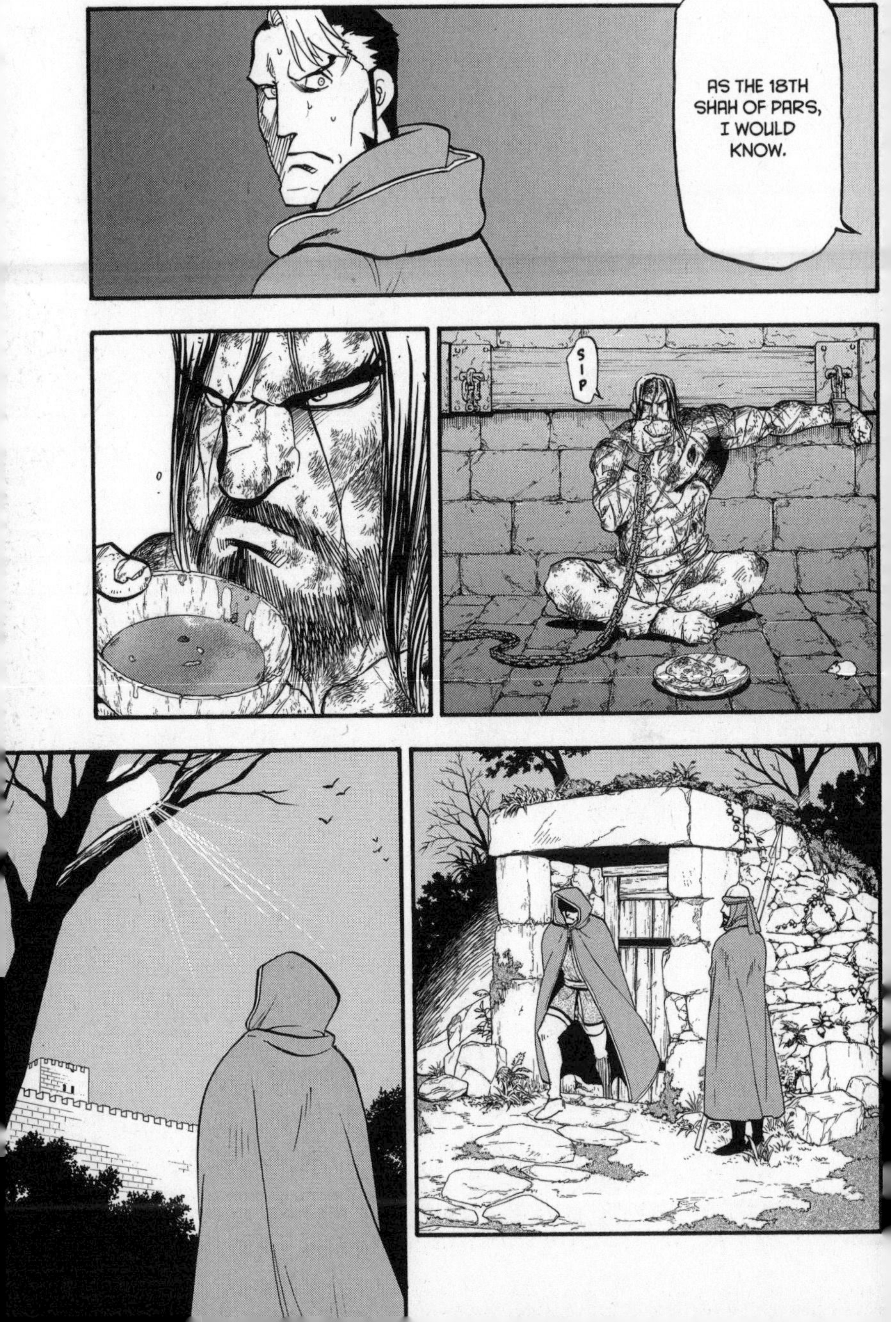
AS THE 18TH SHAH OF PARS, I WOULD KNOW.
SIP

Chapter 57: The Chance Encounter in Early Spring

ON THE FIRST DAY OF THE THIRD MONTH, AN ARMY CONSISTING ONLY OF PARSIANS, LED BY HILMES— ALSO KNOWN AS LORD SILVER MASK— DEPARTED THE ROYAL CAPITAL.

THEY NUMBERED 9,200 CAVALRY-MEN AND 25,400 INFANTRY-MEN...

...AND WERE ACCOMPANIED BY ONE UNIT OF LABORERS TRANSPORTING PROVISIONS.

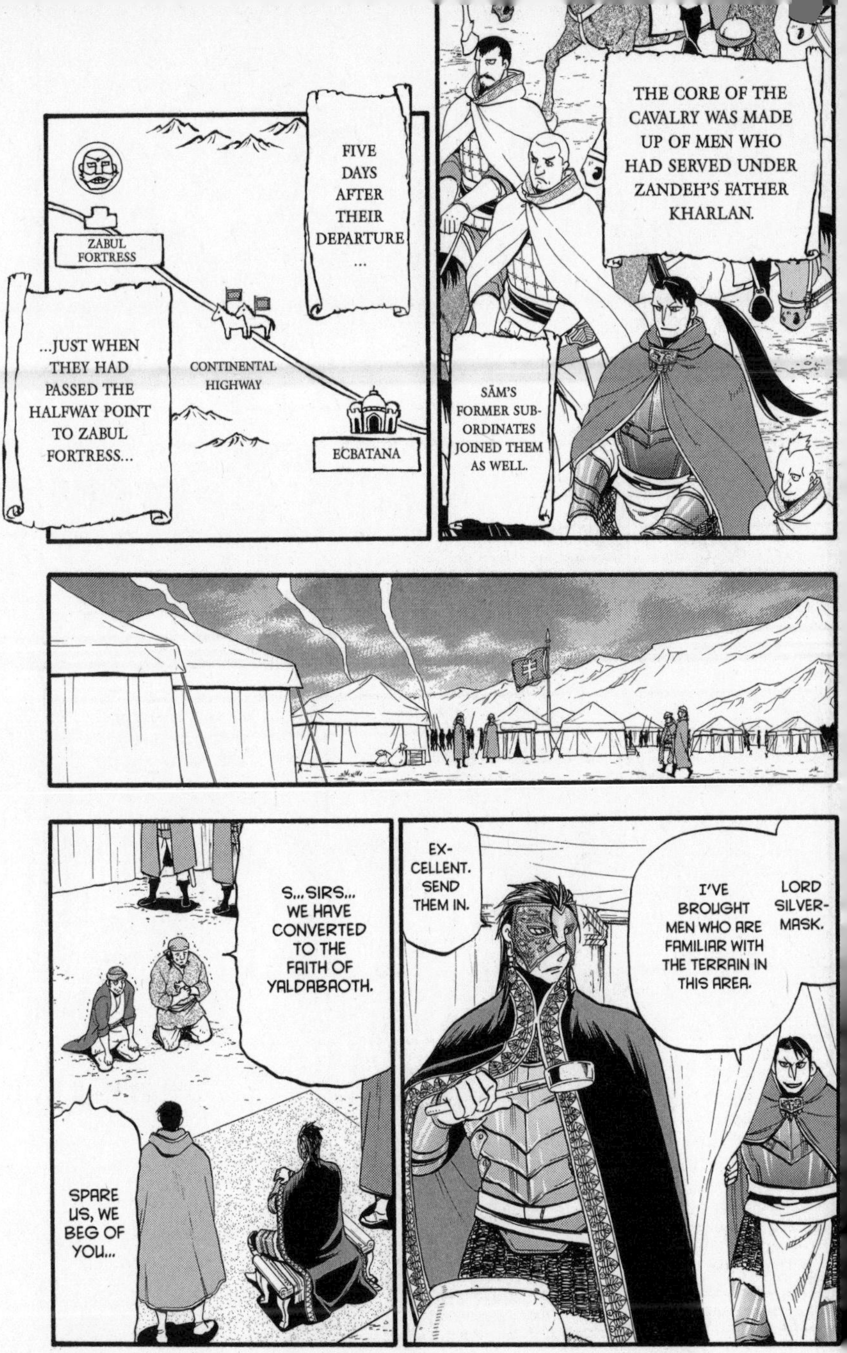
THE CORE OF THE CAVALRY WAS MADE UP OF MEN WHO HAD SERVED UNDER ZANDEH'S FATHER KHARLAN.
SĀM'S FORMER SUB-ORDINATES JOINED THEM AS WELL.
FIVE DAYS AFTER THEIR DEPARTURE ...
ZABUL FORTRESS
CONTINENTAL HIGHWAY
ECBATANA
...JUST WHEN THEY HAD PASSED THE HALFWAY POINT TO ZABUL FORTRESS...
LORD SILVER-MASK.
I'VE BROUGHT MEN WHO ARE FAMILIAR WITH THE TERRAIN IN THIS AREA.
EX-CELLENT. SEND THEM IN.
S... SIRS... WE HAVE CONVERTED TO THE FAITH OF YALDABAOTH.
SPARE US, WE BEG OF YOU...

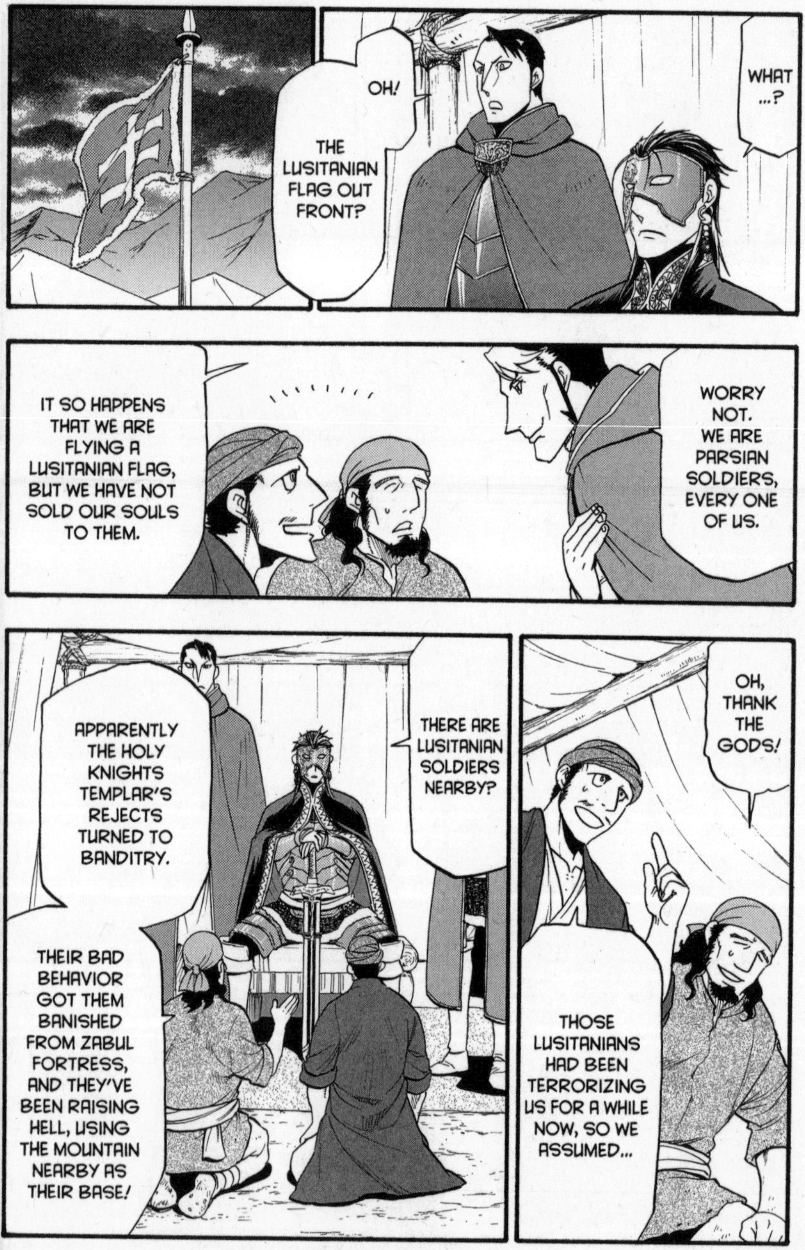
WHAT ...?
OH!
THE LUSITANIAN FLAG OUT FRONT?
WORRY NOT. WE ARE PARSIAN SOLDIERS, EVERY ONE OF US.
IT SO HAPPENS THAT WE ARE FLYING A LUSITANIAN FLAG, BUT WE HAVE NOT SOLD OUR SOULS TO THEM.
OH, THANK THE GODS!
THOSE LUSITANIANS HAD BEEN TERRORIZING US FOR A WHILE NOW, SO WE ASSUMED...
THERE ARE LUSITANIAN SOLDIERS NEARBY?
APPARENTLY THE HOLY KNIGHTS TEMPLAR'S REJECTS TURNED TO BANDITRY.
THEIR BAD BEHAVIOR GOT THEM BANISHED FROM ZABUL FORTRESS, AND THEY'VE BEEN RAISING HELL, USING THE MOUNTAIN NEARBY AS THEIR BASE!

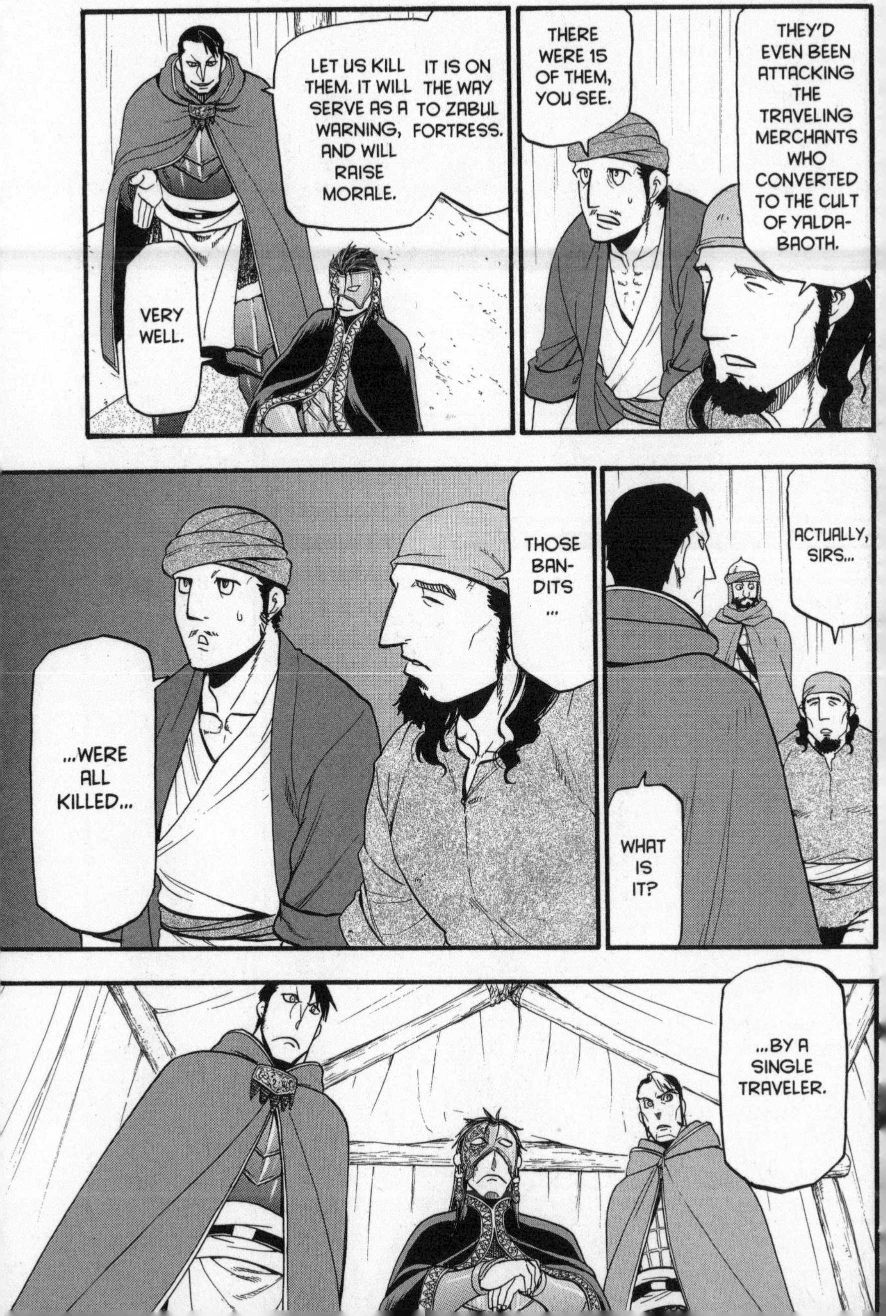
THEY'D EVEN BEEN ATTACKING THE TRAVELING MERCHANTS WHO CONVERTED TO THE CULT OF YALDA-BAOTH.
THERE WERE 15 OF THEM, YOU SEE.
LET US KILL THEM. IT WILL SERVE AS A WARNING, AND WILL RAISE MORALE.
IT IS ON THE WAY TO ZABUL FORTRESS.
VERY WELL.
ACTUALLY, SIRS...
WHAT IS IT?
THOSE BAN-DITS ...
...WERE ALL KILLED...
...BY A SINGLE TRAVELER.

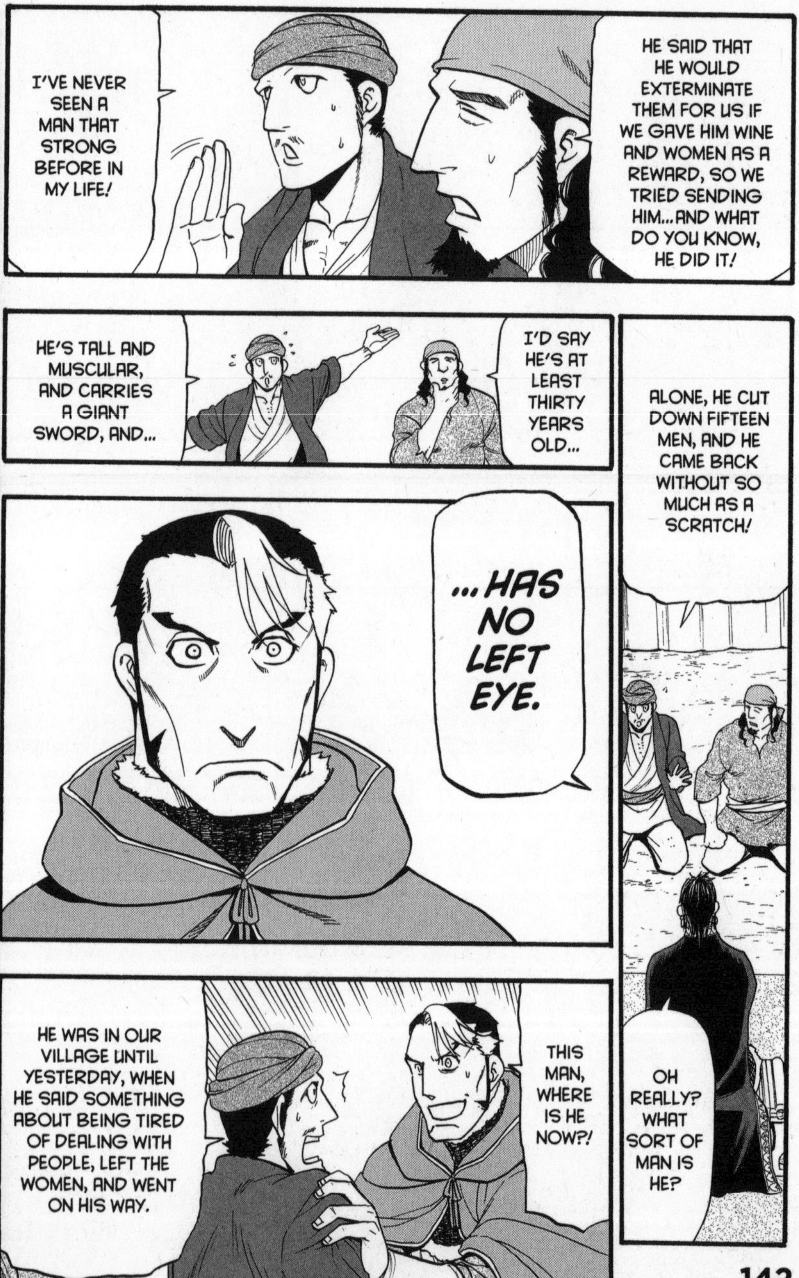
HE SAID THAT HE WOULD EXTERMINATE THEM FOR US IF WE GAVE HIM WINE AND WOMEN AS A REWARD, SO WE TRIED SENDING HIM...AND WHAT DO YOU KNOW, HE DID IT!
I'VE NEVER SEEN A MAN THAT STRONG BEFORE IN MY LIFE!
ALONE, HE CUT DOWN FIFTEEN MEN, AND HE CAME BACK WITHOUT SO MUCH AS A SCRATCH!
OH REALLY? WHAT SORT OF MAN IS HE?
I'D SAY HE'S AT LEAST THIRTY YEARS OLD...
HE'S TALL AND MUSCULAR, AND CARRIES A GIANT SWORD, AND...
...HAS NO LEFT EYE.
THIS MAN, WHERE IS HE NOW?!
HE WAS IN OUR VILLAGE UNTIL YESTERDAY, WHEN HE SAID SOMETHING ABOUT BEING TIRED OF DEALING WITH PEOPLE, LEFT THE WOMEN, AND WENT ON HIS WAY.

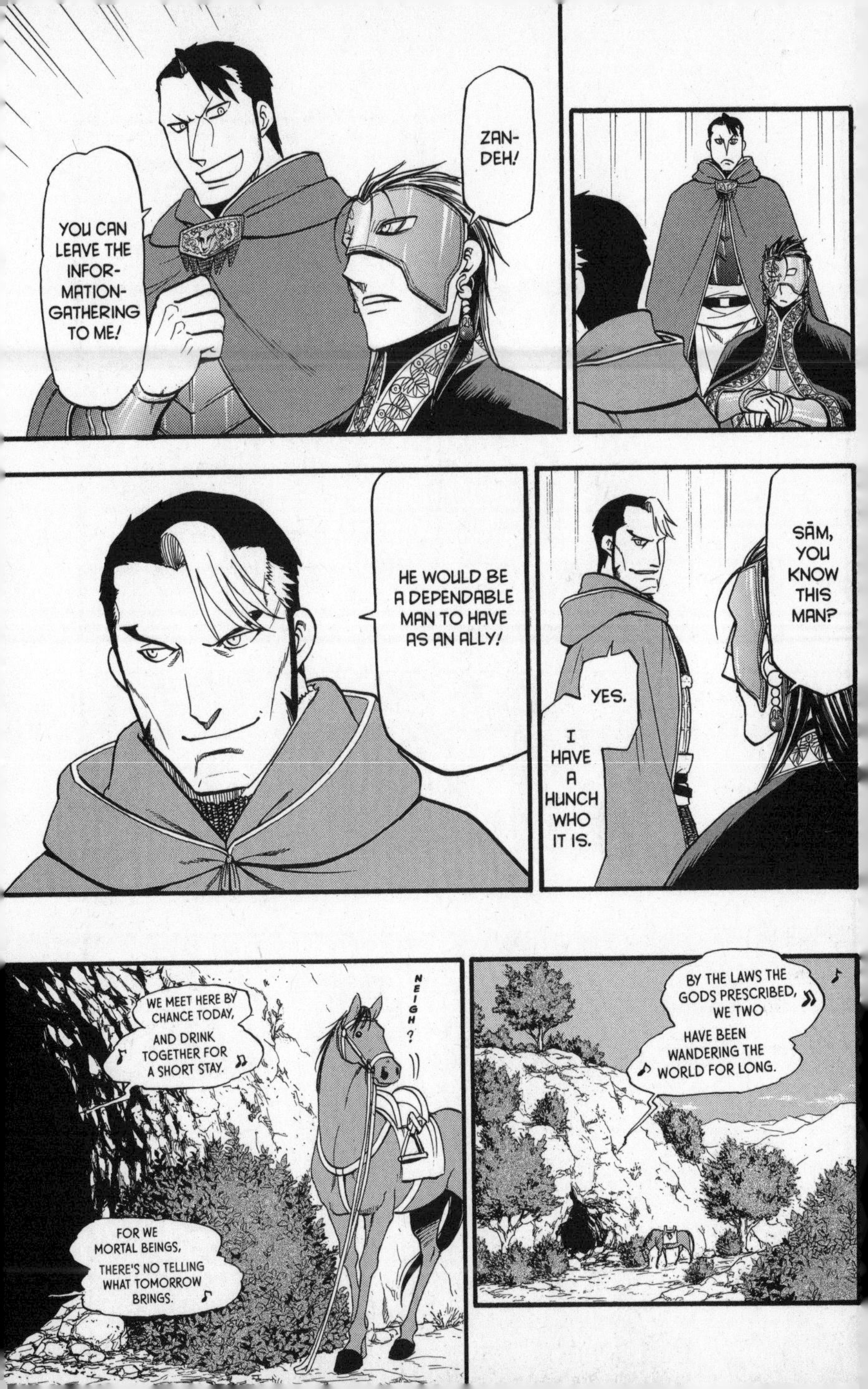
ZAN-DEH!
YOU CAN LEAVE THE INFOR-MATION-GATHERING TO ME!
SĀM, YOU KNOW THIS MAN?
YES.
I HAVE A HUNCH WHO IT IS.
HE WOULD BE A DEPENDABLE MAN TO HAVE AS AN ALLY!
BY THE LAWS THE GODS PRESCRIBED, WE TWO
HAVE BEEN WANDERING THE WORLD FOR LONG.
NEIGH?
WE MEET HERE BY CHANCE TODAY,
AND DRINK TOGETHER FOR A SHORT STAY.
FOR WE MORTAL BEINGS,
THERE'S NO TELLING WHAT TOMORROW BRINGS.

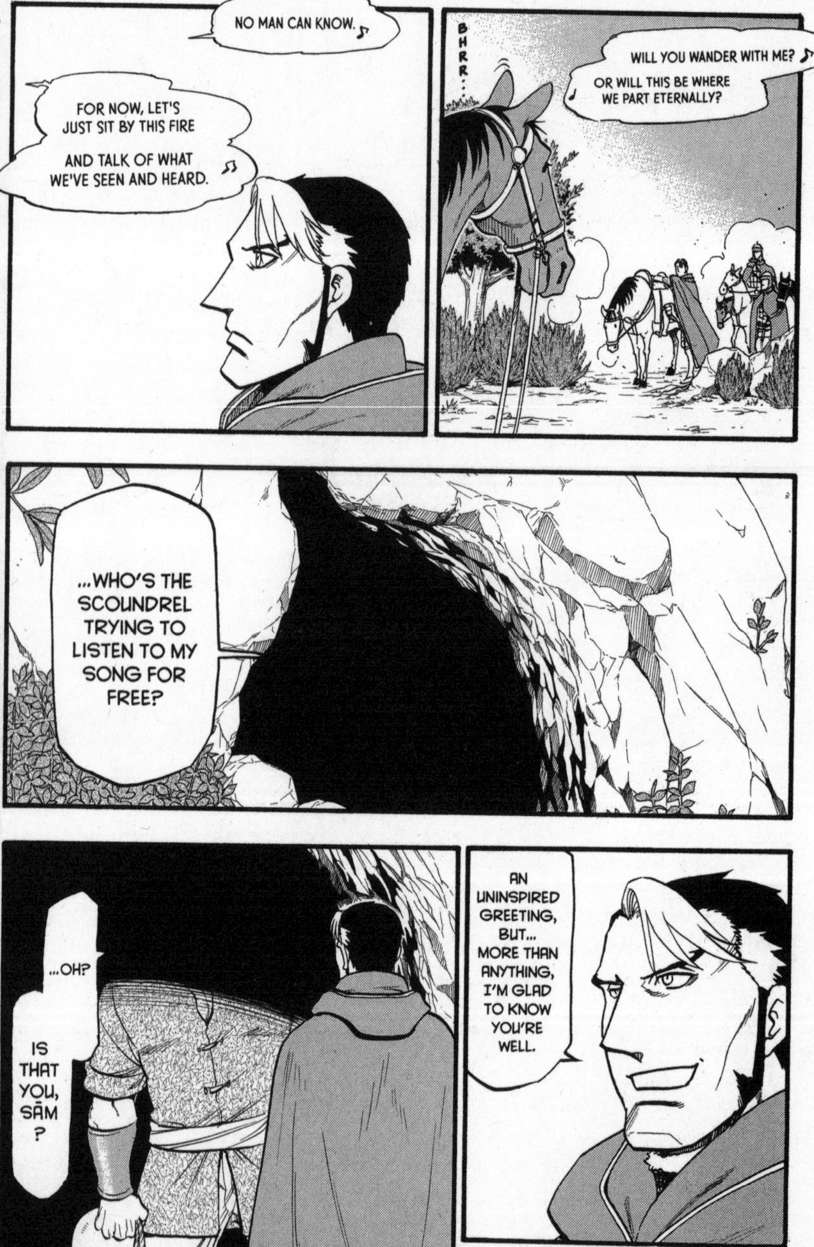
BHRR...
WILL YOU WANDER WITH ME?
OR WILL THIS BE WHERE WE PART ETERNALLY?
NO MAN CAN KNOW.
FOR NOW, LET'S JUST SIT BY THIS FIRE
AND TALK OF WHAT WE'VE SEEN AND HEARD.
...WHO'S THE SCOUNDREL TRYING TO LISTEN TO MY SONG FOR FREE?
AN UNINSPIRED GREETING, BUT... MORE THAN ANYTHING, I'M GLAD TO KNOW YOU'RE WELL.
...OH?
IS THAT YOU, SĀM?

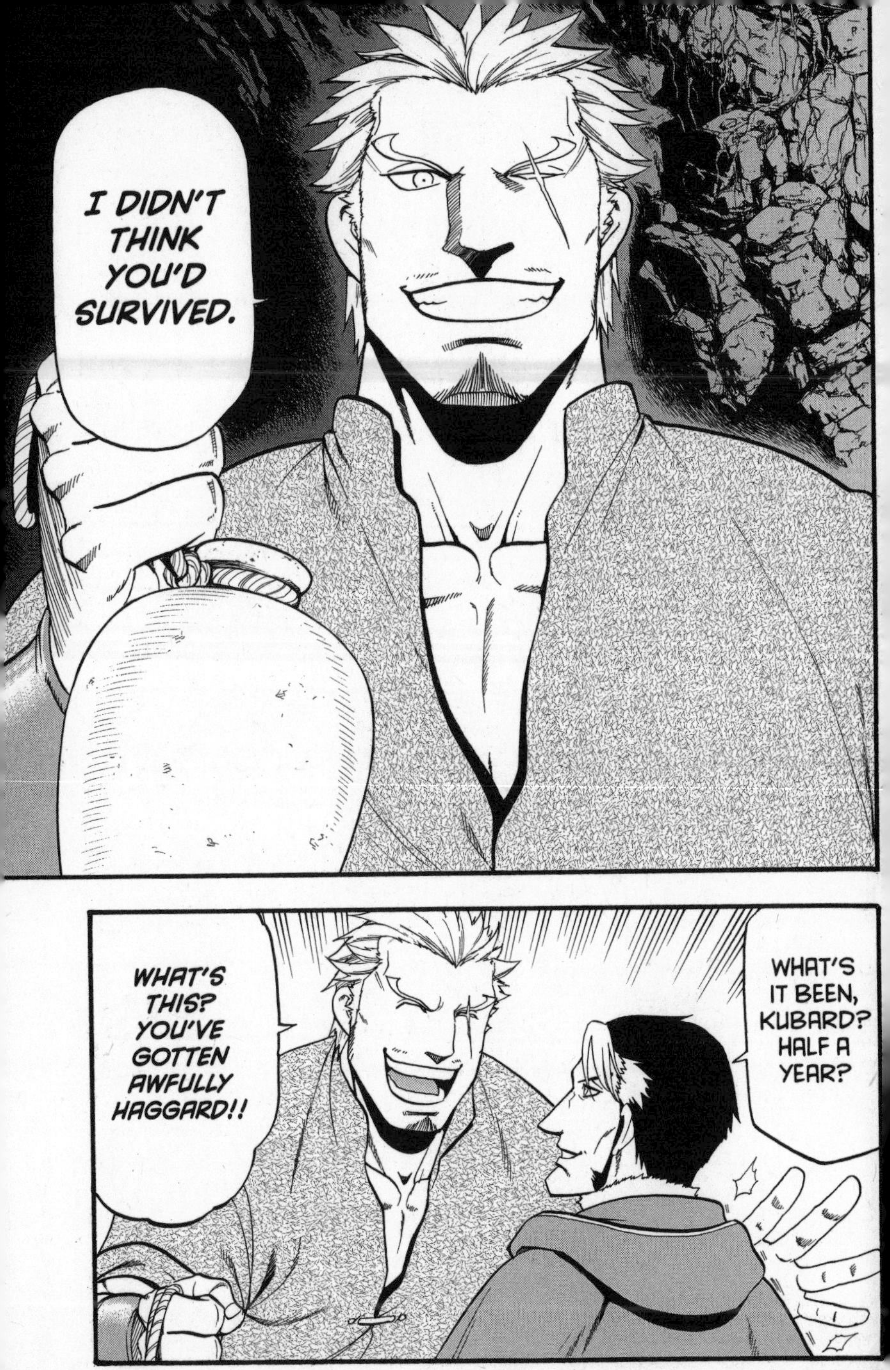
I DIDN'T THINK YOU'D SURVIVED.
WHAT'S IT BEEN, KUBARD? HALF A YEAR?
WHAT'S THIS? YOU'VE GOTTEN AWFULLY HAGGARD!!

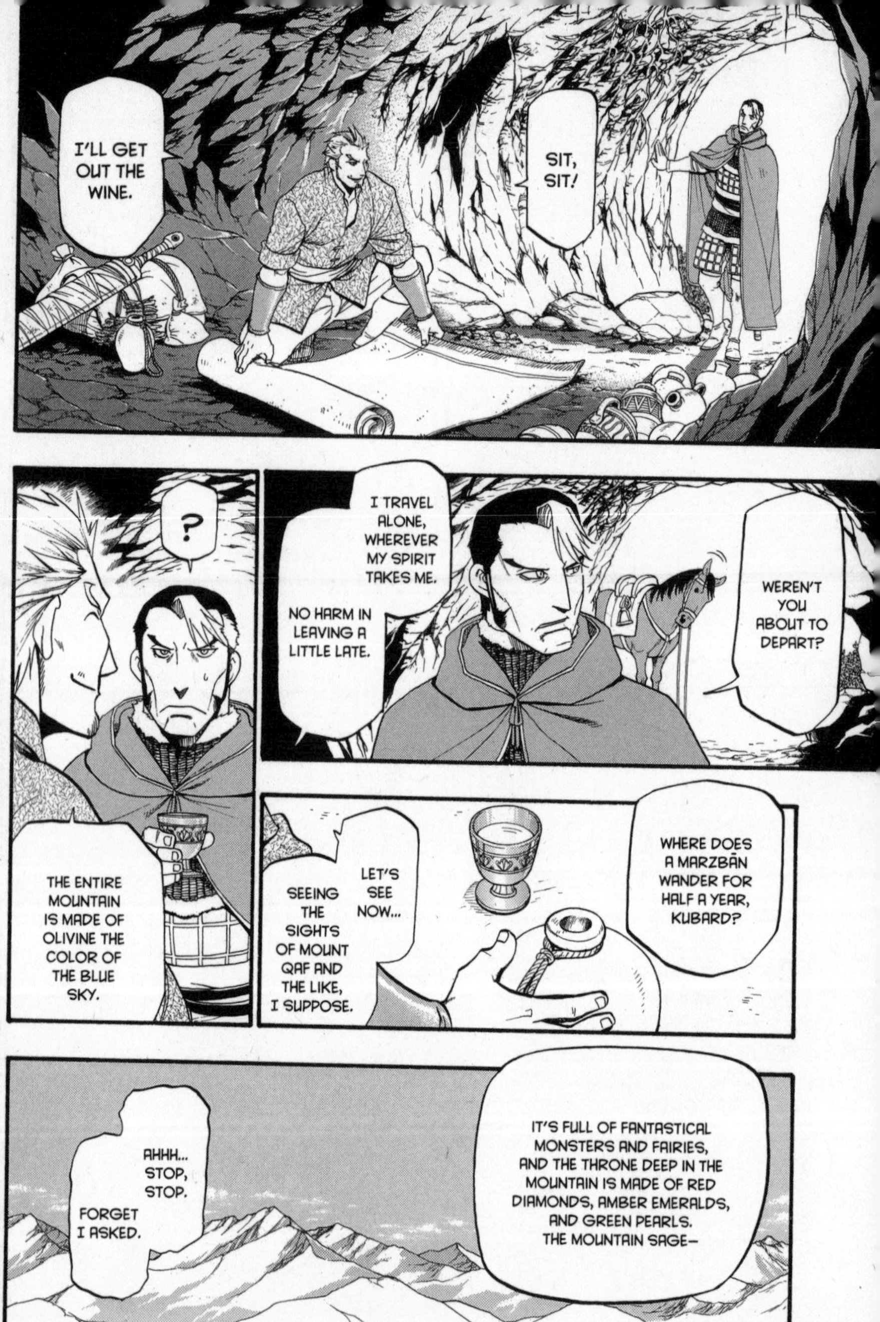
SIT, SIT!
I'LL GET OUT THE WINE.
WEREN'T YOU ABOUT TO DEPART?
I TRAVEL ALONE, WHEREVER MY SPIRIT TAKES ME.
NO HARM IN LEAVING A LITTLE LATE.
WHERE DOES A MARZBĀN WANDER FOR HALF A YEAR, KUBARD?
LET'S SEE NOW...
SEEING THE SIGHTS OF MOUNT QAF AND THE LIKE, I SUPPOSE.
?
THE ENTIRE MOUNTAIN IS MADE OF OLIVINE THE COLOR OF THE BLUE SKY.
IT'S FULL OF FANTASTICAL MONSTERS AND FAIRIES, AND THE THRONE DEEP IN THE MOUNTAIN IS MADE OF RED DIAMONDS, AMBER EMERALDS, AND GREEN PEARLS. THE MOUNTAIN SAGE—
AHHH... STOP, STOP.
FORGET I ASKED.

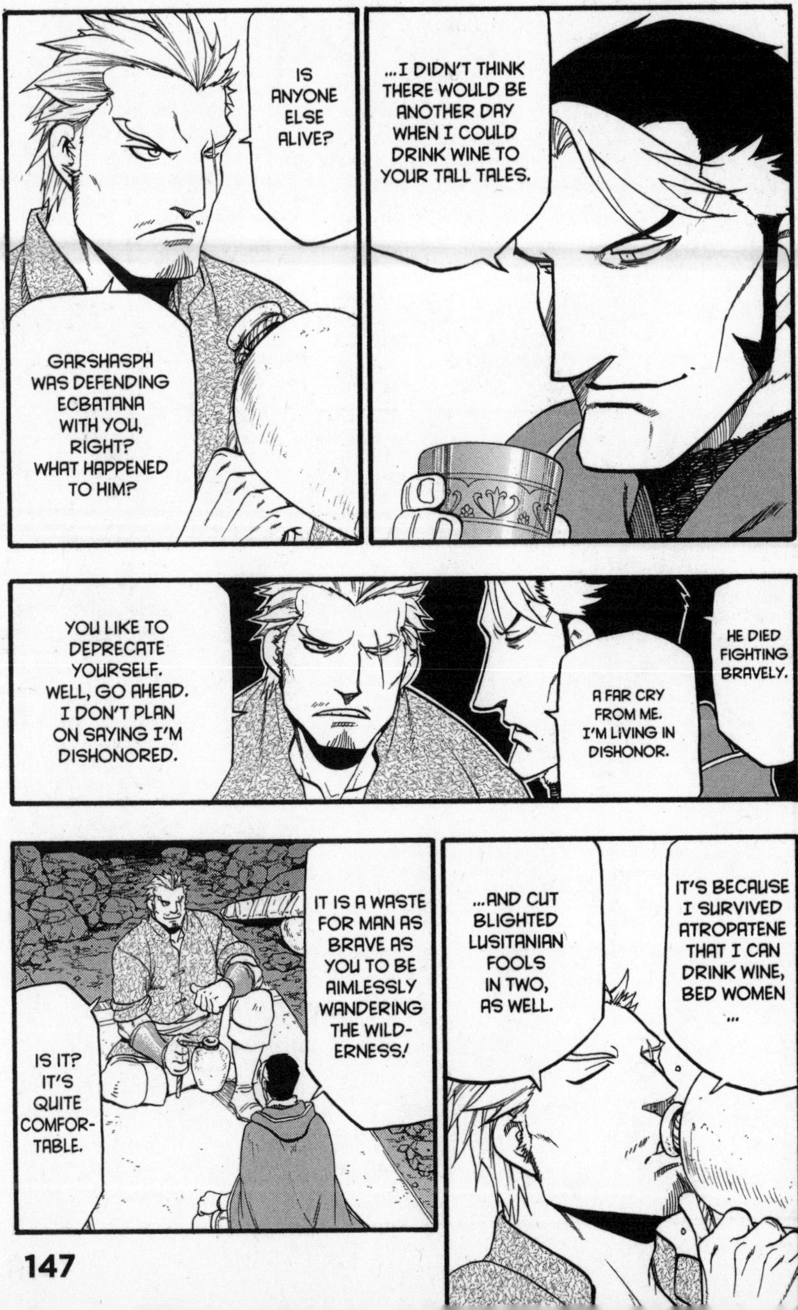
...I DIDN'T THINK THERE WOULD BE ANOTHER DAY WHEN I COULD DRINK WINE TO YOUR TALL TALES.
IS ANYONE ELSE ALIVE?
GARSHASPH WAS DEFENDING ECBATANA WITH YOU, RIGHT? WHAT HAPPENED TO HIM?
HE DIED FIGHTING BRAVELY.
A FAR CRY FROM ME. I'M LIVING IN DISHONOR.
YOU LIKE TO DEPRECATE YOURSELF. WELL, GO AHEAD. I DON'T PLAN ON SAYING I'M DISHONORED.
IT'S BECAUSE I SURVIVED ATROPATENE THAT I CAN DRINK WINE, BED WOMEN ...
...AND CUT BLIGHTED LUSITANIAN FOOLS IN TWO, AS WELL.
IT IS A WASTE FOR MAN AS BRAVE AS YOU TO BE AIMLESSLY WANDERING THE WILDERNESS!
IS IT? IT'S QUITE COMFORTABLE.

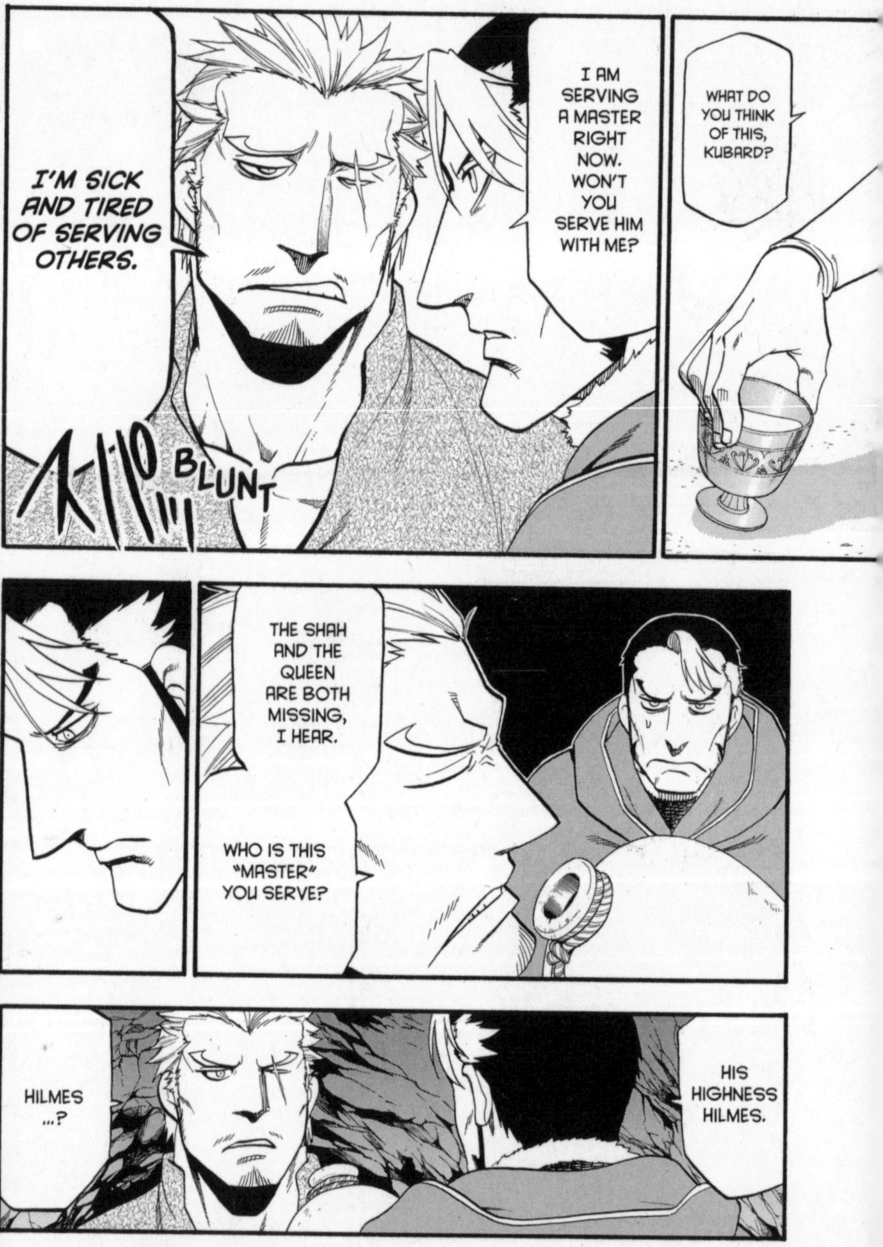
WHAT DO YOU THINK OF THIS, KUBARD?
I AM SERVING A MASTER RIGHT NOW. WON'T YOU SERVE HIM WITH ME?
I'M SICK AND TIRED OF SERVING OTHERS.
BLUNT
THE SHAH AND THE QUEEN ARE BOTH MISSING, I HEAR.
WHO IS THIS "MASTER" YOU SERVE?
HIS HIGHNESS HILMES.
HILMES ...?

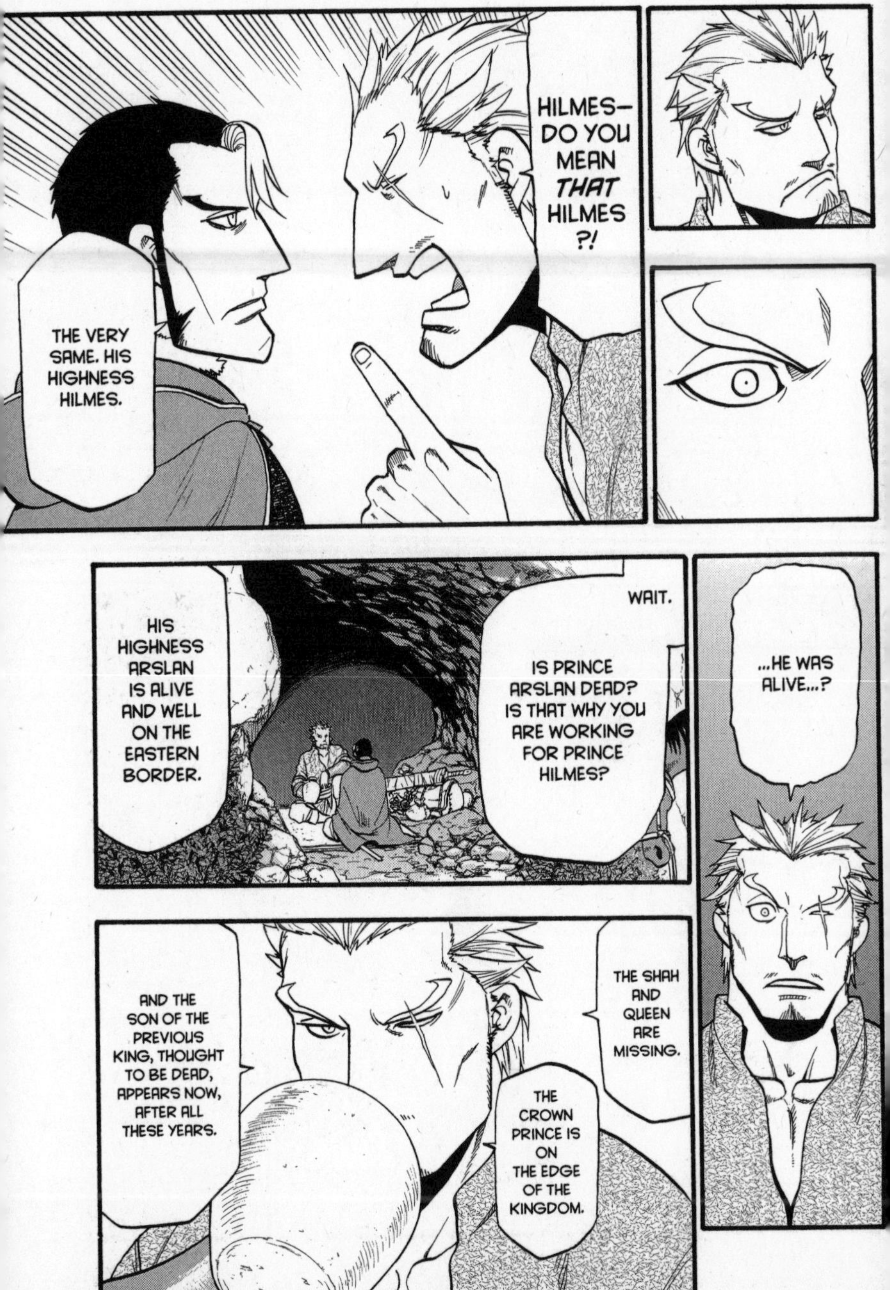
HILMES— DO YOU MEAN *THAT* HILMES ?!
THE VERY SAME. HIS HIGHNESS HILMES.
...HE WAS ALIVE...?
WAIT.
IS PRINCE ARSLAN DEAD? IS THAT WHY YOU ARE WORKING FOR PRINCE HILMES?
HIS HIGHNESS ARSLAN IS ALIVE AND WELL ON THE EASTERN BORDER.
THE SHAH AND QUEEN ARE MISSING.
THE CROWN PRINCE IS ON THE EDGE OF THE KINGDOM.
AND THE SON OF THE PREVIOUS KING, THOUGHT TO BE DEAD, APPEARS NOW, AFTER ALL THESE YEARS.

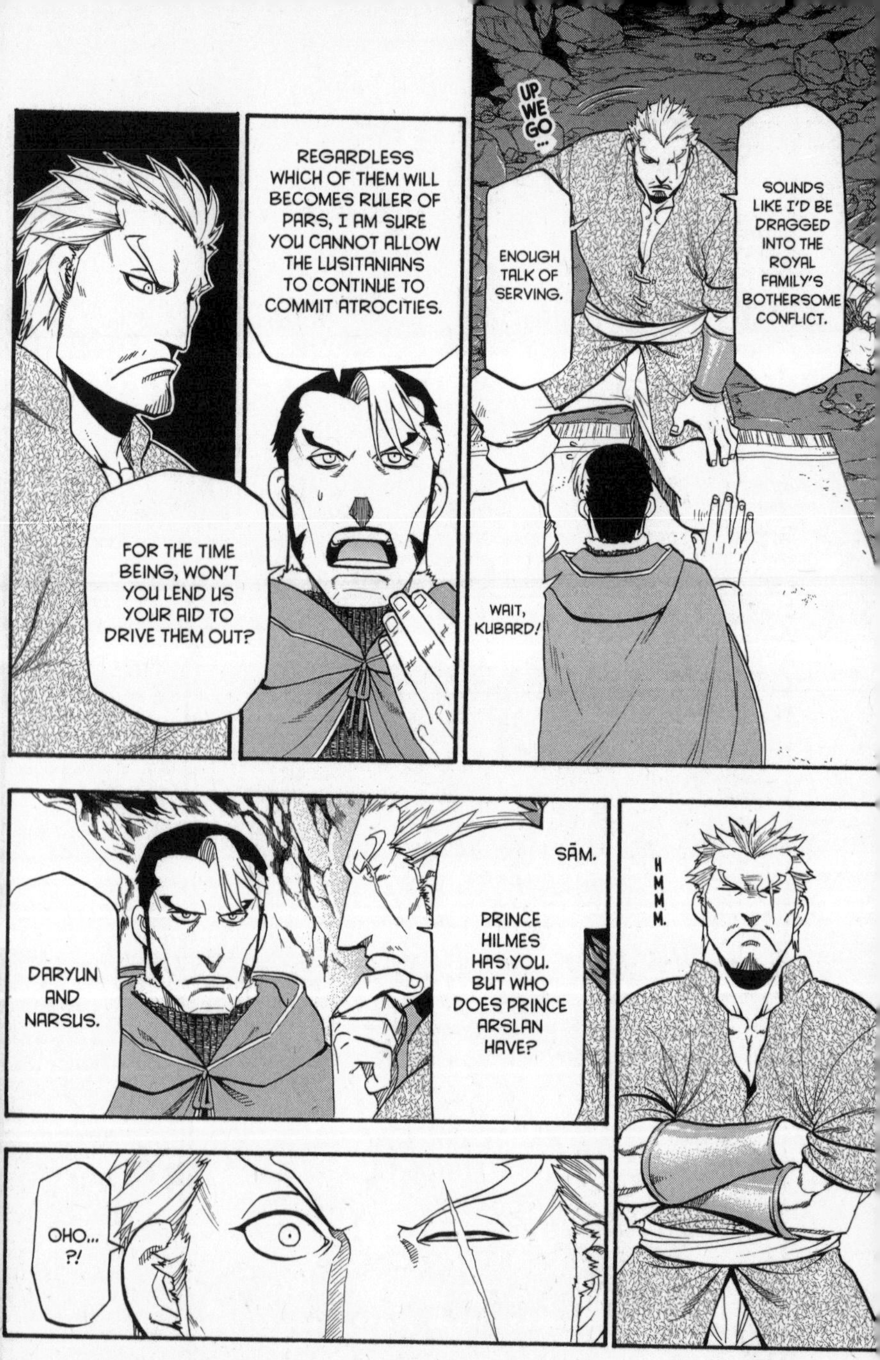
UP WE GO...
SOUNDS LIKE I'D BE DRAGGED INTO THE ROYAL FAMILY'S BOTHERSOME CONFLICT.
ENOUGH TALK OF SERVING.
WAIT, KUBARD!
REGARDLESS WHICH OF THEM WILL BECOMES RULER OF PARS, I AM SURE YOU CANNOT ALLOW THE LUSITANIANS TO CONTINUE TO COMMIT ATROCITIES.
FOR THE TIME BEING, WON'T YOU LEND US YOUR AID TO DRIVE THEM OUT?
HMMMM.
SĀM.
PRINCE HILMES HAS YOU. BUT WHO DOES PRINCE ARSLAN HAVE?
DARYUN AND NARSUS.
OHO... ?!

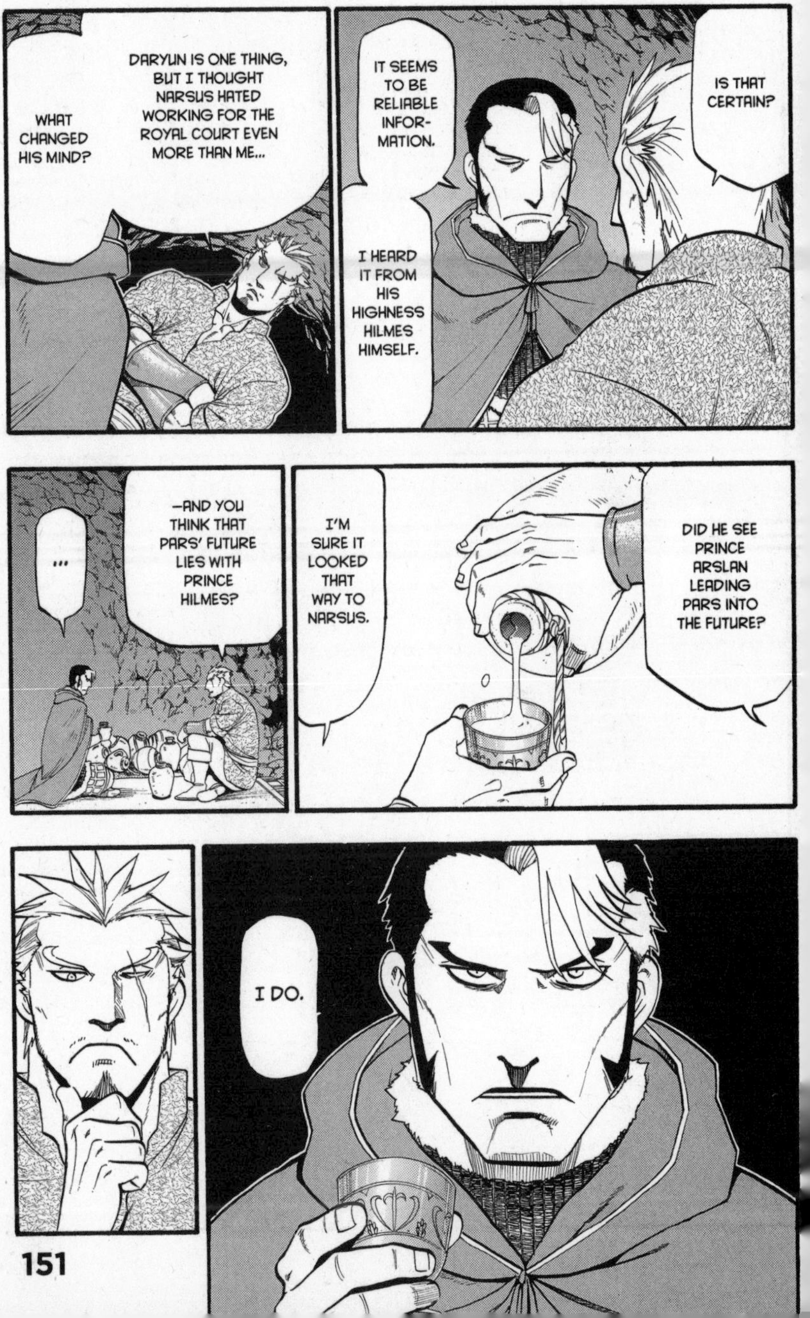
IS THAT CERTAIN?
IT SEEMS TO BE RELIABLE INFORMATION.
I HEARD IT FROM HIS HIGHNESS HILMES HIMSELF.
DARYUN IS ONE THING, BUT I THOUGHT NARSUS HATED WORKING FOR THE ROYAL COURT EVEN MORE THAN ME...
WHAT CHANGED HIS MIND?
DID HE SEE PRINCE ARSLAN LEADING PARS INTO THE FUTURE?
I'M SURE IT LOOKED THAT WAY TO NARSUS.
—AND YOU THINK THAT PARS' FUTURE LIES WITH PRINCE HILMES?
...
I DO.

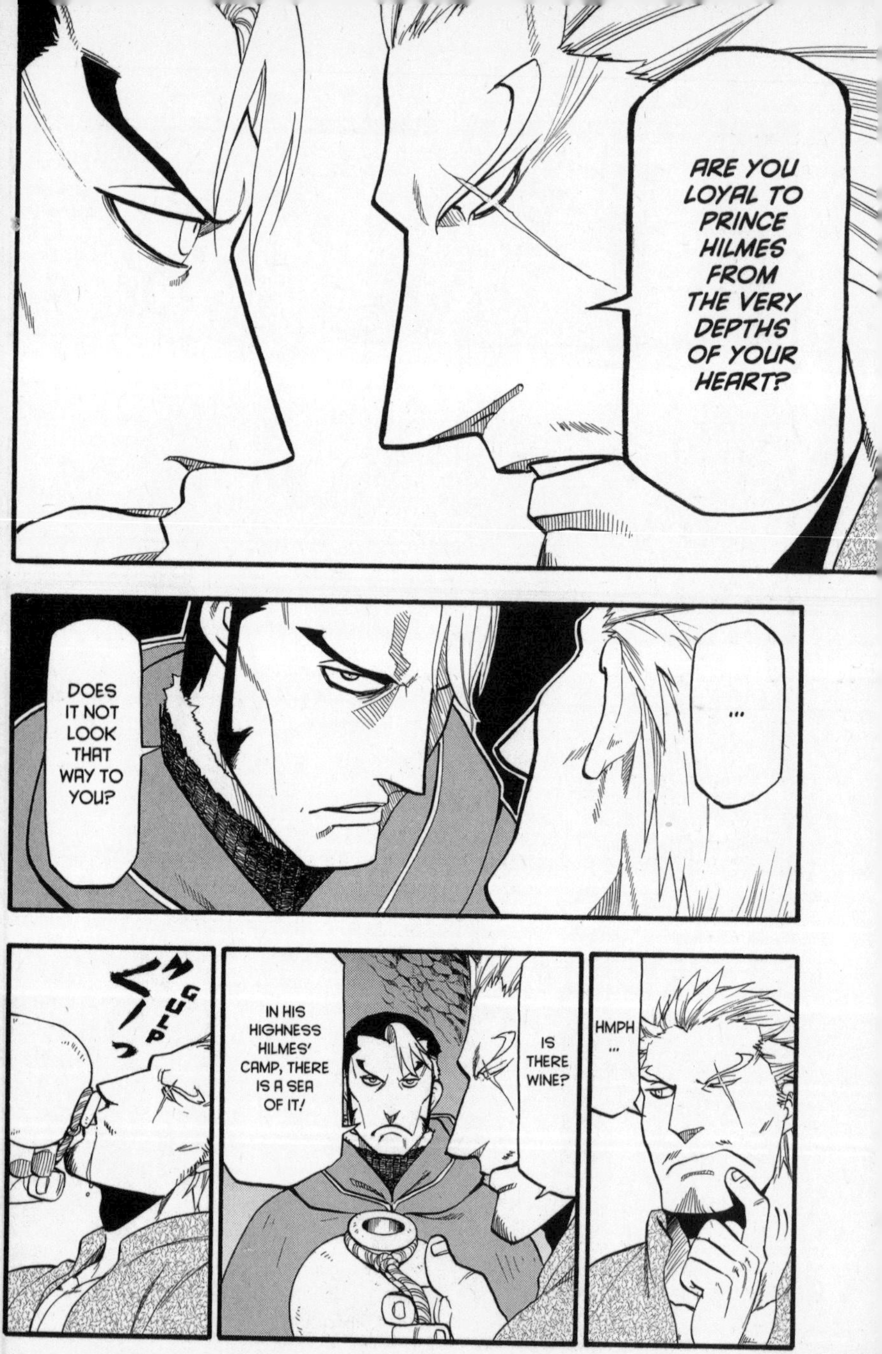
ARE YOU LOYAL TO PRINCE HILMES FROM THE VERY DEPTHS OF YOUR HEART?
...
DOES IT NOT LOOK THAT WAY TO YOU?
HMPH ...
IS THERE WINE?
IN HIS HIGHNESS HILMES' CAMP, THERE IS A SEA OF IT!
GULP

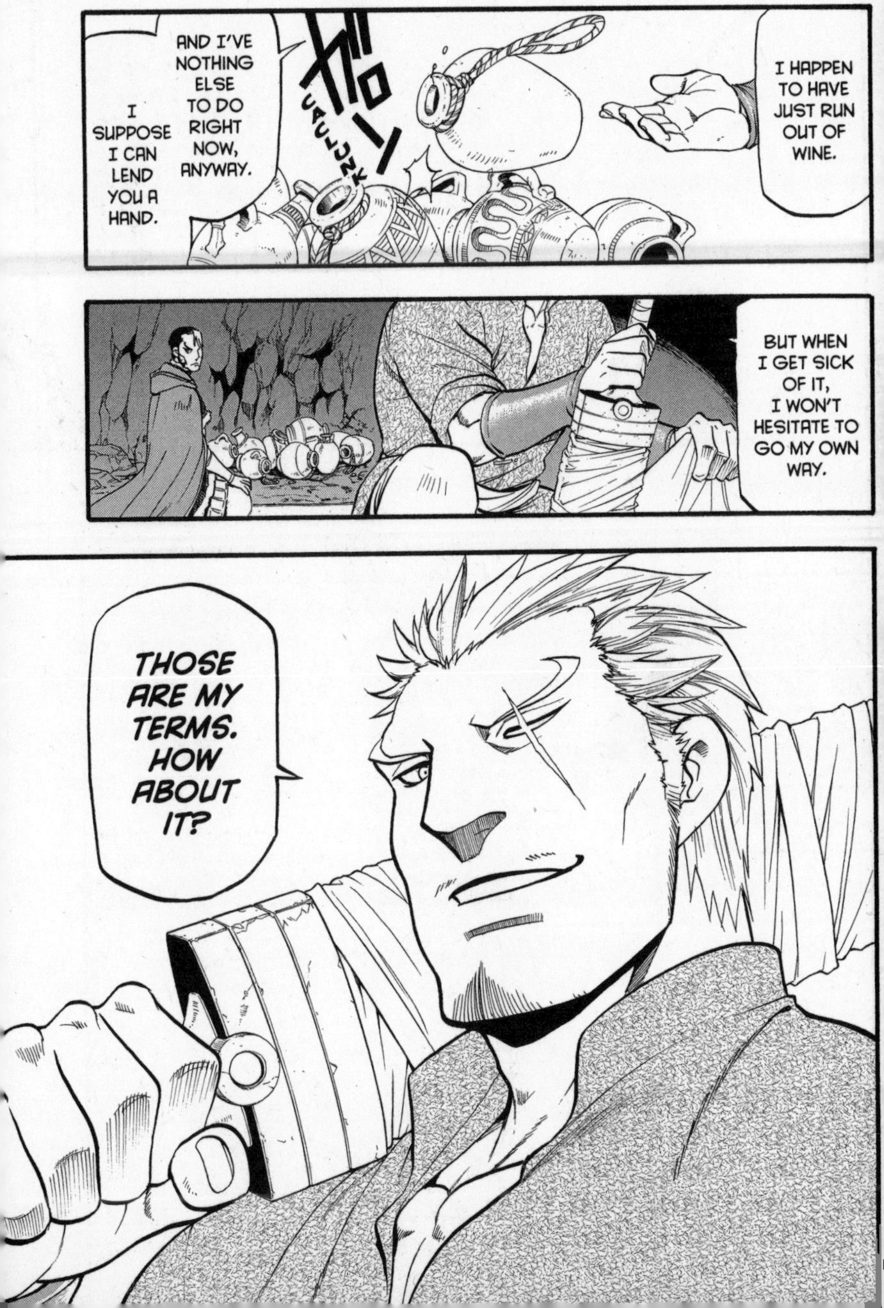
I HAPPEN TO HAVE JUST RUN OUT OF WINE.
AND I'VE NOTHING ELSE TO DO RIGHT NOW, ANYWAY.
I SUPPOSE I CAN LEND YOU A HAND.
BUT WHEN I GET SICK OF IT, I WON'T HESITATE TO GO MY OWN WAY.
THOSE ARE MY TERMS. HOW ABOUT IT?

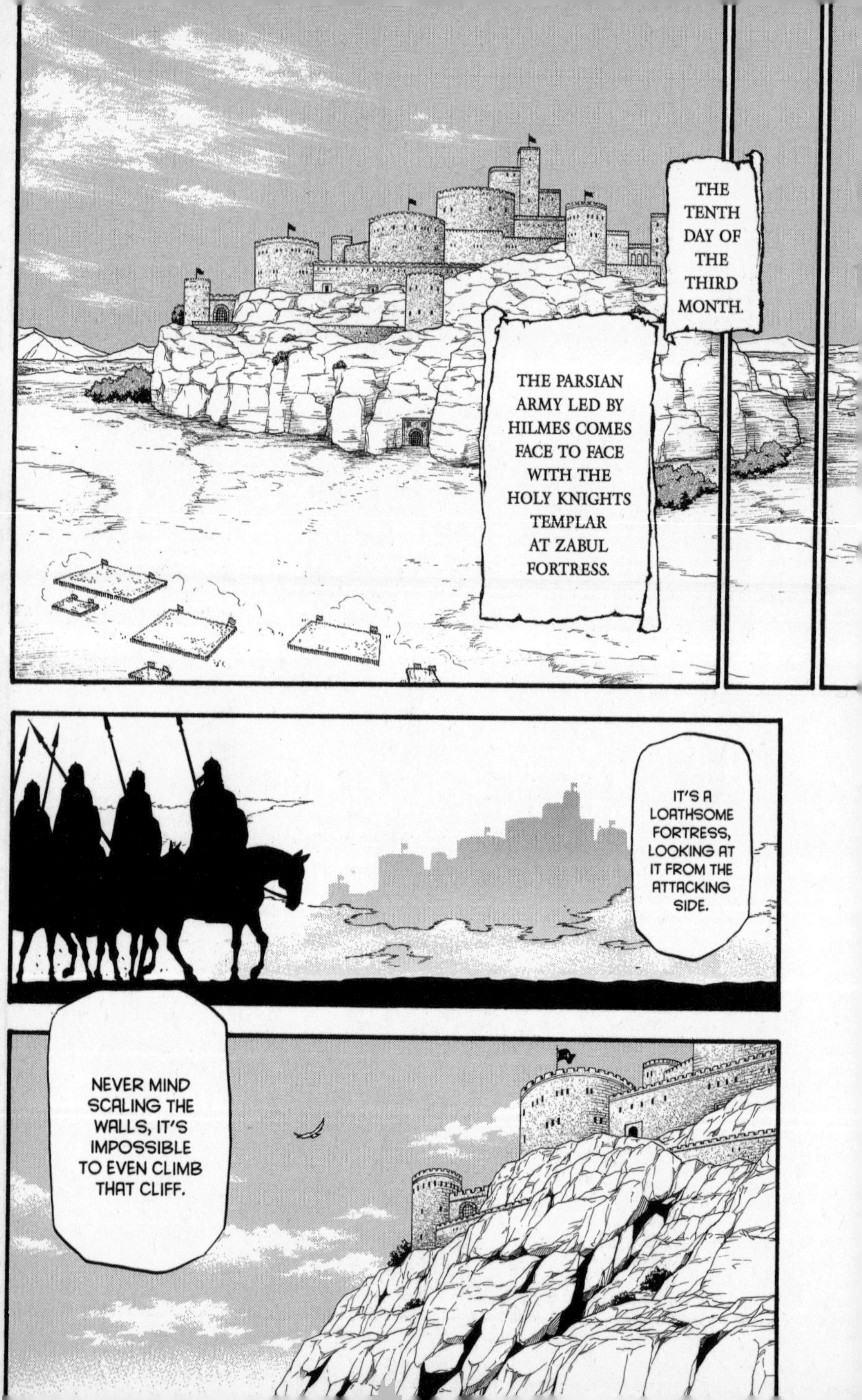
THE TENTH DAY OF THE THIRD MONTH.
THE PARSIAN ARMY LED BY HILMES COMES FACE TO FACE WITH THE HOLY KNIGHTS TEMPLAR AT ZABUL FORTRESS.
IT'S A LOATHSOME FORTRESS, LOOKING AT IT FROM THE ATTACKING SIDE.
NEVER MIND SCALING THE WALLS, IT'S IMPOSSIBLE TO EVEN CLIMB THAT CLIFF.

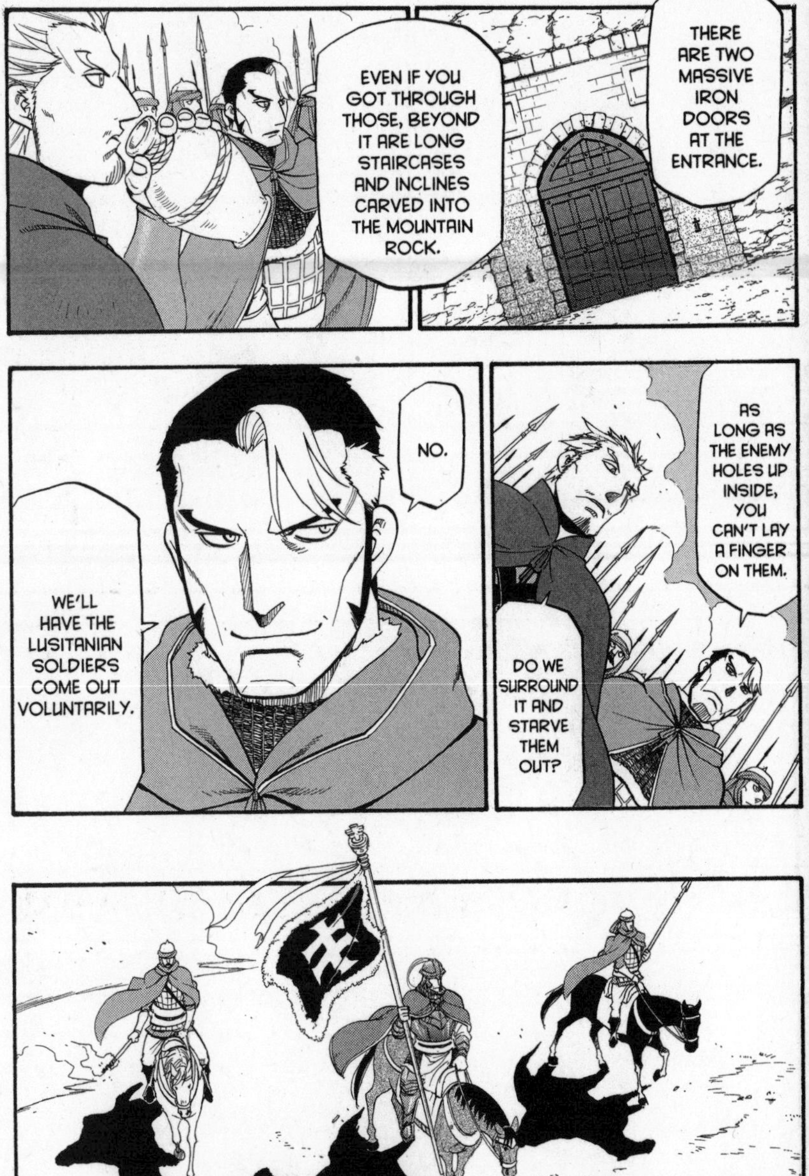
THERE ARE TWO MASSIVE IRON DOORS AT THE ENTRANCE.
EVEN IF YOU GOT THROUGH THOSE, BEYOND IT ARE LONG STAIRCASES AND INCLINES CARVED INTO THE MOUNTAIN ROCK.
AS LONG AS THE ENEMY HOLES UP INSIDE, YOU CAN'T LAY A FINGER ON THEM.
DO WE SURROUND IT AND STARVE THEM OUT?
NO.
WE'LL HAVE THE LUSITANIAN SOLDIERS COME OUT VOLUNTARILY.

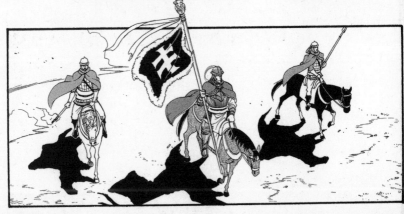

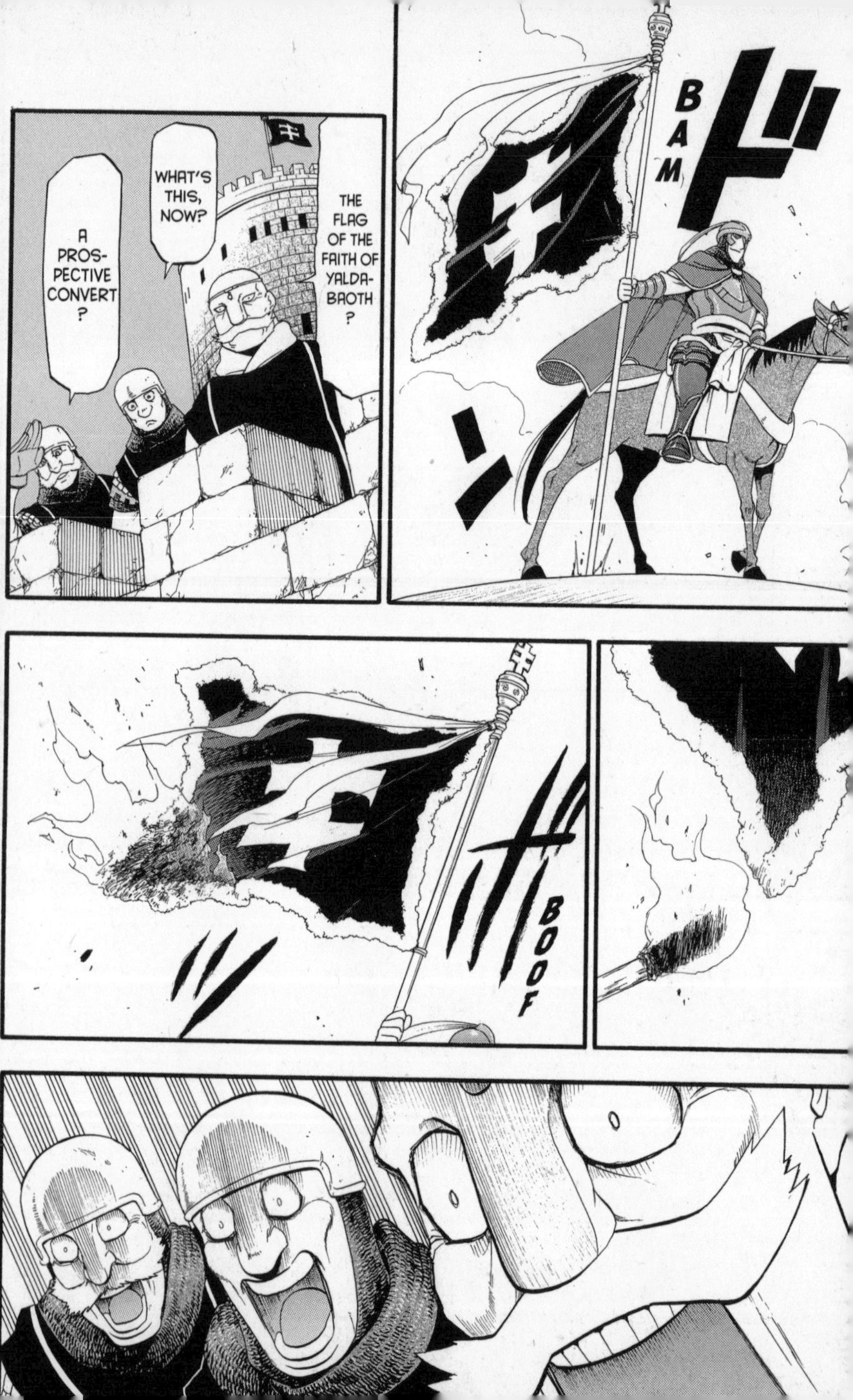
BAM
ドン
THE FLAG OF THE FAITH OF YALDA-BAOTH?
WHAT'S THIS, NOW?
A PROS-PECTIVE CONVERT?
BOOF

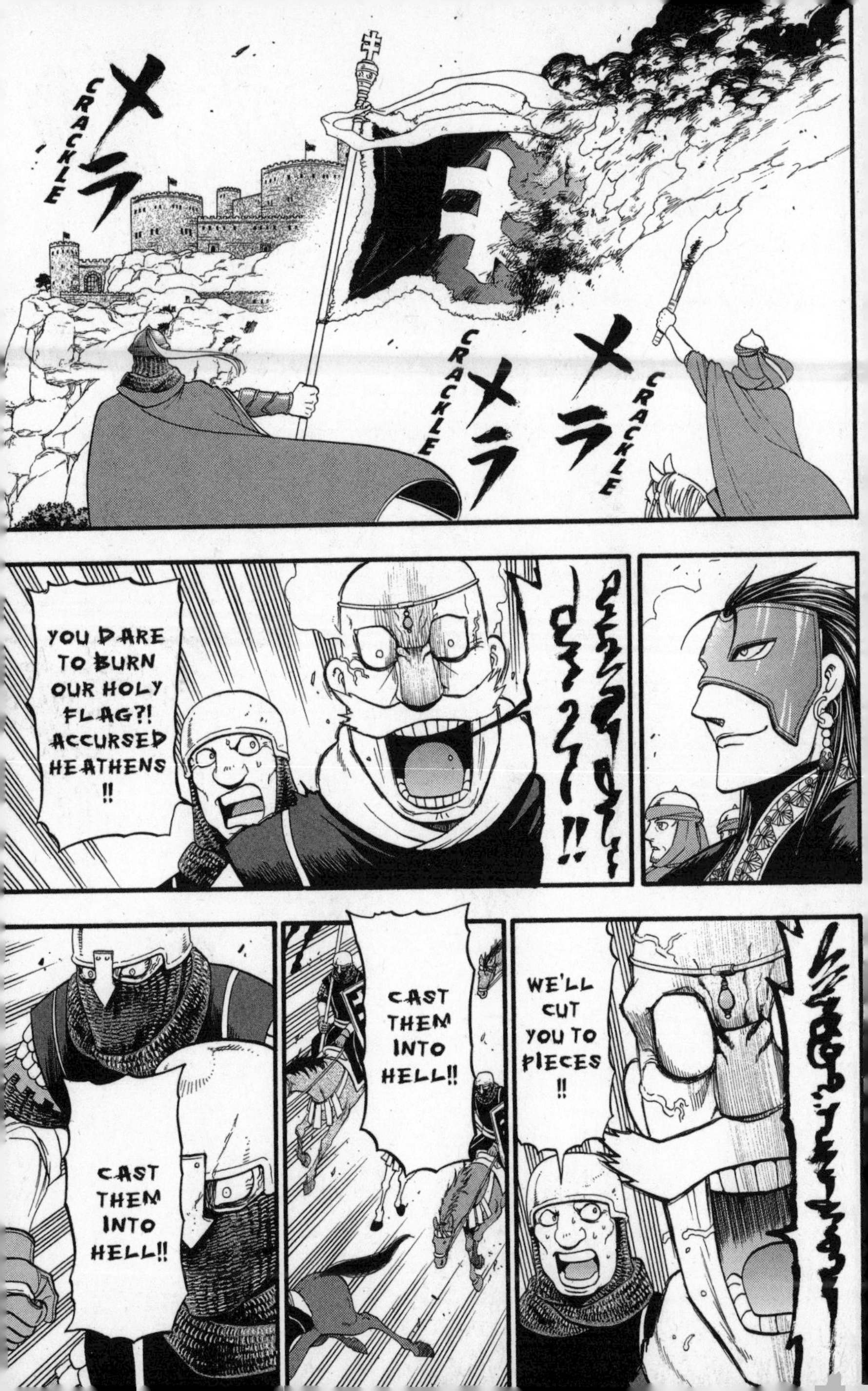

メラ
CRACKLE
メラ
CRACKLE
メラ
CRACKLE
YOU DARE TO BURN OUR HOLY FLAG?! ACCURSED HEATHENS!!
WE'LL CUT YOU TO PIECES!!
CAST THEM INTO HELL!!
CAST THEM INTO HELL!!

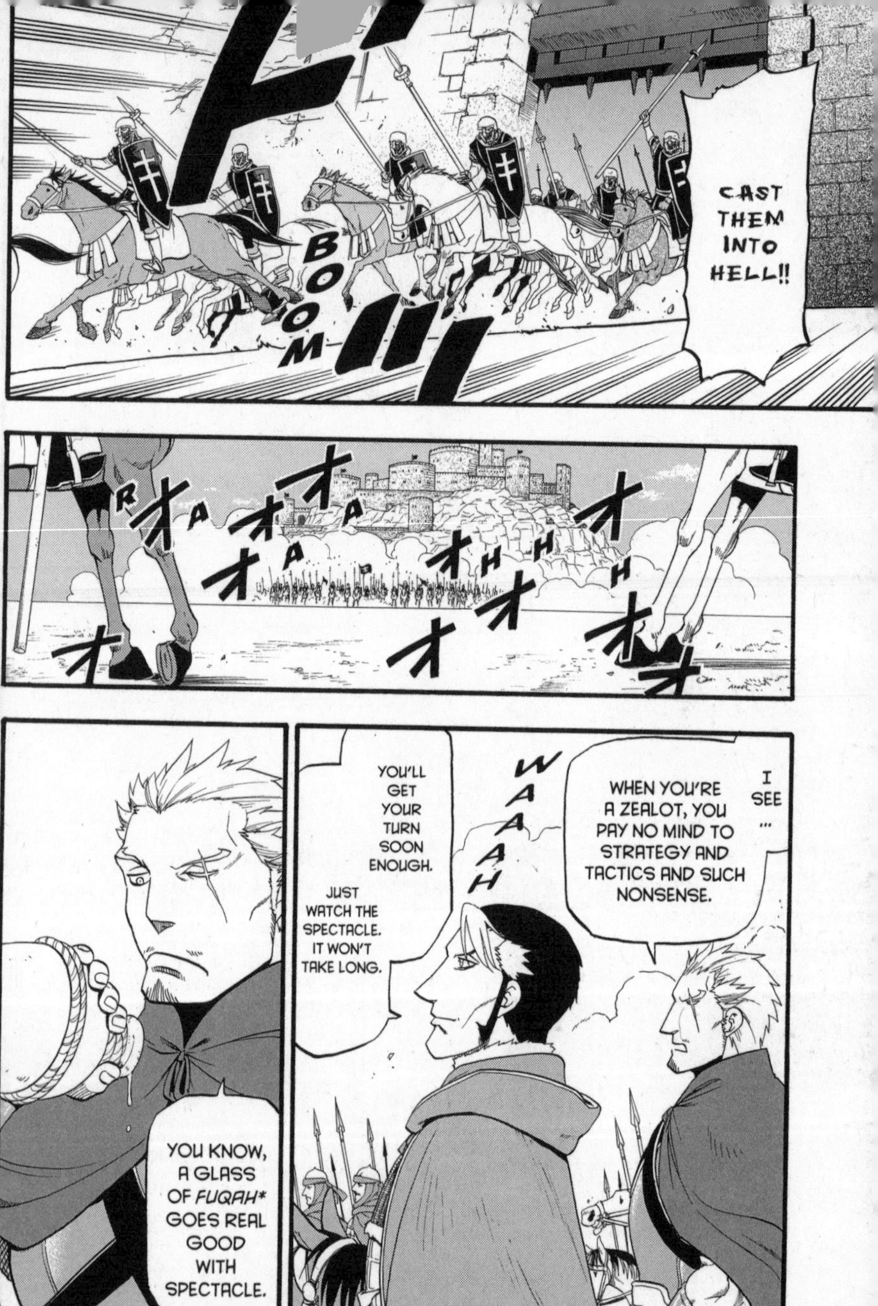
CAST THEM INTO HELL!!
BOOOM
RAAAHHH
I SEE ...
WHEN YOU'RE A ZEALOT, YOU PAY NO MIND TO STRATEGY AND TACTICS AND SUCH NONSENSE.
WAAAAH
YOU'LL GET YOUR TURN SOON ENOUGH.
JUST WATCH THE SPECTACLE. IT WON'T TAKE LONG.
YOU KNOW, A GLASS OF *FUQAH** GOES REAL GOOD WITH SPECTACLE.

*BARLEY WINE

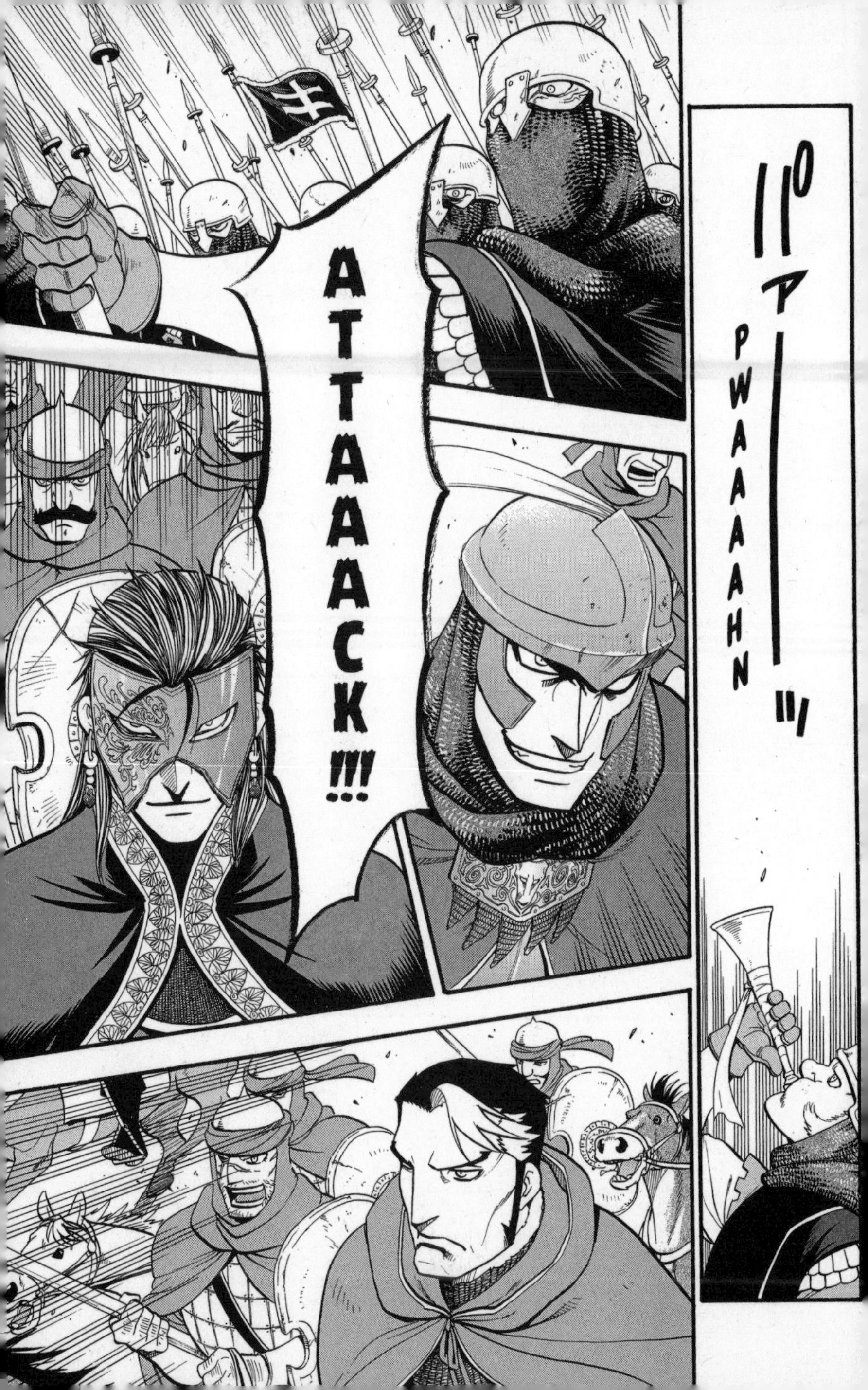
PWAAAAAAHN
ATTAAACK!!!

THE HEROIC LEGEND OF
ARSLAN

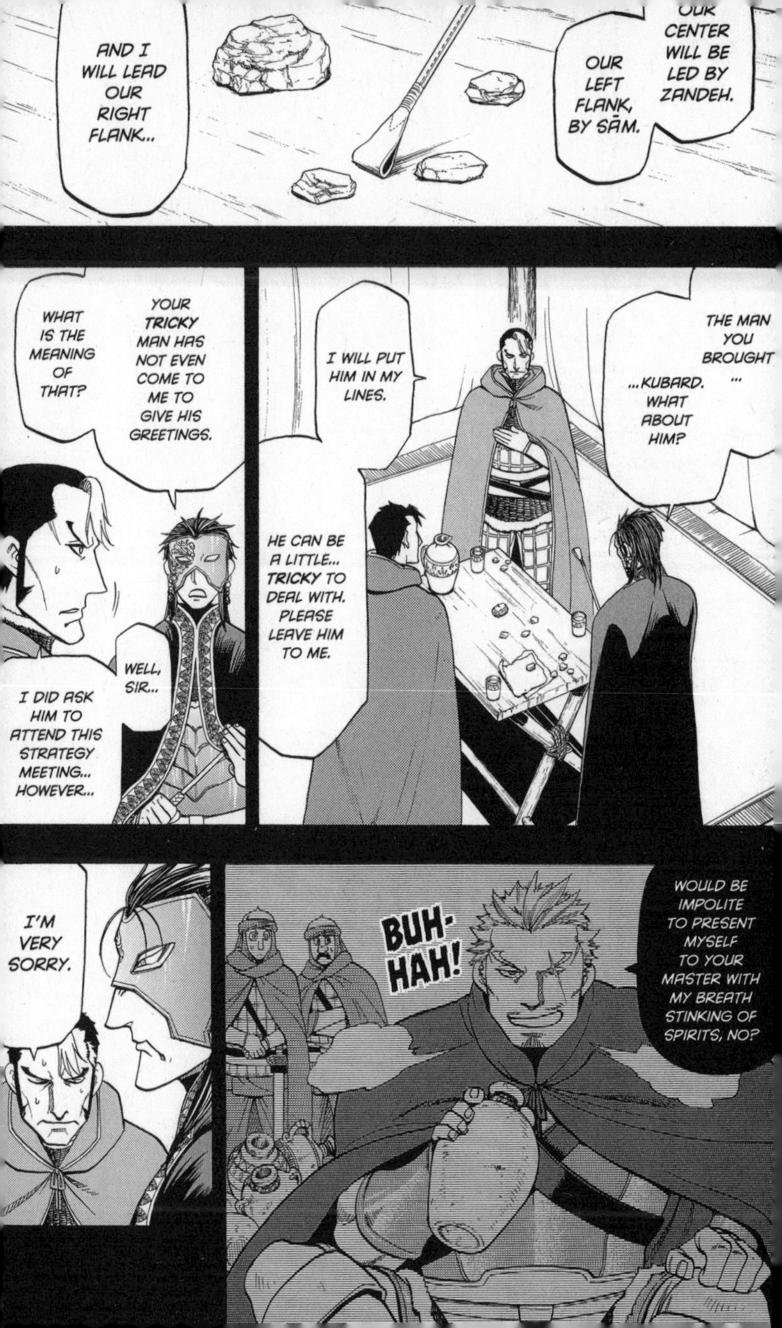
OUR CENTER WILL BE LED BY ZANDEH.
OUR LEFT FLANK, BY SĀM.
AND I WILL LEAD OUR RIGHT FLANK...
THE MAN YOU BROUGHT...
...KUBARD. WHAT ABOUT HIM?
I WILL PUT HIM IN MY LINES.
HE CAN BE A LITTLE... TRICKY TO DEAL WITH. PLEASE LEAVE HIM TO ME.
YOUR TRICKY MAN HAS NOT EVEN COME TO ME TO GIVE HIS GREETINGS.
WHAT IS THE MEANING OF THAT?
WELL, SIR...
I DID ASK HIM TO ATTEND THIS STRATEGY MEETING... HOWEVER...
WOULD BE IMPOLITE TO PRESENT MYSELF TO YOUR MASTER WITH MY BREATH STINKING OF SPIRITS, NO?
BUH-HAH!
I'M VERY SORRY.

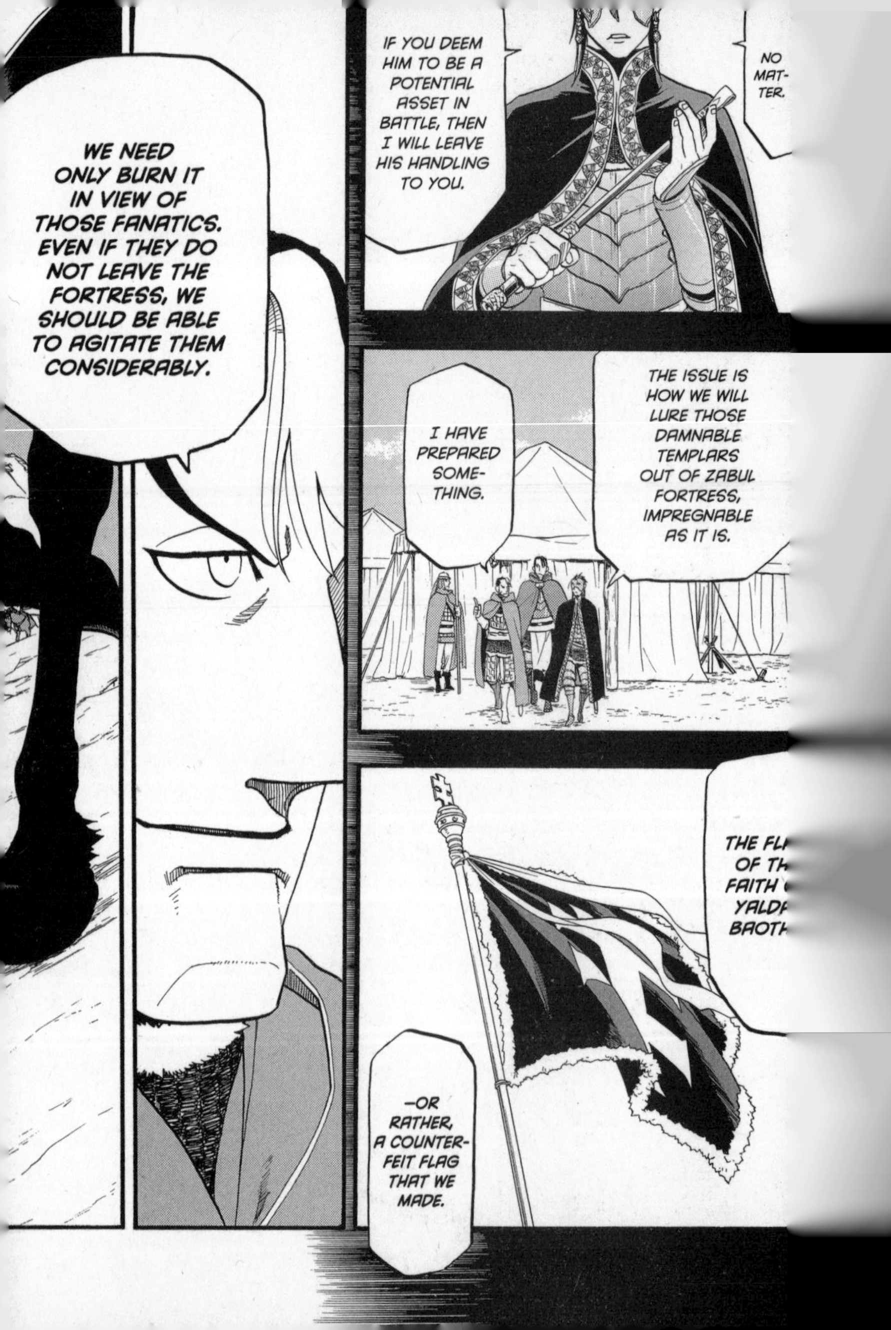
NO MATTER.
IF YOU DEEM HIM TO BE A POTENTIAL ASSET IN BATTLE, THEN I WILL LEAVE HIS HANDLING TO YOU.
THE ISSUE IS HOW WE WILL LURE THOSE DAMNABLE TEMPLARS OUT OF ZABUL FORTRESS, IMPREGNABLE AS IT IS.
I HAVE PREPARED SOMETHING.
THE FL OF TH FAITH YALDA BAOTH
—OR RATHER, A COUNTERFEIT FLAG THAT WE MADE.
WE NEED ONLY BURN IT IN VIEW OF THOSE FANATICS. EVEN IF THEY DO NOT LEAVE THE FORTRESS, WE SHOULD BE ABLE TO AGITATE THEM CONSIDERABLY.

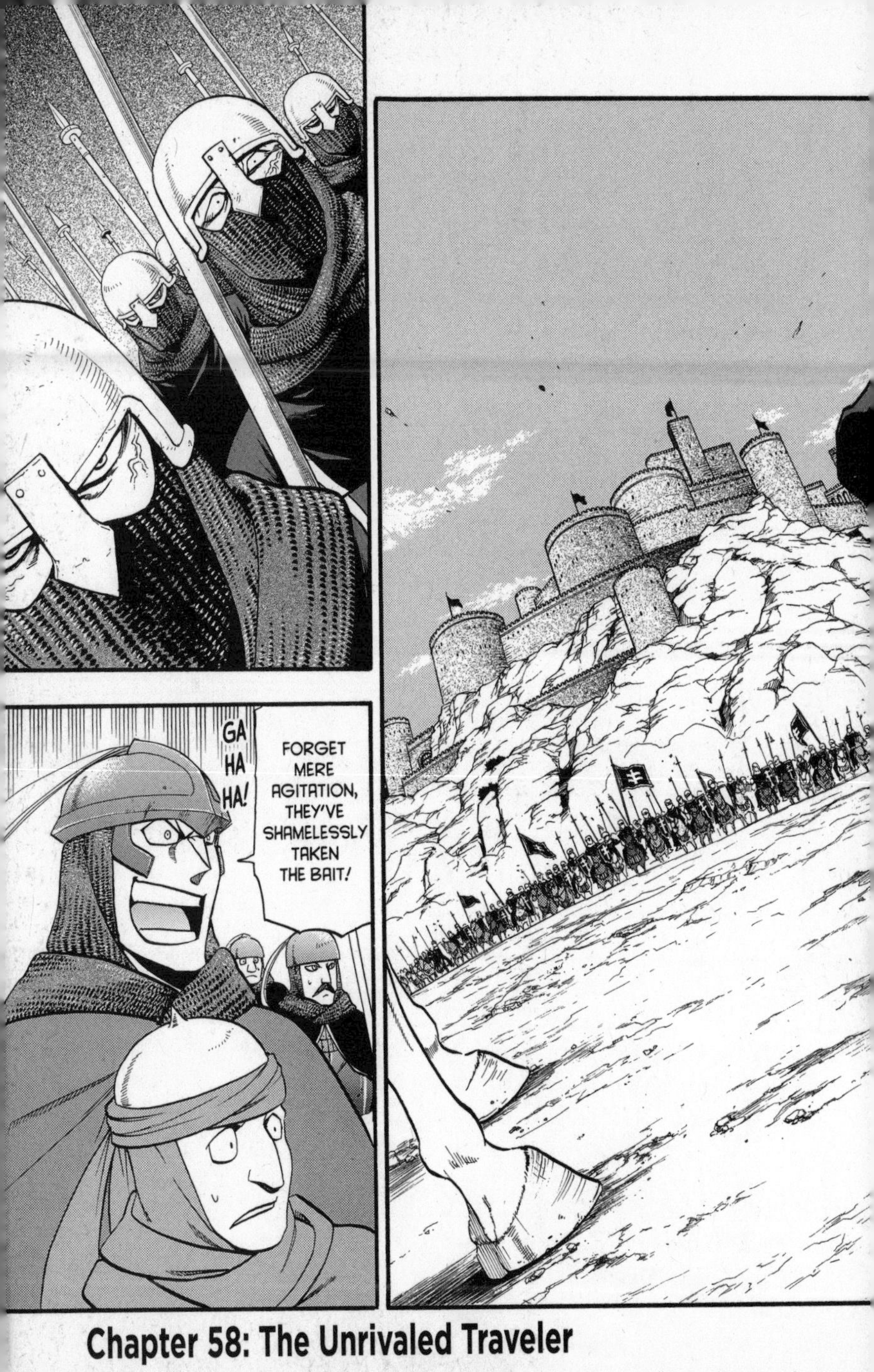
GA HA HA!
FORGET MERE AGITATION, THEY'VE SHAMELESSLY TAKEN THE BAIT!

Chapter 58: The Unrivaled Traveler

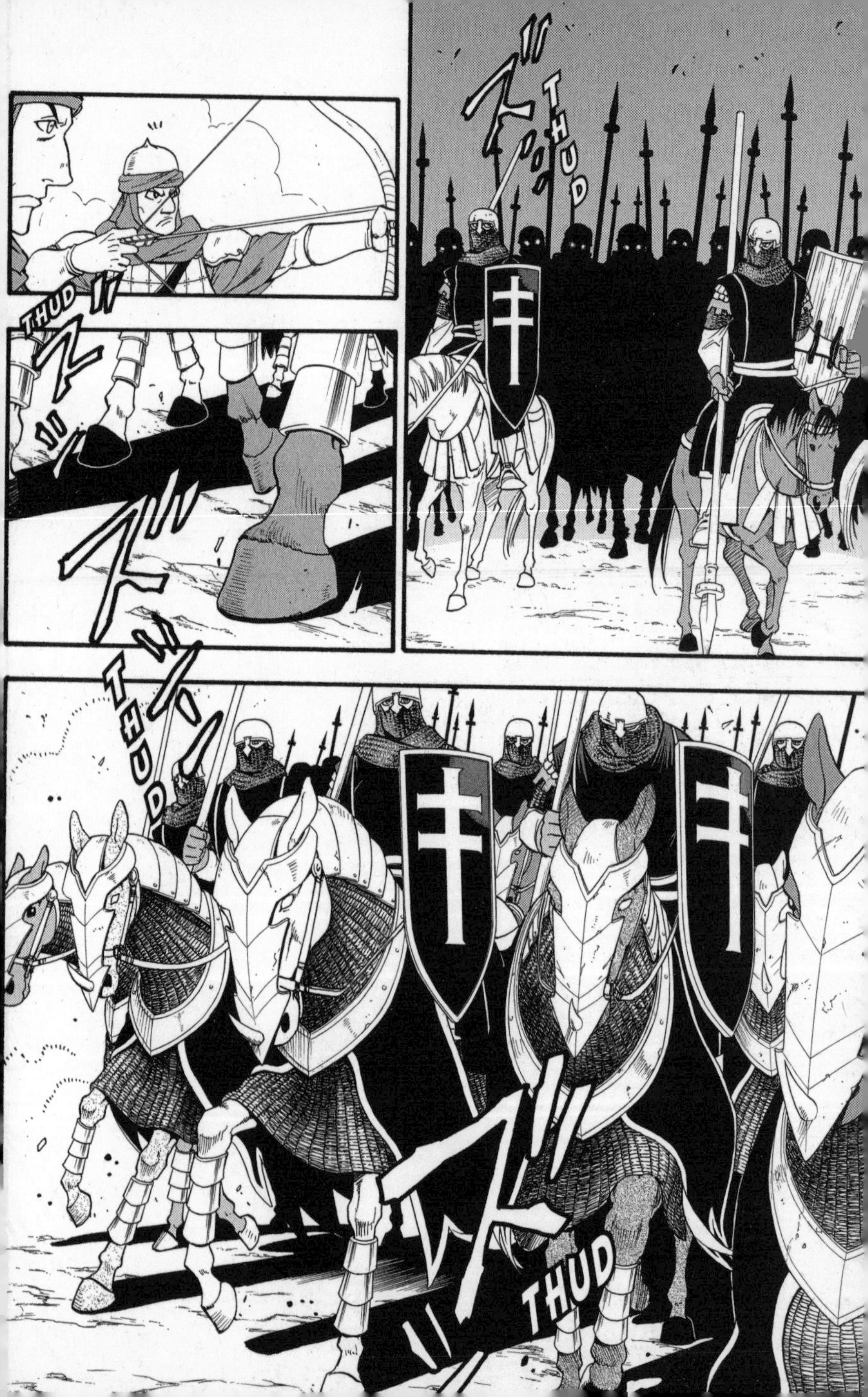
THUD
THUD
THUD
THUD

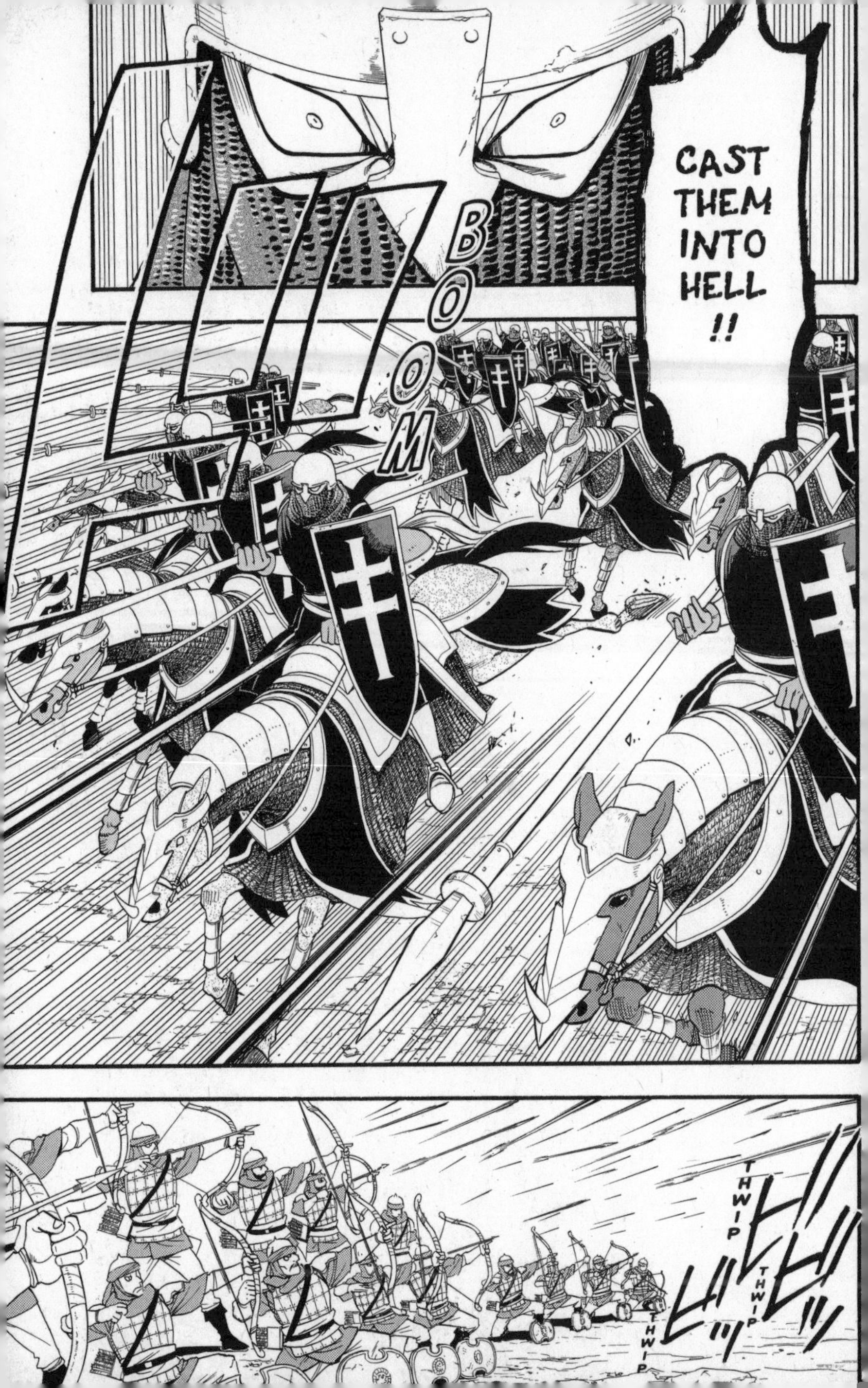
CAST THEM INTO HELL !!
BOOM
THWIP
THWIP
THWIP

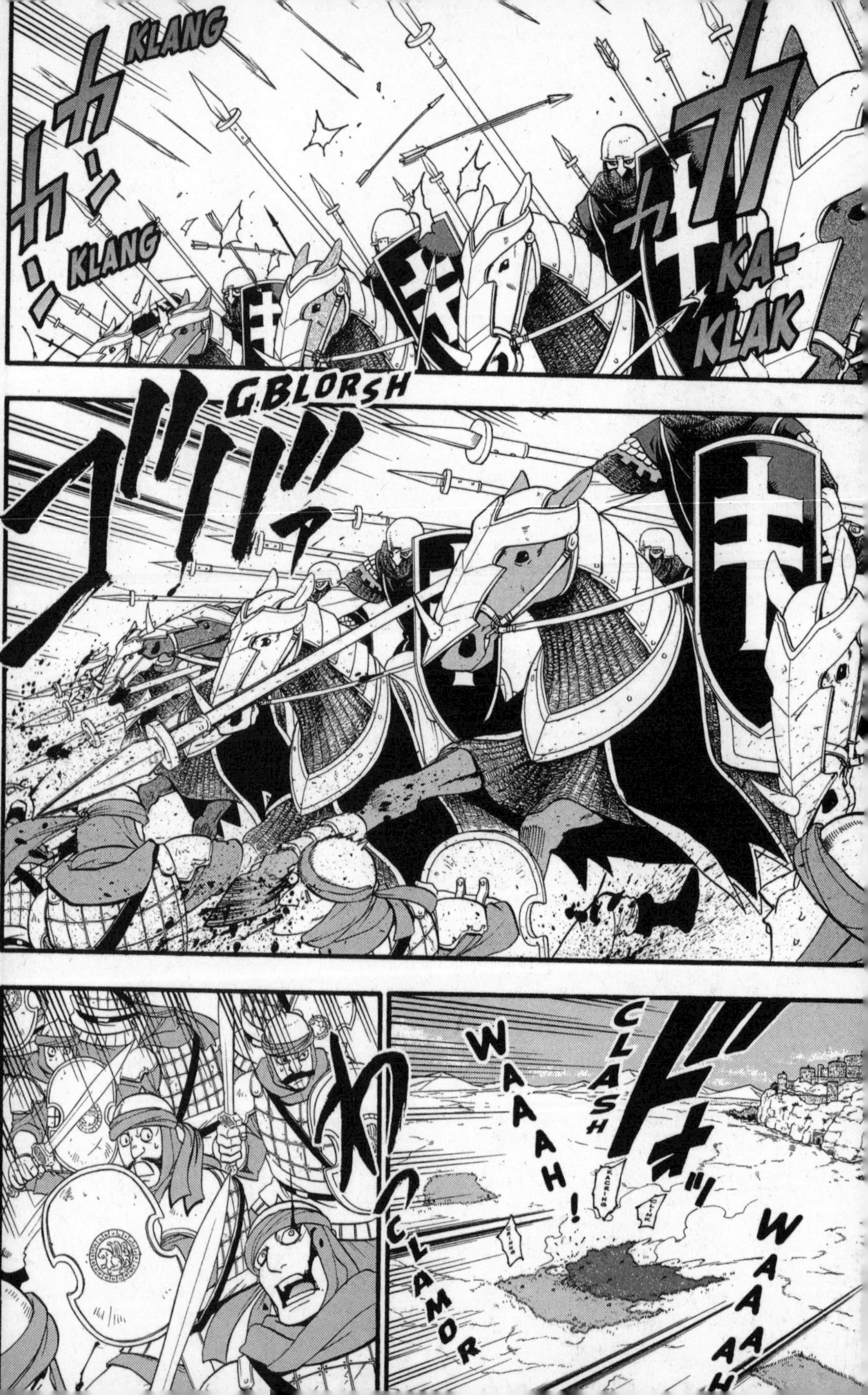
KA-KLAK
KLANG
KLANG
GBLORSH
CLASH
WAAAH!
WAAAAH
CLAMOR

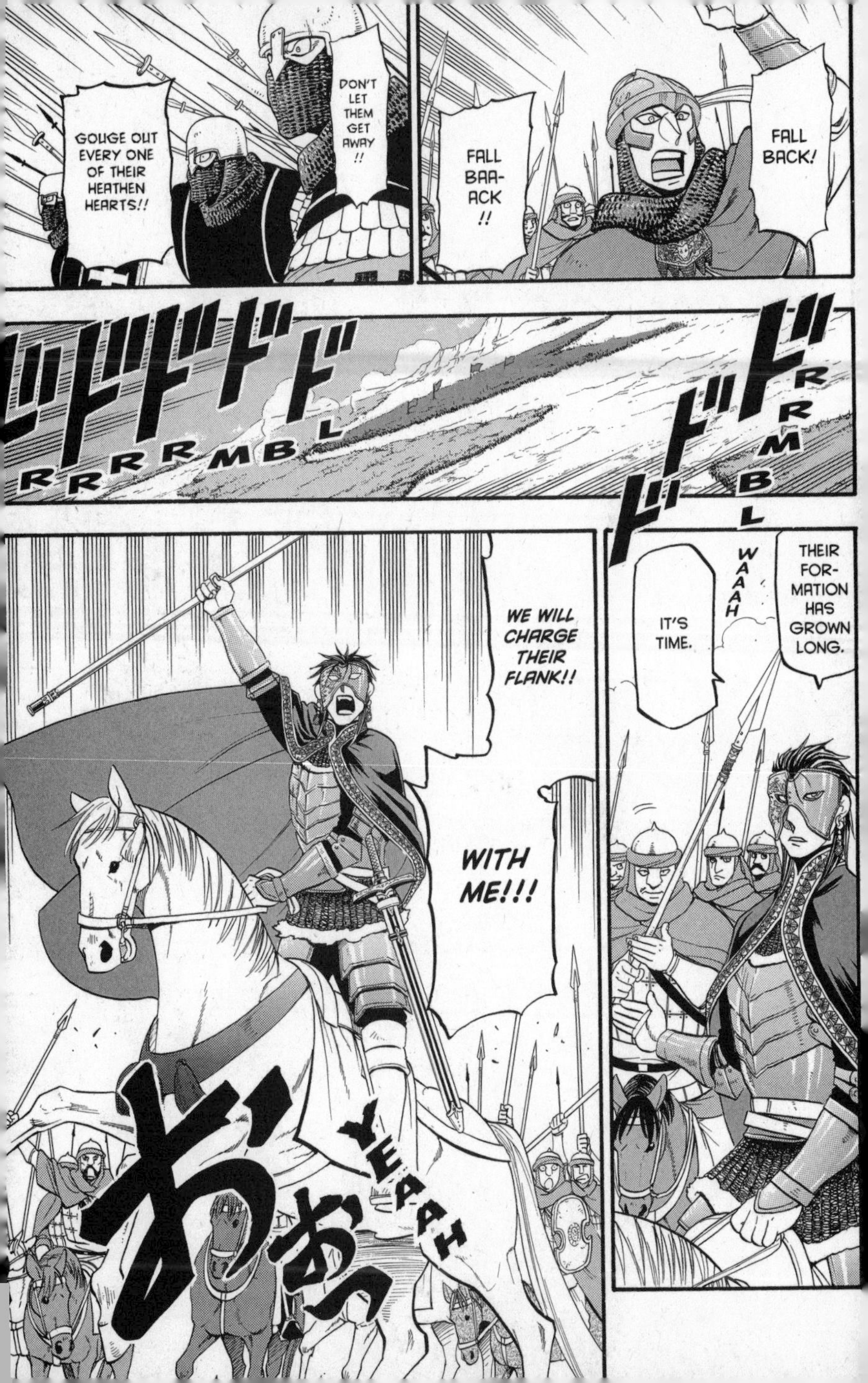
FALL BACK!
FALL BAAACK!!
DON'T LET THEM GET AWAY!!
GOUGE OUT EVERY ONE OF THEIR HEATHEN HEARTS!!
RRRMBL
RRRRRMBL
THEIR FORMATION HAS GROWN LONG.
WAAAH
IT'S TIME.
WE WILL CHARGE THEIR FLANK!!
WITH ME!!!
YEAAAH

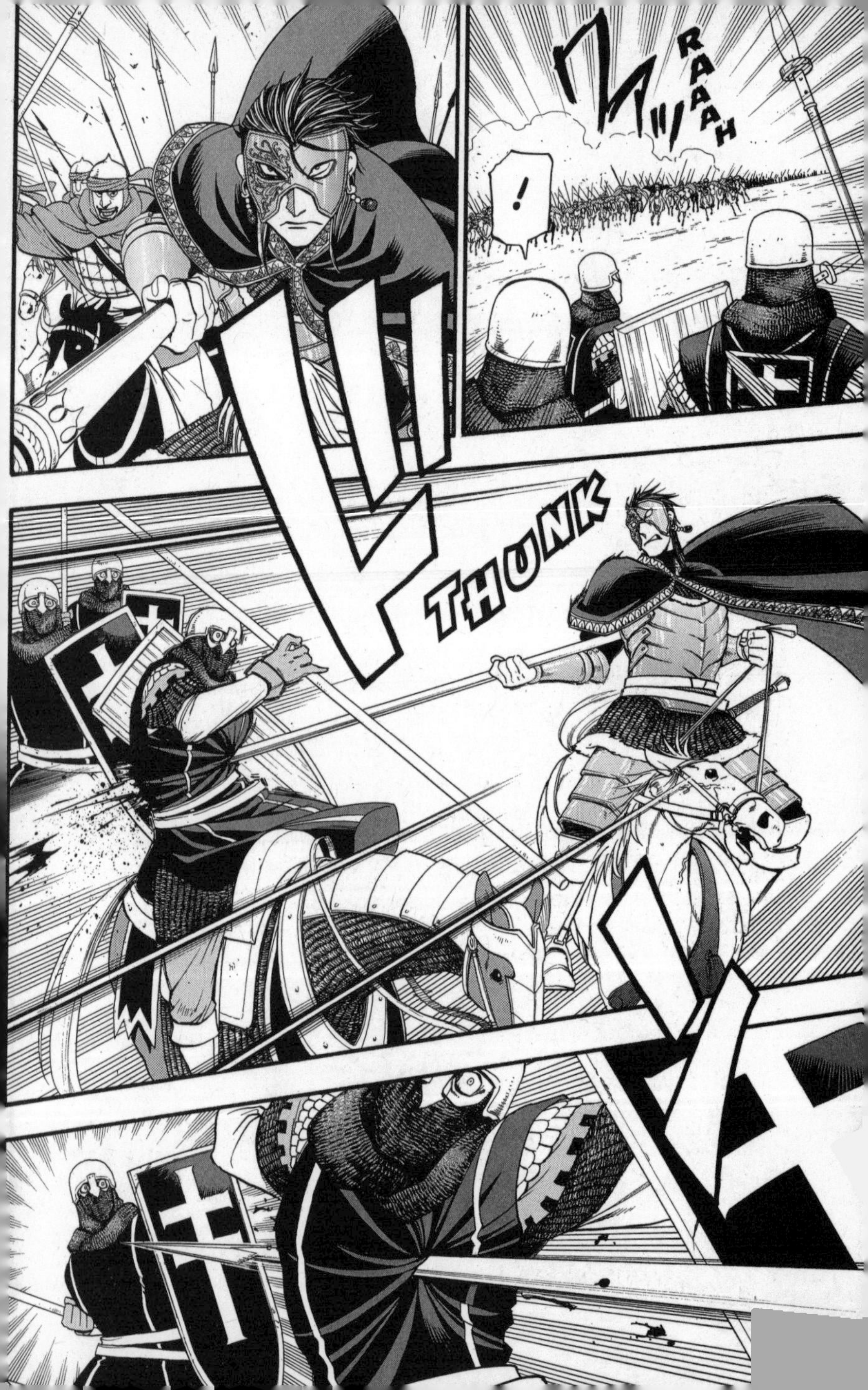
RAAAH
!
THUNK

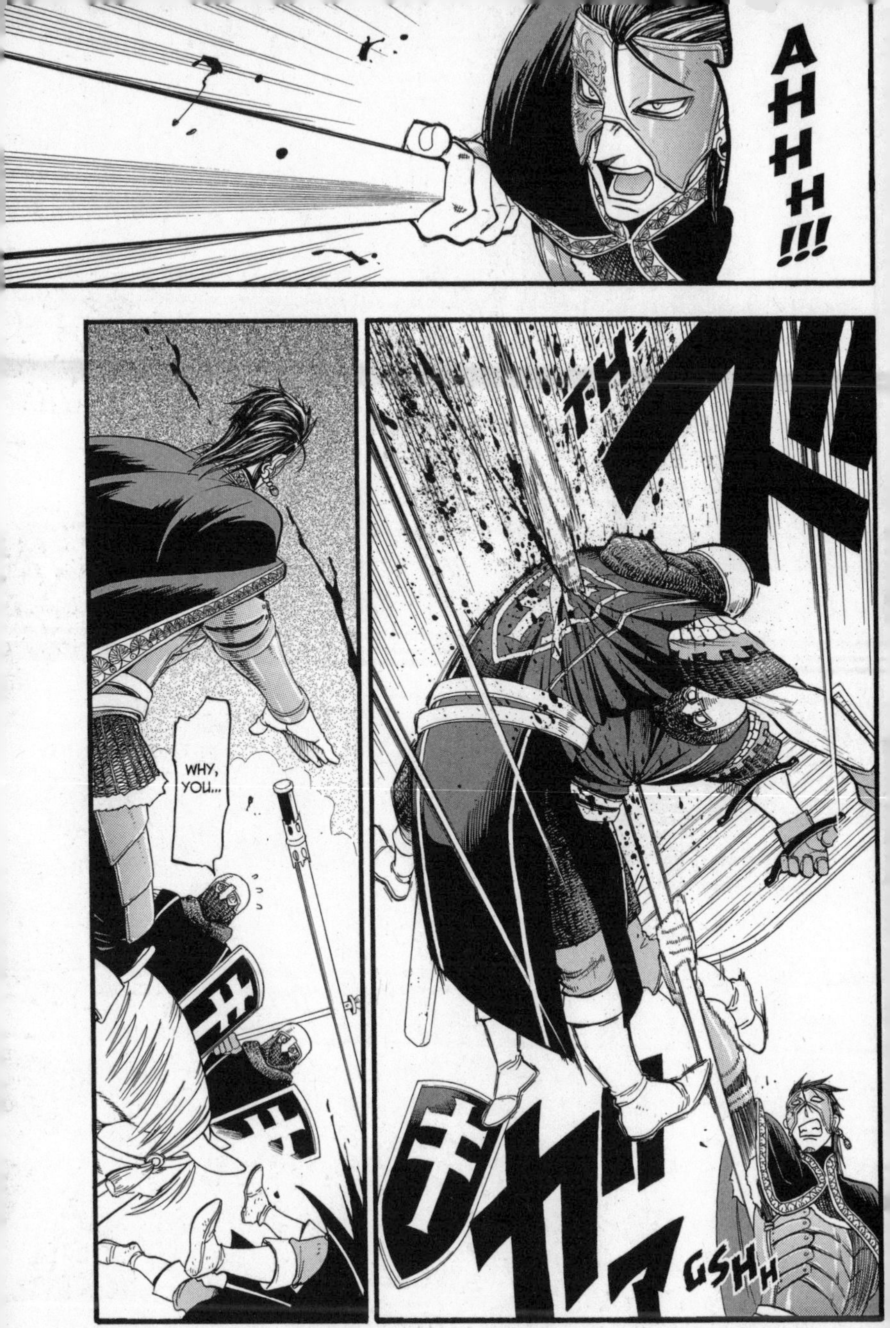
AHHH!!!
TH-
GSHH
WHY, YOU...

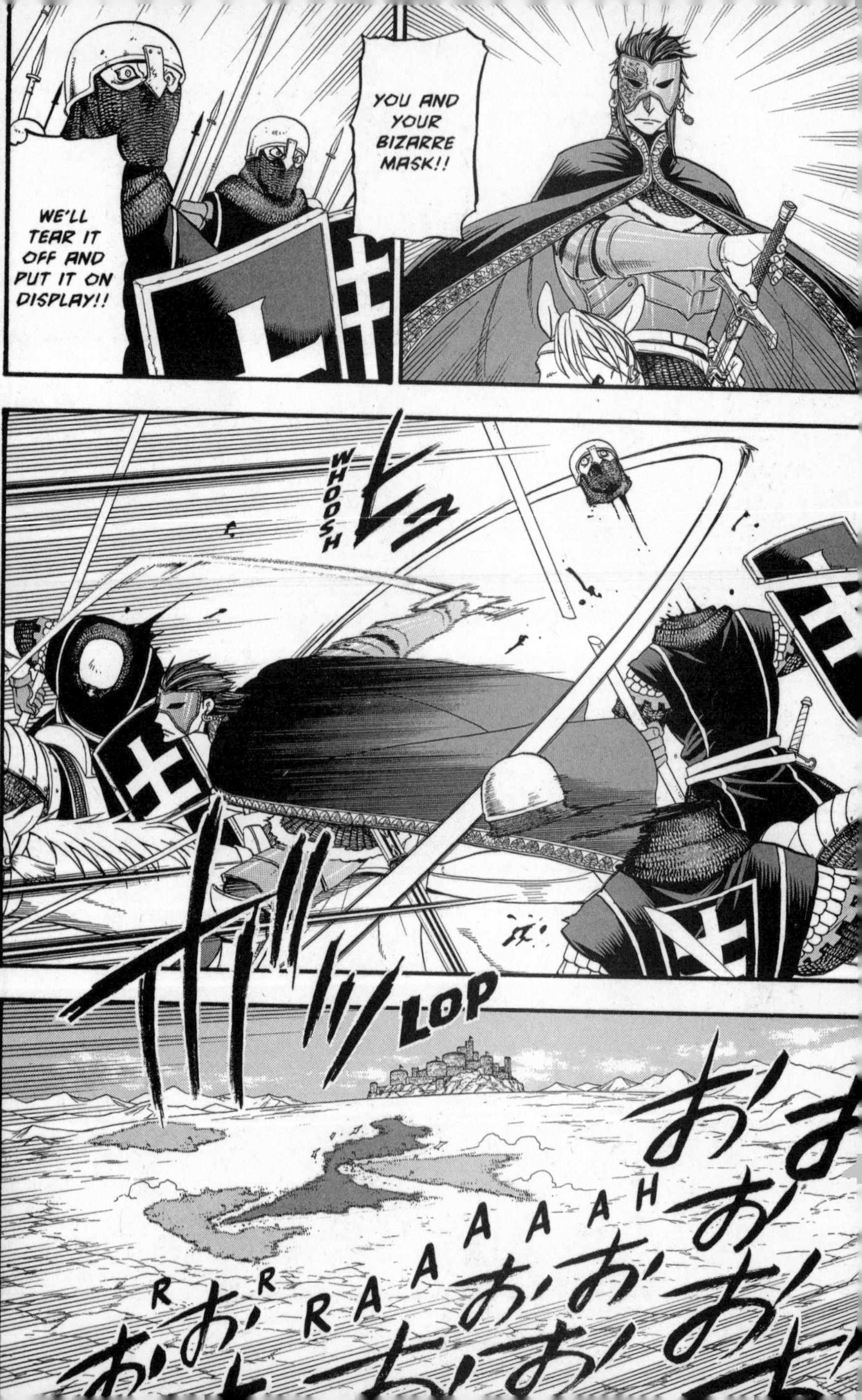
YOU AND YOUR BIZARRE MASK!!
WE'LL TEAR IT OFF AND PUT IT ON DISPLAY!!
WHOOSH
LOP
RRRAAAAAAH

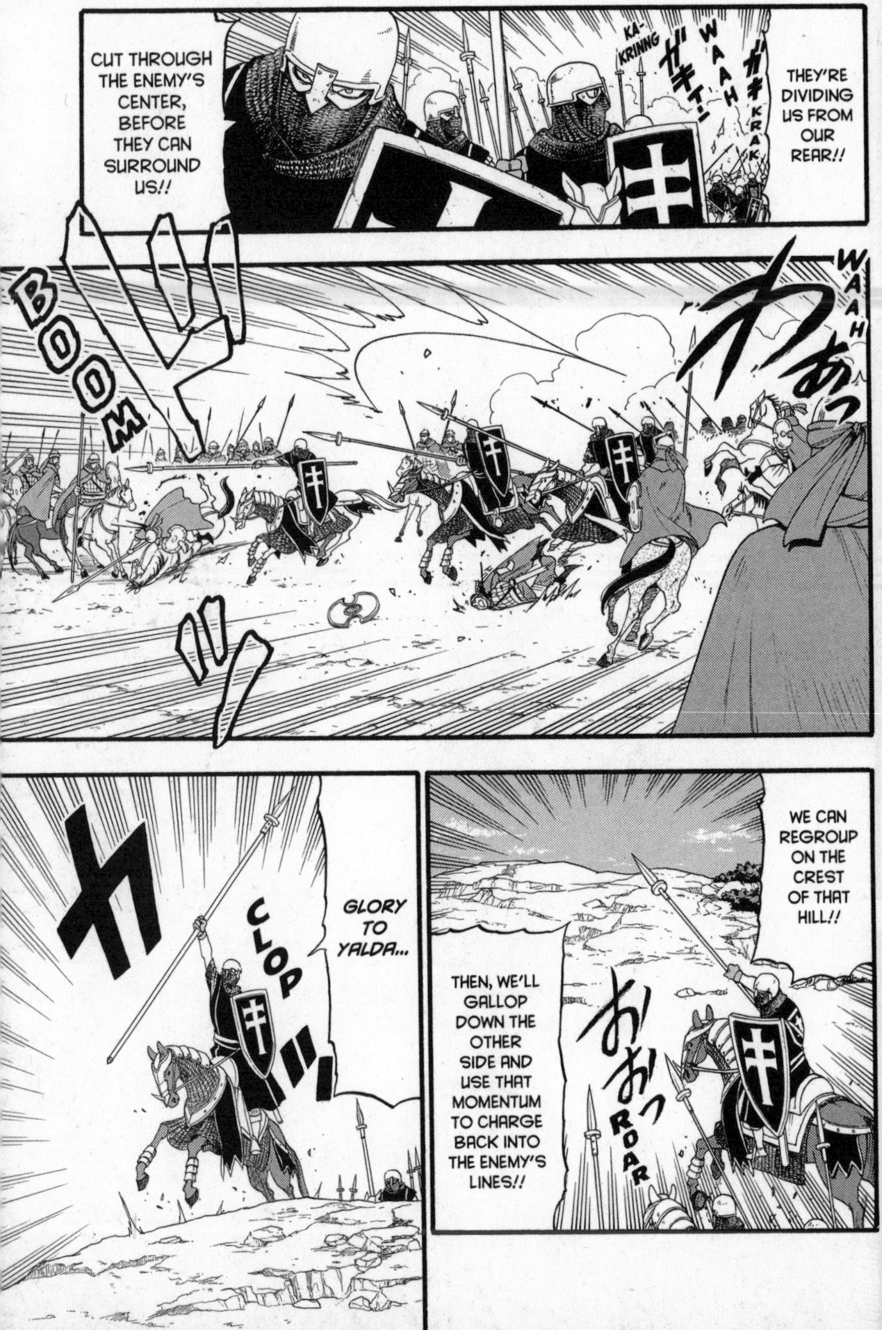
THEY'RE DIVIDING US FROM OUR REAR!!
KRAK
WAAH
KA-KRINNG
CUT THROUGH THE ENEMY'S CENTER, BEFORE THEY CAN SURROUND US!!
WAAH
BOOM
WE CAN REGROUP ON THE CREST OF THAT HILL!!
THEN, WE'LL GALLOP DOWN THE OTHER SIDE AND USE THAT MOMENTUM TO CHARGE BACK INTO THE ENEMY'S LINES!!
ROAR
GLORY TO YALDA...
CLOP

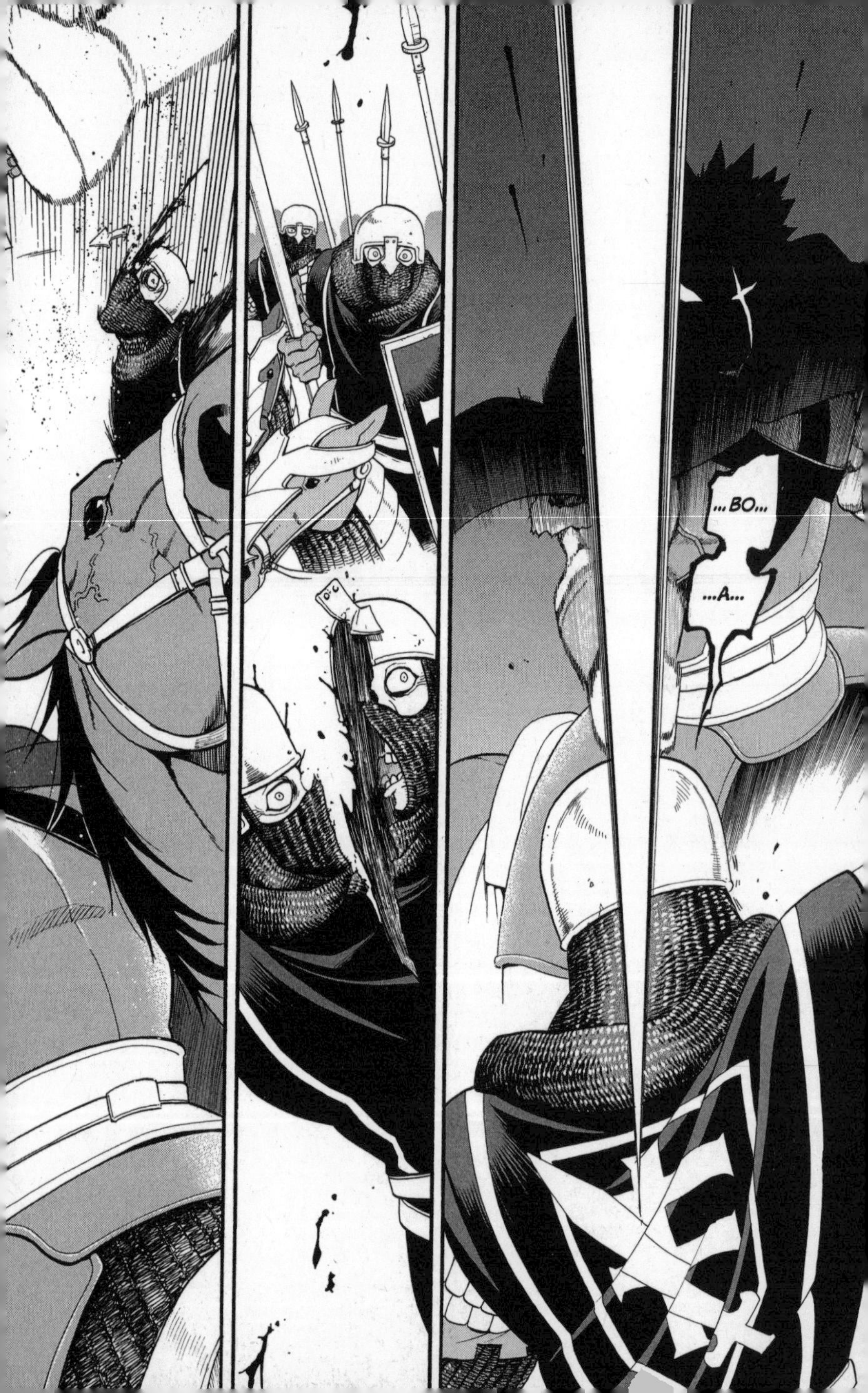
...BO...
...A...

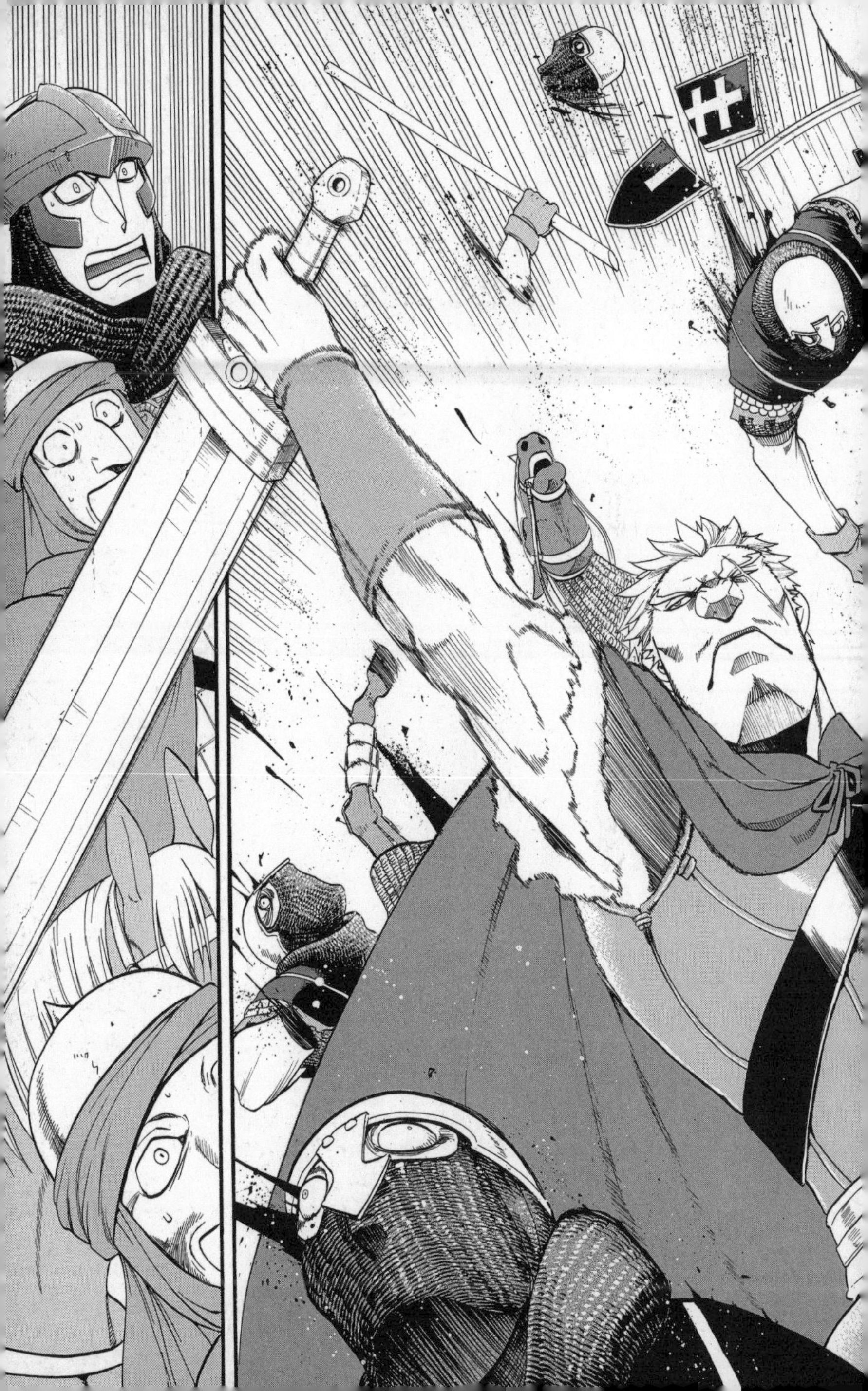

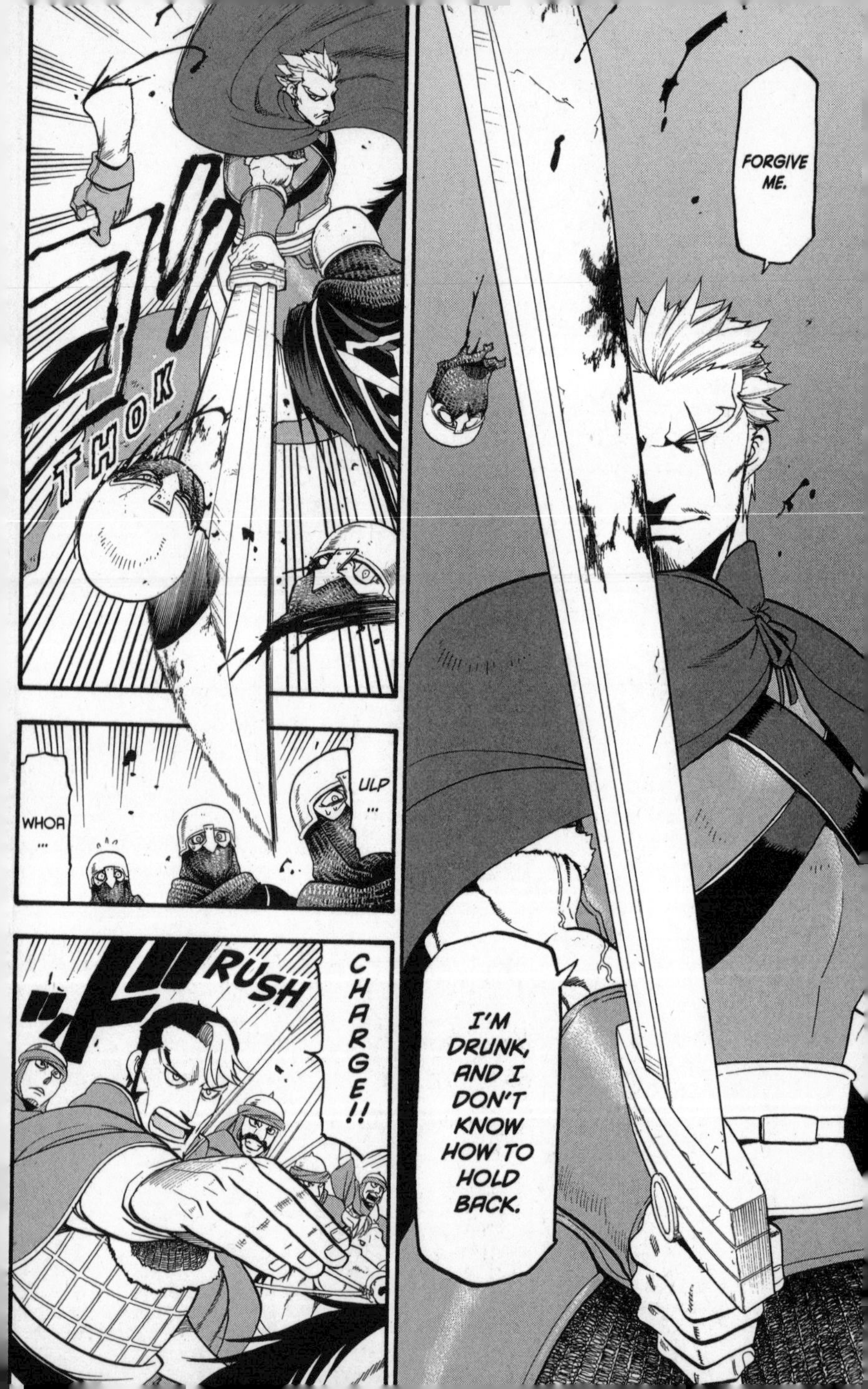
FORGIVE ME.
I'M DRUNK, AND I DON'T KNOW HOW TO HOLD BACK.
THOK
ULP ...
WHOA ...
CHARGE!!
RUSH

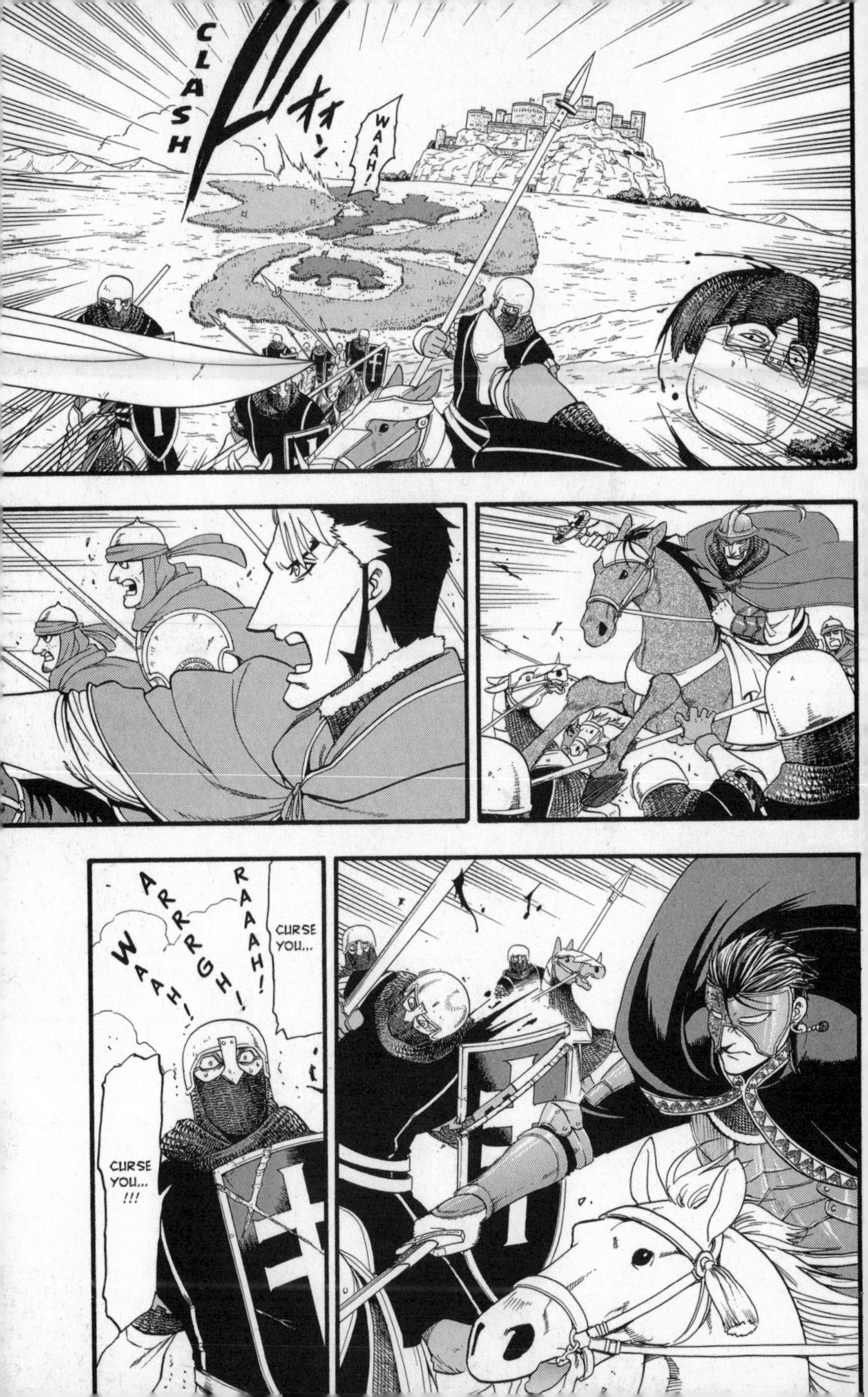
WAAH!
オォン
CLASH
CURSE YOU...
RAAAAH!
ARRRGH!
WAAH!
CURSE YOU... !!!

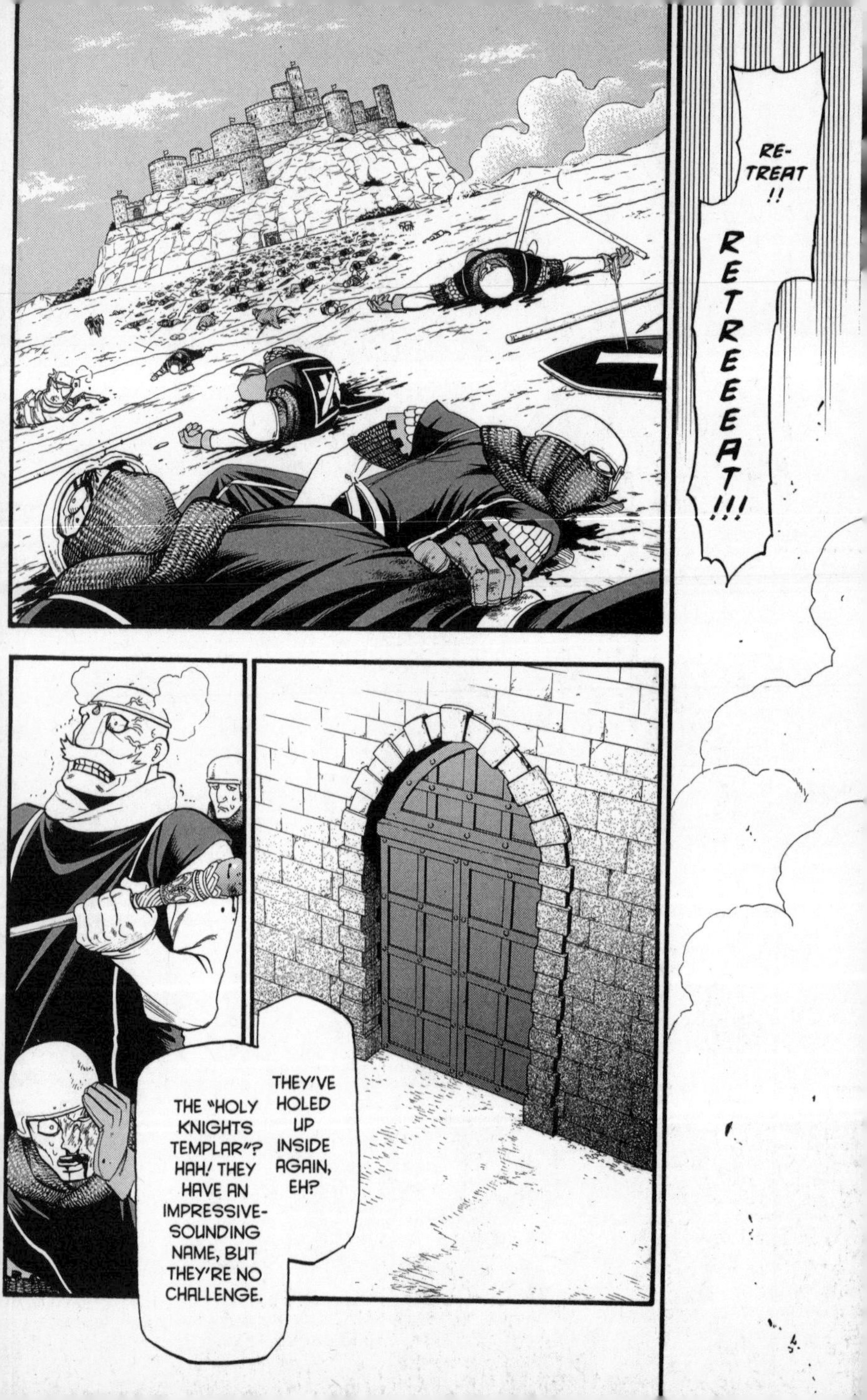
RE-TREAT!!
RETREEEAT!!!
THEY'VE HOLED UP INSIDE AGAIN, EH?
THE "HOLY KNIGHTS TEMPLAR"? HAH! THEY HAVE AN IMPRESSIVE-SOUNDING NAME, BUT THEY'RE NO CHALLENGE.

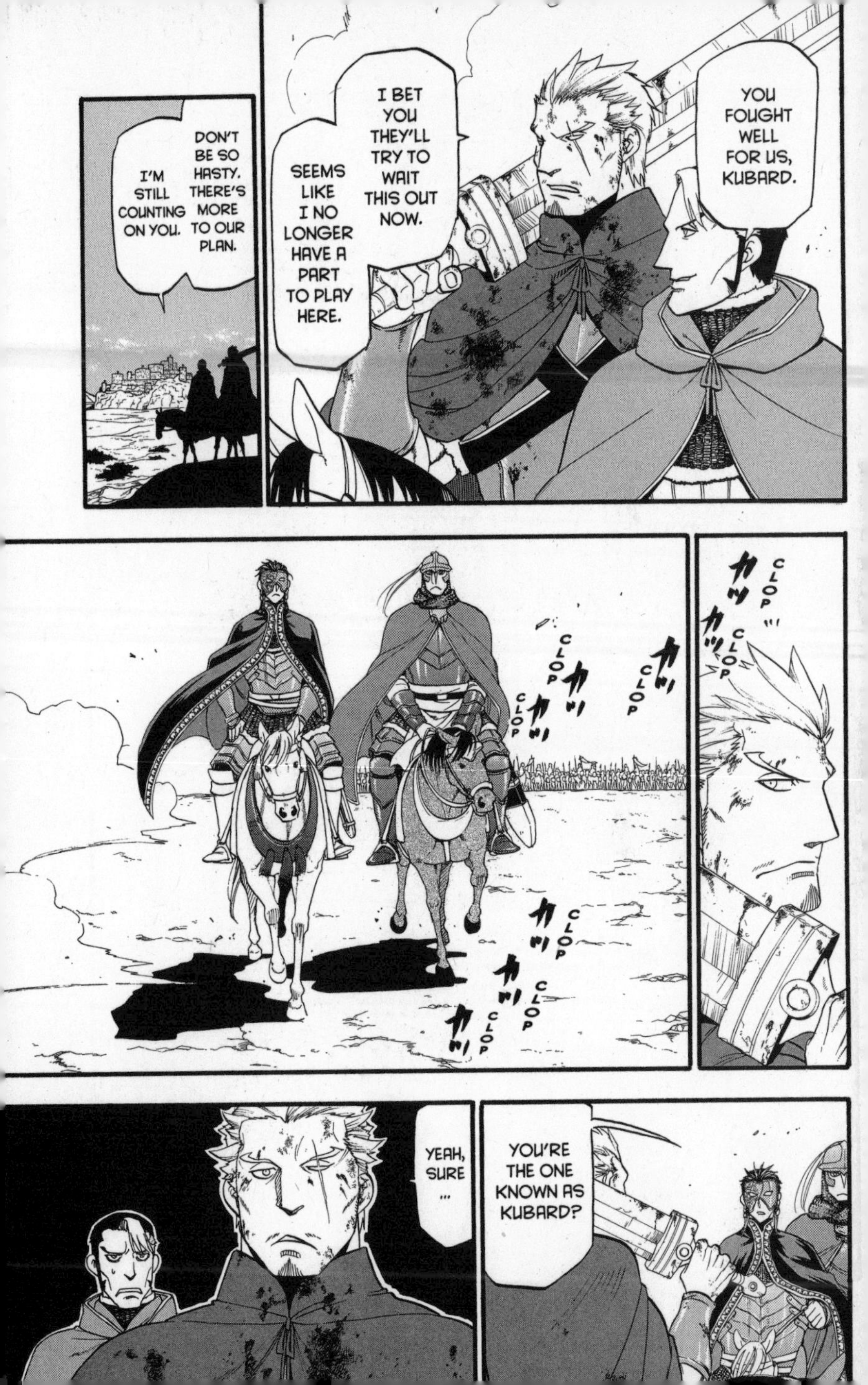
YOU FOUGHT WELL FOR US, KUBARD.
I BET YOU THEY'LL TRY TO WAIT THIS OUT NOW.
SEEMS LIKE I NO LONGER HAVE A PART TO PLAY HERE.
DON'T BE SO HASTY. THERE'S MORE TO OUR PLAN.
I'M STILL COUNTING ON YOU.
CLOP
CLOP
CLOP
CLOP
CLOP
CLOP
CLOP
CLOP
YOU'RE THE ONE KNOWN AS KUBARD?
YEAH, SURE ...

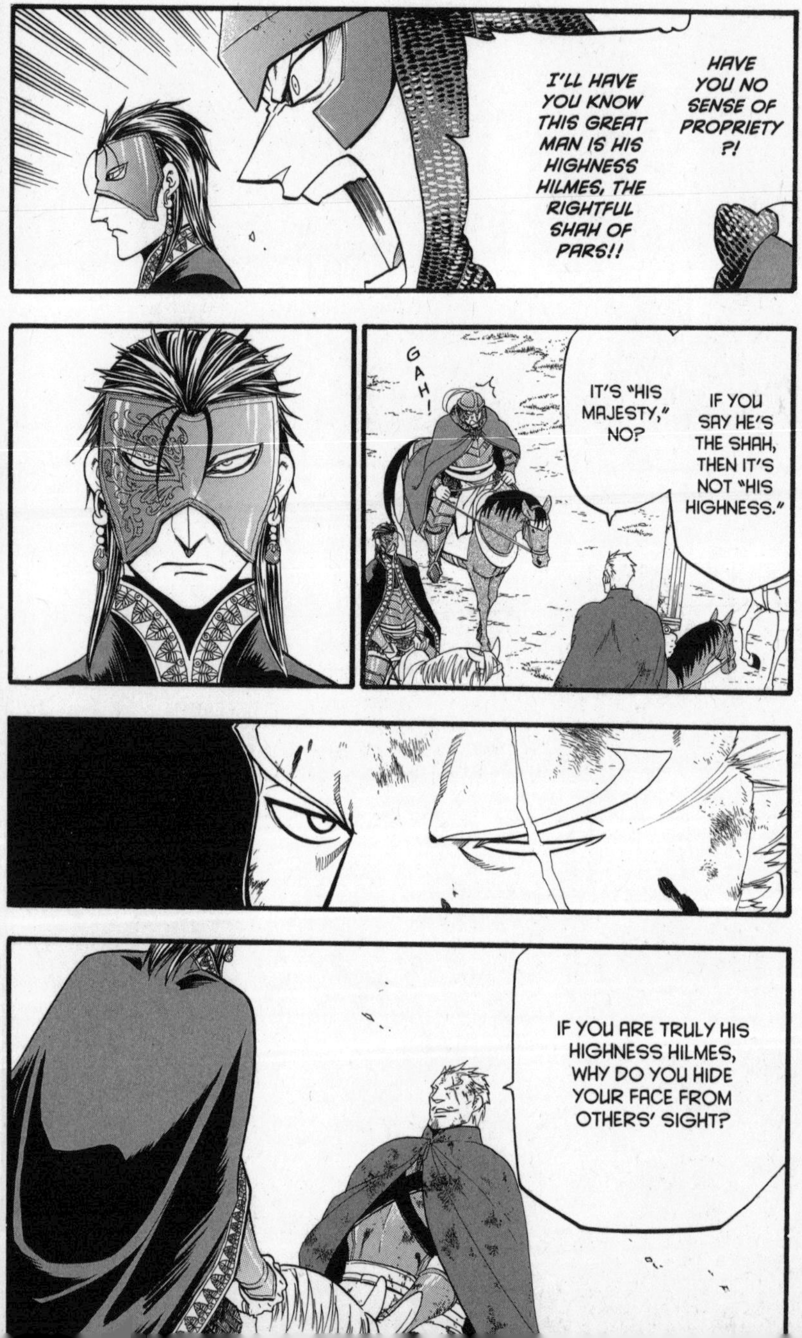
HAVE YOU NO SENSE OF PROPRIETY ?!
I'LL HAVE YOU KNOW THIS GREAT MAN IS HIS HIGHNESS HILMES, THE RIGHTFUL SHAH OF PARS!!
IF YOU SAY HE'S THE SHAH, THEN IT'S NOT "HIS HIGHNESS."
IT'S "HIS MAJESTY," NO?
GAH!
IF YOU ARE TRULY HIS HIGHNESS HILMES, WHY DO YOU HIDE YOUR FACE FROM OTHERS' SIGHT?

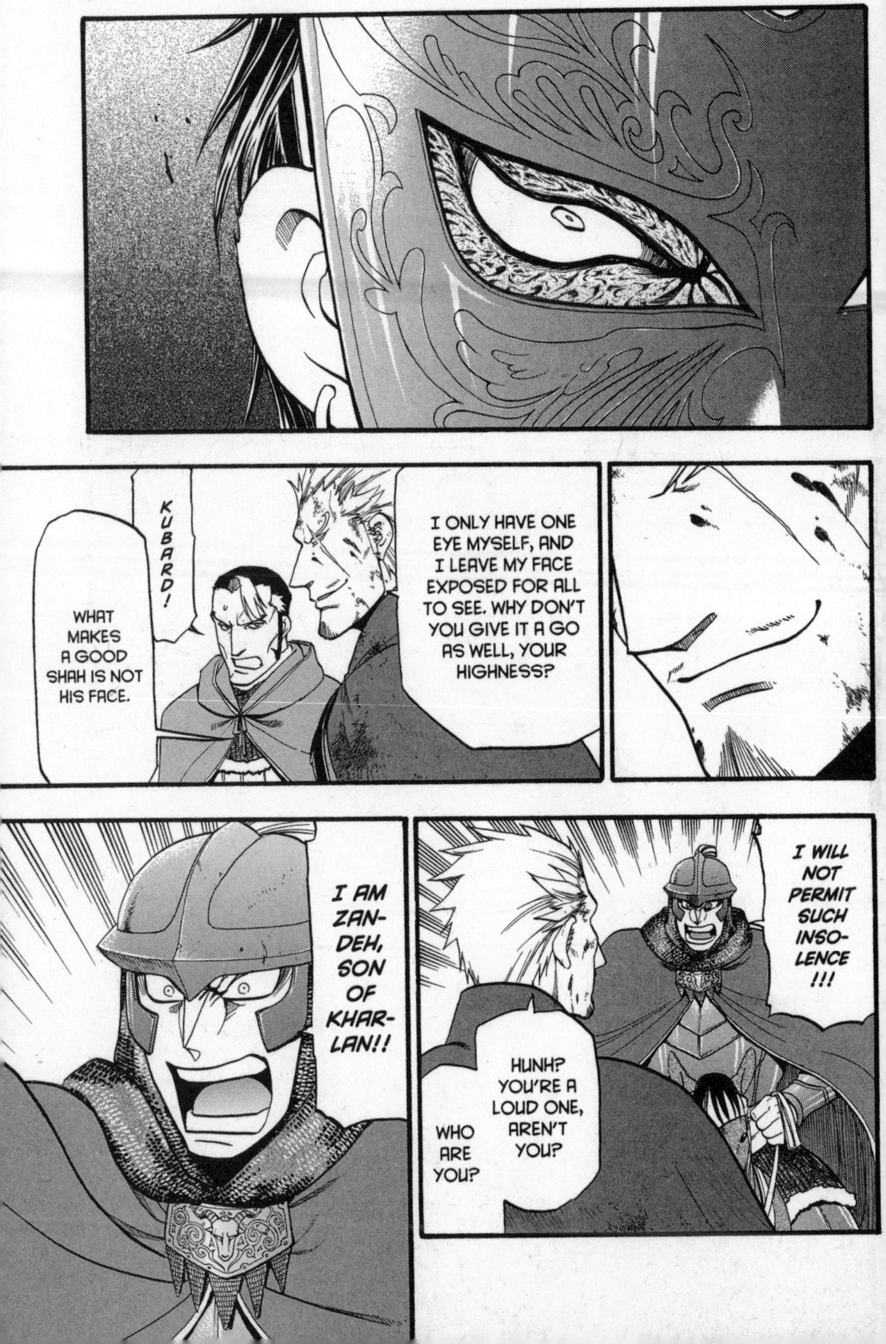
I ONLY HAVE ONE EYE MYSELF, AND I LEAVE MY FACE EXPOSED FOR ALL TO SEE. WHY DON'T YOU GIVE IT A GO AS WELL, YOUR HIGHNESS?
KUBARD!
WHAT MAKES A GOOD SHAH IS NOT HIS FACE.
I WILL NOT PERMIT SUCH INSO-LENCE!!!
HUNH? YOU'RE A LOUD ONE, AREN'T YOU?
WHO ARE YOU?
I AM ZAN-DEH, SON OF KHAR-LAN!!

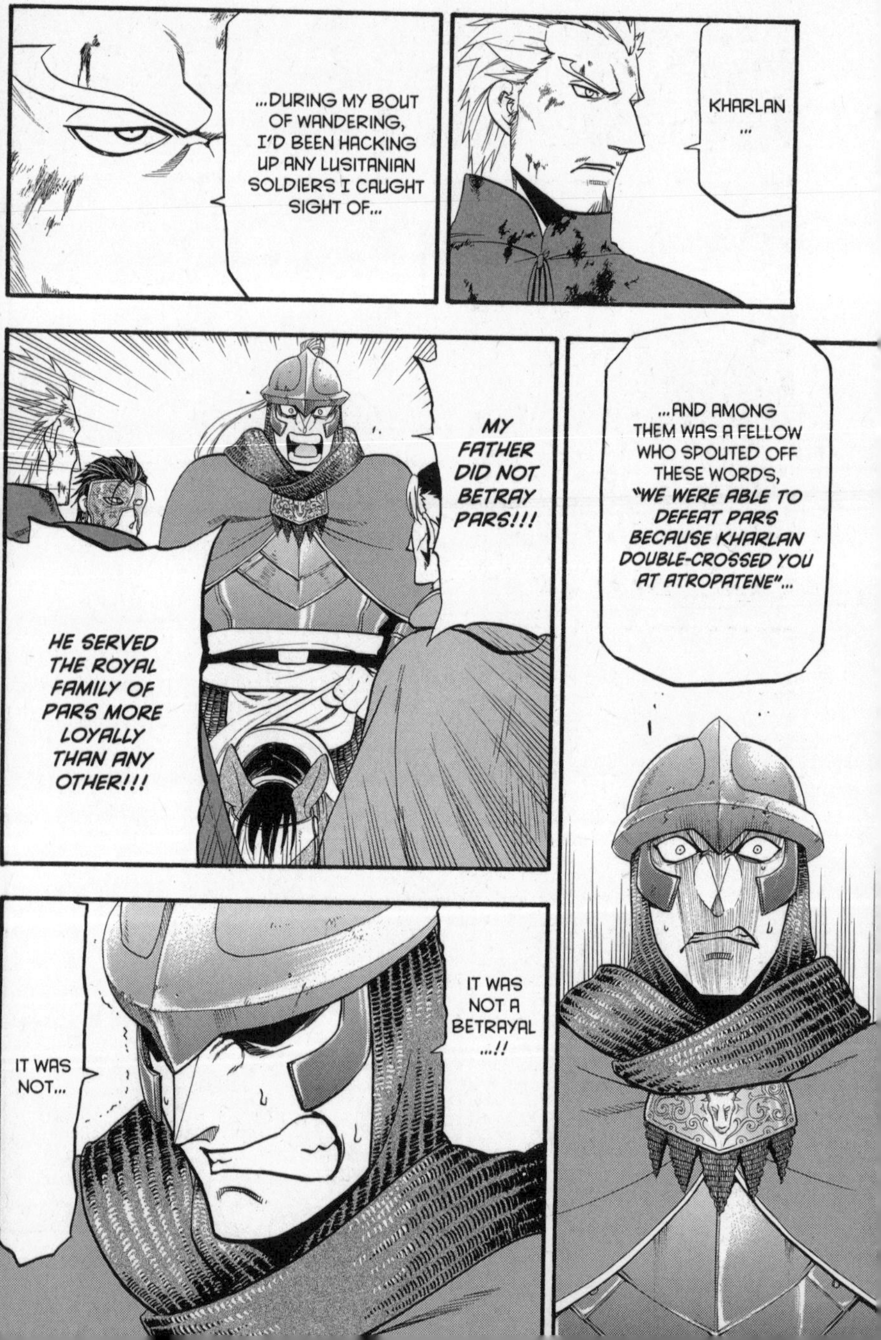
KHARLAN ...
...DURING MY BOUT OF WANDERING, I'D BEEN HACKING UP ANY LUSITANIAN SOLDIERS I CAUGHT SIGHT OF...
...AND AMONG THEM WAS A FELLOW WHO SPOUTED OFF THESE WORDS, "WE WERE ABLE TO DEFEAT PARS BECAUSE KHARLAN DOUBLE-CROSSED YOU AT ATROPATENE"...
MY FATHER DID NOT BETRAY PARS!!!
HE SERVED THE ROYAL FAMILY OF PARS MORE LOYALLY THAN ANY OTHER!!!
IT WAS NOT A BETRAYAL ...!!
IT WAS NOT...

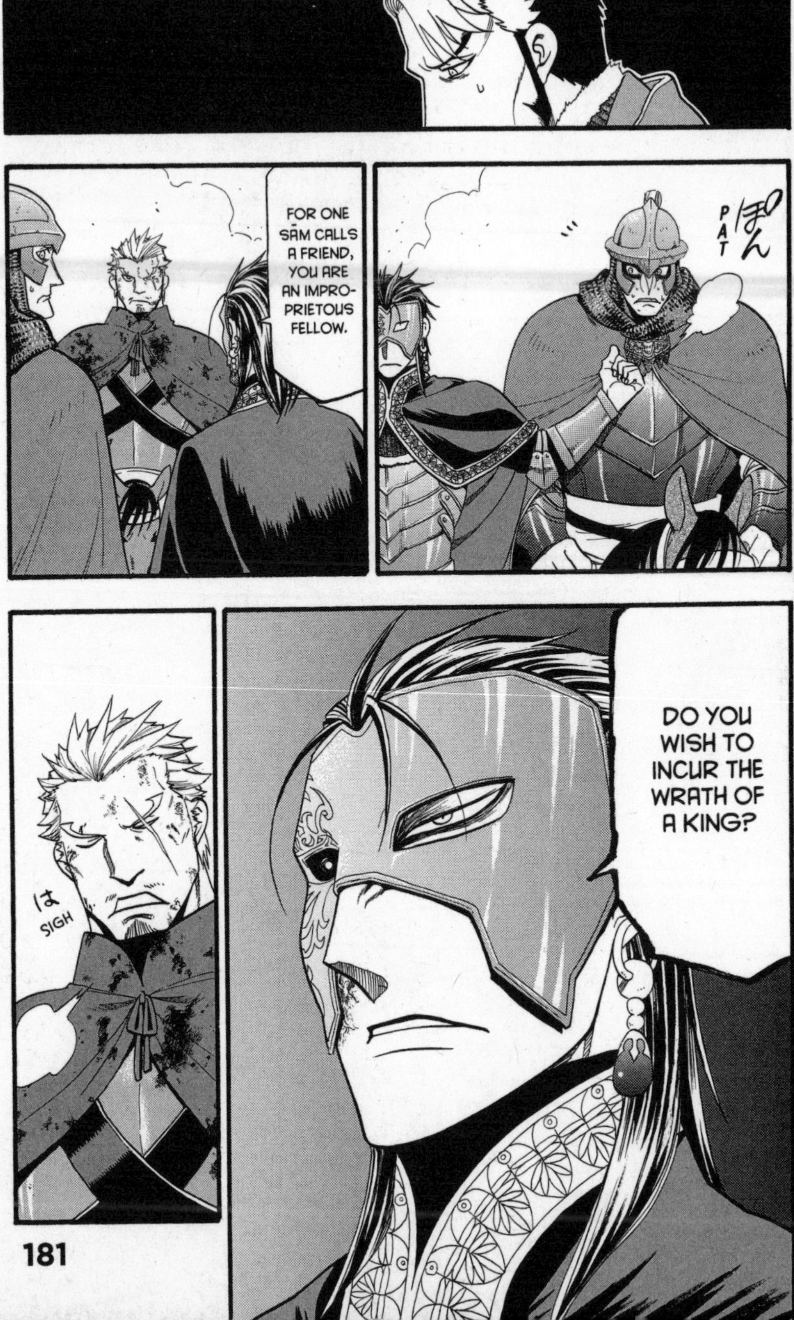
ぽん
PAT
FOR ONE SĀM CALLS A FRIEND, YOU ARE AN IMPRO-PRIETOUS FELLOW.
DO YOU WISH TO INCUR THE WRATH OF A KING?
は
SIGH

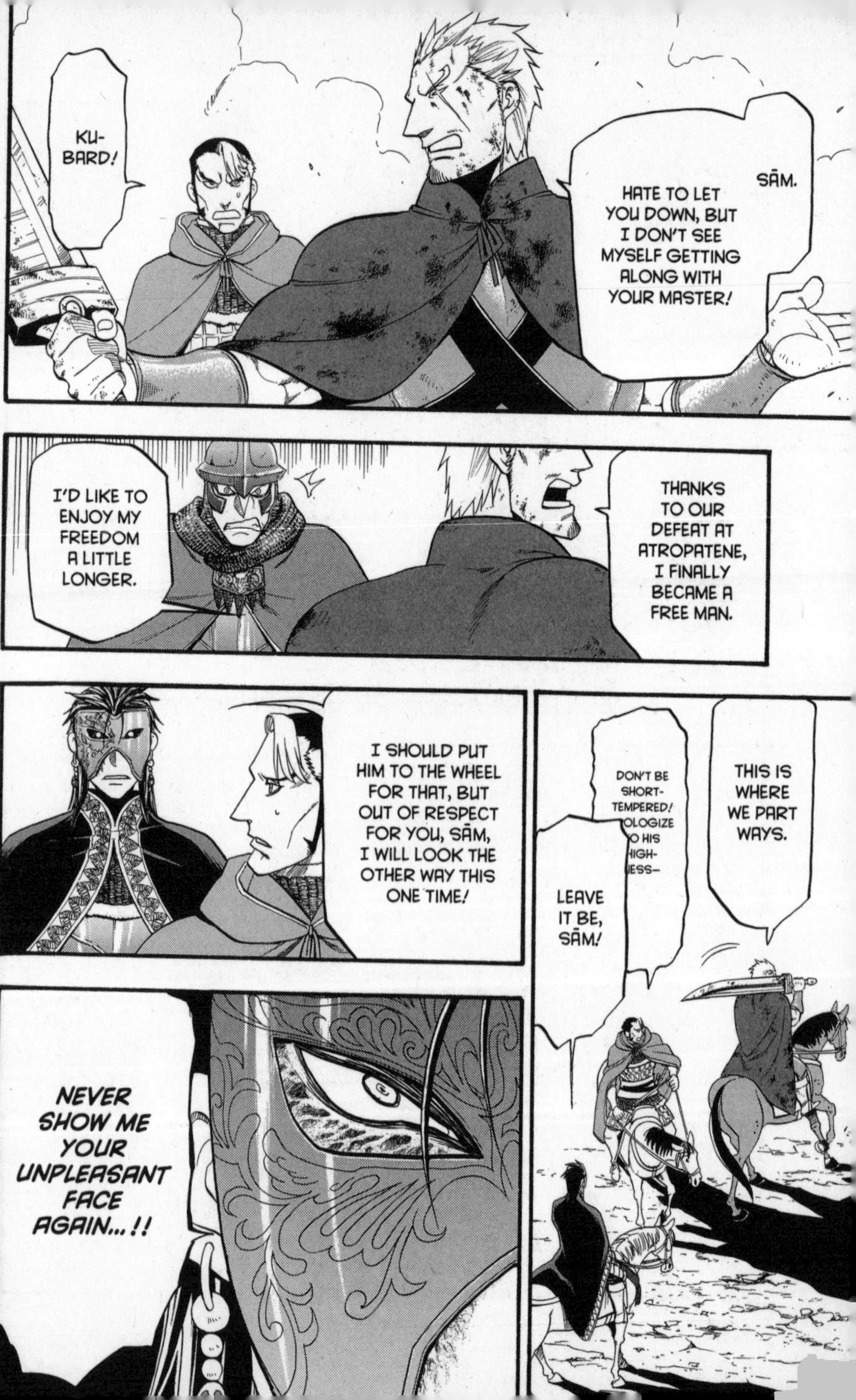
SĀM. HATE TO LET YOU DOWN, BUT I DON'T SEE MYSELF GETTING ALONG WITH YOUR MASTER!
KU-BARD!
THANKS TO OUR DEFEAT AT ATROPATENE, I FINALLY BECAME A FREE MAN.
I'D LIKE TO ENJOY MY FREEDOM A LITTLE LONGER.
THIS IS WHERE WE PART WAYS.
DON'T BE SHORT-TEMPERED! OLOGIZE O HIS HIGH- IESS–
LEAVE IT BE, SĀM!
I SHOULD PUT HIM TO THE WHEEL FOR THAT, BUT OUT OF RESPECT FOR YOU, SĀM, I WILL LOOK THE OTHER WAY THIS ONE TIME!
NEVER SHOW ME YOUR UNPLEASANT FACE AGAIN...!!

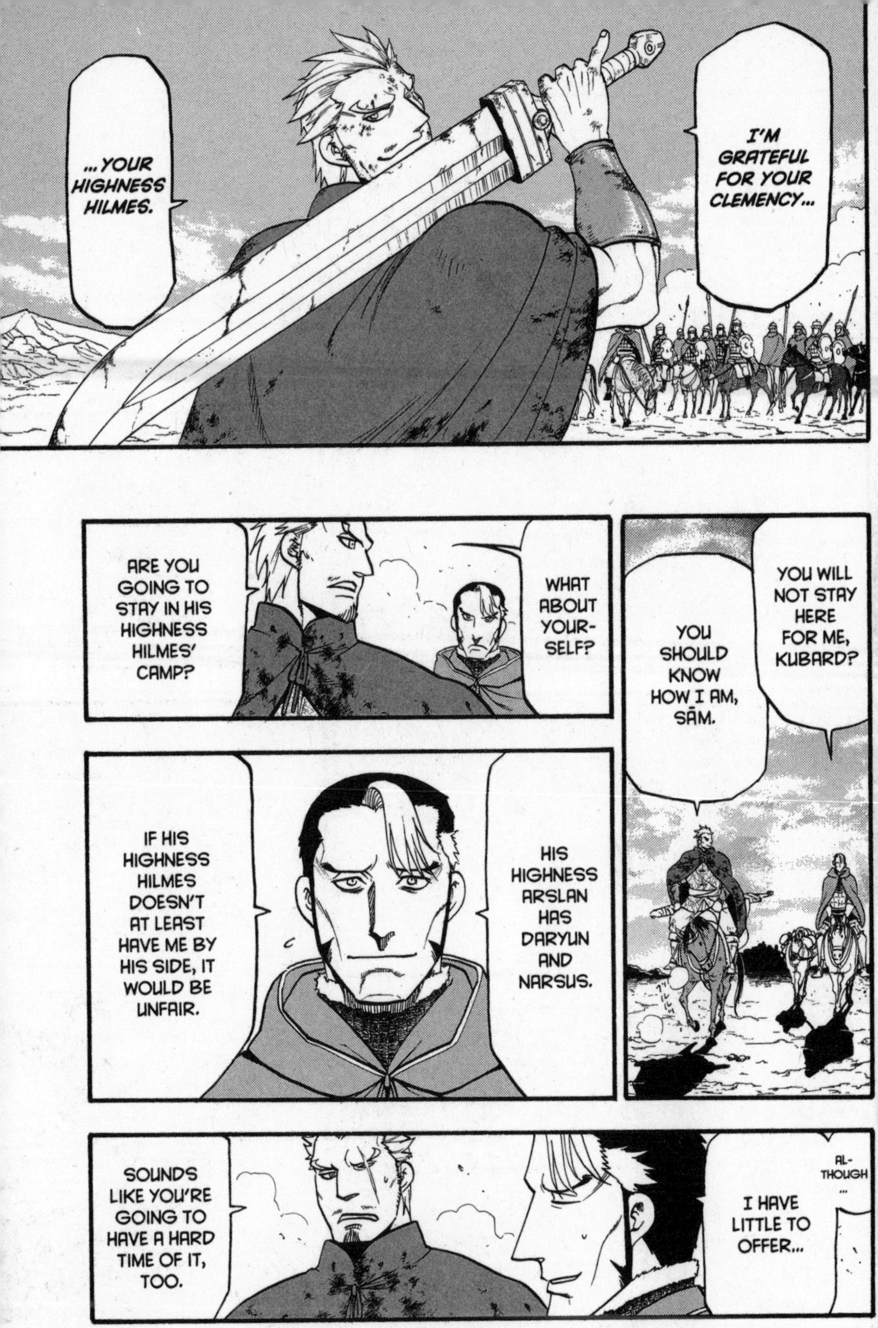
I'M GRATEFUL FOR YOUR CLEMENCY...
...YOUR HIGHNESS HILMES.
YOU WILL NOT STAY HERE FOR ME, KUBARD?
YOU SHOULD KNOW HOW I AM, SĀM.
WHAT ABOUT YOURSELF?
ARE YOU GOING TO STAY IN HIS HIGHNESS HILMES' CAMP?
HIS HIGHNESS ARSLAN HAS DARYUN AND NARSUS.
IF HIS HIGHNESS HILMES DOESN'T AT LEAST HAVE ME BY HIS SIDE, IT WOULD BE UNFAIR.
ALTHOUGH...
I HAVE LITTLE TO OFFER...
SOUNDS LIKE YOU'RE GOING TO HAVE A HARD TIME OF IT, TOO.

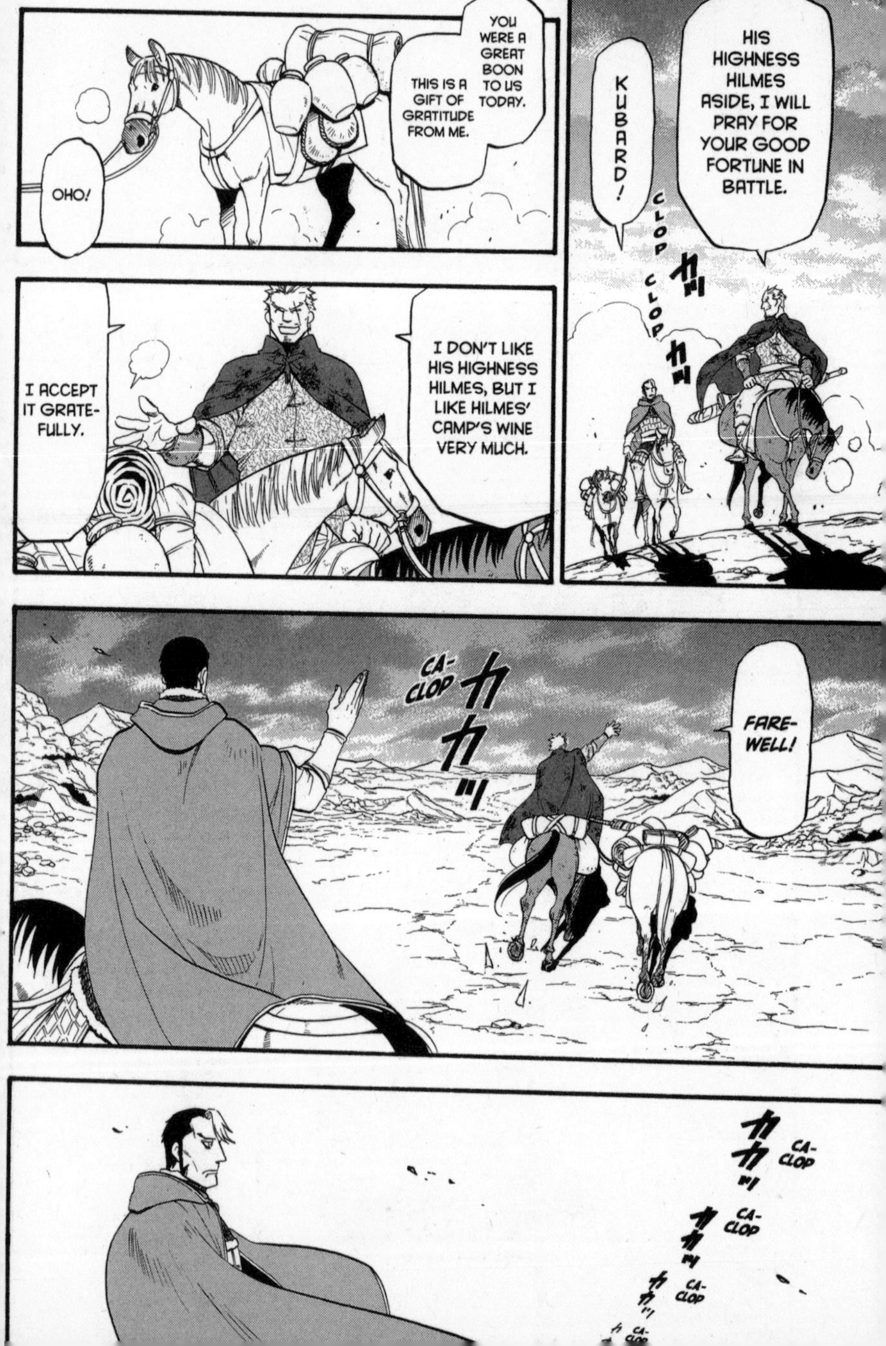
HIS HIGHNESS HILMES ASIDE, I WILL PRAY FOR YOUR GOOD FORTUNE IN BATTLE.
KUBARD!
CLOP CLOP
CLOP
YOU WERE A GREAT BOON TO US TODAY.
THIS IS A GIFT OF GRATITUDE FROM ME.
OHO!
I DON'T LIKE HIS HIGHNESS HILMES, BUT I LIKE HILMES' CAMP'S WINE VERY MUCH.
I ACCEPT IT GRATEFULLY.
FAREWELL!
CA-CLOP
CA-CLOP
CA-CLOP
CA-CLOP
CA-CLOP

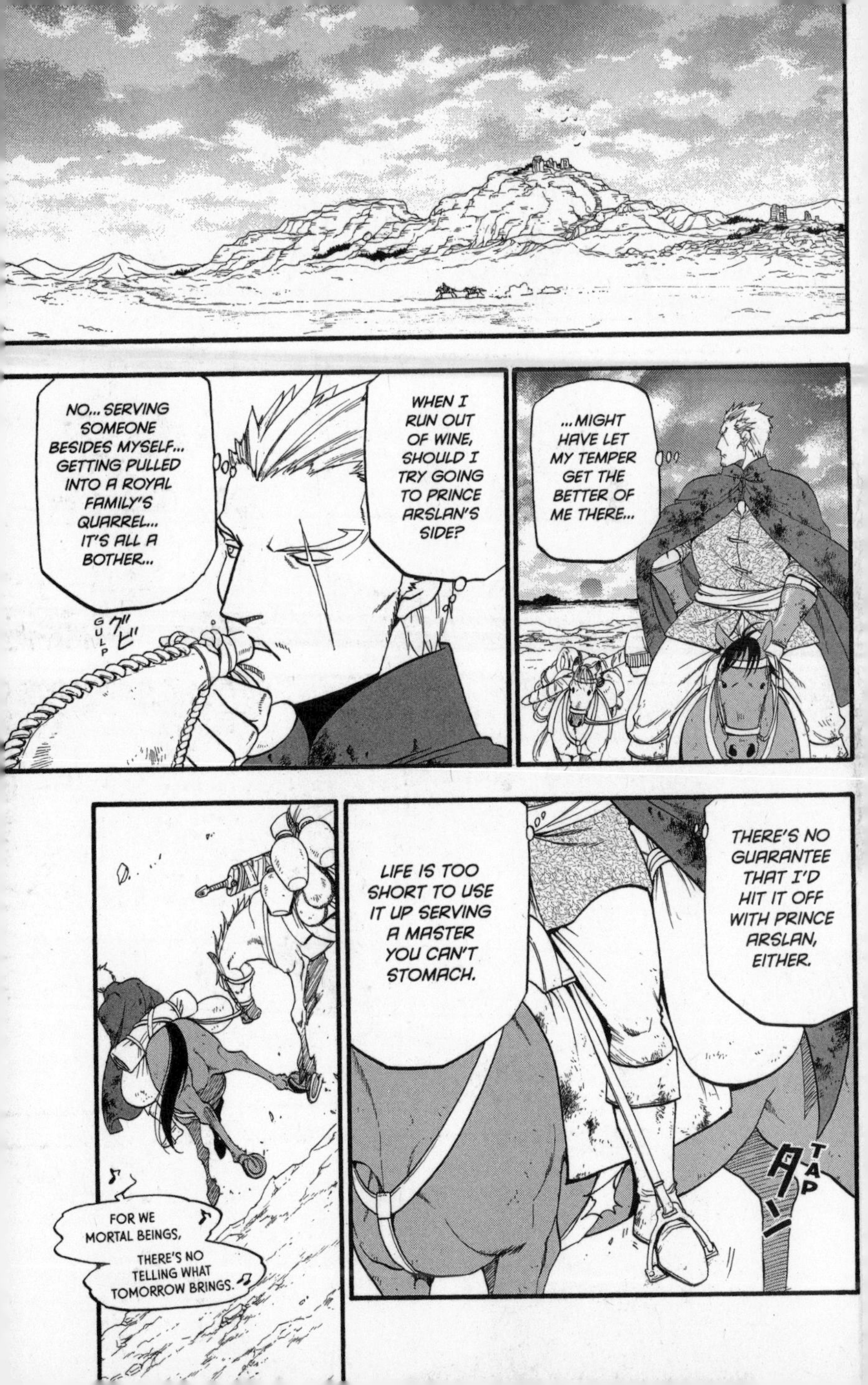
...MIGHT HAVE LET MY TEMPER GET THE BETTER OF ME THERE...
WHEN I RUN OUT OF WINE, SHOULD I TRY GOING TO PRINCE ARSLAN'S SIDE?
NO... SERVING SOMEONE BESIDES MYSELF... GETTING PULLED INTO A ROYAL FAMILY'S QUARREL... IT'S ALL A BOTHER...
GULP
THERE'S NO GUARANTEE THAT I'D HIT IT OFF WITH PRINCE ARSLAN, EITHER.
LIFE IS TOO SHORT TO USE IT UP SERVING A MASTER YOU CAN'T STOMACH.
TAP
FOR WE MORTAL BEINGS, THERE'S NO TELLING WHAT TOMORROW BRINGS.

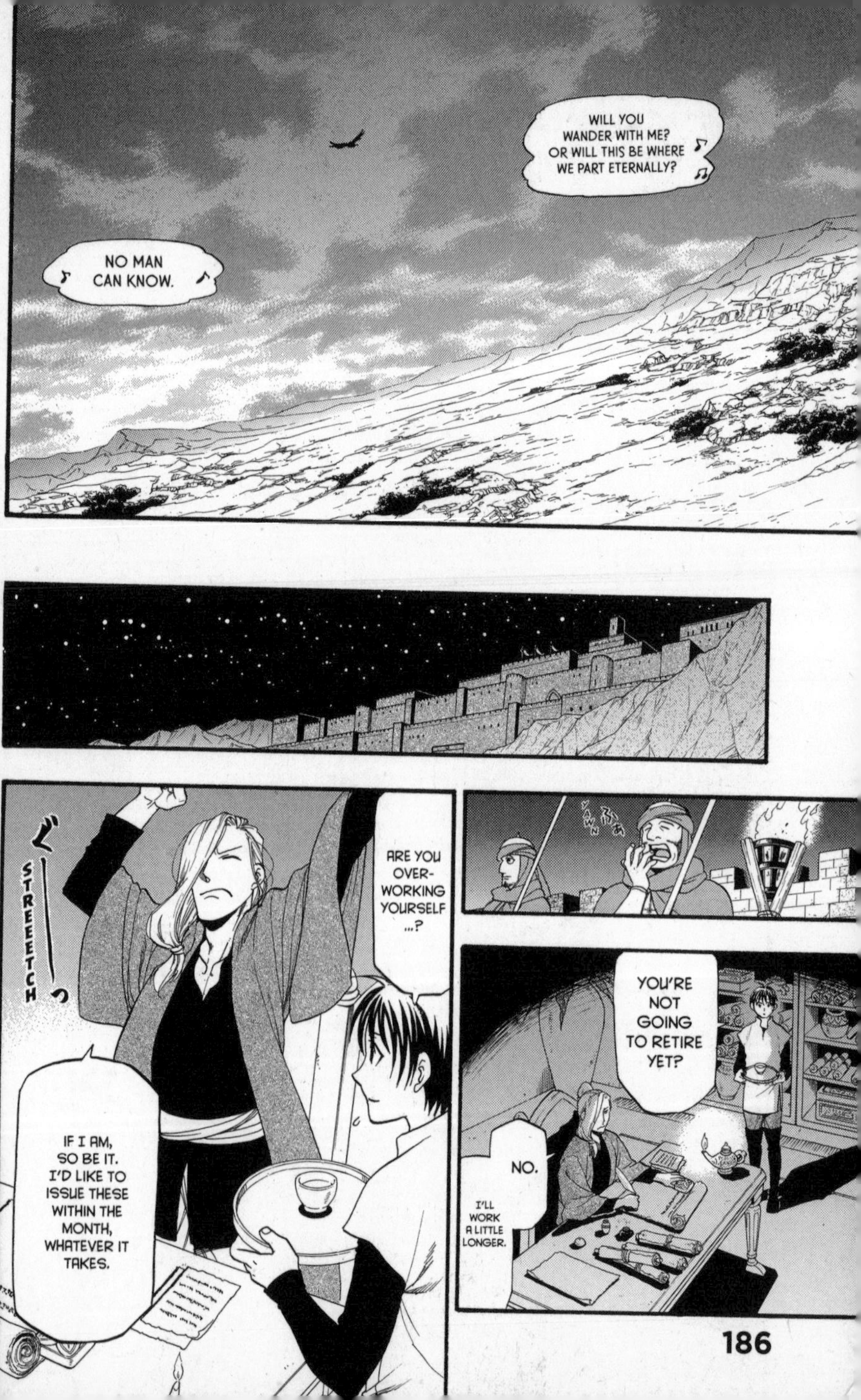
WILL YOU WANDER WITH ME? OR WILL THIS BE WHERE WE PART ETERNALLY?
NO MAN CAN KNOW.
YAWN
YOU'RE NOT GOING TO RETIRE YET?
NO.
I'LL WORK A LITTLE LONGER.
STREEETCH
ARE YOU OVER-WORKING YOURSELF ...?
IF I AM, SO BE IT. I'D LIKE TO ISSUE THESE WITHIN THE MONTH, WHATEVER IT TAKES.

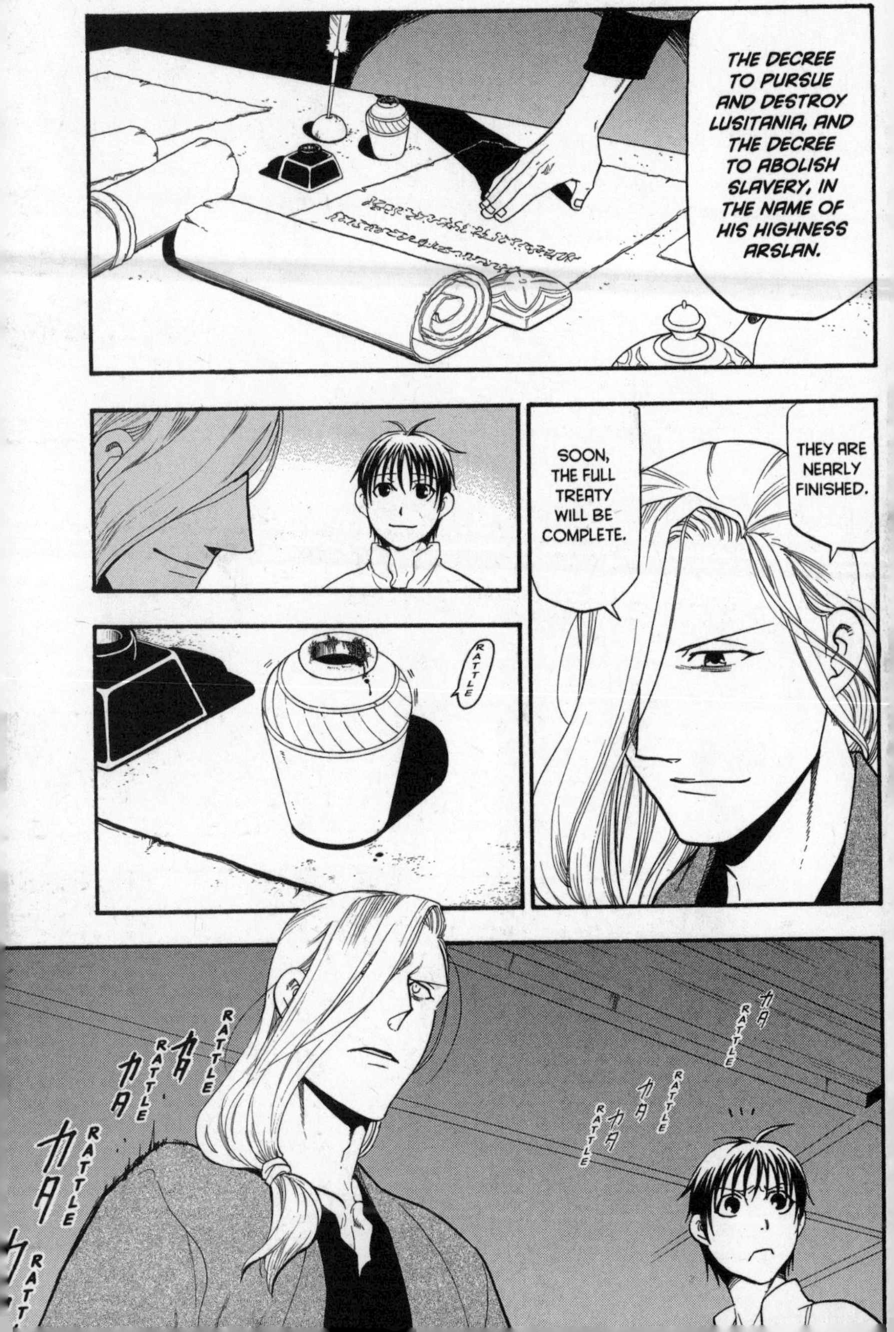
THE DECREE TO PURSUE AND DESTROY LUSITANIA, AND THE DECREE TO ABOLISH SLAVERY, IN THE NAME OF HIS HIGHNESS ARSLAN.
THEY ARE NEARLY FINISHED.
SOON, THE FULL TREATY WILL BE COMPLETE.
RATTLE
カタ RATTLE
カタ RATTLE
カタ RATTLE
カタ RATTLE
カタ RATTLE
カタ RATTLE
カ RATT

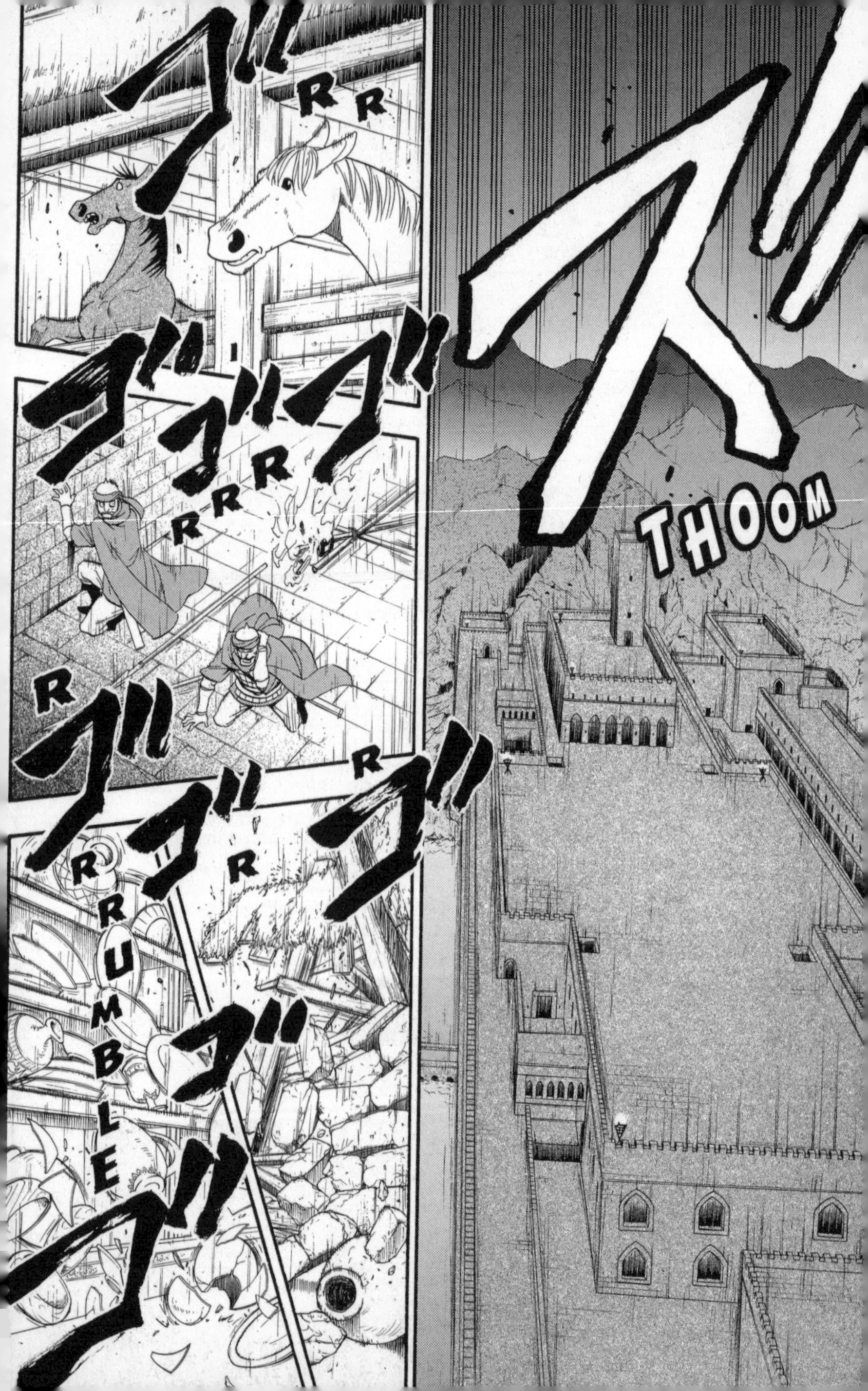
THOOM
RR
RRRR
R
R
R
RRUMBLE

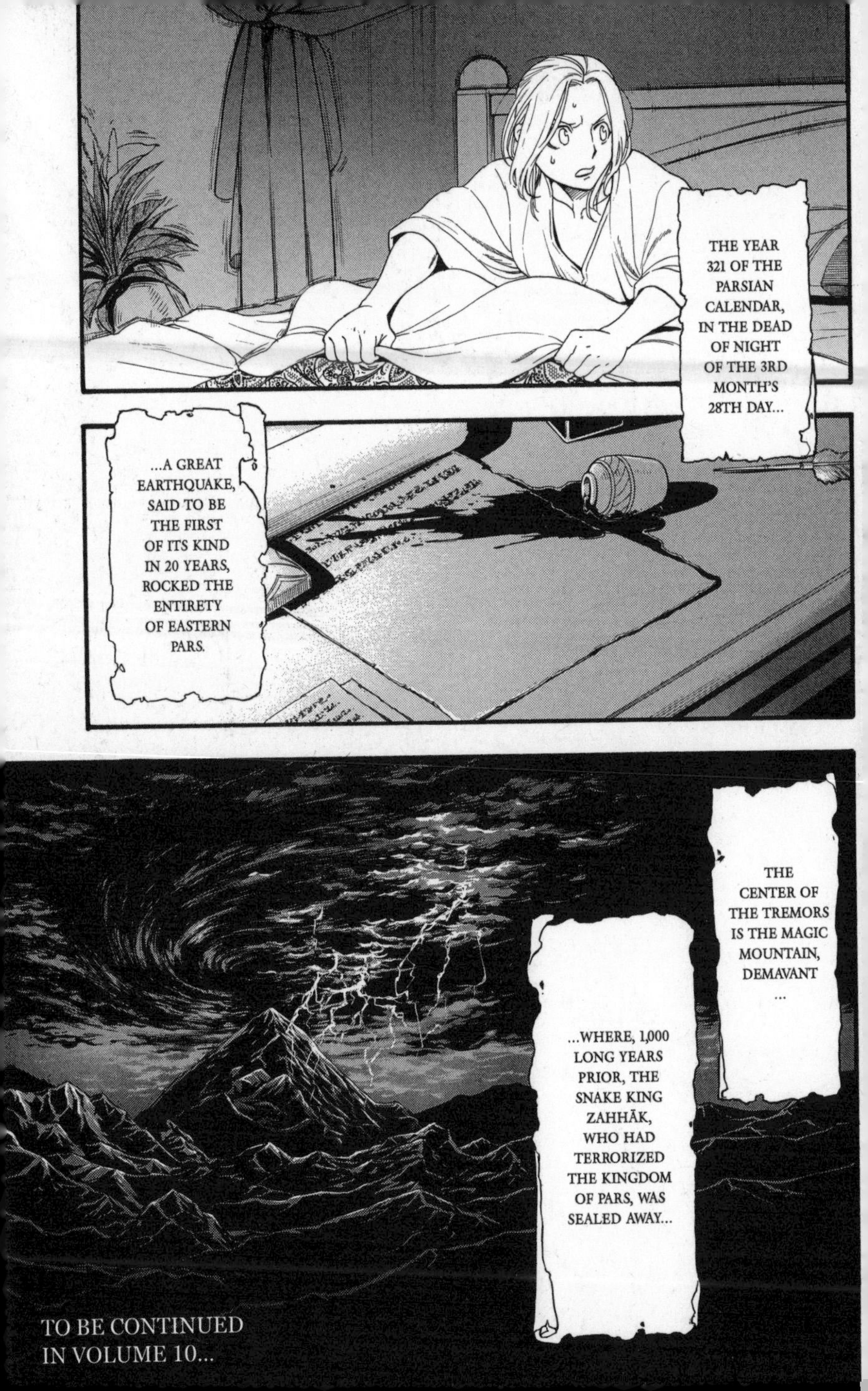
THE YEAR 321 OF THE PARSIAN CALENDAR, IN THE DEAD OF NIGHT OF THE 3RD MONTH'S 28TH DAY...
...A GREAT EARTHQUAKE, SAID TO BE THE FIRST OF ITS KIND IN 20 YEARS, ROCKED THE ENTIRETY OF EASTERN PARS.
THE CENTER OF THE TREMORS IS THE MAGIC MOUNTAIN, DEMAVANT...
...WHERE, 1,000 LONG YEARS PRIOR, THE SNAKE KING ZAHHĀK, WHO HAD TERRORIZED THE KINGDOM OF PARS, WAS SEALED AWAY...
TO BE CONTINUED IN VOLUME 10...

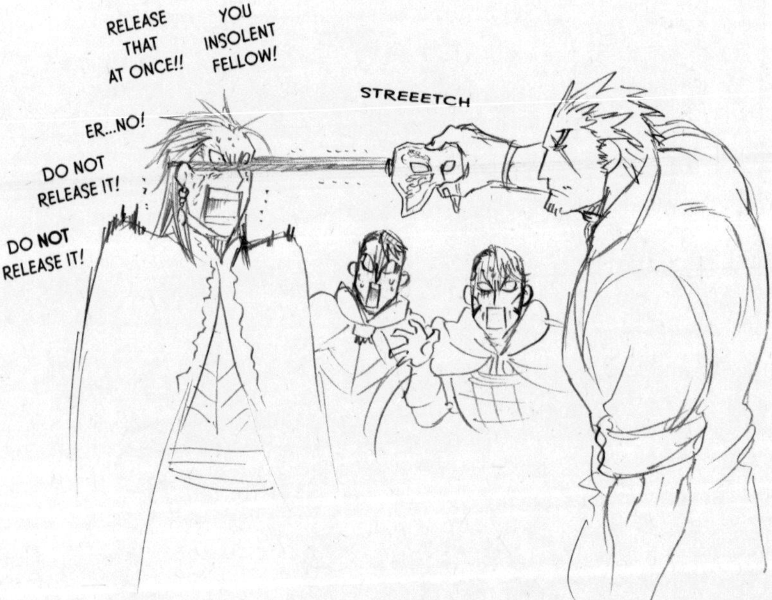
STREEETCH
YOU INSOLENT FELLOW!
RELEASE THAT AT ONCE!!
ER...NO!
DO NOT RELEASE IT!
DO **NOT** RELEASE IT!

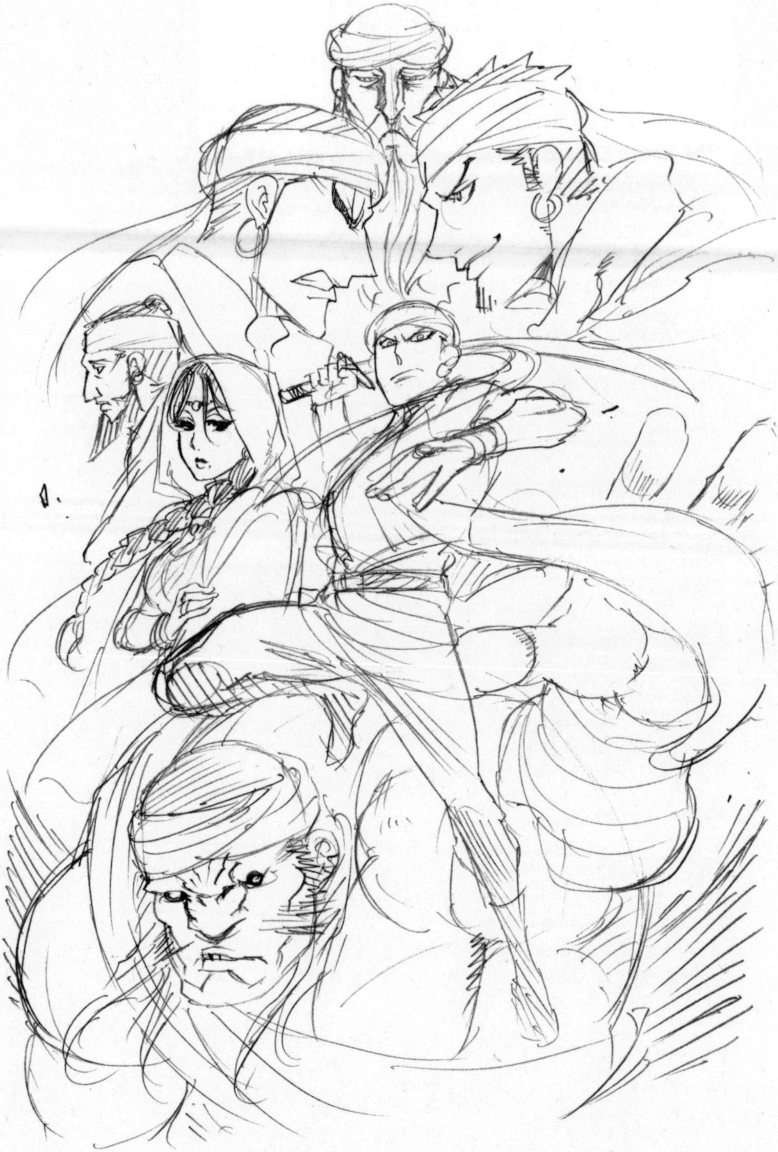

. Names, characters, places, and incidents are the products of the author's imagination or are used fictitiously. Any resemblance to actual events, locales, or persons, living or dead, is entirely coincidental.

A Kodansha Comics Trade Paperback Original.

The Heroic Legend of Arslan volume 9 copyright © 2018 Hiromu Arakawa & Yoshiki Tanaka
English translation copyright © 2018 Hiromu Arakawa & Yoshiki Tanaka

Published in the United States by Kodansha Comics,
an imprint of Kodansha USA Publishing, LLC, New York.

Publication rights for this English edition arranged through Kodansha Ltd., Tokyo.

First published in Japan in 2018 by Kodansha Ltd., Tokyo, as *Arslan Senki* volume 9.

ISBN 978-1-63236-680-1

Printed in the United States of America.

www.kodanshacomics.com

9 8 7 6 5 4 3 2 1

Translation: Amanda Haley
Lettering: James Dashiell
Editing: Ajani Oloye